Introduction

to

Linear Models

Joe H. Ward, Jr.

Air Force Human Resources Laboratory,
Brooks Air Force Base, Texas

Earl Jennings

University of Texas at Austin

Prentice-Hall, Inc.   Englewood Cliffs, New Jersey

Library of Congress Cataloging in Publication Data

WARD, JOE H. JR.
Introduction to linear models.

(Prentice-Hall series in educational measurement, research, and statistics)
Includes bibliography
1. Electronic data processing—Social sciences—Statistical methods. I. Jennings, Earl, joint author. II. Title
HA33.W35   519.5   72–5128
ISBN 0–13–486175–2

Prentice-Hall Series in Educational Measurement, Research, and Statistics

Gene V Glass, Editor

Printed in the United States of America

10 9 8 7 6 5 4 3 2 1

Prentice-Hall International, Inc., *London*
Prentice-Hall of Australia, Pty. Ltd., *Sydney*
Prentice-Hall of Canada, Ltd., *Toronto*
Prentice-Hall of India Private Limited, *New Delhi*
Prentice-Hall of Japan, Inc., *Tokyo*

Contents

4

A ONE-ATTRIBUTE MODEL WITH MULTIPLE
CATEGORIES 53

5

LINEAR INDEPENDENCE, LINEAR DEPENDENCE, AND
EQUIVALENT MODELS 77

6

A ONE-ATTRIBUTE MODEL WITH ORDERED
CATEGORIES 92

7
A TWO-ATTRIBUTE MODEL WITH MULTIPLE CATEGORIES 113

8
A TWO-ATTRIBUTE MODEL WITH ONE ATTRIBUTE ORDERED 133

9
A TWO-ATTRIBUTE MODEL WITH BOTH ATTRIBUTES ORDERED 156

10
APPLICATIONS OF THE PRINCIPLES OF MODEL DEVELOPMENT TO ONE-ATTRIBUTE PROBLEMS 184

11
APPLICATIONS TO ONE-ATTRIBUTE PROBLEMS USING POLYNOMIAL FORMS 200

12
APPLICATIONS TO TWO-ATTRIBUTE PROBLEMS   230

13
APPLICATION TO PROBLEMS INVOLVING SEVERAL ATTRIBUTES   243

Illustrations

Tables

Preface

The advent of high-speed computers has made feasible the utilization of statistical and computational procedures previously considered impratical. Expansion of research capabilities has encouraged investigators in business, industry, government, and universities to study broad problems which they had never before thought of as possible areas of research.

Many research workers do not know how to make full use of the combined statistical and computer techniques available. Because they were trained before the development of modern computer technology, they are most familiar with traditional analytical procedures, dictated in part by limited equipment such as desk calculators. Such workers have been concerned with "matching experimental subjects," "equating cell frequencies" in analysis of variance, and similar devices for fitting research problems into "standard" designs. Few feel competent enough to generate the models required to handle their own problems in a more meaningful way. The main purpose of this book is to present (and encourage) a general approach which enables investigators to formulate models and obtain results (via a computer) that aid in obtaining meaningful answers to research questions.

There are many approaches to the formulation and analysis of research problems. In some situations an informal, nonmathematical approach may be most appropriate while in others it is desirable to develop a more formal model of the problem to be studied. One effective approach in many situations is a **general linear mathematical model,** a direct and powerful approach to the effective formulation and solution of a wide variety of research problems. Certain widely used procedures such as analysis of variance and analysis of covariance are special cases of this general approach.

Investigators who have access to high-speed computers have little need to restrict the number of variables and interactions considered when applying the linear model to complex problems. Research workers who master appropriate ways of formulating problems for machine analyses command one of the most powerful statistical tools available.

Most of the books currently available on the topic of linear models emphasize the powerful statistical properties and/or computing expressions which can be used to calculate the quantities of interest. In our judgement such presentations tempt many investigators to attempt to fit their problem to a model rather than encouraging them to formulate a model to fit their problem. Our primary goal in this book is to help develop the capability of exploiting general linear models in order to reach conclusions about research questions. Such a goal involves developing in research workers the ability to transfer a few fundamental concepts to specific problem situations.

Since our aim is to concentrate on model development, many topics related to the use of linear models are not discussed in detail; e.g., confidence intervals, proofs of theorems, matrices, properties of estimators, probability, and distribution theory. These topics are treated in other books listed in the reference section. Although a mastery of such topics is invaluable to exploit the power of the general linear model fully, we have concentrated on those concepts we believe will broaden the horizons of research workers and improve the effectiveness of their handling of research problems.

The content of this work can be separated into two major categories: model development and computing procedures. Except for some elementary models in the early chapters, the discussion of computing procedures is limited to a description of how to use the computer program provided in Appendix E. Desirable prerequisite skills include experience in using punched cards and some practice in writing simple FORTRAN assignment statements. Chapters 14 and 15 can be covered profitably anytime after Chapter 6.

An understanding of the content associated with model development also requires as prerequisite skills some understanding of the associative, commutative, and distributive properties of addition and multiplication. Previous exposure to such terms as *mean, standard deviation, correlation coefficients, F distribution,* and *normal distribution* is highly desirable.

As a prospective reader of this book, you can expect to profit from the experience in many ways. The set of activities listed below are those which a researcher should be able to perform after reading this book.

1. State research questions in a "natural language" form. Example:
   a. Do third-grade girls read *better* than third-grade boys?
   b. Does typing performance *depend* on finger dexterity?
   c. Is the *effect* of sleep deprivation on discrimination reaction time constant across levels of sleep deprivation?
   d. If the effect of age is *controlled for,* is Drug *a superior* to Drug *b* in reducing pain?

e. Does the difference in Drug a and Drug b in reducing pain *depend* on age?

2. Give a persuasive argument as to why and how comparisons among *expected values* of variables can be used as a basis for deciding answers to questions such as those listed in 1.

3. Translate *natural language* questions into a symbolic expression that relates expected values in a model independent form.

Example:

a. The expected reading speed of a third-grade girl is equal to the expected reading speed of a third-grade boy.

$$\mathscr{E}(g) = \mathscr{E}(b)$$

b. The expected typing score of an individual with i hours of practice is equal to the expected typing score of an individual with j hours of practice.

$$\mathscr{E}(i) = \mathscr{E}(j)$$

c. The expected change in discrimination reaction time per unit change in sleep deprivation is a constant.

$$\frac{\mathscr{E}(i) - \mathscr{E}(j)}{i - j} = c$$

d. The pain reduction expected for an individual who took Drug a at a given age (say j) is equal to the pain reduction expected for an individual with the same age who took Drug b.

$$\mathscr{E}(a, j) = \mathscr{E}(b, j)$$

e. The expected difference between Drug a and b is the same at age i as it is at age j.

$$\mathscr{E}(a, i) - \mathscr{E}(b, i) = \mathscr{E}(a, j) - \mathscr{E}(b, j)$$

4. Write a linear model in vector notation which will produce good estimates of the expected vales which are to be compared. This model will be referred to as the *full* or starting model.

5. Investigate the properties of the model so as to identify what assumptions are being made. In connection with this, the researcher should be able to distinguish between a model which is known to be *true* and a model the truth of which depends on certain assumptions being true.

6. Substitute for the expected values expressed in 3, their estimates in symbolic form from the model generated in 4.

7. State the restrictions on the parameters of the model which are implied by simplifying the mathematical espressions of 6.

8. Impose the restrictions identified in 7 on the model generated in 4 to produce a *restricted* model.
9. Investigate the properties of the restricted model so as to verify that the estimates of the expected values are related in the manner specified in 3.
10. Find numerical least squares solutions for linear models.
11. Compare the full and restricted models by constructing an appropriate test statistic on the basis of which a decision is reached about 3 and by inference about 1.

This approach is based upon material developed at the Air Force Personnel Research Laboratory, Lackland Air Force Base, Texas, and was first documented by Robert Bottenberg and Joe Ward in *Applied Multiple Linear Regression* (1963). The instructional approach has been further developed through courses of instruction by Earl Jennings (at The University of Texas at Austin), Ward (at The University of Hawaii), and Bottenberg, Jennings, and Ward (for the American Educational Research Association). A list of all the individuals to whom we feel indebted would necessarily be incomplete, but special recognition is offered to Robert Bottenberg. Any merit this work possesses is due in large part to our interaction with him.

1

Problem Analysis, Models, and Vectors

1.1
INTRODUCTION

The primary purpose of this book is to identify and to illustrate several concepts that we believe are of general value in numerous problem situations. In general, we will argue that after the relevant components of a problem situation have been identified, a model can be formulated and manipulated that will reduce the uncertainty about an appropriate course of action in the context of a given problem situation. Although we regard the skills required in problem specification to be of crucial importance, very little space is devoted to them. Rather, we will concentrate on the skills required for the formulation and manipulation of models and the inferences that may be drawn from them.

1.2
PROBLEM SPECIFICATION

Every problem situation has its own unique characteristics, which makes it difficult to list or even describe everything an investigator must think about in problem specification. The comments in this section should therefore be taken as examples of what we mean by problem specification, not as an exhaustive consideration of the topic.

Many problem situations involve the following components:

1. an *individual* or *decision maker* (or a group of individuals),
2. an *outcome* or *objective* that the decision maker desires,

3. *alternative activities* related to the attainment of desired outcomes,

4. *uncertainty* by the decision maker as to which *activity* is the "best."

For example, an educator (*decision maker*) may desire to provide "excellent" typing instruction for students (his *objective*). There may be several alternative instructional systems (*alternative activities*) that are related to typing performance, but the educator is not sure (*uncertainty*) which method is the "best." The decision maker's problem is to choose the "best" method. In this particular example, the outcome would most likely be *quantitatively defined*; that is, we could *measure* the extent to which an outcome is obtained. Thus the outcome might be measured as "number of words per minute." It is also possible to use a *qualitative definition*; that is, the outcome is either obtained or not. Hence the desired outcome might be defined as: "All students attain at least 25 words per minute." Some examples of the objectives desired by the decision maker might be

1. to maximize typing performance at a fixed expenditure,

2. to attain the qualitative outcome at minimum cost by all students (at least 25 words per minute),

3. a combination—maximize the performance at a fixed expenditure but increase the expenditure if required to insure at least 25 words per minute from every student.

Generally, we will want to translate a decision maker's problem into a precise form. This requires careful identification of the components of the problem. Among the components that must be identified are

1. the decision maker,

2. the objectives,

3. the alternative activities,

4. the measures of performance efficiency,

5. the variables that can be controlled and the variables that cannot be controlled,

6. the context of the problem.

The identification and precise description of components of the problem are referred to as **problem specification**—the most important and difficult aspect of dealing with problem situations.

Prediction

In many problem situations decision makers have a need to predict the outcomes of alternative courses of action. Every person, confronted with even simple problem situations, incorporates some type of prediction system in selecting alternative activities. For example, an individual must predict the effects of eating alternative products on his objective of "satisfying hunger" or "maximizing health." Obviously, some alternative products (e.g., those labeled "poison, for external use only") are easy to reject, whereas other choices are more difficult.

Some problems may require prediction of *future* outcomes, whereas others may involve the prediction of outcomes that occur almost *simultaneously* with the availability of the information used as a basis for prediction. An example of the prediction of *future* outcomes is the desire to predict the performance of college students from information available when the students are in high school. Another example is the prediction of the future yield of a farm product from knowledge of fertilizer used, soil characteristics, moisture content, and other information.

An example of the prediction of nearly *simultaneously* occurring events is the prediction of the amount of gasoline in a tank from information given by the fuel indicator on the car's dashboard. This information varies almost simultaneously with the amount of gasoline in the tank. We could regard this example as a measurement or estimation problem rather than one of prediction, but the practical value of predicting (estimating) the amount of gasoline in a tank is apparent to every driver. Another example is the desire to predict (or diagnose) the occurrence of a disease from knowledge of such easily obtainable information as the number of a certain type of cell occurring in a blood sample. The cells may occur in the blood as a result of the disease, or perhaps both the cells and the disease are the result of a third factor. In any event, it is desirable to diagnose (predict) the disease as soon as possible.[1]

In this book the term **prediction** will include *all* situations in which we wish to predict (or estimate) an outcome, objective, or measure of performance from knowledge of other information. In most problem situations, the prediction requirements will cause the outcome (e.g., measure of performance) to be predicted (or estimated) in terms of (1) aspects of the situation that can be controlled and (2) aspects of the situation that cannot be controlled.

The prediction problem requires the description or representation of the outcome measure in terms of other relevant information (called *predictor information*). A key component of problem specification is the

---

[1] Of course, it would be even more desirable to predict the future occurrence of the disease. In most situations in which some outcome is predictable from other information, the question of *causation* can be entertained. However, cause and effect linkages are frequently very difficult to establish. Although basic understandings are enhanced when such linkages can be determined, efficacious decisions can frequently be made without reference to causation when predictability exists.

identification or definition of the information to be used as predictors and outcome measures. The prediction problem can be handled more easily if the relevant information and their relations are identified. This is accomplished through **models**.

1.3
MODELS

In *Scientific Method* (1962, p. 108), Ackoff presents a useful description of models:

> The word *model* is used as a noun, adjective, and verb, and in each instance it has a slightly different connotation. As a noun "model" is a *representation* in the sense in which an architect constructs a small-scale model of a building or a physicist a large-scale model of an atom. As an adjective "model" implies a degree of *perfection* or idealization, as in reference to a model home, a model student, or a model husband. As a verb "to model" means *to demonstrate*, to reveal, to show what a thing is like.
>
> Scientific models have all these connotations. They are representations of states, objects, and events. They are idealized in the sense that they are less complicated than reality and hence easier to use for research purposes. These models are easier to manipulate and "carry about" than the real thing. The simplicity of models, compared with reality, lies in the fact that only the relevant properties of reality are represented. For example, in a road map, which is a model of a portion of the earth's surface, vegetation is not shown, since it is not relevant with respect to the use of the map. In a model of a portion of the solar system the balls representing planets need not be made of the same material or have the same temperature as the planets themselves.[2]

Ackoff then describes three types of models:

1. The *iconic model* is a large- or small- scale representation of the "real thing." Iconic models *look like* what they represent. An example is a scale model of an airplane.

2. The *analogue model* uses one property to represent a different property. A slide rule is an analogue model in which distances are used to represent logarithms.

3. In *symbolic models* the properties to be represented are expressed symbolically. For example, the distance a body falls (d) in a given amount of time (t) can be represented by an equation $(d = 16.1t^2)$. The equation is a symbolic model. Models using symbols that represent numbers are referred to as *mathematical models*.

---

[2]From R. L. Ackoff, *Scientific Method: Optimizing Applied Research Decisions.* Copyright © 1962 by John Wiley & Sons, Inc. Reprinted by permission.

The models used throughout this book will be mathematical models and will take the form of equations. The outcome measure (or *measure of interest*) will be on the left side, and the *predictor information* will be on the right side. Thus

Measure of interest = Function of predictor information

An accurate and unambiguous notation to describe this general form is required. Although a number of different notations meet the requirements, no single style best fits all the models discussed. For example, Sir Ronald Fisher (see Wishart, 1934) points out that the analysis of variance is not a mathematical theorem but a convenient way of arranging the arithmetic. Historically, it appears that the notation chosen for the discussion of a particular type of model has largely been dictated by a desire to produce arithmetic simplicity. Now, however, adopting a notation that produces arithmetic simplicity is not as important, due to the widespread availability of computers. Moreover, an emphasis on computational ease can produce some undesirable educational results, since fundamental similarities between various models are obscured when different notations are used.

1.4
VECTORS

One major objective of this book is to provide investigators with techniques that are useful in conceptualizing and resolving research problems. An essential step in problem solution is the development of an appropriate model. We shall adopt a symbolic language that will enable us to express precisely the relevant aspects of the problem in a form that is easily translated for computers. The language used for all models throughout this book is **vector notation.** The vector concepts, which are introduced in this section, are fundamental to our technique of formulating research problems for analysis. Although we may forfeit some arithmetic simplicities for some models, we will gain conceptual simplicity and generality.

Vector Representation of Information

One of our first tasks is to find some means of representing large quantities of information in a concise and orderly manner. In almost every case, vector notation can be used to organize our information efficiently.

In the models to be discussed, it will be possible to identify a collection of *entities,* each of which has a number associated with it; this collection of numbers will be referred to as the **variable of interest.** For example, the entities might be students, and the number associated with each student might be his typing-test score; or the entities might be plots of ground, and the number associated with each plot might be bushels of corn yielded per plot. Furthermore, the entities may be classified into subcollections or *categories* according to some other *attribute*. For example, students may be classified into the categories "male" or "female" according to the attribute "sex" or into the categories "freshman, sophomore, junior, or senior" according to the attribute "grade in school." Entities may be classified into categories on a number of attributes simultaneously. For example, plots of ground could be classified into categories on the basis of which fertilizer (say *A* or *B*) was used and simultaneously on the basis of how much rain had fallen on the plots (say heavy, moderate, or light). Consider the examples shown in Table 1.1.

In the first two examples in this table, the same entities (students) have been classified according to sex *or* according to grade. The ways in which the entities are classified are dictated by the nature of the problem. In the third

Table 1.1

Entities	Variable of interest	Number of attributes	Names of attributes	Categories	Number of mutually exclusive categories
Students	Score on a typing test	1	Sex	Girls Boys	2
Students	Score on a typing test	1	Grade	Freshman Sophomore Junior Senior	4
Plots of ground	Bushels of corn	2	Brand of fertilizer	A B	6
			Amount of rainfall	Light Moderate Heavy	
Public school teachers	Annual salary	3	Sex	Male Female	306
			Level	Elementary Junior Secondary	
			State	Alabama Alaska . . . Wyoming	

example, the entities (plots of ground) have been classified on two attributes (brand of fertilizer and amount of rainfall) simultaneously, which results in six (2×3) mutually exclusive categories. In the last example, teachers have been classified on three attributes simultaneously, which results in

$$2 \times 3 \times 51 = 306$$

mutually exclusive categories. Notice that there are 2 sexes, 3 teaching levels, and 51 states of residence (including the District of Columbia).

Examples such as these could be expanded indefinitely; hence the freedom one possesses in definition should be clearly understood. For example, entities might be classrooms rather than students, and the value associated with each classroom (variable of interest) might be the class-average typing score. In Section 1.2, the general concepts of outcomes and predictors were discussed. In the context of this discussion, the variable of interest would be numbers associated with outcomes, and the attributes would be predictors. Observe that a particular collection of numbers could be regarded as the variable of interest in one problem situation but as predictor information in another. In the first example in Table 1.1, a rating of on-the-job proficiency might become available at a later date; thus this rating might become the variable of interest, and the entities (employees) could be classified into a number of categories reflecting typing speed at the time they were students.

The major point is that we need a concise, efficient and unambiguous way of organizing information about a given problem situation. Vector notation enables us to do this.

1.5
DEFINITION OF A VECTOR AND ITS ELEMENTS

A **vector** is an ordered set of numbers. The numbers are called **elements** or **components** of the vector. In some sciences the word vector has specific connotations (e.g., direction and magnitude of force), but the term as we shall use it refers to an *ordered set of numbers*. The ordering is only by position, and there is no special ordering of the size of the elements.

A *row vector*, as the name indicates, is a vector in which the elements are arranged in a row. Similarly, a *column vector* is one in which the elements are arranged in a column. Examples of these are

$$\text{Row vectors:} \quad (4, 3.6, -2), (1, -1, 1), (4, 3, 165, 82, -4)$$

$$\text{Column vectors:} \quad \begin{bmatrix} 35 \\ 6 \\ 4 \\ -2 \\ 1.6 \end{bmatrix} \begin{bmatrix} 1.5 \\ -.6 \\ 3.0 \end{bmatrix} \begin{bmatrix} 1 \\ 1 \\ 1 \end{bmatrix} \begin{bmatrix} 0 \\ 0 \end{bmatrix} \begin{bmatrix} 1 \\ 0 \\ 1 \\ 0 \end{bmatrix}$$

Throughout this book, the vectors will be defined as **column vectors** unless otherwise indicated.

The Dimension of a Vector

The number of elements in a vector is referred to as the **dimension** of that vector. This is an important distinguishing characteristic of any vector. In the examples just given, a count of the elements in each of the three row vectors indicates that the dimensions of these vectors are 3, 3, and 5, respectively. Similarly, the five column vectors are of dimensions 5, 3, 3, 2, and 4, respectively. The dimension of a vector is sometimes called the **order** of the vector.

1.6
VECTOR NOTATION

No one form of vector notation has been universally adopted. The notation used in this book, like in others, enables the investigator to represent numerical values in an orderly fashion. An additional advantage of any vector notation is the compactness with which ordered arrays of numbers can be represented. Since we will primarily use column vectors, our notation will be in terms of column vectors. *Our general practice will be to represent vectors with either*

1. uppercase letters without subscripts (e.g., $\mathbf{Y}, \mathbf{Z}, \mathbf{X}, \mathbf{E}$), or
2. uppercase letters with superscripts in parentheses (e.g., $\mathbf{X}^{(1)}, \mathbf{X}^{(2)}, \mathbf{E}^{(1)}, \mathbf{E}^{(2)}, \mathbf{X}^{(b)}, \mathbf{X}^{(g)}$).

We will use lowercase letters with or without subscripts to represent single numbers (e.g., $a_1, a_2, b_1, b_2, a, w, p$). Three column vectors of dimension 10 could be represented as

$$\mathbf{Y} = \begin{bmatrix} y_1 \\ y_2 \\ \cdot \\ \cdot \\ \cdot \\ y_{10} \end{bmatrix} \qquad \mathbf{X} = \begin{bmatrix} x_1 \\ x_2 \\ \cdot \\ \cdot \\ \cdot \\ x_{10} \end{bmatrix} \qquad \mathbf{E} = \begin{bmatrix} e_1 \\ e_2 \\ \cdot \\ \cdot \\ \cdot \\ e_{10} \end{bmatrix}$$

where the vertical dots indicate the unwritten elements.

Whenever we have many vectors, we will use superscripts in parentheses. For example, if we wish to define column vectors $\mathbf{X}^{(1)}, \mathbf{X}^{(2)}, \mathbf{X}^{(3)}$, and $\mathbf{X}^{(4)}$—each of dimension 5—the elements will be indicated as

$$\mathbf{X}^{(1)} = \begin{bmatrix} x_{11} \\ x_{21} \\ x_{31} \\ x_{41} \\ x_{51} \end{bmatrix} \quad \mathbf{X}^{(2)} = \begin{bmatrix} x_{12} \\ x_{22} \\ x_{32} \\ x_{42} \\ x_{52} \end{bmatrix} \quad \mathbf{X}^{(3)} = \begin{bmatrix} x_{13} \\ x_{23} \\ x_{33} \\ x_{43} \\ x_{53} \end{bmatrix} \quad \mathbf{X}^{(4)} = \begin{bmatrix} x_{14} \\ x_{24} \\ x_{34} \\ x_{44} \\ x_{54} \end{bmatrix}$$

Each element has two subscripts: *the first subscript indicates the element number within the vector, and the second subscript indicates the vector number.*

x_{11} is the first element in vector $\mathbf{X}^{(1)}$.
x_{42} is the fourth element in vector $\mathbf{X}^{(2)}$.
x_{33} is the third element in vector $\mathbf{X}^{(3)}$.
x_{54} is the fifth element in vector $\mathbf{X}^{(4)}$.

Representing Information in Vector Form

Assume we wish to represent the age and sex of a group of 150 students. Then define

$\mathbf{X}^{(1)}$ = a vector of dimension 150 representing age, with elements defined as
x_{11} = age in years for student number 1
x_{21} = age in years for student number 2

x_i = age in years for student number i

$x_{150,1}$ = age in years for student number 150

$\mathbf{X}^{(2)}$ = a vector of dimension 150, with elements defined indicating female as
x_{12} = 1 if sex of student number 1 is a girl, 0 otherwise
x_{22} = 1 if sex of student number 2 is a girl, 0 otherwise

x_{i2} = 1 if sex of student number i is a girl, 0 otherwise

$x_{150,2}$ = 1 if sex of student number 150 is a girl, 0 otherwise

$\mathbf{X}^{(3)}$ = a vector of dimension 150 with elements defined indicating male as

$x_{13} = 1$ if sex of student number 1 is a boy, 0 otherwise

$x_{23} = 1$ if sex of student number 2 is a boy, 0 otherwise

$x_{i3} = 1$ if sex of student number i is a boy, 0 otherwise

$x_{150,3} = 1$ if sex of student number 150 is a boy, 0 otherwise

The data may appear as

$$\mathbf{X}^{(1)} = \begin{bmatrix} 14 \\ 13 \\ 12 \\ 12 \\ 10 \\ \cdot \\ \cdot \\ \cdot \\ 11 \end{bmatrix} \quad \mathbf{X}^{(2)} = \begin{bmatrix} 1 \\ 1 \\ 0 \\ 1 \\ 0 \\ \cdot \\ \cdot \\ \cdot \\ 1 \end{bmatrix} \quad \mathbf{X}^{(3)} = \begin{bmatrix} 0 \\ 0 \\ 1 \\ 0 \\ 1 \\ \cdot \\ \cdot \\ \cdot \\ 0 \end{bmatrix}$$

In this example

student number 1 is 14 years old and a girl.
student number 2 is 13 years old and a girl.
student number 3 is 12 years old and a boy.
student number 4 is 12 years old and a girl.
student number 5 is 10 years old and a boy.
student number 150 is 11 years old and a girl.

Note that if $x_{i2} = 1$, then $x_{i3} = 0$ and vice versa.

1.7
EQUALITY OF TWO VECTORS

Two column vectors (or two row vectors) are said to be equal if and only if they have the same dimension and the corresponding elements have the same values. Define two column vectors, **U** and **V**, that have the same number of elements, n.

$$\mathbf{U} = \begin{bmatrix} u_1 \\ u_2 \\ \cdot \\ \cdot \\ \cdot \\ u_n \end{bmatrix} \qquad \mathbf{V} = \begin{bmatrix} v_1 \\ v_2 \\ \cdot \\ \cdot \\ \cdot \\ v_n \end{bmatrix}$$

If we write $\mathbf{U} = \mathbf{V}$, then all of the following statements are true.

$$u_1 = v_1$$
$$u_2 = v_2$$
$$\cdot \qquad \cdot$$
$$\cdot \qquad \cdot$$
$$\cdot \qquad \cdot$$
$$u_n = v_n$$

Examples of Equality of Vectors.   Let

$$\mathbf{X} = \begin{bmatrix} 1.5 \\ 4.0 \\ -3 \\ 0 \end{bmatrix} \quad \text{and} \quad \mathbf{Y} = \begin{bmatrix} 1.5 \\ 4.0 \\ -3 \\ 0 \end{bmatrix}$$

Then we can write

$$\mathbf{X} = \mathbf{Y}$$

since every one of the corresponding pairs of elements are equal.

Let

$$\mathbf{E} = \begin{bmatrix} e_1 \\ e_2 \\ e_3 \\ e_4 \\ e_5 \end{bmatrix} \quad \text{and} \quad \mathbf{F} = \begin{bmatrix} 1 \\ 0 \\ -1 \\ 0 \\ 1 \end{bmatrix}$$

Then writing

$$\mathbf{E} = \mathbf{F}$$

is simply an abbreviated way of writing the following statements.

$$e_1 = 1$$
$$e_2 = 0$$
$$e_3 = -1$$
$$e_4 = 0$$
$$e_5 = 1$$

Note that the following vectors are not equal because the corresponding elements are not equal.

$$\begin{bmatrix} 1 \\ 2 \\ 4 \end{bmatrix} \neq \begin{bmatrix} 1 \\ 4 \\ 2 \end{bmatrix}$$

1.8
TWO IMPORTANT VECTOR OPERATIONS

Several arithmetic operations with vectors will be used frequently in formulating and analyzing problems. The operations involve only simple arithmetic, but vector representation enables one to think of many such operations simultaneously rather than one at a time. This advantage exists because we agree, by definition, to work with corresponding vector elements and to adhere to the order relation of these elements within the vector. Two of the most frequently used operations are (1) *the multiplication of a vector by a number* and (2) *the addition of two vectors*. These two operations when combined provide the powerful idea of linear combination of vectors, described in Section 1.9.

Multiplication of a Vector by a Number

The multiplication of a vector by a number is defined as *the multiplication of each element of the vector by that number*. This operation results in a new vector that has the same dimension as the original vector. Each element in the new vector is the same multiple of the corresponding element of the original vector.

If, therefore,

$$\mathbf{W} = \begin{bmatrix} w_1 \\ w_2 \\ \cdot \\ \cdot \\ \cdot \\ w_n \end{bmatrix}$$

then

$$k\mathbf{W} = \begin{bmatrix} kw_1 \\ kw_2 \\ \cdot \\ \cdot \\ \cdot \\ kw_n \end{bmatrix}$$

Example of Multiplication of a Vector by a Number. Assume that we have a vector, **H**, that has six elements, each representing the height of students in inches.

$$\mathbf{H} = \begin{bmatrix} h_1 \\ h_2 \\ h_3 \\ h_4 \\ h_5 \\ h_6 \end{bmatrix} = \begin{bmatrix} 72 \\ 63 \\ 69 \\ 69 \\ 63 \\ 66 \end{bmatrix}$$

If we wish to convert height in inches to height in feet, we can define a new vector, **F** as

$$\mathbf{F} = (1/12)\mathbf{H}$$

The extended form of this statement is

$$\begin{matrix} \mathbf{F} & & \mathbf{H} \\ \begin{bmatrix} f_1 \\ f_2 \\ f_3 \\ f_4 \\ f_5 \\ f_6 \end{bmatrix} = 1/12 & \begin{bmatrix} 72 \\ 63 \\ 69 \\ 69 \\ 63 \\ 66 \end{bmatrix} = \begin{bmatrix} 1/12(72) \\ 1/12(63) \\ 1/12(69) \\ 1/12(69) \\ 1/12(63) \\ 1/12(66) \end{bmatrix} = \begin{bmatrix} 6.00 \\ 5.25 \\ 5.75 \\ 5.75 \\ 5.25 \\ 5.50 \end{bmatrix} \end{matrix}$$

and

$$f_1 = 6.00$$
$$f_2 = 5.25$$
$$f_3 = 5.75$$
$$f_4 = 5.75$$
$$f_5 = 5.25$$
$$f_6 = 5.50$$

In the form $\mathbf{F} = (1/12)\mathbf{H}$, it appears as if only one multiplication is involved, but the expression represents many multiplication operations. Such concise representation of large amounts of information is one of the advantages of vector representation.

Addition of Two Vectors

The addition of two vectors (either two row vectors or two column vectors) is defined as *the addition of each element in one vector to the corresponding element in the other.* The vectors being added must be of the same type (i.e., both row or both column), and both must have the same dimension. This operation yields a new vector in which each element is equal to the sum of the corresponding elements in the first two vectors. Thus the addition of the two n-element column vectors, **W** and **B**, would yield a new vector, **Z**.

$$\mathbf{Z} = \mathbf{W} + \mathbf{B} = \begin{bmatrix} w_1 \\ w_2 \\ \cdot \\ \cdot \\ \cdot \\ w_n \end{bmatrix} + \begin{bmatrix} b_1 \\ b_2 \\ \cdot \\ \cdot \\ \cdot \\ b_n \end{bmatrix} = \begin{bmatrix} w_1 + b_1 \\ w_2 + b_2 \\ \cdot \\ \cdot \\ \cdot \\ w_n + b_n \end{bmatrix}$$

Example of the Addition of Two Vectors. Assume that 50 students have taken a psychological test that has a *verbal* score and a *quantitative* score. Then, to obtain the total score, we can let

$$\mathbf{V} = \begin{bmatrix} v_1 \\ v_2 \\ \cdot \\ \cdot \\ \cdot \\ v_{50} \end{bmatrix} = \begin{bmatrix} 40 \\ 60 \\ \cdot \\ \cdot \\ \cdot \\ 35 \end{bmatrix}$$

where

$$v_1 = \text{verbal score of student } 1 = 40$$
$$v_2 = \text{verbal score of student } 2 = 60$$
$$\cdot \qquad \cdot \qquad \cdot$$
$$\cdot \qquad \cdot \qquad \cdot$$
$$\cdot \qquad \cdot \qquad \cdot$$
$$v_{50} = \text{verbal score of student } 50 = 35$$

$$\mathbf{Q} = \begin{bmatrix} q_1 \\ q_2 \\ \cdot \\ \cdot \\ \cdot \\ q_{50} \end{bmatrix} = \begin{bmatrix} 70 \\ 40 \\ \cdot \\ \cdot \\ \cdot \\ 60 \end{bmatrix}$$

where

$$q_1 = \text{quantitative score of student } 1 = 70$$
$$q_2 = \text{quantitative score of student } 2 = 40$$
$$\cdot \qquad \cdot \qquad \cdot$$
$$\cdot \qquad \cdot \qquad \cdot$$
$$\cdot \qquad \cdot \qquad \cdot$$
$$q_{50} = \text{quantitative score of student } 50 = 60$$

Then the total-score vector, **T**, can be defined as

$$\mathbf{T} = \begin{bmatrix} t_1 \\ t_2 \\ \cdot \\ \cdot \\ \cdot \\ t_{50} \end{bmatrix}$$

where

$$t_1 = \text{total score of student 1}$$
$$t_2 = \text{total score of student 2}$$

$$t_{50} = \text{total score of student 50}$$

And the numerical values for the elements of **T** can be determined from

$$
\begin{matrix} \mathbf{T} & & \mathbf{V} & & \mathbf{Q} \end{matrix}
$$

$$
\begin{bmatrix} t_1 \\ t_2 \\ \cdot \\ \cdot \\ \cdot \\ t_{50} \end{bmatrix} = \begin{bmatrix} v_1 \\ v_2 \\ \cdot \\ \cdot \\ \cdot \\ v_{50} \end{bmatrix} + \begin{bmatrix} q_1 \\ q_2 \\ \cdot \\ \cdot \\ \cdot \\ q_{50} \end{bmatrix} = \begin{bmatrix} v_1 + q_1 \\ v_2 + q_2 \\ \cdot \\ \cdot \\ \cdot \\ v_{50} + q_{50} \end{bmatrix} = \begin{bmatrix} 40 + 70 \\ 60 + 40 \\ \cdot \\ \cdot \\ \cdot \\ 35 + 60 \end{bmatrix} = \begin{bmatrix} 110 \\ 100 \\ \cdot \\ \cdot \\ \cdot \\ 95 \end{bmatrix}
$$

Then $t_1 = 110$, $t_2 = 100$, and $t_{50} = 95$.

The concise expression $\mathbf{T} = \mathbf{V} + \mathbf{Q}$ looks as if only one sum is to be computed, but vector notation allows such simple expressions to represent many summing operations. This can be done because, in adding two vectors, we work with corresponding elements and adhere to the position relation of the elements within the vectors.

1.9
LINEAR COMBINATIONS OF VECTORS

Given, two column vectors (or two row vectors), **Y** and **Z**, each of dimension n, and the numbers a_1 and a_2. If we form a new n-dimensional column (or row) vector, **X**, by the relationship

$$\mathbf{X} = a_1\mathbf{Y} + a_2\mathbf{Z}$$

X is said to be a **linear combination** of **Y** and **Z**.

In extended form

$$
\begin{array}{ccc}
\mathbf{X} & \mathbf{Y} & \mathbf{Z}
\end{array}
$$

$$
\begin{bmatrix} x_1 \\ x_2 \\ \cdot \\ \cdot \\ \cdot \\ x_n \end{bmatrix} = a_1 \begin{bmatrix} y_1 \\ y_2 \\ \cdot \\ \cdot \\ \cdot \\ y_n \end{bmatrix} + a_2 \begin{bmatrix} z_1 \\ z_2 \\ \cdot \\ \cdot \\ \cdot \\ z_n \end{bmatrix} = \begin{bmatrix} a_1 y_1 + a_2 z_1 \\ a_1 y_2 + a_2 z_2 \\ \cdot \\ \cdot \\ \cdot \\ a_1 y_n + a_2 z_n \end{bmatrix}
$$

Then

$$
x_1 = a_1 y_1 + a_2 z_1
$$
$$
x_2 = a_1 y_2 + a_2 z_2
$$
$$
\begin{array}{ccc} \cdot & \cdot & \cdot \\ \cdot & \cdot & \cdot \\ \cdot & \cdot & \cdot \end{array}
$$
$$
x_n = a_1 y_n + a_2 z_n
$$

Example of Linear Combination of Two Vectors. Assume that the vectors, **V** and **Q**, represent *verbal* and *quantitative* part scores for four students.

$$
\mathbf{V} = \begin{bmatrix} 25 \\ 35 \\ 20 \\ 10 \end{bmatrix} \qquad \mathbf{Q} = \begin{bmatrix} 32 \\ 24 \\ 12 \\ 47 \end{bmatrix}
$$

Assume that for each student we wish to obtain a weighted total-test score, where each verbal score is to be multiplied by the number $w_1 = 2.6$ and each quantitative score is to be multiplied by $w_2 = 2.0$. Then we can express the total-test score vector, **S**, as a linear combination of **V** and **Q**.

$$
\mathbf{S} = w_1 \mathbf{V} + w_2 \mathbf{Q}
$$

The steps in computing the numerical values of the elements of **S** are

$$
\mathbf{S} = \begin{bmatrix} s_1 \\ s_2 \\ s_3 \\ s_4 \end{bmatrix} = w_1 \begin{bmatrix} v_1 \\ v_2 \\ v_3 \\ v_4 \end{bmatrix} + w_2 \begin{bmatrix} q_1 \\ q_2 \\ q_3 \\ q_4 \end{bmatrix} = \begin{bmatrix} w_1 v_1 + w_2 q_1 \\ w_1 v_2 + w_2 q_2 \\ w_1 v_3 + w_2 q_3 \\ w_1 v_4 + w_2 q_4 \end{bmatrix}
$$

$$
\mathbf{S} = \begin{bmatrix} s_1 \\ s_2 \\ s_3 \\ s_4 \end{bmatrix} = 2.6 \begin{bmatrix} 25 \\ 35 \\ 20 \\ 10 \end{bmatrix} + 2.0 \begin{bmatrix} 32 \\ 24 \\ 12 \\ 47 \end{bmatrix} = \begin{bmatrix} 2.6(25) + 2.0(32) \\ 2.6(35) + 2.0(24) \\ 2.6(20) + 2.0(12) \\ 2.6(10) + 2.0(47) \end{bmatrix}
$$

$$\mathbf{S} = \begin{bmatrix} s_1 \\ s_2 \\ s_3 \\ s_4 \end{bmatrix} = \begin{bmatrix} 65 + 64 \\ 91 + 48 \\ 52 + 24 \\ 26 + 94 \end{bmatrix} = \begin{bmatrix} 129 \\ 139 \\ 76 \\ 120 \end{bmatrix}$$

Now that the linear combination of two vectors has been defined, observe that the sum of two vectors can be written as

$$\mathbf{S} = 1(\mathbf{X}) + 1(\mathbf{Y})$$

The sum is a special linear combination in which the multipliers are equal to one. Also, if a vector, **A**, is written as

$$\mathbf{A} = a_1\mathbf{X} + 0(\mathbf{Y})$$

then

$$\mathbf{A} = a_1\mathbf{X}$$

Thus multiplication of a vector by a number is a special case of the linear combination of two vectors. In this special case, we say either that **A** is a *multiple* of **X** or that **A** is a *linear combination* of **X**.

1.10
LINEAR COMBINATION OF ANY NUMBER OF VECTORS

In some situations, we may wish to form vectors that are linear combinations of many vectors. The procedure is analogous to that described for the two-vector case. Suppose, for example, the psychological test described previously yielded a spatial perception part-score as well as the verbal and quantitative part-scores, which were weighted in the composite represented by the vector **S**. We wish to form a weighted total-score composite that includes all three part-scores.

Let **P** denote the vector in which the elements are the spatial perception scores of the same individuals whose verbal and quantitative scores are the corresponding elements in vectors **V** and **Q**. Let w_3 be the weight to be applied to **P**. A new vector, **C**, representing the weighted composite of the three part-scores, can be expressed as

$$\mathbf{C} = (1.0)\,\mathbf{S} + w_3\mathbf{P}$$

That is, **C** is a linear combination of **S** and **P**, where **S** is multiplied by the number 1.0. However, we know that **S** itself is a linear combination of **V** and **Q**; that is,

$$\mathbf{S} = w_1\mathbf{V} + w_2\mathbf{Q}$$

Therefore, by substituting its equivalent for $\mathbf{S}$, we can write

$$\mathbf{C} = w_1\mathbf{V} + w_2\mathbf{Q} + w_3\mathbf{P}$$

From this we see that vector $\mathbf{C}$ represents a weighted composite of verbal, quantitative, and spacial perception part-score vectors $\mathbf{V}, \mathbf{Q}$, and $\mathbf{P}$. The principles illustrated here can be stated in the form of a definition.

Definition of a Linear Combination of a Set of Vectors

Given a set of vectors $\mathbf{X}^{(1)}, \mathbf{X}^{(2)}, \ldots, \mathbf{X}^{(k)}$, each of dimension n, and the numbers $a_1, a_2, \ldots, a_k$. If we form a new n-dimensional vector, $\mathbf{Y}$, by the relationship

$$\mathbf{Y} = a_1\mathbf{X}^{(1)} + a_2\mathbf{X}^{(2)} + \cdots + a_k\mathbf{X}^{(k)}$$

vector $\mathbf{Y}$ is said to be a **linear combination** of the vectors $\mathbf{X}^{(1)}, \mathbf{X}^{(2)}, \ldots, \mathbf{X}^{(k)}$.

Example of Total-Test Score as a Linear Combination of Three Part-Scores. Verbal and quantitative part-scores in vectors $\mathbf{V}$ and $\mathbf{Q}$ were specified for four individuals in the numerical example in Section 1.9. Assume now that spatial perception part-scores, such as those just described, are available for the same four individuals. The scores are represented in vector $\mathbf{P}$.

$$\mathbf{P} = \begin{bmatrix} 18 \\ 3 \\ 12 \\ 6 \end{bmatrix}$$

We wish to obtain a weighted composite of the three part-scores in which the scores in $\mathbf{P}$ are weighted by the number $w_3 = 1/3$, and the scores in $\mathbf{V}$ and $\mathbf{Q}$ are again weighted 2.6 and 2.0, respectively. The weighted total-test composite vector, $\mathbf{C}$, is expressed as

$$\mathbf{C} = w_1\mathbf{V} + w_2\mathbf{Q} + w_3\mathbf{P}$$

The substitutions and computations necessary to obtain the weighted composite scores for the four individuals are

$$\mathbf{C} = \begin{bmatrix} c_1 \\ c_2 \\ c_3 \\ c_4 \end{bmatrix} = 2.6\begin{bmatrix} 25 \\ 35 \\ 20 \\ 10 \end{bmatrix} + 2.0\begin{bmatrix} 32 \\ 24 \\ 12 \\ 47 \end{bmatrix} + 1/3\begin{bmatrix} 18 \\ 3 \\ 12 \\ 6 \end{bmatrix}$$

$$= \begin{bmatrix} 2.6(25) + 2.0(32) + 1/3(18) \\ 2.6(35) + 2.0(24) + 1/3(3) \\ 2.6(20) + 2.0(12) + 1/3(12) \\ 2.6(10) + 2.0(47) + 1/3(6) \end{bmatrix}$$

$$\mathbf{C} = \begin{bmatrix} c_1 \\ c_2 \\ c_3 \\ c_4 \end{bmatrix} = \begin{bmatrix} 65 + 64 + 6 \\ 91 + 48 + 1 \\ 52 + 24 + 4 \\ 26 + 94 + 2 \end{bmatrix} = \begin{bmatrix} 135 \\ 140 \\ 80 \\ 122 \end{bmatrix}$$

We could have obtained these weighted total-test scores in another way. $\mathbf{C}$ can be expressed in terms of $\mathbf{S}$ and $\mathbf{P}$, and the four individual scores in $\mathbf{S}$ can be computed (see Section 1.9). We can then use this information as follows:

$$\mathbf{C} = \mathbf{S} + w_3\mathbf{P}$$

$$\mathbf{C} = \begin{bmatrix} c_1 \\ c_2 \\ c_3 \\ c_4 \end{bmatrix} = \begin{bmatrix} 129 \\ 139 \\ 76 \\ 120 \end{bmatrix} + 1/3 \begin{bmatrix} 18 \\ 3 \\ 12 \\ 6 \end{bmatrix} = \begin{bmatrix} 129 + 1/3(18) \\ 139 + 1/3(3) \\ 76 + 1/3(12) \\ 120 + 1/3(6) \end{bmatrix}$$

$$\mathbf{C} = \begin{bmatrix} c_1 \\ c_2 \\ c_3 \\ c_4 \end{bmatrix} = \begin{bmatrix} 129 + 6 \\ 139 + 1 \\ 76 + 4 \\ 120 + 2 \end{bmatrix} = \begin{bmatrix} 135 \\ 140 \\ 80 \\ 122 \end{bmatrix}$$

1.11
TWO IMPORTANT PROPERTIES OF VECTOR OPERATIONS

The two properties of vector operations described in this section are based on the properties of ordinary numbers. These properties are important in simplifying the models to be developed in subsequent chapters.

Given two vectors, $\mathbf{X}$ and $\mathbf{Y}$, each of dimension n, and two numbers, a_1 and a_2, then

Property 1: $a_1(\mathbf{X} + \mathbf{Y}) = a_1\mathbf{X} + a_1\mathbf{Y}$

Property 2: $(a_1 + a_2)\mathbf{X} = a_1\mathbf{X} + a_2\mathbf{X}$

If we let

$$\mathbf{X} = \begin{bmatrix} 1 \\ 1 \\ 0 \end{bmatrix} \quad \text{and} \quad \mathbf{Y} = \begin{bmatrix} 3 \\ 4 \\ 2 \end{bmatrix}$$

and the two numbers

$$a_1 = 4 \quad \text{and} \quad a_2 = 3$$

then, an example of Property 1 would be

$$4(\mathbf{X} + \mathbf{Y}) = 4\mathbf{X} + 4\mathbf{Y}$$

$$4\left(\begin{bmatrix} 1 \\ 1 \\ 0 \end{bmatrix} + \begin{bmatrix} 3 \\ 4 \\ 2 \end{bmatrix} \right) = 4\begin{bmatrix} 1 \\ 1 \\ 0 \end{bmatrix} + 4\begin{bmatrix} 3 \\ 4 \\ 2 \end{bmatrix}$$

$$4\begin{bmatrix} 1+3 \\ 1+4 \\ 0+2 \end{bmatrix} = \begin{bmatrix} 4(1) \\ 4(1) \\ 4(0) \end{bmatrix} + \begin{bmatrix} 4(3) \\ 4(4) \\ 4(2) \end{bmatrix}$$

$$4\begin{bmatrix} 4 \\ 5 \\ 2 \end{bmatrix} = \begin{bmatrix} 4 \\ 4 \\ 0 \end{bmatrix} + \begin{bmatrix} 12 \\ 16 \\ 8 \end{bmatrix}$$

$$\begin{bmatrix} 4(4) \\ 4(5) \\ 4(2) \end{bmatrix} = \begin{bmatrix} 4+12 \\ 4+16 \\ 0+8 \end{bmatrix}$$

$$\begin{bmatrix} 16 \\ 20 \\ 8 \end{bmatrix} = \begin{bmatrix} 16 \\ 20 \\ 8 \end{bmatrix}$$

And an example of Property 2 would be

$$(4 + 3)\mathbf{X} = 4\mathbf{X} + 3\mathbf{X}$$

$$(4 + 3)\begin{bmatrix} 1 \\ 1 \\ 0 \end{bmatrix} = 4\begin{bmatrix} 1 \\ 1 \\ 0 \end{bmatrix} + 3\begin{bmatrix} 1 \\ 1 \\ 0 \end{bmatrix}$$

$$7\begin{bmatrix} 1 \\ 1 \\ 0 \end{bmatrix} = \begin{bmatrix} 4(1) \\ 4(1) \\ 4(0) \end{bmatrix} + \begin{bmatrix} 3(1) \\ 3(1) \\ 3(0) \end{bmatrix}$$

$$\begin{bmatrix} 7(1) \\ 7(1) \\ 7(0) \end{bmatrix} = \begin{bmatrix} 4 \\ 4 \\ 0 \end{bmatrix} + \begin{bmatrix} 3 \\ 3 \\ 0 \end{bmatrix}$$

$$\begin{bmatrix} 7 \\ 7 \\ 0 \end{bmatrix} = \begin{bmatrix} 4+3 \\ 4+3 \\ 0+0 \end{bmatrix}$$

$$\begin{bmatrix} 7 \\ 7 \\ 0 \end{bmatrix} = \begin{bmatrix} 7 \\ 7 \\ 0 \end{bmatrix}$$

1.12
SUMMARY

To formulate problems for analysis, we have adopted vector notation, a *symbolic* language that enables us to specify *models* in a form that is easily translated for computers. *Vectors*, used as the basic units in formulating problems, permit large amounts of data to be represented in an orderly way. *Linear combination of a set of vectors* provides the basic tool for the formulation of models to be used in the solution of problems.

* * *

In this chapter, only a few concepts of vector algebra were discussed, but in the following chapters, vector concepts are used to define models for a wide variety of problems. Additional reading in sources such as Bashaw (1969) and Murdoch (1957) will be helpful, and more advanced coverage can be found in Scheffé (1959, Appendix I).

EXERCISES

1. What is the dimension of each of the column vectors shown below?

A	B	C	D	E
$\begin{bmatrix} 1 \\ 3 \\ 5 \\ 7 \end{bmatrix}$	$\begin{bmatrix} 1 \\ 0 \\ 1 \end{bmatrix}$	$\begin{bmatrix} 1 \\ 1 \\ 1 \\ 1 \end{bmatrix}$	$[3.5]$	$\begin{bmatrix} -1.0 \\ 1.5 \\ 0.0 \\ -6.3 \\ 4.2 \end{bmatrix}$

2. Which of the following notations represent a *single number* and which represent a *vector*?

$$y_1, \, x_{1,1}, \, \mathbf{X}, \, \mathbf{Y}, \, \mathbf{Y}^{(1)}, \, \mathbf{E}^{(2)}, \, e_{3,2}, \, \mathbf{X}^{(b,k)}, \, a, \, \mathbf{A}, \, \mathbf{A}^{(1)}, \, n, \, \mathbf{N}, \, \mathbf{P}, \, r, \, \mathbf{E}$$

3. Create a problem situation of your own similar to the following example. Define five vectors, represent them in extended form by alphabetic letters, and indicate the appearance of numerical values.

Example: Information is to be described about 475 students in a school. The information involves age, hair color, and aptitude-test score.

Define vectors:

A = a vector of dimension 475 with the elements of **A** being the ages of the students. (Assume the students are in alphabetic order and the *first* element in **A** is the age of the *first* student in alphabetic order, etc.)

$\mathbf{H}^{(r)}$ = a vector of dimension 475 with the elements of $\mathbf{H}^{(r)}$ equal to 1, if the corresponding element of **A** is associated with a student having red hair—the value of 0 otherwise.

$\mathbf{H}^{(b)}$ = a vector of dimension 475 with the elements of $\mathbf{H}^{(b)}$ equal to 1, if the corresponding element of **A** is associated with a student having blonde hair—the value of 0 otherwise.

$\mathbf{H}^{(n)}$ = a vector of dimension 475 with the elements of $\mathbf{H}^{(n)}$ equal to 1, if the corresponding element of **A** is *not* associated with a student having red or blonde hair—the value of 0 otherwise.

T = a vector of dimension 475 with the elements of **T** equal to the test scores associated with the corresponding students in vector **A**. (Assuming that each student has a test score.)

Extended form using letters:

$$\mathbf{A} = \begin{bmatrix} a_1 \\ a_2 \\ \cdot \\ \cdot \\ \cdot \\ a_{475} \end{bmatrix} \quad \mathbf{H}^{(r)} = \begin{bmatrix} h_{1r} \\ h_{2r} \\ \cdot \\ \cdot \\ \cdot \\ h_{475,r} \end{bmatrix} \quad \mathbf{H}^{(b)} = \begin{bmatrix} h_{1b} \\ h_{2b} \\ \cdot \\ \cdot \\ \cdot \\ h_{475,b} \end{bmatrix}$$

$$\mathbf{H}^{(n)} = \begin{bmatrix} h_{1n} \\ h_{2n} \\ \cdot \\ \cdot \\ \cdot \\ h_{475,n} \end{bmatrix} \quad \mathbf{T} = \begin{bmatrix} t_1 \\ t_2 \\ \cdot \\ \cdot \\ \cdot \\ t_{475} \end{bmatrix}$$

Extended form using numbers:

$$\mathbf{A} = \begin{bmatrix} 14 \\ 18 \\ 13 \\ 19 \\ 12 \\ \cdot \\ \cdot \\ \cdot \\ 15 \end{bmatrix} \quad \mathbf{H}^{(r)} = \begin{bmatrix} 1 \\ 0 \\ 1 \\ 1 \\ 0 \\ \cdot \\ \cdot \\ \cdot \\ 0 \end{bmatrix} \quad \mathbf{H}^{(b)} = \begin{bmatrix} 0 \\ 0 \\ 0 \\ 0 \\ 1 \\ \cdot \\ \cdot \\ \cdot \\ 1 \end{bmatrix}$$

$$\mathbf{H}^{(n)} = \begin{bmatrix} 0 \\ 1 \\ 0 \\ 0 \\ 0 \\ \cdot \\ \cdot \\ \cdot \\ 0 \end{bmatrix} \qquad \mathbf{T} = \begin{bmatrix} 75 \\ 84 \\ 92 \\ 63 \\ 25 \\ \cdot \\ \cdot \\ \cdot \\ 86 \end{bmatrix}$$

4. Indicate the sets of vectors that are equal to each other.

A	B	C	D	E	F
$\begin{bmatrix} 3/2 \\ 8/2 \\ 6/2 \end{bmatrix}$	$\begin{bmatrix} 3/2 \\ 8/2 \\ 6/2 \\ 4/2 \end{bmatrix}$	$\begin{bmatrix} 1.5 \\ 4 \\ 3 \end{bmatrix}$	$\begin{bmatrix} 3/2 \\ 4 \\ 3 \\ 8/2 \end{bmatrix}$	$\begin{bmatrix} 3 \\ 8 \\ 6 \\ 4 \end{bmatrix}$	$\begin{bmatrix} 1 \\ 0 \\ 0 \\ 1 \end{bmatrix}$

G	H	I	J	K	L
$\begin{bmatrix} 0 \\ 1 \\ 1 \\ 0 \end{bmatrix}$	$\begin{bmatrix} -1 \\ 0 \\ 0 \\ -1 \end{bmatrix}$	$\begin{bmatrix} 2 \\ 0 \\ 0 \\ 2 \end{bmatrix}$	$\begin{bmatrix} 1 \\ 0 \\ 0 \\ 1 \end{bmatrix}$	$\begin{bmatrix} 4/5 \\ 0 \\ 1/3 \\ 1 \end{bmatrix}$	$\begin{bmatrix} 6 \\ 16 \\ 2 \\ 8 \end{bmatrix}$

Use the following vectors and numbers in Exercises 5–14.

$$\mathbf{X} \qquad \mathbf{W} \qquad \mathbf{Y}$$

$$\begin{bmatrix} 3 \\ 7 \\ 5 \\ 4 \\ 1 \end{bmatrix} \qquad \begin{bmatrix} 4 \\ 2 \\ 1 \\ 3 \\ 7 \end{bmatrix} \qquad \begin{bmatrix} 1 \\ 0 \\ 0 \\ 1 \\ -1 \end{bmatrix} \qquad \begin{matrix} b = 2 \\ c = .5 \\ d = -1 \end{matrix}$$

Example: $b\mathbf{X} + d\mathbf{W} =$

$$2\begin{bmatrix} 3 \\ 7 \\ 5 \\ 4 \\ 1 \end{bmatrix} + (-1)\begin{bmatrix} 4 \\ 2 \\ 1 \\ 3 \\ 7 \end{bmatrix} = \begin{bmatrix} 6 - 4 \\ 14 - 2 \\ 10 - 1 \\ 8 - 3 \\ 2 - 7 \end{bmatrix} = \begin{bmatrix} 2 \\ 12 \\ 9 \\ 5 \\ -5 \end{bmatrix}$$

5. $c\mathbf{Y} =$

6. $bc\mathbf{X} =$

7. $b\mathbf{X} + c\mathbf{X} =$

8. $(b + c)\mathbf{X} =$

9. $b\mathbf{X} + b\mathbf{W} =$

10. $b(\mathbf{X} + \mathbf{W}) =$

11. $\mathbf{W} - c\mathbf{W} =$

12. $\mathbf{X} + \mathbf{W} - \mathbf{Y} =$

13. $b\mathbf{X} + \mathbf{W} + d\mathbf{Y} =$

14. $\mathbf{Y} - b\mathbf{X} - d\mathbf{W} =$

2

An Elementary
One-Attribute Model

2.1
INTRODUCTION

In this chapter, we will present a very simple problem utilizing the important concept of linear combination of vectors. The use of vector concepts in problem formulation provides results that are consistent with our intuitive ideas in the simplest problems. But more importantly, the use of vector concepts provides solutions for more complicated problems. By learning a few basic ideas and through extensive practice, it is possible to analyze effectively a wide variety of important questions.

In a large number of problems, some type of analysis is required of values that have been observed on some *variable of interest, dependent variable,* or *criterion variable.* In general, these observations can be classified as coming from one or more groups or categories of persons, objects, or events. The way in which these observations are classified is determined by the question that motivated their collection. In this particular problem, we will analyze a single variable of interest (typing performance), whose values are classified as coming from the members of a single group.

2.2
ANALYSIS OF AN ILLUSTRATIVE PROBLEM
INVOLVING ONLY ONE CATEGORY

For purposes of illustration, consider a problem concerning typing performance in a school. Suppose the question at issue is whether it is appropriate to say that the typing performance of students who have completed typing instruction during a particular year is equal to some previously specified level of performance. (The specified level may have been established by the State Certification Committee.)

In analyzing the problem, one of the first questions is: "What do we mean by *level* of typing performance?" If different persons have different typing scores, our question might have an ambiguous answer. For example, if every person in our present group has a score higher than the specified value, we could probably agree that the answer to our question is: "Yes, our students do differ from the specified value." However, what if some students have a higher score and some have a lower score than the specified value? What should we do? An appropriate course of action will depend partially on what we intend to do with the answer and partially on how much we are willing to pay to find the answer.

One course of action is to choose a single value to represent the level of performance for the entire group. One might say: "Why not use the *average* of all typing scores as the level of performance and compare this average with the specified value?" This is a reasonable suggestion. Of course, there are other indicators of the level of typing performance; the mode, median, maximum, minimum, or some other value might be chosen by individuals in different situations. As we shall see, the average is actually the number that evolves as the level indicator when the problem is analyzed in terms of the concept of linear combination of vectors.

Note that the recommended course of action is an arbitrary way of arriving at a yes or no answer to a question that probably does not have a yes or no answer. We have not specified very precisely which students we are concerned about. Are they students of a particular class, a school, an entire school district, or perhaps an entire state? As the number of students involved grows larger, the expense associated with gathering and analyzing the data also increases. In order to reduce the cost, we may have to accept a certain degree of uncertainty in our answer. In this case, rather than calculate the average of all typing scores, we have selected only a sample of scores and have estimated the average of all scores on the basis of the sampled values. Then we are in a position to compare the estimated average with the value specified by the State Certification Committee.

2.3
DEFINING THE VECTOR OF INTEREST
AND THE PREDICTOR VECTORS

The first step in the application of vector concepts to the solution of our problem is to define the information of major concern. We must study typing

performance, and a typing-test score is used as the indicator of typing performance. The typing-test scores are represented as the *elements of a vector*,
and this vector is referred to as the **vector of interest**. (We will assume that
typing-test scores are available for each of n students.) These n scores can then
be represented by a vector, $\mathbf{Y}$, of dimension n, where n is the number of
typing test scores.

$\mathbf{Y} =$ a vector in which each element is a typing-test score observed
on a member of the particular group of students.

The extended form of $\mathbf{Y}$ is

$$\mathbf{Y} = \begin{bmatrix} y_1 \\ y_2 \\ \cdot \\ \cdot \\ \cdot \\ y_n \end{bmatrix}$$

where

$$y_1 = \text{typing test score for student 1}$$

$$y_2 = \text{typing test score for student 2}$$

$$y_n = \text{typing test score for student } n$$

After defining the vector of interest $(\mathbf{Y})$, the next goal is to express it in
terms of other appropriately defined vectors. But the only information we
have about the typing-test scores in vector $\mathbf{Y}$ is that they were observed from
a particular group of students. We therefore define a vector, $\mathbf{U}$, of dimension
n, which expresses this information.

$\mathbf{U} =$ a vector in which each element is a 1, if the corresponding typing
score in $\mathbf{Y}$ is one from our group of students. Of course, since all
elements of $\mathbf{Y}$ are from our particular group, there are n 1's in
the vector—one corresponding to each element in $\mathbf{Y}$. A vector with
every element equal to 1 is called a **unit vector**.

The extended form of $\mathbf{U}$ is

$$\mathbf{U} = \begin{bmatrix} 1 \\ 1 \\ \cdot \\ \cdot \\ \cdot \\ 1 \end{bmatrix}$$

Next we will attempt to express $\mathbf{Y}$ as a *linear combination* of $\mathbf{U}$. Can we find a single number a_0 such that $\mathbf{Y} = a_0\mathbf{U}$ is true? Observe the detailed elements to decide if the expression can be true.

$$
\begin{matrix} \mathbf{Y} & & \mathbf{U} \end{matrix}
$$

$$
\begin{bmatrix} y_1 \\ y_2 \\ \cdot \\ \cdot \\ \cdot \\ y_n \end{bmatrix} = a_0 \begin{bmatrix} 1 \\ 1 \\ \cdot \\ \cdot \\ \cdot \\ 1 \end{bmatrix}
$$

Let the vector $a_0\mathbf{U}$ be given the name $\mathbf{S}$.

$$
\begin{matrix} \mathbf{U} & & \mathbf{S} & & \mathbf{S} \end{matrix}
$$

$$
a_0 \begin{bmatrix} 1 \\ 1 \\ \cdot \\ \cdot \\ \cdot \\ 1 \end{bmatrix} = \begin{bmatrix} s_1 \\ s_2 \\ \cdot \\ \cdot \\ \cdot \\ s_n \end{bmatrix} = \begin{bmatrix} a_0 \\ a_0 \\ \cdot \\ \cdot \\ \cdot \\ a_0 \end{bmatrix}
$$

Observe that every element of $\mathbf{S}$ has the same value a_0. Therefore, it is obvious that the statement

$$\mathbf{Y} = a_0\mathbf{U} = \mathbf{S}$$

is generally not true; that is,

$$\mathbf{Y} \neq a_0\mathbf{U}$$

$$\mathbf{Y} \neq \mathbf{S}$$

This statement would be true only when all the elements of $\mathbf{Y}$ are equal; that is,

$$y_1 = y_2 = \cdots = y_n$$

However, it is possible to define a vector that represents the difference or residual between the observed values in $\mathbf{Y}$ and the values in $\mathbf{S}$.

2.4
DEFINING THE RESIDUAL OR ERROR VECTOR

The *residual* or *error vector*, $\mathbf{E}$, is defined as

$$\mathbf{E} = \mathbf{Y} - \mathbf{S} = \mathbf{Y} - a_0\mathbf{U} \tag{2.1}$$

The extended form is

$$
\begin{array}{cccccc}
\mathbf{E} & \mathbf{Y} & \mathbf{S} & \mathbf{Y} & \mathbf{S} & \mathbf{Y-S}
\end{array}
$$

$$
\begin{bmatrix} e_1 \\ e_2 \\ \cdot \\ \cdot \\ \cdot \\ e_n \end{bmatrix}
=
\begin{bmatrix} y_1 \\ y_2 \\ \cdot \\ \cdot \\ \cdot \\ y_n \end{bmatrix}
-
\begin{bmatrix} s_1 \\ s_2 \\ \cdot \\ \cdot \\ \cdot \\ s_n \end{bmatrix}
=
\begin{bmatrix} y_1 \\ y_2 \\ \cdot \\ \cdot \\ \cdot \\ y_n \end{bmatrix}
-
\begin{bmatrix} a_0 \\ a_0 \\ \cdot \\ \cdot \\ \cdot \\ a_0 \end{bmatrix}
=
\begin{bmatrix} y_1 - a_0 \\ y_2 - a_0 \\ \cdot \\ \cdot \\ \cdot \\ y_n - a_0 \end{bmatrix}
$$

Therefore, we can now express the vector $\mathbf{Y}$ as a linear combination of $\mathbf{U}$ and $\mathbf{E}$.

$$
\mathbf{Y} = \mathbf{S} + \mathbf{E} = a_0\mathbf{U} + \mathbf{E} \tag{2.2}
$$

2.5
INTRODUCTION OF NUMERICAL VALUES

Before continuing our discussion, it may be helpful to look at these concepts in terms of specific values. Assume for simplicity that typing scores are available from only four students.

Student 1 has a typing score of 50.
Student 2 has a typing score of 60.
Student 3 has a typing score of 30.
Student 4 has a typing score of 40.

Thus the vector $\mathbf{Y}$ has four elements.

$$
\mathbf{Y} = \begin{bmatrix} y_1 \\ y_2 \\ y_3 \\ y_4 \end{bmatrix} = \begin{bmatrix} 50 \\ 60 \\ 30 \\ 40 \end{bmatrix}
$$

Then

$$
\begin{array}{ccccccc}
\mathbf{Y} & = & a_0\mathbf{U} & + & \mathbf{E} & = & \mathbf{S} & + & \mathbf{E}
\end{array}
$$

$$
\begin{bmatrix} 50 \\ 60 \\ 30 \\ 40 \end{bmatrix}
= a_0 \begin{bmatrix} 1 \\ 1 \\ 1 \\ 1 \end{bmatrix}
+ \begin{bmatrix} e_1 \\ e_2 \\ e_3 \\ e_4 \end{bmatrix}
= \begin{bmatrix} a_0 \\ a_0 \\ a_0 \\ a_0 \end{bmatrix}
+ \begin{bmatrix} e_1 \\ e_2 \\ e_3 \\ e_4 \end{bmatrix}
$$

From the definition of $\mathbf{E}$ in (2.1), we can make the substitution and write

$$\mathbf{E} = \mathbf{Y} - \mathbf{S} \tag{2.3}$$

$$\begin{bmatrix} 50 - a_0 \\ 60 - a_0 \\ 30 - a_0 \\ 40 - a_0 \end{bmatrix} = \begin{bmatrix} 50 \\ 60 \\ 30 \\ 40 \end{bmatrix} - \begin{bmatrix} a_0 \\ a_0 \\ a_0 \\ a_0 \end{bmatrix}$$

The magnitude of the elements in $\mathbf{E}$, the residual vector, indicates an inability to express $\mathbf{Y}$ as a linear combination of $\mathbf{U}$. All elements of $\mathbf{E}$ will be zero only when $\mathbf{Y}$ can be expressed as an exact linear combination of $\mathbf{U}$. An examination of (2.3) reveals that $\mathbf{Y} = a_0\mathbf{U}$ (and all the values of $\mathbf{E}$ are zero) only when all the elements of $\mathbf{Y}$ have the same value.

If it is generally impossible to have the elements of $\mathbf{E}$ all equal to zero, it would be nice to have the values of $\mathbf{E}$ very small. The next question then is: "What value do we assign to a_0 so that the elements of $\mathbf{E}$ will be small?"

2.6
SELECTING A VALUE FOR a_0

The number of different values for a_0 is unlimited, so we will select several different values for a_0 and examine the resulting elements of $\mathbf{E}$.

First, assume that $a_0 = 35$. Then express $\mathbf{Y}$ as

$$\mathbf{Y} = 35\mathbf{U} + \mathbf{E}^{(1)}$$

where $\mathbf{E}^{(1)}$ is the error vector obtained as a result of using $a_0 = 35$. Now compute the values for the elements of $\mathbf{E}^{(1)}$ that make $\mathbf{Y} = 35\mathbf{U} + \mathbf{E}^{(1)}$ a true statement.

$$\begin{array}{ccc} \mathbf{Y} & \mathbf{U} & \mathbf{E}^{(1)} \end{array}$$

$$\begin{bmatrix} 50 \\ 60 \\ 30 \\ 40 \end{bmatrix} = 35\begin{bmatrix} 1 \\ 1 \\ 1 \\ 1 \end{bmatrix} + \begin{bmatrix} e_{11} \\ e_{21} \\ e_{31} \\ e_{41} \end{bmatrix}$$

$$\begin{bmatrix} 50 \\ 60 \\ 30 \\ 40 \end{bmatrix} = \begin{bmatrix} 35 \\ 35 \\ 35 \\ 35 \end{bmatrix} + \begin{bmatrix} 15 \\ 25 \\ -5 \\ 5 \end{bmatrix}$$

The elements of $\mathbf{E}^{(1)}$ were determined as follows:

$$e_{11} = 50 - 35 = 15$$

$$e_{21} = 60 - 35 = 25$$

$$e_{31} = 30 - 35 = -5$$

$$e_{41} = 40 - 35 = 5$$

Each element of $\mathbf{E}^{(1)}$ can be observed, but we need a single indicator to represent the general size of the errors. We could use the largest absolute value in the residual vector as the single indicator of error size, or we could use the sum of the absolute values of the residuals. *The indicator we will use in this book to represent error size is* **the sum of the squares of the elements of the error vector.**

For $\mathbf{E}^{(1)}$, let q_1 be the error sum of squares. Then

$$q_1 = (e_{11})^2 + (e_{21})^2 + (e_{31})^2 + (e_{41})^2$$

$$q_1 = (15)^2 + (25)^2 + (-5)^2 + (5)^2$$

$$q_1 = 225 + 625 + 25 + 25$$

$$q_1 = 900$$

which is the error sum of squares using $a_0 = 35$.

Next, let $a_0 = 45$. Then

$$\mathbf{Y} = 45\mathbf{U} + \mathbf{E}^{(2)}$$

where $\mathbf{E}^{(2)}$ is the error vector obtained by using $a_0 = 45$.

Next, compute the values for elements of $\mathbf{E}^{(2)}$.

$$
\begin{matrix}
\mathbf{Y} & & \mathbf{U} & & \mathbf{E}^{(2)} \\
\begin{bmatrix} 50 \\ 60 \\ 30 \\ 40 \end{bmatrix} & = 45 & \begin{bmatrix} 1 \\ 1 \\ 1 \\ 1 \end{bmatrix} & + & \begin{bmatrix} e_{12} \\ e_{22} \\ e_{32} \\ e_{42} \end{bmatrix}
\end{matrix}
$$

$$
\begin{bmatrix} 50 \\ 60 \\ 30 \\ 40 \end{bmatrix} = \begin{bmatrix} 45 \\ 45 \\ 45 \\ 45 \end{bmatrix} + \begin{bmatrix} 5 \\ 15 \\ -15 \\ -5 \end{bmatrix}
$$

The elements of $\mathbf{E}^{(2)}$ were determined as follows:

$$e_{12} = 50 - 45 = 5$$

$$e_{22} = 60 - 45 = 15$$

$$e_{32} = 30 - 45 = -15$$

$$e_{42} = 40 - 45 = -5$$

Now that the elements of $\mathbf{E}^{(2)}$ are known, we can compute the error sum of squares as the indicator of error size. Let

$$q_2 = (e_{12})^2 + (e_{22})^2 + (e_{32})^2 + (e_{42})^2$$

Then

$$q_2 = (5)^2 + (15)^2 + (-15)^2 + (-5)^2$$
$$q_2 = 25 + 225 + 225 + 25$$
$$q_2 = 500$$

we can compare $q_1 = 900$ with $q_2 = 500$. Note that when $a_0 = 45$, we obtain a smaller error sum of squares than when $a_0 = 35$. We will say that the value $a_0 = 45$ is "better" than $a_0 = 35$ because the error sum of squares is smaller.

Now select a third value for a_0. Let $a_0 = 55$. Then

$$\mathbf{Y} = 55\mathbf{U} + \mathbf{E}^{(3)}$$

where $\mathbf{E}^{(3)}$ is the error vector obtained by using $a_0 = 55$.

Next, compute the values for the elements of $\mathbf{E}^{(3)}$.

$$
\begin{matrix}
\mathbf{Y} & \mathbf{U} & \mathbf{E}^{(3)}
\end{matrix}
$$

$$
\begin{bmatrix} 50 \\ 60 \\ 30 \\ 40 \end{bmatrix} = 55 \begin{bmatrix} 1 \\ 1 \\ 1 \\ 1 \end{bmatrix} + \begin{bmatrix} e_{13} \\ e_{23} \\ e_{33} \\ e_{33} \end{bmatrix}
$$

$$
\begin{bmatrix} 50 \\ 60 \\ 30 \\ 40 \end{bmatrix} = \begin{bmatrix} 55 \\ 55 \\ 55 \\ 55 \end{bmatrix} + \begin{bmatrix} -5 \\ 5 \\ -25 \\ -15 \end{bmatrix}
$$

The elements of $\mathbf{E}^{(3)}$ were determined as follows:

$$e_{13} = 50 - 55 = -5$$
$$e_{23} = 60 - 55 = 5$$
$$e_{33} = 30 - 55 = -25$$
$$e_{43} = 40 - 55 = -15$$

From the elements of $\mathbf{E}^{(3)}$ we can then compute

$$q_3 = (e_{13})^2 + (e_{23})^2 + (e_{33})^2 + (e_{43})^2$$
$$q_3 = (-5)^2 + (5)^2 + (-25)^2 + (-15)^2$$
$$q_3 = 25 + 25 + 625 + 225$$
$$q_3 = 900$$

Observe that when

$$a_0 = 35, \qquad q_1 = 900$$
$$a_0 = 45, \qquad q_2 = 500$$
$$a_0 = 55, \qquad q_3 = 900$$

We can therefore say that $a_0 = 45$ is the "best" value of the three because the error sum of squares is smallest. In a similar way, we can let

$$a_0 = 43$$

and compute $\mathbf{E}^{(4)}$ and q_4, and let

$$a_0 = 47$$

and compute $\mathbf{E}^{(5)}$ and q_5.

Table 2.1   THE ERROR SUM OF SQUARES RESULTING FROM FIVE VALUES OF a_0

Assumed Value for a_0	*Error Sum of Squares*
35	$q_1 = 900$
43	$q_4 = 516$
45	$q_2 = 500$
47	$q_5 = 516$
55	$q_3 = 900$

Examination of Table 2.1 reveals that of the five values chosen, $a_0 = 45$ gives the smallest error sum of squares, and we would therefore select it as the "best" value from the five.

In general, we will choose from the infinite set of possible numbers a value for a_0 that will produce the smallest error sum of squares. The value of a_0 that produces the smallest error sum of squares is called the *least-squares value* or *least-squares weight*.[1] The method used to minimize the error sum of squares is known as the *least-squares procedure*.

2.7
THE LEAST-SQUARES VALUE FOR a_0

In Section 2.2, the question was asked: "Why not use the *average* of all the typing scores to indicate the level of performance?" It turns out that for any problem in which $\mathbf{Y}$ is expressed as

$$\mathbf{Y} = a_0 \mathbf{U} + \mathbf{E}$$

---

[1]A computer program for computing least-squares weights is discussed in Chapter 14.

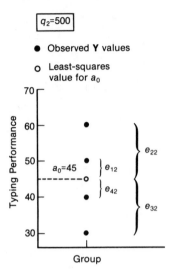

FIG. 2.1 Deviations of Observed Values from the Least Squares Value.

*the least-squares value for a_0 is the arithmetic average of all the values in the **Y** vector.* Moreover, if the values in **Y** have been selected in a certain way (called *random sampling*) from a larger collection of values, the obtained value of a_0 can be regarded as a "good" estimate of the average of the larger collection. For the numerical example just given, we observe that the average value of the elements of **Y** is

$$\text{Average} = (50 + 60 + 30 + 40)/4$$
$$\text{Average} = 180/4 = 45$$

Hence the best model to use is

$$\mathbf{Y} = 45\mathbf{U} + \mathbf{E}^{(2)} \tag{2.4}$$

Another look at Table 2.1 reveals that the error sum of squares resulting from $a_0 = 45$ is 500. The value 500—resulting from using the arithmetic average—is the smallest error sum of squares possible. Furthermore, there is no other value for a_0 that will produce an error sum of squares equal to or less than 500. Figure 2.1 is a pictorial representation of the typing scores, the average, and the elements of $\mathbf{E}^{(2)}$.

2.8
SUMMARY OF PROBLEM FORMULATION

Our problem was to determine if it is appropriate to claim that the level of typing performance of a group of students is equal to a specified constant. Our first task was to select *an indicator of level of performance*. Knowledge of *vector concepts* was used to express a sample of typing scores (vector $\mathbf{Y}$) as *a linear combination of a simple vector* ($\mathbf{U}$), which contains only 1's and *a residual vector* ($\mathbf{E}$).

The value used for a_0 (the weight used with $\mathbf{U}$) is the one that minimizes the sum of the squared differences between the observed values in $\mathbf{Y}$ and the values in $\mathbf{S}$. The *least-squares procedure* was used to obtain the value, and for this particular problem, the *average* of the $\mathbf{Y}$ values was the *least-squares weight*.

The *error sum of squares* is an indicator of the degree to which the value of a_0 fails to be equal to each value in $\mathbf{Y}$. The magnitude of the error sum of squares is also heavily influenced by the number of elements in $\mathbf{Y}$. Dividing the error sum of squares by the number of elements in $\mathbf{Y}$ produces a value that is called the *sample variance*. In general, the variance is a more informative number than is the error sum of squares.

2.9
COMPARING THE LEVEL OF PERFORMANCE WITH A SPECIFIED VALUE

Now return to the question of whether it is appropriate to say that the level of typing performance is equal to some specified value. We will translate this problem into the mathematical model described in Section 2.4 by relation (2.2); that is,

$$\mathbf{Y} = a_0\mathbf{U} + \mathbf{E}$$

We decided that the single weight a_0 would be used to indicate the performance level for the entire group of students. And, furthermore, we decided to use the least-squares value as the best numerical value for a_0.

Now the question is: "How reasonable is it to say that the level of performance (called a_0 in our model) is equal to a specified value?" For our sample problem, assume that the State Certification Committee has specified the value 32 as the desired level of typing performance. In terms of the mathematical model, the question can then be restated as: "Is $a_0 = 32$ a reasonable statement?" In Table 2.1 several values for a_0 were tried; however 32 was not among them. The value 35 was the closest to 32, and $a_0 = 35$ produced an error sum of squares $q_1 = 900$.

To investigate how reasonable the statement $a_0 = 32$ is, we will again attempt to express $\mathbf{Y}$ by using a specified value (32) as the numerical value for a_0. From an examination of the pattern of error sums of squares in Table 2.1, we might guess that the error sum of squares when $a_0 = 32$ will be greater than 900. Using the numerical data and the procedure in Section 2.6,

$$\mathbf{Y} = 32\mathbf{U} + \mathbf{D}^{(1)} \tag{2.5}$$

where $\mathbf{D}^{(1)}$ is the error vector obtained by considering $a_0 = 32$.

$$
\begin{array}{ccc}
\mathbf{Y} & \mathbf{U} & \mathbf{D}^{(1)} \\
\begin{bmatrix} 50 \\ 60 \\ 30 \\ 40 \end{bmatrix} = 32 & \begin{bmatrix} 1 \\ 1 \\ 1 \\ 1 \end{bmatrix} + & \begin{bmatrix} d_{11} \\ d_{21} \\ d_{31} \\ d_{41} \end{bmatrix}
\end{array}
$$

$$
\begin{bmatrix} 50 \\ 60 \\ 30 \\ 40 \end{bmatrix} = \begin{bmatrix} 32 \\ 32 \\ 32 \\ 32 \end{bmatrix} + \begin{bmatrix} 18 \\ 28 \\ -2 \\ 8 \end{bmatrix}
$$

The elements of $\mathbf{D}^{(1)}$ were determined as follows:

$$
\begin{aligned}
d_{11} &= 50 - 32 = 18 \\
d_{21} &= 60 - 32 = 28 \\
d_{31} &= 30 - 32 = -2 \\
d_{41} &= 40 - 32 = 8
\end{aligned}
$$

Now that the elements of $\mathbf{D}^{(1)}$ are available, we can compute the error sum of squares. Let

$$
\begin{aligned}
q_6 &= (d_{11})^2 + (d_{21})^2 + (d_{31})^2 + (d_{41})^2 \\
q_6 &= (18)^2 + (28)^2 + (-2)^2 + (8)^2 \\
q_6 &= 324 + 784 + 4 + 64 \\
q_6 &= 1176
\end{aligned}
$$

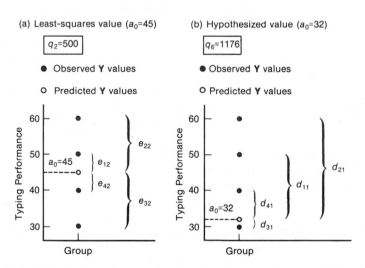

FIG. 2.2 Deviations of Observed Values from the Least Squares and Hypothesized Values.

We now have the error sum of squares $q_6 = 1176$ by considering $a_0 = 32$ and the error sum of squares $q_2 = 500$ by using the least-squares value for a_0. Figure 2.2 is a pictorial representation of the data with the least-squares value 45 and the specified value 32.

2.10
COMPARING ERROR SUMS OF SQUARES

We now seek a means of deciding if 32 is a reasonable value to use for a_0—is $a_0 = 32$ a reasonable statement? Two problems are immediately apparent. One has to do with the ambiguous meaning of the word reasonable. What seems to be "reasonable" to one individual may not strike another as being reasonable at all. The second problem is somewhat more subtle. We have previously stated that 45 is the "best" value for a_0. What meaning can be attached to the search for a *reasonable* value when we already have the *best* value?

If the values in **Y** are observations on *all* of the individuals of concern, then 45 is the average of those values, and it is clear that 45 does not equal 32. Whether one thinks 32 is close enough to 45 to be a reasonable substitute is simply a matter of opinion. However, if the values in **Y** are observations on a *sample* of all the individuals, then 45 is the average of the sampled observations but not necessarily the average of all the individuals concerned. As a matter of fact, it is possible that the average of all potential observations is 32, and the average of the sampled values is 45. We are then in a position to entertain the question: "How likely is it that a random collection of observations would generate a value of 45 if the corresponding value on all potential observations is 32?"

If certain underlying assumptions[2] are met, we can actually assign an exact probability value to the likelihood of drawing a sample with an average of 45 from a larger collection whose average is 32. For the time being, we appeal to your intuition by directing your attention to Table 2.1. Note that as values for a_0 get farther from 45, the error sum of squares gets larger. If the error sum of squares using the value 32 ($q_6 = 1176$) is "appreciably larger" than the error sum of squares for the least-squares value 45 ($q_2 = 500$), we will conclude that it is reasonable to say that the level of typing performance for the students of concern *does* differ from the value of 32.[3]

---

[2] These assumptions are discussed in some detail in Sections 4.8, 4.10, and Appendix B.

[3] A similar procedure could be used to investigate values (i.e., 45.6, 12.5, or any other number) other than 32. If we use the designation c_0 to represent any constant that might be selected, then the general problem is to decide how likely it is that we could get a value of a_0 by sampling from a larger collection whose corresponding value is c_0.

2.11
SUMMARY

In this chapter we have followed eight basic steps in the construction of a problem-solution model.

1. *State the problem in natural language.* The example problem was to determine whether it is appropriate to say that the level of typing performance of a group of students is equal to a specified constant.

2. *Define the vector of interest and the predictor vectors.* Typing-test score was defined as the vector of interest ($\mathbf{Y}$). The unit vector ($\mathbf{U}$) was the only predictor vector.

3. *Express the vector of interest* ($\mathbf{Y}$) *as a linear combination of the unit vector* ($\mathbf{U}$) *and a residual vector* ($\mathbf{E}$).

$$\mathbf{Y} = a_0\mathbf{U} + \mathbf{E}$$

4. *Select a value for a_0 that minimizes the sum of squares of the elements of* $\mathbf{E}$. In the example, the *least-squares value* was the *average* of the typing-test scores. The numerical value for the least-squares weight was 45.

$$\mathbf{Y} = 45\mathbf{U} + \mathbf{E}^{(2)}$$

5. *Compute the error sum of squares.* In the example, the error sum of squares using the least-squares value 45 for a_0 was

$$q_2 = 500$$

6. *Make an appropriate statement in terms of the predicted scores in the model.* In the example, we considered whether 32 was an appropriate value for level of performance (a_0).

7. *Impose the restriction implied by the statement on the original model, and determine the error sum of squares.*

$$\mathbf{Y} = 32\mathbf{U} + \mathbf{E}^{(6)}$$

The error sum of squares using 32 was

$$q_6 = 1176$$

8. *Compare the error sum of squares using the assigned value (32 or $q_6 = 1176$) with the error sum of squares using the least-squares value (45 or $q_2 = 500$).* If the error sums of squares are *nearly equal*, then it is reasonable to use the assigned value (32) as the level-of-performance indicator. If the error sums of squares *differ appreciably*, it is reasonable to reject 32 as an appropriate value.

These steps are special cases of the activities listed in the Preface, and they will be extended in future chapters as the models become more complex.

EXERCISES

Apply the eight steps in the Summary to the following two problems.

1. IQ scores from a sample of 12 children were obtained and a question was raised about whether the average value of the population from which the sample was drawn is equal to 100. The data are given below.

   85,   100,   110,   112,   114,   116,   117,   118,   121,   128,   129,   130

2. Six measurements were made to estimate the value of pi (π). It is argued that 3.140 is an appropriate value. The data are given below.

   3.142,   3.142,   3.141,   3.142,   3.140,   3.143

3

A One-Attribute Model
with Two Categories

3.1
INTRODUCTION

In Chapter 2 all observations were from only one category. In this chapter we will consider problems that allow observations to be classified into two categories. The descriptions of the problems are deliberately similar to those in Chapter 2 to emphasize a common strategy in problem formulation and analysis. Our aim is to increase the complexity of the discussed models in a manner that will make any model look familiar. As this practice is continued throughout the book, it will become apparent that even the most complex models require only slight modifications of the previous ones.

3.2
ANALYSIS OF A PROBLEM
INVOLVING TWO CATEGORIES

This illustration considers another problem involving typing performance. Suppose the question is whether it is appropriate to say that the typing performance of girls who have completed typing instruction is equal to the typing performance of boys. A typing-test score will again be used as an indicator of a student's typing performance.

In analyzing the problem, one of the first questions is: "What is meant by *level* of typing performance for the girls and for the boys?" Preferably, a single value should represent the level of typing performance for boys and another for girls. We might also ask: "Why not use the *average* of the boys' typing scores as their level of performance? Then the girls' average can be compared with the boys'." This is a reasonable approach.[1] As in Chapter 2, we will use vector concepts in problem formulation that will provide results consistent with our intuitive ideas in the simplest problems. But, most importantly, the use of vector concepts will provide for the solution of more complicated problems.

3.3
DEFINING THE VECTOR OF INTEREST
AND THE PREDICTOR VECTORS

As before, the first step in the solution of this problem is to define the information of major concern. The typing-test scores will again be represented as the elements of a vector, and also, as before, this vector will be referred to as the *vector of interest*.

We will assume that typing-test scores are available for a total of n students. Of these n students, there are n_b boys and n_g girls. Therefore,

$$n = n_b + n_g$$

and

Y = a vector in which the elements are typing-test scores observed on n students.

The vector definition does not imply any special ordering of the elements in **Y**. For clarity, however, the elements of **Y** obtained from girls are listed first. The extended form of **Y** is

$$\mathbf{Y} = \begin{bmatrix} y_1 \\ y_2 \\ \cdot \\ \cdot \\ \cdot \\ y_{n_g} \\ \cdot \\ \cdot \\ \cdot \\ y_n \end{bmatrix} \begin{matrix} \left. \begin{matrix} \\ \\ \\ \\ \\ \end{matrix} \right\} \longrightarrow \text{These } n_g \text{ values were observed on girls.} \\ \\ \left. \begin{matrix} \\ \\ \\ \\ \end{matrix} \right\} \longrightarrow \text{These } n_b \text{ values were observed on boys.} \end{matrix}$$

After defining the vector of interest, **Y**, the next step is to express it in terms

---

[1]Later it will become evident that these two averages are actually the two numbers that evolve from the use of vector concepts.

of appropriately defined vectors. It will therefore be necessary to define some vectors to be used to predict **Y**.

A method was needed in Chapter 2 to designate membership in only *one* group—the one representing any student who took typing. In the present problem, it is necessary to refer to levels of performance in *two* groups—boys and girls. Therefore, two vectors, each of dimension n, that will allow for the representation of the two levels of performance are defined.

$\mathbf{X}^{(g)}$ = a vector in which an element has the value 1 if the corresponding typing score in **Y** is a girl's; otherwise an element has the value 0. This vector will have n_g elements with values equal to 1 and n_b elements with values equal to 0.

$\mathbf{X}^{(b)}$ = a vector in which an element has the value 1 if the corresponding typing score in **Y** is a boy's; otherwise an element has the value 0. This vector will have n_b elements with values equal to 1 and n_g elements with values equal to 0.

Keeping in mind that the girls' scores have been arbitrarily listed first, the extended forms of $\mathbf{X}^{(g)}$ and $\mathbf{X}^{(b)}$ are

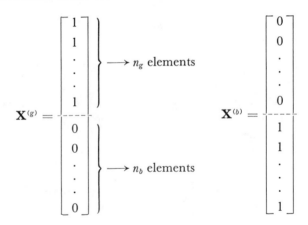

Observe that the first n_g elements of $\mathbf{X}^{(g)}$ contain 1's, and the remaining n_b elements of $\mathbf{X}^{(g)}$ contain 0's. Conversely, the first n_g elements of $\mathbf{X}^{(b)}$ contain 0's, and the remaining n_b elements of $\mathbf{X}^{(b)}$ contain 1's.

Next, an attempt will be made to express **Y** as a linear combination of $\mathbf{X}^{(g)}$ and $\mathbf{X}^{(b)}$. Can two numbers a_g and a_b be found such that the following equation is true?

$$\mathbf{Y} = a_g \mathbf{X}^{(g)} + a_b \mathbf{X}^{(b)}$$

Observe the detailed elements to decide if the expression is generally true.

$$
\mathbf{Y} \qquad\qquad \mathbf{X}^{(g)} \qquad\qquad \mathbf{X}^{(b)}
$$

$$
\begin{bmatrix} y_1 \\ y_2 \\ \cdot \\ \cdot \\ \cdot \\ \cdot \\ \cdot \\ \cdot \\ \cdot \\ \cdot \\ \cdot \\ \cdot \\ \cdot \\ y_n \end{bmatrix}
= a_g
\begin{bmatrix} 1 \\ 1 \\ \cdot \\ \cdot \\ \cdot \\ 1 \\ \hline 0 \\ 0 \\ \cdot \\ \cdot \\ \cdot \\ \cdot \\ \cdot \\ 0 \end{bmatrix}
+ a_b
\begin{bmatrix} 0 \\ 0 \\ \cdot \\ \cdot \\ \cdot \\ 0 \\ \hline 1 \\ 1 \\ \cdot \\ \cdot \\ \cdot \\ \cdot \\ \cdot \\ 1 \end{bmatrix}
$$

A new name is now given to the vector resulting from the linear combination

$$
a_g \mathbf{X}^{(g)} + a_b \mathbf{X}^{(b)}
$$

Let

$$
a_g \mathbf{X}^{(g)} + a_b \mathbf{X}^{(b)} = \mathbf{T}
$$

and observe the extended form of $\mathbf{T}$.

$$
\mathbf{X}^{(g)} \qquad\qquad \mathbf{X}^{(b)} \qquad\qquad \mathbf{T}
$$

$$
a_g
\begin{bmatrix} 1 \\ 1 \\ \cdot \\ \cdot \\ \cdot \\ 1 \\ \hline 0 \\ 0 \\ \cdot \\ \cdot \\ \cdot \\ \cdot \\ \cdot \\ 0 \end{bmatrix}
+ a_b
\begin{bmatrix} 0 \\ 0 \\ \cdot \\ \cdot \\ \cdot \\ 0 \\ \hline 1 \\ 1 \\ \cdot \\ \cdot \\ \cdot \\ \cdot \\ \cdot \\ 1 \end{bmatrix}
=
\begin{bmatrix} t_1 \\ t_2 \\ \cdot \\ \cdot \\ \cdot \\ \cdot \\ \cdot \\ \cdot \\ \cdot \\ \cdot \\ \cdot \\ \cdot \\ \cdot \\ t_n \end{bmatrix}
=
\begin{bmatrix} a_g \\ a_g \\ \cdot \\ \cdot \\ \cdot \\ a_g \\ \hline a_b \\ a_b \\ \cdot \\ \cdot \\ \cdot \\ \cdot \\ \cdot \\ a_b \end{bmatrix}
$$

Note that the first n_g elements of $\mathbf{T}$ have the same value, a_g, and that the last n_b elements of $\mathbf{T}$ have the same value, a_b. Therefore, it is obvious that the statement

$$
\mathbf{Y} = a_g \mathbf{X}^{(g)} + a_b \mathbf{X}^{(b)} = \mathbf{T}
$$

is generally not true; that is,

$$Y \neq a_g X^{(g)} + a_b X^{(b)}$$

$$Y \neq T$$

The only time the statement would be true is when all the girls had the same typing scores and all boys had identical scores. However, as before, it is possible to define a vector that represents the difference or residual between the observed values in **Y** and the values in **T**.

3.4
DEFINING THE RESIDUAL OR ERROR VECTOR

The residual or error vector, **R**, is defined as

$$R = Y - T = Y - [a_g X^{(g)} + a_b X^{(b)}] \qquad (3.1)$$

Note that **R** represents the residual vector in this chapter (instead of **E**) to clarify the difference between the models. The extended form is

$$
\begin{array}{cccc}
\mathbf{R} & \mathbf{Y} & \mathbf{T} & \mathbf{Y} - \mathbf{T} \\
\begin{bmatrix} r_1 \\ r_2 \\ \cdot \\ \cdot \\ \cdot \\ r_{n_g} \\ \cdot \\ \cdot \\ \cdot \\ r_n \end{bmatrix}
& = &
\begin{bmatrix} y_1 \\ y_2 \\ \cdot \\ \cdot \\ \cdot \\ y_{n_g} \\ \cdot \\ \cdot \\ \cdot \\ y_n \end{bmatrix}
& -
\begin{bmatrix} a_g \\ a_g \\ \cdot \\ \cdot \\ \cdot \\ a_g \\ \cdot \\ \cdot \\ \cdot \\ a_b \end{bmatrix}
& =
\begin{bmatrix} y_1 - a_g \\ y_2 - a_g \\ \cdot \\ \cdot \\ \cdot \\ y_{n_g} - a_g \\ \cdot \\ \cdot \\ \cdot \\ y_n - a_b \end{bmatrix}
\end{array}
$$

Therefore, **Y** can be expressed as a linear combination of $X^{(g)}$, $X^{(b)}$, and **R**.

$$Y = T + R = a_g X^{(g)} + a_b X^{(b)} + R \qquad (3.2)$$

3.5
INTRODUCTION OF NUMERICAL VALUES

The numerical values in Chapter 2 will be used to illustrate this problem. The typing scores are as follows

Girl student 1:	50
Girl student 2:	60
Boy student 1:	30
Boy student 2:	40

The vector **Y** has four elements and appears as

$$\mathbf{Y} = \begin{bmatrix} y_1 \\ y_2 \\ y_3 \\ y_4 \end{bmatrix} = \begin{bmatrix} 50 \\ 60 \\ 30 \\ 40 \end{bmatrix}$$

Then

$$\mathbf{Y} = a_g \mathbf{X}^{(g)} + a_b \mathbf{X}^{(b)} + \mathbf{R} = \mathbf{T} + \mathbf{R}$$

$$\begin{bmatrix} 50 \\ 60 \\ 30 \\ 40 \end{bmatrix} = a_g \begin{bmatrix} 1 \\ 1 \\ 0 \\ 0 \end{bmatrix} + a_b \begin{bmatrix} 0 \\ 0 \\ 1 \\ 1 \end{bmatrix} + \begin{bmatrix} r_1 \\ r_2 \\ r_3 \\ r_4 \end{bmatrix} = \begin{bmatrix} a_g \\ a_g \\ a_b \\ a_b \end{bmatrix} + \begin{bmatrix} r_1 \\ r_2 \\ r_3 \\ r_4 \end{bmatrix}$$

From the definition of **R** (3.1), substitution can then be made.

$$\begin{bmatrix} 50 \\ 60 \\ 30 \\ 40 \end{bmatrix} = \begin{bmatrix} a_g \\ a_g \\ a_b \\ a_b \end{bmatrix} + \begin{bmatrix} 50 - a_g \\ 60 - a_g \\ 30 - a_b \\ 40 - a_b \end{bmatrix} \tag{3.3}$$

The elements in **R**, the residual vector, indicate the inability to express **Y** as a linear combination of $\mathbf{X}^{(g)}$ and $\mathbf{X}^{(b)}$. All of the elements in **R** will be zero only when all of the girls' scores are the same and when all of the boys' scores are identical. If it is generally impossible to have the elements in **R** equal to zero, then it is desirable to have the values in **R** as *small* as possible. The next step, therefore, is to select values for a_g (the predicted score for girls) and a_b (the predicted score for boys) so that the elements of **R** will be small.

3.6
SELECTING VALUES FOR a_g AND a_b

In Chapter 2 the *least-squares values* were chosen as the *best* to be used. We will again compute values for a_g and a_b that will minimize the sum of squares of the elements of the residual vector, and we will again examine the error sum of squares resulting from several sets of values for a_g and a_b.

Assume that $a_g = 57$ and $a_b = 33$; then

$$\mathbf{Y} = 57\mathbf{X}^{(g)} + 33\mathbf{X}^{(b)} + \mathbf{R}^{(1)}$$

where $\mathbf{R}^{(1)}$ is the error vector obtained as a result of using $a_g = 57$ and $a_b = 33$. The elements of $\mathbf{R}^{(1)}$ can then be determined.

$$
\begin{array}{cccc}
\mathbf{Y} & \mathbf{X}^{(g)} & \mathbf{X}^{(b)} & \mathbf{R}^{(1)}
\end{array}
$$

$$
\begin{bmatrix} 50 \\ 60 \\ 30 \\ 40 \end{bmatrix} = 57 \begin{bmatrix} 1 \\ 1 \\ 0 \\ 0 \end{bmatrix} + 33 \begin{bmatrix} 0 \\ 0 \\ 1 \\ 1 \end{bmatrix} + \begin{bmatrix} r_{11} \\ r_{21} \\ r_{31} \\ r_{41} \end{bmatrix}
$$

$$
\begin{bmatrix} 50 \\ 60 \\ 30 \\ 40 \end{bmatrix} = \begin{bmatrix} 57 \\ 57 \\ 33 \\ 33 \end{bmatrix} + \begin{bmatrix} -7 \\ 3 \\ -3 \\ 7 \end{bmatrix}
$$

$$
r_{11} = 50 - 57 = -7
$$
$$
r_{21} = 60 - 57 = 3
$$
$$
r_{31} = 30 - 33 = -3
$$
$$
r_{41} = 40 - 33 = 7
$$

After the elements of $\mathbf{R}^{(1)}$ have been determined, the error sum of squares can be computed. Let

$$
q_1 = (r_{11})^2 + (r_{21})^2 + (r_{31})^2 + (r_{41})^2
$$

Then

$$
q_1 = (-7)^2 + (3)^2 + (-3)^2 + (7)^2
$$
$$
q_1 = 49 + 9 + 9 + 49
$$
$$
q_1 = 116, \text{ the error sum of squares using } a_g = 57
$$
$$
\text{and } a_b = 33.
$$

The results of several pairs of values for a_g and a_b are summarized in Table 3.1, which shows that of the five pairs of values, $a_g = 55$ and $a_b = 35$

Table 3.1 THE ERROR SUM OF SQUARES RESULTING FROM FIVE PAIRS OF VALUES FOR a_g AND a_b

\multicolumn{2}{c}{*Assumed values*}	*Error sum of squares*
a_g	a_b	
57	33	$q_1 = 116$
55	33	$q_2 = 108$
55	35	$q_3 = 100$
56	34	$q_4 = 104$
57	35	$q_5 = 108$

give the smallest error sum of squares ($q_3 = 100$). Therefore, the values $a_g = 55$ and $a_b = 35$ are the *best* pair from the five.

In general, we will choose a pair of values for a_g and a_b that will produce the *smallest error sum of squares* and that, as before, will be called the *least-squares values* or *least-squares weights*.

3.7
THE LEAST-SQUARES VALUES FOR a_g AND a_b

In Section 3.2 a question was raised about using the *average* of the girls' typing scores as their level of performance. Consideration was also given to using the *average* of the boys' typing scores as the boys' level. It turns out that for the problem in which $\mathbf{Y}$ is expressed as

$$\mathbf{Y} = a_g\mathbf{X}^{(g)} + a_b\mathbf{X}^{(b)} + \mathbf{R}$$

the least-squares value for a_g *is the average* of all the girls' $\mathbf{Y}$ values, and the least-squares value for a_b *is the average* of all the boys' $\mathbf{Y}$ values.

Using the numerical values in Section 3.5, the average value of the $\mathbf{Y}$ elements from girls is $(50 + 60)/2 = 55$, and the average value of the $\mathbf{Y}$ elements from boys is $(30 + 40)/2 = 35$. The *best* model to be used is, therefore,

$$\mathbf{Y} = 55\mathbf{X}^{(g)} + 35\mathbf{X}^{(b)} + \mathbf{R}^{(3)}$$

where $\mathbf{R}^{(3)}$ is the error vector. From Table 3.1, the error sum of squares that resulted from using $a_g = 55$ and $a_b = 35$ is 100. In this particular model, no other pair of numbers will produce an error sum of squares equal to or less than 100. Figure 3.1 is a pictorial representation of these data.

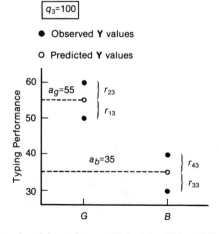

FIG. 3.1 Observed and Least Squares Values for Girls and Boys.

3.8
SUMMARY OF PROBLEM FORMULATION

The problem was to determine if we could say that the level of typing performance for girls was equal to the level for boys. Knowledge of vector concepts was used to express the typing scores (vector $\mathbf{Y}$) as a linear combination of predictor vectors $\mathbf{X}^{(g)}$ and $\mathbf{X}^{(b)}$ and a residual vector, $\mathbf{R}$. The least-squares values were used for a_g (the weight used with $\mathbf{X}^{(g)}$) and a_b (the weight used with $\mathbf{X}^{(b)}$).

3.9
COMPARING THE LEVEL OF PERFORMANCE
OF GIRLS WITH THE LEVEL OF PERFORMANCE
OF BOYS

Return now to the question of whether it is appropriate to say that the level of typing performance of girls is equal to that of the boys. This problem can be translated into the language of the mathematical model described in (3.2).

$$\mathbf{Y} = a_g\mathbf{X}^{(g)} + a_b\mathbf{X}^{(b)} + \mathbf{R}$$

The single weight a_g was used as the level of performance for the girls, and the single weight a_b indicated the boys' level. Furthermore, the least-squares values were used as the *best* for a_g and a_b. Now, how reasonable is it to say that the number used as the level of performance for girls (a_g in the model) is equal to the level of performance of boys (a_b in the model)? In terms of the mathematical model, is

$$a_g = a_b$$

a reasonable statement?

To investigate this question, first choose a different name to represent the common value for a_g and a_b. Let the claimed statement be

$$a_g = a_b = a_c$$

where a_c is the designation of the weight to be used for both groups. Then try to express $\mathbf{Y}$ using the *same value*, a_c, for both the girl and boy groups. Thus

$$\mathbf{Y} = a_c\mathbf{X}^{(g)} + a_c\mathbf{X}^{(b)} + \mathbf{K} \tag{3.4}$$

where $\mathbf{K}$ is the error vector. The next step is to collect all the vectors multiplied by a_c (see Section 1.11).

$$\mathbf{Y} = a_c(\mathbf{X}^{(g)} + \mathbf{X}^{(b)}) + \mathbf{K}$$

Now, observe the sum $(\mathbf{X}^{(g)} + \mathbf{X}^{(b)})$ of the vectors $\mathbf{X}^{(g)}$ and $\mathbf{X}^{(b)}$ in the numerical example

$$\mathbf{X}^{(g)} + \mathbf{X}^{(b)} = \mathbf{U}$$

$$\begin{bmatrix} 1 \\ 1 \\ 0 \\ 0 \end{bmatrix} + \begin{bmatrix} 0 \\ 0 \\ 1 \\ 1 \end{bmatrix} = \begin{bmatrix} 1 \\ 1 \\ 1 \\ 1 \end{bmatrix}$$

The sum $\mathbf{X}^{(g)} + \mathbf{X}^{(b)}$ is a vector containing all 1's. This special vector, $\mathbf{U}$, with elements containing all 1's was referred to in Chapter 2 as the *unit vector*. Therefore, the model (3.4) becomes

$$\mathbf{Y} = a_c \mathbf{U} + \mathbf{K} \tag{3.5}$$

which is identical to the starting model (2.2) in Chapter 2.

The value chosen as the *best* for a_c will again be the *least-squares value*. In Section 2.7 we indicated that the *average* value in $\mathbf{Y}$ is the least-squares value. The least-squares value for the sample data was 45. Therefore, $a_c = 45$ is the least-squares value, and we can write

$$\mathbf{Y} = 45\mathbf{U} + \mathbf{K} \tag{3.6}$$

where $\mathbf{K}$ is the error vector obtained as a result of using the least-squares value for $a_c = 45$. The model (2.4) is the same as (3.6), and $\mathbf{K} = \mathbf{E}^{(2)}$. The computations are the same as in Section 2.6.

$$\begin{array}{ccc} \mathbf{Y} & \mathbf{U} & \mathbf{K} \end{array}$$

$$\begin{bmatrix} 50 \\ 60 \\ 30 \\ 40 \end{bmatrix} = 45 \begin{bmatrix} 1 \\ 1 \\ 1 \\ 1 \end{bmatrix} + \begin{bmatrix} k_1 \\ k_2 \\ k_3 \\ k_4 \end{bmatrix}$$

$$\begin{bmatrix} 50 \\ 60 \\ 30 \\ 40 \end{bmatrix} = \begin{bmatrix} 45 \\ 45 \\ 45 \\ 45 \end{bmatrix} + \begin{bmatrix} 5 \\ 15 \\ -15 \\ -5 \end{bmatrix}$$

And the elements of $\mathbf{K}$ can be determined exactly as the elements of $\mathbf{E}^{(2)}$ in Section 2.6.

$$k_1 = 50 - 45 = \quad 5$$
$$k_2 = 60 - 45 = \quad 15$$
$$k_3 = 30 - 45 = -15$$
$$k_4 = 40 - 45 = \quad -5$$

Let

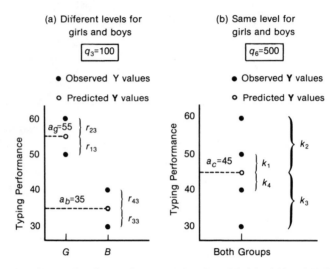

FIG. 3.2 Observed and Least Squares Values from Models (3.2) and (3.5).

$$q_6 = (k_1)^2 + (k_2)^2 + (k_3)^2 + (k_4)^2$$
$$q_6 = (5)^2 + (15)^2 + (-15)^2 + (-5)^2$$
$$q_6 = 25 + 225 + 225 + 25$$
$$q_6 = 500$$

Two error sums of squares are now available:

1. the error sum of squares $q_6 = 500$, resulting from using a *common value* ($a_c = 45$) for the level of performance of boys and girls, and
2. the error sum of squares $q_3 = 100$, resulting from using *different values* ($a_g = 55$, $a_b = 35$) for girls and boys.

Figure 3.2 is a pictorial representation of the data, using the two different models.

3.10
COMPARING ERROR SUMS OF SQUARES

The approach used in Chapter 2 will now be used to decide the reasonability of the statement

$$a_g = a_b = a_c$$

The least-squares values $a_g = 55$ and $a_b = 35$ were accepted as the *best* values to use as the levels of typing performance for girls and boys. The error sum of squares using *different* least-squares values for girls and boys

($a_g = 55$ and $a_b = 35$) will be compared with the error sum of squares using the *same* least-squares value ($a_c = 45$).

If the error sum of squares ($q_6 = 500$) obtained from using the same value for boys and girls is appreciably larger than the error sum of squares using different levels ($q_3 = 100$), we can conclude that *it is not appropriate to claim that the level of typing performance for girls is equal to the level of performance for boys.*

The reasoning is similar to that used in Section 2.10. If the values in **Y** are only a *sample* of the potential values for all of the boys and girls, then a_g and a_b are *estimates* of the corresponding averages of all girls and all boys. It may very well be that the corresponding averages for all boys and girls are equal. If so, how likely is it that a difference of $55 - 35 = 20$ could be observed from a random collection of observations? In general, a large difference between q_6 and q_3 is unlikely if the overall boy and girl averages are equal.

3.11
SUMMARY

We have followed ten important steps in this chapter.

1. *State the problem in natural language.* The example we used was to determine if it is appropriate to say that the level of typing performance of girl students who have completed typing instruction is equal to the level of typing performance of boys.

2. *Define the vector of interest and the predictor vectors.* The typing-test score was defined as the vector of interest, **Y**. A vector, $\mathbf{X}^{(g)}$, was defined to represent the *girl* category, and a vector, $\mathbf{X}^{(b)}$, was defined to represent the *boy* category.

3. *Express the vector of interest,* **Y**, *as a linear combination of the vectors* $\mathbf{X}^{(g)}$ *and* $\mathbf{X}^{(b)}$ *and a residual vector,* **R**.

$$\mathbf{Y} = a_g\mathbf{X}^{(g)} + a_b\mathbf{X}^{(b)} + \mathbf{R}$$

4. *Select values for* a_g *and* a_b *that minimize the sum of squares of the elements of* **R**. In our example the *least-squares value* for a_g was the *average* of the typing test scores of the girls; and the *least-squares value* for a_b was the *average* of the boys' typing-test scores. The numerical value for the *least-squares weights* was $a_g = 55$ and $a_b = 35$. The model used was

$$\mathbf{Y} = 55\mathbf{X}^{(g)} + 35\mathbf{X}^{(b)} + \mathbf{R}^{(3)}$$

5. *Compute the error sum of squares.* In our example the error sum of squares using $a_g = 55$ and $a_b = 35$ was

$$q_3 = 100$$

6. *Make an appropriate statement in terms of predicted scores in the model.* In our example we considered whether it was appropriate to say that the predicted girls' typing score is equal to the predicted boys' score. In terms of the model, the predicted girls' score is a_g, and the predicted boys' score is a_b. Is it reasonable to use a common numerical value, a_c, for a_b and a_g?

7. *Impose the restriction implied by the statement on the original model.* The restricted model was

$$\mathbf{Y} = a_c \mathbf{U} + \mathbf{K}$$

8. *Compute the least-squares values for the weights of the restricted model.* The least-squares value for $a_c = 45$, and the restricted model was

$$\mathbf{Y} = 45\mathbf{U} + \mathbf{K}$$

9. *Compute the error sum of squares.* The error sum of squares was

$$q_6 = 500$$

10. *Compare the error sum of squares from the restricted model* ($q_6 = 500$) *with the error sum of squares from the full model* ($q_3 = 100$). If the error sums of squares are *nearly equal*, it is reasonable to use a common value to represent the predicted typing performance for boys and girls. We can therefore say that the level of typing performance for girls is equal to the level of performance for boys. However, if the error sums of squares[2] *differ appreciably*, then the levels are different.

EXERCISES

Apply the ten steps in the Summary to the following exercises.

1. An experiment was performed comparing the effects of two different methods of instruction on achievement performance in abstract mathematics. At the end of the experiment, each group was given an objective test. The variable of interest was "number of correct answers." The data for the two groups are

Group 1	Group 2
60, 61, 62, 64, 66, 67, 68	74, 72, 68, 64, 62

2. An experiment was performed comparing the effects of two different methods for reducing the weight of adult males. At the end of the experiment, the following weight losses were recorded for the two methods.

Method A	Method B
1, 10, 4, 3, 12	18, 9, 10, 16, 7

---

[2]The comparisons of these error sums of squares will be discussed in Section 4.8.

4

A One-Attribute Model
with Multiple Categories

4.1
INTRODUCTION

In Chapter 3 we presented an analysis of a two-category problem. We will now extend this analysis to a four-category problem. In addition, we will present a discussion of the comparison of error sums of squares for full and restricted models. The procedures will be similar to those described in Chapter 3; however there will be less detailed description.

4.2
ANALYSIS OF A PROBLEM INVOLVING FOUR CATEGORIES

This example considers another problem involving typing performance. Suppose the problem is whether it is appropriate to say that the typing performances of freshmen, sophomores, juniors, and seniors are equal. Again, we will use a typing-test score as the indicator of student performance. The analysis will be conducted similar to our previous examples. Recall that in those cases, we argued that a reasonable way to arrive at a decision was to characterize each group by a single number, referred to as an *average*. But, before any future discussions of problem analysis and solutions can be efficiently conducted, certain ideas must be clearly fixed by adopting a more technical vocabulary.

Populations

In Chapter 2 we indicated that it is normal to want the conclusions to be true for individuals other than those for whom data were observed. This larger set of individuals is called a **population.** In general, *a population is a well-defined collection of persons, objects, or events.* An important fact is that a *population is essentially created by definition.* The same collection of persons, objects, or events might be defined as one population, two populations, or many populations. Consider all of the students currently enrolled in first-year typing at the high-school level in a specified city. In Chapter 2 such a collection of persons was considered a single population. However, that same group of individuals is composed of males and females and, therefore, could be considered two populations, as in Chapter 3. Moreover, that same collection of persons can be classified into four distinct groups—freshmen, sophomores, juniors, and seniors—and could therefore be regarded as four populations, as in our present example. The point is: Populations, as the term is used here, are not defined by the nature of the material in some mystical fashion but are defined *arbitrarily* by the investigator who has a problem. The investigator "makes up" definitions that he feels are relevant to his problem.

Probably the best way to define a population is simply to list all its members. In practice, such a procedure frequently creates insurmountable problems, particularly when the population is very large. A more common procedure is to *state a rule on the basis of which a decision can be made as to whether a given object is a member of a specified population.*

Variable of Interest

In most situations, interest is not primarily in the population itself but in some characteristic of it, such as typing skill. In general, *we have some way of assigning a number to every member of a population,* and this collection of numbers is called a **variable.** In our present example, a typing test could be given to every member of the four different populations.

Suppose the results were summarized, obtaining the values shown in Table 4.1. The values under the column labeled f indicate the number of persons in each population attaining the test score represented in the column to the left. For example, there were two freshmen who attained a score of 35, and there were 90 juniors who attained a score of 33. The column labeled f/n is a proportion indicating the relative frequency of the various test scores' values in each population (e.g., 35% of the seniors achieved a score of 32). Note also that 35% of the sophomores had a score of 32. However, 10% of the sophomores had a score of 29, while only 7.5% of the seniors had a score of 29. On the other hand, 7.5% of the seniors achieved a score of 34, but only 2.5% of the sophomores achieved that value. From this example you should be able to appreciate the logical problems involved in attempting to get a simple yes or no answer to the question: "Do sophomores and seniors type equally well?"

As indicated previously, one way of evading such logical problems is to characterize each group by a single value and then compare those values. The problem then is to choose a good number to characterize each group. Our conclusion may depend on what number is chosen. For example, the most frequent value attained by each class is 31 for freshmen, 32 for sophomores, 33 for juniors, and 32 for seniors. On this basis, we could conclude that the four classes do not type equally well (although two of them do) and that juniors are the "best" typists.

Table 4.1 SUMMARY OF RESULTS OF TYPING TEST

Population

Score	Freshman f	f/n	Sophomore f	f/n	Junior f	f/n	Senior f	f/n
28	3	.030	3	.015	10	.025	1	.005
29	10	.100	20	.100	40	.100	15	.075
30	15	.150	30	.150	50	.125	25	.125
31	25	.250	40	.200	60	.150	35	.175
32	20	.200	70	.350	80	.200	70	.350
33	15	.150	30	.150	90	.225	35	.175
34	10	.100	5	.025	50	.125	15	.075
35	2	.020	2	.010	20	.050	4	.020
Σ	100	1.000	200	1.000	400	1.000	200	1.000

Expected Values

Another way of characterizing each group by a single number is to calculate a quantity called the expected value. *The* **expected value** *of a discrete variable is the weighted sum of the values assumed by the variable and the associated probability that the variable takes on that value.* For example, the expected value of the variable "typing performance" for freshmen can be calculated as

$$\mathcal{E}(\text{fr}) = (28)(.03) + (29)(.10) + (30)(.15)$$
$$+ (31)(.25) + (32)(.20) + (33)(.15)$$
$$+ (34)(.10) + (35)(.02)$$
$$= 0.84 + 2.90 + 4.50 + 7.75$$
$$+ 6.40 + 4.95 + 3.40 + 0.70$$
$$= 31.34$$

The corresponding values for the other three classes are obtained in the same way.

$$\mathcal{E}(\text{soph}) = (28)(.015) + \cdots + (35)(.010) = 31.37$$
$$\mathcal{E}(\text{jr}) = (28)(.025) + \cdots + (35)(.050) = 31.82$$
$$\mathcal{E}(\text{sr}) = (28)(.005) + \cdots + (35)(.020) = 31.95$$

On the basis of the expected values, we could conclude that the classes do not type equally well and that seniors are the "best" typists. To some degree, this conclusion contradicts our previous conclusion. The point is: There is no "right" method for answering research questions. We argue here—and implicitly in the remainder of this book—that comparing expected values is a "good" way, or at least not an unreasonable way, to arrive at conclusions about research questions. If you do not find this argument persuasive, then it is unlikely that you will find these models very useful.

Estimating Expected Values

The expected values just shown characterize the four populations. These values are referred to as **parameters**; they are also called **means**. In practice, for one reason or another, an investigator is unable to determine the values of the parameters (i.e., the expected values or means), so he must be content with *estimates* of the parameter values based on *samples* of members from the populations of interest. In many situations, the cost of measuring every member of each population is too great, relative to one's need for an answer. In other situations, the population(s) may not even exist. For example, if the effect of some new drug is being studied, it may be administered to (say) only 20 individuals, and these may be the only persons who have ever taken or who will ever take the drug. Nonetheless, we would like the conclusions to be valid for persons who might have taken or who might take the drug. The 20 individuals are regarded as a sample from a population of these individuals. Such a population is frequently referred to as a **hypothetical population.**

There are a number of different ways in which expected values might be estimated from a sample. Obviously, we would like to choose a "good" method. As we have already indicated, the method recommended in this book is a *least-squares procedure*, and the values obtained, which estimate the expected values, are called *least-squares estimates.* Up to this point, the only least-squares estimates we have discussed have been arithmetic averages. But, as we will discover in Chapter 6, the values of the least-squares estimates of the expected values will depend on how a model is defined, and these estimates may not be arithmetic averages. For this reason, *we will use the general term* **predicted values** *to refer to the least-squares estimates of the expected values or parameter means.*

In general, estimating expected values by the least-squares method has a number of desirable properties (see Section 5.2), if the model is true (see Section 6.15) and if the observed members of the populations have been randomly selected. *A sample of size n is said to be* **random** *if every possible combination of n members has an equal chance of being the one selected.*

In this section a few paragraphs have been devoted to some concepts about which an entire book could easily be written. Additional reading in other sources will prove invaluable.[1] Our primary purpose here has been to indicate in a slightly more formal, though incomplete, way some of the features of statistical reasoning and logic that are implicit in our discussion of models. In particular, it will be our invariable practice to assume (argue implicitly) that a comparison among expected values is a reasonable way to arrive at decisions. In general, the steps listed in the Preface will be followed.

Returning to our example, we can argue that if we reject the hypothesis

$$\mathscr{E}(\text{fr}) = \mathscr{E}(\text{soph}) = \mathscr{E}(\text{jr}) = \mathscr{E}(\text{sr})$$

then it is reasonable to conclude that the four groups do not type equally well. This mathematical expression is simply a "shorthand" used to save space. It should be read to mean: "The expected value of the typing speed variable defined across the freshman population is equal to the expected value of the typing speed variable defined across the sophomore population . . ." We now turn to the construction of a model to estimate the expected values.

---

[1]An excellent source is *Statistical Methods in Education and Psychology* by Gene Glass and Julian Stanley (Englewood Cliffs, N.J.: Prentice-Hall, 1970), particularly pages 57–72, 212–214, 220–223, and 240–256.

4.3
DEFINING THE VECTOR OF INTEREST
AND THE PREDICTOR VECTORS

A specific example is used in which there is a total of $n = 20$ students who have typing-test scores. Data are available for five students in each of the four grades.

$\mathbf{Y}$ = a vector of dimension 20 in which each element is a typing-test score observed on a student.

The elements in the vectors can be written in an arbitrary order, but to clarify the presentation, we will list the elements so that freshman scores are first, followed by those of the sophomores, juniors, and seniors. And, as before, the vectors representing the group membership are defined as

$\mathbf{X}^{(9)}$ = a vector of dimension 20 in which an element has the value 1 if the corresponding typing score in $\mathbf{Y}$ is from a freshman; otherwise the element has the value 0.

$\mathbf{X}^{(10)}$ = a vector of dimension 20 in which an element has the value 1 if the corresponding typing score in $\mathbf{Y}$ is from a sophomore; otherwise the element has the value 0.

Using an abbreviated definition to describe the remaining two vectors, they are defined as

$\mathbf{X}^{(11)}$ = 1 if a junior; 0 otherwise.

$\mathbf{X}^{(12)}$ = 1 if a senior; 0 otherwise.

As in Chapter 3, $\mathbf{Y}$ is expressed as a linear combination of $\mathbf{X}^{(9)}$, $\mathbf{X}^{(10)}$, $\mathbf{X}^{(11)}$, $\mathbf{X}^{(12)}$, and a residual vector $\mathbf{E}$. Using the weights $a_9, a_{10}, a_{11}, a_{12}$, we can write.

$$\mathbf{Y} = a_9\mathbf{X}^{(9)} + a_{10}\mathbf{X}^{(10)} + a_{11}\mathbf{X}^{(11)} + a_{12}\mathbf{X}^{(12)} + \mathbf{E}^{(1)} \qquad (4.1)$$

When numerical values for $\mathbf{Y}, \mathbf{X}^{(9)}, \mathbf{X}^{(10)}, \mathbf{X}^{(11)}$, and $\mathbf{X}^{(12)}$ are introduced (see Section 4.4), the least-squares values for a_9, a_{10}, a_{11}, and a_{12} can be obtained. Then the elements of $\mathbf{E}^{(1)}$ and the sum of squares of the elements of $\mathbf{E}^{(1)}$ can be computed.

4.4
INTRODUCTION OF NUMERICAL VALUES

The data for this example are displayed in terms of the vector definitions given in the preceding section. Thus the extended forms of the vectors are

Y	$\mathbf{X}^{(9)}$	$\mathbf{X}^{(10)}$	$\mathbf{X}^{(11)}$	$\mathbf{X}^{(12)}$
16	1	0	0	0
48	1	0	0	0
40	1	0	0	0
40	1	0	0	0
32	1	0	0	0
40	0	1	0	0
24	0	1	0	0
64	0	1	0	0
56	0	1	0	0
48	0	1	0	0
64	0	0	1	0
56	0	0	1	0
48	0	0	1	0
72	0	0	1	0
56	0	0	1	0
80	0	0	0	1
72	0	0	0	1
72	0	0	0	1
64	0	0	0	1
72	0	0	0	1

Again, the least-squares values will be selected for a_9, a_{10}, a_{11}, and a_{12}. These least-squares values, as before, are the averages of the typing-test scores for each of the four groups.

$$a_9 = (16 + 48 + 40 + 40 + 32)/5 = 35.2$$

$$a_{10} = (40 + 24 + 64 + 56 + 48)/5 = 46.4$$

$$a_{11} = (64 + 56 + 48 + 72 + 56)/5 = 59.2$$

$$a_{12} = (80 + 72 + 72 + 64 + 72)/5 = 72.0$$

The extended form of the model can be written, including the error vector $\mathbf{E}^{(1)}$, which results when the least-squares values for a_9, a_{10}, a_{11}, and a_{12} are used. The extended form of the model is

$$Y = 35.2\,X^{(9)} + 46.4\,X^{(10)} + 59.2\,X^{(11)} + 72.0\,X^{(12)} + E^{(1)}$$

Y	X⁽⁹⁾	X⁽¹⁰⁾	X⁽¹¹⁾	X⁽¹²⁾	E⁽¹⁾	
16	1	0	0	0	−19.2	← $e_{1,1}$
48	1	0	0	0	12.8	
40	1	0	0	0	4.8	
40	1	0	0	0	4.8	
32	1	0	0	0	−3.2	
40	0	1	0	0	−6.4	← $e_{6,1}$
24	0	1	0	0	−22.4	
64	0	1	0	0	17.6	
56	0	1	0	0	9.6	
48	0	1	0	0	1.6	
64	0	0	1	0	4.8	← $e_{11,1}$
56	0	0	1	0	−3.2	
48	0	0	1	0	−11.2	
72	0	0	1	0	12.8	
56	0	0	1	0	−3.2	
80	0	0	0	1	8.0	← $e_{16,1}$
72	0	0	0	1	0.0	
72	0	0	0	1	0.0	
64	0	0	0	1	−8.0	
72	0	0	0	1	0.0	

We can calculate several elements of $E^{(1)}$.

$$e_{1,1} = 16 - 35.2(1) - 46.4(0) - 59.2(0) - 72.0(0)$$
$$e_{6,1} = 40 - 35.2(0) - 46.4(1) - 59.2(0) - 72.0(0)$$
$$e_{11,1} = 64 - 35.2(0) - 46.4(0) - 59.2(1) - 72.0(0)$$
$$e_{16,1} = 80 - 35.2(0) - 46.4(0) - 59.2(0) - 72.0(1)$$
$$e_{1,1} = 16 - 35.2 = -19.2$$
$$e_{6,1} = 40 - 46.4 = -6.4$$
$$e_{11,1} = 64 - 59.2 = 4.8$$
$$e_{16,1} = 80 - 72.0 = 8.0$$

The error sum of squares q_1 can be computed, and the result is

$$q_1 = (-19.2)^2 + (12.8)^2 + (4.8)^2 + \cdots + (-8.0)^2 + (0.0)^2$$
$$q_1 = 1996.8$$

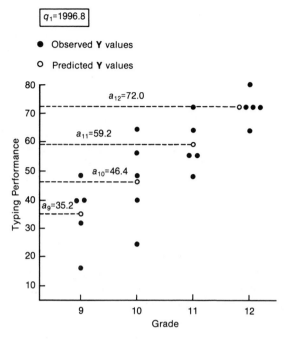

FIG. 4.1 Observed and Least Squares Values from Model (4.1).

Figure 4.1 is a pictorial representation of the data.

Now, returning to our problem, is it appropriate to say that the levels of typing performance for freshmen, sophomores, juniors, and seniors are equal? Or, how reasonable is it to use the same numerical value to represent the levels of typing performance for all four groups of students? The problem can be stated in terms of model (4.1).

$$\mathbf{Y} = a_9\mathbf{X}^{(9)} + a_{10}\mathbf{X}^{(10)} + a_{11}\mathbf{X}^{(11)} + a_{12}\mathbf{X}^{(12)} + \mathbf{E}^{(1)}$$

Now, consider the problem similar to the two-group problem of Section 3.9. The following represent the levels of typing performance for the students indicated.

$$a_9 = \text{freshmen}$$

$$a_{10} = \text{sophomores}$$

$$a_{11} = \text{juniors}$$

$$a_{12} = \text{seniors}$$

Furthermore, the least-squares values

$$a_9 = 35.2$$

$$a_{10} = 46.4$$

$$a_{11} = 59.2$$

$$a_{12} = 72.0$$

are the *best* values to use as indicators of the levels of typing performance for the four groups. These values, which are obtained on a sample from the four populations, are referred to as the *predicted values* (see Section 4.2) because they are the values that would be predicted for a member of each population. *The predicted values are estimates of the expected values.*

As in Chapter 3, we now ask the question: "How reasonable is it to say that

$$a_9 = a_{10} = a_{11} = a_{12} = a_c$$

where a_c is the common value to be used to indicate the levels of typing for all four groups?" From a statistical point of view, the question is: "How likely is it that predicted values could be achieved, differing as those shown above, if the sampling has been random from populations that have the same expected value?" The appropriateness of this statement is examined by using the common value a_c as the level of typing performance for all four groups. The least-squares value for a_c will be used as the indicator for the common level of performance.

4.5
THE RESTRICTED MODEL

The restriction

$$a_9 = a_{10} = a_{11} = a_{12} = a_c$$

is imposed on the full model by substitution and is written

$$\mathbf{Y} = a_c\mathbf{X}^{(9)} + a_c\mathbf{X}^{(10)} + a_c\mathbf{X}^{(11)} + a_c\mathbf{X}^{(12)} + \mathbf{E}^{(2)}$$

where $\mathbf{E}^{(2)}$ is the residual in the restricted model. Then, using one of the vector properties in Chapter 1 (Section 1.11), we can write

$$\mathbf{Y} = a_c(\mathbf{X}^{(9)} + \mathbf{X}^{(10)} + \mathbf{X}^{(11)} + \mathbf{X}^{(12)}) + \mathbf{E}^{(2)}$$

But, noticing that $(\mathbf{X}^{(9)} + \mathbf{X}^{(10)} + \mathbf{X}^{(11)} + \mathbf{X}^{(12)}) = \mathbf{U}$ (a unit vector of dimension 20, with each element $= 1$), we can write

$$\mathbf{Y} = a_c\mathbf{U} + \mathbf{E}^{(2)} \tag{4.2}$$

4.6
THE LEAST-SQUARES VALUE FOR a_c

The least-squares value is used as the best value of a_c and is the *average* of the elements of **Y**. Then,

$$a_c = (16 + 48 + 40 + \cdots + 64 + 72)/20 = 53.2$$

Using the least-squares value, we can write

$$\mathbf{Y} = 53.2\mathbf{U} + \mathbf{E}^{(2)}$$

where $\mathbf{E}^{(2)}$ is the residual vector obtained as a result of using $a_c = 53.2$ as the level of typing performance for all four groups. The extended form of the restricted model is

Y	**U**	$\mathbf{E}^{(2)}$	
16	1	−37.2	← $e_{1,2}$
48	1	−5.2	
40	1	−13.2	
40	1	−13.2	
32	1	−21.1	
40	1	−13.2	
24	1	−29.2	
64	1	10.8	
56	1	2.8	
48	1	−5.2	
64	1	10.8	
56	1	2.8	
48	1	−5.2	
72	1	18.8	
56	1	2.5	
80	1	26.8	
72	1	18.8	
72	1	18.8	
64	1	10.8	
72	1	18.8	← $e_{20,2}$

with $\mathbf{Y} = 53.2 \, \mathbf{U} + \mathbf{E}^{(2)}$

$$e_{1,2} = 16 - 53.2(1) = -37.2$$
$$e_{20,2} = 72 - 53.2(1) = 18.8$$

Then the error sum of squares, q_2, can be computed, and the result is

$$q_2 = (-37.2)^2 + (-5.2)^2 + \cdots + (18.8)^2$$
$$q_2 = 5795.2$$

4.7
COMPARING THE ERROR SUMS OF SQUARES

Two error sums of squares are now available.

$q_2 = 5795.2$, resulting from using a *common value* $(a_c = 53.2)$ for the level of typing performance for all students.

$q_1 = 1996.8$, resulting from using *different values* $(a_9 = 35.2, a_{10} = 46.4, a_{11} = 59.2, a_{12} = 72.0)$ for the four groups.

Figure 4.2 is a pictorial representation of the data, using the two different models.

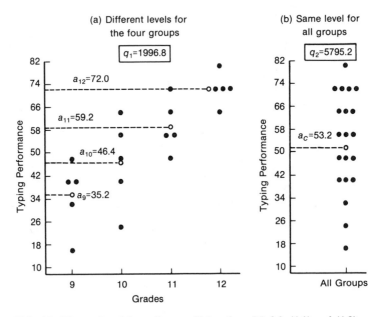

FIG. 4.2 Observed and Least Squares Values from Models (4.1) and (4.2).

We will use the same approach as before in deciding the reasonability of the statement: "All four groups have the same level of typing performance." That is, is it appropriate to say

$$a_9 = a_{10} = a_{11} = a_{12} = a_c$$

From a statistical point of view, the question is: "How likely is it that the four expected values are equal?" If they are all equal, then

$$\mathscr{E}(\text{fr}) = \mathscr{E}(\text{soph}) = \mathscr{E}(\text{jr}) = \mathscr{E}(\text{sr})$$

Since these four expected values are estimated by the predicted values

$$a_9 = 35.2$$
$$a_{10} = 46.4$$
$$a_{11} = 59.2$$
$$a_{12} = 72.0$$

the extent to which the predicted values are unequal is evidence of the lack of equality of the expected values. One way of measuring the extent to which the predicted values differ is to note the difference between $q_1 = 1996.8$ (the error sum of squares in the model that allowed the estimates to be *different*) and $q_2 = 5795.2$ (the error sum of squares in the model that required the estimates to be the *same*, i.e., $a_c = 53.2$).

If the error sum of squares ($q_2 = 5795.2$) using the common value is *appreciably larger* than the error sum of squares ($q_1 = 1996.8$) using different levels, the conclusion will be: "It is not appropriate to say that levels of typing performance for all four groups are equal." *Generally, the error sum of squares in the restricted model (q_2) will be larger than the error sum of squares in the full model (q_1).*[2] The q_1 and q_2 will be equal only when the least-squares weights (a_9, a_{10}, a_{11}, a_{12}) have exactly the relations implied by the restrictions. In no case will q_1 be larger than q_2. Additional discussion of the comparison of q_1 with q_2 will be presented in the next section.

Our problem can be approached in another way: "How valuable for prediction is the *information* about class membership?" If we are *allowed to use the information* expressing membership in the four groups for prediction of typing performance, the error sum of squares $q_1 = 1996.5$ is observed. But, if we are *not allowed to use the information* (and must make the same prediction for all students), the error sum of squares $q_2 = 5792.2$ is observed. If a large amount of error is introduced as a result of *giving up* information about class membership, then we have an indication of the *value of the information*.

[2]For a more complete explanation of *full* and *restricted models*, see Section 6.14.

4.8
STATISTICAL CONSIDERATIONS IN COMPARING
ERROR SUMS OF SQUARES—USE OF THE *F* STATISTIC

Of the three examples presented in Chapters 2, 3, and 4, each terminated with the need for a method of comparing the error sums of squares between the full and restricted models. In this section a procedure is discussed briefly to assist in deciding the appropriateness of the restriction that has been imposed on the full model. The computed number used as a basis for decision is based on statistical considerations. It is called the *F* **statistic**.

Our three previous problems were stated in terms of *the appropriateness or reasonability of a statement*. This form of stating the problem was used to postpone a discussion of certain statistical concepts. Now we will present an introduction to hypothesis testing; a more extensive discussion of the assumptions associated with these statistical tests can be found in Appendix B.

Error sums of squares are used to determine the confidence that should exist in conclusions about the *appropriateness of a statement* or, in a statistical context, about a *hypothesis*. The use of error sums of squares to determine confidence in the hypothesis is based, in part, on how the choice of a sample of observations can affect the findings. Consider, for example, the problem of differences in typing performance among the four categories of students (see Section 4.2). In a study of this type, the number of observations available from each of the four categories is likely to be small compared to the actual numbers in the four categories. Had observations been obtained on the entire population of students from the four categories, the computed values for the weights a_9, a_{10}, a_{11}, a_{12}, and a_c would have been unique values. However, when a sample from each of the four categories is chosen, the computed values for a_9, a_{10}, a_{11}, a_{12}, and a_c are not necessarily equal to the values that would have been obtained from the entire population.

When unknown values such as a_9, a_{10}, a_{11}, a_{12}, and a_c are quantities that characterize an entire population, they are called parameters (Section 4.2). Greek letters are frequently used to denote parameters, but any type of letter symbol can be used. *When parameters are estimated from a sample, the sample values are called estimates* (see Section 4.2). Whenever statements (hypotheses) are made about a model, they are statements about relations among the parameters. Since the estimates do not necessarily agree exactly with the parameter values, conclusions about hypotheses are *inferences* in which we have varying degrees of confidence. The problem of statistical inference is the validity of hypotheses about parameter values. Thus, any conclusion about the truth of a hypothesis must be qualified by expressing the degree to which the hypothesis is correctly accepted as true or rejected as false.

The certainty with which a hypothesis is accepted or rejected is usually stated in terms of the probability that the hypothesis would have been rejected as false when, in fact, it is true. Such a probability statement for the examples discussed in this book can be based upon the value obtained for the F statistic, which results from an appropriate comparison of two sums of squares. *The* **first error sum of squares** *is obtained by estimating the parameters of the full model. The* **second error sum of squares** *is obtained by estimating the parameters under the restrictions implied by the hypothesis.* These two error sums of squares, the number of predictor vectors in the two models, and the dimension of the vectors form the basis for the F computation. This F statistic is Snedecor's F ratio, commonly used with analysis of variance techniques (see Glass & Stanley, 1970, pp. 233–8).

Different samples drawn at random from a population in which the hypothesis is true would yield different values for the F statistic. The probability can be determined of obtaining a value as large as the one observed in the available sample. Published tables show the values of F, associated with the proportion of times that samples drawn from a population in which the hypotheses are true, would yield a computed F value greater than the tabled value. The computer program described in Chapter 14 provides the proportion of times that samples drawn from populations in which the hypotheses are true would yield computed F values greater than the F value computed from the sample determined in the analysis. If the decision maker decides that the probability (p_1) is small, he will reject the hypothesis; however this rejection must be qualified by the fact that the conclusion might be in error. The degree of confidence in not erroneously rejecting a hypothesis is expressed by the quantity $(1 - p_1)$. On the other hand, if the probability is sufficiently large, the decision maker may decide to accept the hypothesis. Peculiarities of the sample chosen may lead to the erroneous acceptance of the hypothesis. Thus inferences based on the results for a sample may involve two types of error: *Type I, a rejection of a hypothesis that is true* and *Type II, an acceptance of a hypothesis that is false.*

The value of F^3 can be computed for the problems in this book. The decision maker can either use tables of the F statistic or the computer-generated probability associated with the F. The computation of the F value is

$$F = \frac{(q_r - q_f)/(df)_1}{q_f/(df)_2}$$

where

q_f = minimized error sum of squares obtained from using the least-squares values in the full or unrestricted model.

q_r = minimized error sum of squares obtained from using the least-squares values in the model restricted by the hypothesis.

---

[3]Note that the letter "F" is a single number—not a vector. It will be reserved for the F statistic and will not be used to represent a vector.

$(df)_1 = n_f - n_r =$ the difference between the number of linearly independent predictor vectors in the unrestricted (or full) model, n_f, and the number of linearly independent predictor vectors[4] in the restricted model, n_r. $(df)_1$ is sometimes referred to as as the **numerator degrees of freedom.**

$(df)_2 = n - n_f =$ the number of elements in each vector (the dimension of the vectors), n, minus the number of linearly independent predictor vectors in the full model, n_f. $(df)_2$ is sometimes referred to as the **denominator degrees of freedom.**

4.9
COMPUTATION OF *F* FOR THE PROBLEMS IN CHAPTERS 2, 3, AND 4

F Value for Problem in Chapter 2

From Section 2.4, eq. (2.2), the full model was

$$\mathbf{Y} = a_0 \mathbf{U} + \mathbf{E}$$

The least-squares value (45) was used as the best estimate of the parameter a_0. Sometimes, we write $a_0 = 45$, meaning that "45" is the *least-squares estimate of a_0*. The value of 45 is an estimate of the expected value. We do not mean that the parameter a_0 has the value 45. **Throughout this book, we will assume that the parameters are unknown and that the numerical values obtained by the least-squares procedure are estimates of the parameters.**

Using (Section 2.7)

$$\mathbf{Y} = 45\mathbf{U} + \mathbf{E}^{(2)} \tag{4.3}$$

the error sum of squares $q_2 = 500$ was obtained (Section 2.7). The *hypothesis* was

$$a_0 = 32$$

When we say that the hypothesis is $a_0 = 32$, we mean that the unknown parameter has the value 32. But, as indicated earlier, the statement $a_0 = 45$ means that the least-squares estimate of the value of the parameter a_0 is 45. Imposing the restrictions implied by the hypothesis results in the following restricted model.

$$\mathbf{Y} = 32\mathbf{U} + \mathbf{D}^{(1)}$$

---

[4]A detailed discussion of the meaning of *number of linearly independent predictors* is presented in Chapter 5.

The error sum of squares was $q_6 = 1176$ (Section 2.7). Next, the full model is observed. The vector **U** is the only predictor vector associated with an unknown parameter, a_0. Therefore,

$$n_f = 1$$

Observing the restricted model, there are *no* unknown parameters to be estimated. Therefore,

$$n_r = 0$$

Since the number of elements in each vector was 4, $n = 4$. Now the F value can be computed.

$$F = \frac{(q_r - q_f)/(df)_1}{q_f/(df)_2}$$

q_f = error sum of squares from full model = 500

q_r = error sum of squares from restricted model = 1176

$(df)_1 = n_f - n_r = 1 - 0 = 1$

$(df)_2 = n - n_f = 4 - 1 = 3$

$$F = \frac{(1176 - 500)/1}{500/3}$$

$$F = \frac{676}{166.67}$$

$$F = 4.1$$

The computer program in Chapter 14 will provide a probability $p_1 =$ approximately 0.14.

The Meaning of the Probability Value. This concept is best understood if we consider what the results might be if certain assumptions are made and the study is repeated. First of all, we assumed that the expected value is equal to 32, although the estimate of the expected value is 45. Suppose another sample of size four is drawn from the population and another estimate of the expected value is calculated. Very probably, the calculated value will be neither 32 nor 45. As a result, if the value of F is calculated using data from the second sample, it would likely be a value different from 4.1. If this process were repeated a large number of times, a large number of F's would be generated. If certain other assumptions are true (see Appendix B), then the form of the distribution of these values is known. Only 14% of the observed F values will equal or exceed 4.1. If the probability value is very small, we are forced to the conclusion that some of the assumptions that were made are not tenable. The most important of these is that the expected value is equal to 32, and, in practice, this assumption is rejected when the probability value is small.

F Value for Problem in Chapter 3

From Section 3.4, the equation of the full model is

$$\mathbf{Y} = a_g \mathbf{X}^{(g)} + a_b \mathbf{X}^{(b)} + \mathbf{R}$$

The least-squares values, used as estimates of the unknown parameters, are $a_g = 55$ and $a_b = 35$. Then, from Section 3.7,

$$\mathbf{Y} = 55 \mathbf{X}^{(g)} + 35 \mathbf{X}^{(b)} + \mathbf{R}^{(3)}$$

the full model error sum of squares $q_3 = 100$ was obtained. The hypothesis is

$$a_g = a_b = a_c$$

The restricted model (3.5) is

$$\mathbf{Y} = a_c \mathbf{U} + \mathbf{K}$$

and the least-squares estimate of $a_c = 45$. Then, from

$$\mathbf{Y} = 45 \mathbf{U} + \mathbf{K}$$

the restricted model sum of squares was $q_6 = 500$. There are two predictor vectors, $\mathbf{X}^{(g)}$ and $\mathbf{X}^{(b)}$, associated with the two unknown parameters, a_g and a_b, in the full model. Therefore,

$$n_f = 2$$

In the restricted model there is one predictor vector, $\mathbf{U}$, associated with the unknown parameter, a_c. Therefore,

$$n_r = 1$$

and the dimension of the vectors is $n = 4$. The value of F is

$$F = \frac{(q_r - q_f)/(df)_1}{q_f/(df)_2} = \frac{(q_r - q_f)/(n_f - n_r)}{q_f/(n - n_f)}$$

$$F = \frac{(500 - 100)/(2 - 1)}{(100)/(4 - 2)} = \frac{400/1}{100/2}$$

$$F = 8.0$$

The probability value associated with $F = 8$, with 1 and 2 degrees of freedom, is approximately 0.11. We can infer from this that if the comparison just made was repeated a large number of times (each time with new samples of the same size), only 11% of the obtained F values would exceed 8, if the expected values for boys and girls are equal.

F Value for Problem of Chapter 4

The full model (4.1) was

$$\mathbf{Y} = a_9 \mathbf{X}^{(9)} + a_{10} \mathbf{X}^{(10)} + a_{11} \mathbf{X}^{(11)} + a_{12} \mathbf{X}^{(12)} + \mathbf{E}^{(1)}$$

The least-squares values (from Section 4.4) were

$$a_9 = 35.2, \qquad a_{10} = 46.4, \qquad a_{11} = 59.2, \qquad a_{12} = 72.0$$

and the error sum of squares for the full model was $q_1 = 1996.8$. The hypothesis was that the parameters

$$a_9 = a_{10} = a_{11} = a_{12} = a_c \text{ (a common value)}$$

The restricted model was

$$\mathbf{Y} = a_c\mathbf{U} + \mathbf{E}^{(2)}$$

and the least-squares estimate for a_c was 53.2. The error sum of squares for the restricted model was $q_2 = 5795.2$. There are four predictor vectors

$$\mathbf{X}^{(9)}, \quad \mathbf{X}^{(10)}, \quad \mathbf{X}^{(11)}, \quad \mathbf{X}^{(12)}$$

associated with the four unknown parameters

$$a_9, \quad a_{10}, \quad a_{11}, \quad a_{12}$$

in the full model. Therefore,

$$n_f = 4$$

The restricted model has only one predictor vector, $\mathbf{U}$, associated with one parameter, a_c. Therefore,

$$n_r = 1$$

There were 20 elements in each vector. Therefore,

$$n = 20$$

The value of F is

$$F = \frac{(q_r - q_f)/(n_f - n_r)}{q_f/(n - n_f)}$$

$$F = \frac{(5795.2 - 1996.8)/(4 - 1)}{1996.8/(20 - 4)}$$

$$F = 10.1$$

The probability associated with this F is less than 0.01. On the basis of this value, the hypothesis

$$\mathscr{E}(\text{fr}) = \mathscr{E}(\text{soph}) = \mathscr{E}(\text{jr}) = \mathscr{E}(\text{sr})$$

would ordinarily be rejected. In natural language, we would conclude that the four classes do not type equally well, since it is very improbable that estimates of the expected values of 35.2, 46.4, 59.2, and 72.0 could have been obtained if they were, in fact, all equal. The probability associated with F is that of making a Type I error (see Section 4.8). When this probability is sufficiently small, the result is frequently summarized by the expressions "statistically significant" or "the differences between the classes were found to be statistically significant."

4.10
DECISION RULES

Comparing the error sums of squares in full and restricted models is a generally accepted way of making decisions. We emphasize this method in this book at the expense of alternative "decision rules," which could be discussed. For this reason, it is important to place the concept of **decision rules** in a more general context.

It is not at all unusual for an investigator to get so involved in the technical details of data manipulation and statistical considerations that he fails to bring his common sense to bear on the problem that motivated the data collection in the first place. Remember that decisions are made every day by competent people without reliance on any formal models or statistical considerations. Some of these decisions are "good" and some are "bad," according to standards that may themselves vary from person to person. Although such an individual may have a "model in his head," it will be of little help to others unless it can be described in some reasonably precise way. *The primary reason for formalizing models and decision rules is that individuals less gifted than the originator can also make "good" decisions.*

In many cases, it is possible to automate the decision-making process to the point that human supervision is almost unnecessary. In other cases, individuals with very little ability and a minimum amount of training can function effectively if a model is sufficiently developed. But, even if you have decided to define a problem in terms of a relatively formal model by using some of the techniques described in this book or in other sources, you will still be faced with additional, complex problems.

Consider the problem of *measurement*. In the example problems in the first four chapters, we have been concerned with a measure of typing performance. There are an infinite number of ways of arranging the test situation (i.e., length of time, degree of noise, electric vs. manual machine, etc.) and of scoring the test (i.e., number of errors, number of words, number of words corrected for number of errors, etc.), and the conclusion reached might be somewhat different in every situation. Even if we are satisfied with our variable of interest, it is not necessarily self-obvious that an examination of the probability value associated with an F statistic, based on a comparison of two error sums of squares, is an appropriate decision rule.

Consider the question of possible male–female differences in typing performance. What is meant when the conclusion is that girls are better typists than boys? This could mean that every girl types better than every boy, but generally, this is not what is meant. Statements of this type are usually so uninteresting or such a part of ordinary observation (i.e., every dog has more legs than every human) as to be trivial as a research topic. This conclusion could also mean: If you take a boy and a girl at random from a defined group, you will be right more often than not if you choose the girl as the better typist. If this is what we mean, the appropriate way to proceed will depend, in part, on the way typing-performance scores are distributed among males and females. Suppose that 25% of the girls have very high scores and 75% have very low scores. Furthermore, suppose that all the boys have scores that fall between the high and low scores for girls. In such a case, the odds would favor selection of the boy as the better typist of a randomly selected pair, but the *expected value* of the girls might still be higher than the *expected value* of the boys. If so, the average of a random selection of girls would probably be higher than the average of a random selection of boys.

The procedures discussed in this book involve estimating expected values and are technically appropriate only when statements are made about expected values. In practice, we would like to be able to conclude that both of these statements are true. If certain distributional requirements are met (described in Appendix B as assumptions of normality and homogeneity of variance), then both claims are equally valid.

Another difficulty in using the probability value as a decision rule concerns confusion that sometimes surrounds the word *significant*. When used in statistical literature, it is a shorthand way of making a long and involved statement. Consider the problem discussed in Section 4.4, where the probability associated with an F statistic of 10.1 was less than 0.01. Frequently, a summary statement of the following kind is made: "Significant differences were found among the classes." This is a shorthand way of stating: "If the measure of typing performance is normally distributed in each of the four classes, and the variance of the typing scores is equal in the four classes, then an observed F value of 10.1 is very improbable, if the expected values of the four classes are equal, because if the study were repeated a great number of times with random samples of five from each class, only a few F values (less than 1 in 100) would exceed 10.1." In effect, this statement concludes that one or more of the antecedent conditions was not fulfilled. In practice, the existence of all conditions is normally assumed, except equal expected values, which is rejected because of the improbable F value.

Unfortunately, sometimes a finding judged as "significant" in the purely statistical sense is translated to mean "important" or "useful." In some cases, this occurs out of ignorance, but usually it avoids the problem of defining the term *important*. Even if an observed difference can be safely accepted as being "true," that difference may be large enough to be important in some situations but not in others. The value to be attached to units comprising the variable of interest is also involved. If it is discovered, for example, that students taught by a new method achieve an average performance five units higher than students taught by an old method, should a change be recommended? If there is any additional expense or inconvenience associated with this change, it is clear that a decision cannot be made until it is known specifically how valuable five units of achievement are. Frequently, this kind of information is unavailable, or there is disagreement about the value. Consequently, statistics limits us to making statements about the relative degree of certainty we have in the truth of a given proposition, but it expresses no value judgments about the "truth" revealed. On the other hand, a lack of specificity or general agreement about the value of one unit of the variable of interest does not necessarily imply that statements of value cannot be made. For example, although there may be disagreement about the value of five units, if the observed difference were 100 units, a general agreement might exist that whatever the value per unit, the difference in number is great enough to justify a change.

Statistical decision rules can be useful in the sense that with fixed sample sizes, the more improbable an observed difference, the more probable that a relatively large difference truly exists. The difficulty is that if a difference truly exists (even though it is small), almost any probability value desired can be achieved by choosing larger samples.

EXERCISES

The methods in this chapter should be applied to the four exercises below.[5] The final result should include not only the F statistic but a natural-language statement of the conclusions.

1. An experimenter seeks to determine the relative effectiveness of four different levels of learner activity on learning about the English monetary system. Forty experimental subjects are randomly placed among the four levels (10 to each level) of learner activity: (1) outline the instructional material; (2) write a summary of the material; (3) study an instructional program of the material; (4) study the program on a teaching machine. Ten subjects studied English money under each of these conditions on five successive days; then a 100-item, multiple-choice test on the English money system is given. A person's "score" is the number of items answered correctly on the 100-item test. These scores appear in the following table:

[5]The problems are taken from *Statistical Methods in Education and Psychology* (Englewood Cliffs, N.J.: Prentice-Hall, 1970) by Gene V. Glass and Julian C. Stanley. Copyright 1970 by Prentice-Hall, Inc. Reprinted by permission. The approaches used here can be directly related to the procedures used in the Glass and Stanley book, particularly on pp. 358, 360, 378 and 379.

SCORES ON A 100-ITEM TEST ON THE ENGLISH MONETARY SYSTEM FOR 40
SUBJECTS STUDYING UNDER FOUR LEVELS OF LEARNER ACTIVITY

1	2	3	4
	Written		*Teaching*
Outline	*Summary*	*Program*	*Machine*
26	51	52	41
34	50	64	49
46	33	39	56
48	28	54	64
42	47	58	72
49	50	53	65
74	48	77	63
61	60	56	87
51	71	63	77
53	42	59	62

2. Three methods of teaching foreign language are compared. To evaluate the instruction, a 50-item vocabulary test is administered to the 24 students in the experiment; 8 students were in each group. The following data, expressed as "number of correct items out of 50," were obtained.

Aural-oral Method	*Translation Method*	*Combined Methods*
$X_{11} = 19$	$X_{12} = 21$	$X_{13} = 17$
$X_{21} = 37$	$X_{22} = 18$	$X_{23} = 20$
$X_{31} = 28$	$X_{32} = 15$	$X_{33} = 28$
$X_{41} = 31$	$X_{42} = 23$	$X_{43} = 30$
$X_{51} = 29$	$X_{52} = 20$	$X_{53} = 13$
$X_{61} = 25$	$X_{62} = 22$	$X_{63} = 18$
$X_{71} = 36$	$X_{72} = 26$	$X_{73} = 19$
$X_{81} = 33$	$X_{82} = 14$	$X_{83} = 23$

3. A group of 30 persons are randomly split into three groups of 10 each. Group I receives organizing material before studying instructional materials on mathematics; group II receives the "organizer" after studying the mathematics; group III receives no organizing material in connection with studying the mathematics instructional materials. On a 10-item test, on the mathematics covered in the instructional materials, the following scores were earned.

Group I (pre-organizer)	Group II (post-organizer)	Group III (no organizer)
4	5	5
5	4	4
3	4	6
6	7	2
6	8	2
3	7	2
3	6	6
4	4	4
4	4	3
2	7	4

4. Test to see whether there is any difference between the weight loss in the four groups shown below. The data represents weight loss in pounds of subjects under four different diets.

Diet A	Diet B	Diet C	Diet D
$X_{11} = 6$	$X_{12} = 11$	$X_{13} = 21$	$X_{14} = 5$
$X_{21} = 8$	$X_{22} = 13$	$X_{23} = 20$	$X_{24} = 9$
$X_{31} = 3$	$X_{32} = 15$	$X_{33} = 17$	$X_{34} = 10$
$X_{41} = 5$		$X_{43} = 16$	$X_{44} = 7$
$X_{51} = 6$			$X_{54} = 7$

5

Linear Independence,
Linear Dependence, and
Equivalent Models

5.1
INTRODUCTION

In this chapter the concepts of linear independence and dependence will be introduced and discussed in terms of the example models of the first four chapters. Although these concepts are easy to understand, they are extremely important, since they provide a framework for the simple solution of a large number of problems that might otherwise prove difficult to resolve. For example, even professional statisticians sometimes disagree about the appropriate degrees of freedom to be used in evaluating a hypothesis (see Engelhart, 1967; Seal, 1967). If the concepts in this chapter are fully understood, this problem should never arise. In addition, we will show that any model can be written in a number of different ways. The value of being able to recognize the essential features of a model written in different ways will not be apparent in elementary models, but you will discover its importance as the models become more complex.

5.2
MODELS WITH UNIQUE SOLUTIONS

Consider the example model we discussed in Section 2.5.

$$Y \quad = \quad a_0 U \ + \quad E \qquad (5.1)$$

$$\begin{bmatrix} 50 \\ 60 \\ 30 \\ 40 \end{bmatrix} = 45 \begin{bmatrix} 1 \\ 1 \\ 1 \\ 1 \end{bmatrix} + \begin{bmatrix} 5 \\ 15 \\ -15 \\ -5 \end{bmatrix}$$

In this model there is only one predictor vector, U, and the least-squares value for a_0 was determined to be 45. Furthermore, in Section 2.7 we showed that no value other than 45 would produce a value for the error sum of squares equal to or less than 500. We can therefore say that this model has a **unique least-squares solution.**

It is possible to formulate a model (deliberately or accidentally) that does not have a unique least-squares solution. But, before we consider a model that does not have a unique solution, the predictor vector U should be examined. Why was the predictor vector defined in this way rather than some other way? For example, why not use a vector containing 2's rather than 1's? The answer is that by using a predictor vector containing all 1's, the least-squares value turns out to be the arithmetic average of the values in the vector Y. As we discussed in Chapter 4, this value is an estimate of a parameter value. It is preferable that the estimate be a "good" one in the sense that it is "close" to the parameter value. Unfortunately, the only way it can be known how close the estimate is to the true value is to know the true value and note the difference. But, if the true parameter value were known, we would not need an estimate of it. The result is that *there is no way to be sure just how "good" any particular estimate is.*

On the other hand, it is possible to determine if an *estimating procedure* has certain properties that can be regarded as desirable. These properties are generally defined by terms such as *unbiased, efficient, and consistent* (see Glass and Stanley, 1970, p. 250–56). For our purposes, we will simply claim— without proof—that estimating parameters by least squares is a procedure that has desirable properties if certain assumptions[1] are met.

5.3
EXAMPLE OF AN EQUIVALENT MODEL

We will now consider another model for estimating level of performance, using the sample data from Section 2.5.

$$Y = b_0 T + E \qquad (5.2)$$

---

[1]These assumptions are discussed in Appendix B.

where **T** is a vector containing a two as each element. The extended forms of the vectors with the least-squares solution are

$$\mathbf{Y} = b_0\mathbf{T} + \mathbf{E}$$

$$\begin{bmatrix} 50 \\ 60 \\ 30 \\ 40 \end{bmatrix} = 22.5 \begin{bmatrix} 2 \\ 2 \\ 2 \\ 2 \end{bmatrix} + \begin{bmatrix} 5 \\ 15 \\ -15 \\ -5 \end{bmatrix}$$

The least-squares value for b_0 turns out to be 22.5, and the error sum of squares is 500. By following the procedure described in Section 2.6, we can demonstrate that there is no other value for b_0, other than 22.5, that will yield a value for the error sum of squares equal to or less than 500. Note also that the predicted level of performance is

$$b_0(2) = 22.5(2) = 45$$

which is the same value that was obtained for the predicted level of performance in model (5.1). The reason is that **T** is a linear combination of **U** (i.e., **T** = 2**U**). In model (5.1) any vector that is a linear combination of **U** could be substituted for **U**, and the same predicted value, the same error vector, and the same error sum of squares would be achieved. (But the least-squares weight would not be the same.) At this point, models (5.1) and (5.2) will simply be defined as **equivalent models.**[2]

5.4
HYPOTHESIS TESTING WITH AN EQUIVALENT MODEL

The problem in Section 2.9 was to determine whether the claim of an expected level of performance equal to 32 was a reasonable statement. Pursuing the same question but using model (5.2), $b_0(2)$ becomes the estimate of the expected level of performance. If the claim is true, then the restriction implied is

$$b_0(2) = 32$$

or

$$b_0 = 32/2 = 16$$

which is the restriction required to test the hypothesis. Substituting $b_0 = 16$ into model (5.2) yields

---

[2]A formal definition is given in Section 5.12.

$$Y = 16T + E^{(2)}$$

which can be written

$$Y - 16T = E^{(2)}$$

The extended forms of the vectors are

$$Y - 16T = E^{(2)}$$

$$\begin{bmatrix} 50 - 32 \\ 60 - 32 \\ 30 - 32 \\ 40 - 32 \end{bmatrix} = \begin{bmatrix} 18 \\ 28 \\ -2 \\ 8 \end{bmatrix}$$

Note that $E^{(2)}$ is identical to $D^{(1)}$ in (2.9), and the error sum of squares (1176) is also the same. In summary: the equivalent models produce the same predicted values and error sums of squares, and the conclusion is identical when the same question is posed.

5.5
MODELS WITHOUT UNIQUE SOLUTIONS

In Section 3.5 a model was formulated to investigate possible sex differences in typing performance. The example data and the least-squares solution are

$$Y = a_g X^{(g)} + a_b X^{(b)} + R^{(1)} \tag{5.3}$$

$$\begin{bmatrix} 50 \\ 60 \\ 30 \\ 40 \end{bmatrix} = 55 \begin{bmatrix} 1 \\ 1 \\ 0 \\ 0 \end{bmatrix} + 35 \begin{bmatrix} 0 \\ 0 \\ 1 \\ 1 \end{bmatrix} + \begin{bmatrix} -5 \\ +5 \\ -5 \\ +5 \end{bmatrix}$$

The error sum of squares is 100.

We will now consider the formulation of another model to investigate the same question.

$$Y = a_0 U + a_1 X^{(g)} + a_2 X^{(b)} + R^{(1)} \tag{5.4}$$

$$\begin{bmatrix} 50 \\ 60 \\ 30 \\ 40 \end{bmatrix} = 45 \begin{bmatrix} 1 \\ 1 \\ 1 \\ 1 \end{bmatrix} + 10 \begin{bmatrix} 1 \\ 1 \\ 0 \\ 0 \end{bmatrix} - 10 \begin{bmatrix} 0 \\ 0 \\ 1 \\ 1 \end{bmatrix} + \begin{bmatrix} -5 \\ +5 \\ -5 \\ +5 \end{bmatrix}$$

Note that an additional predictor vector, the *unit vector*, has been included. A least-squares solution for the weights is given as

$$a_0 = 45$$
$$a_1 = 10$$
$$a_2 = -10$$

The error sum of squares is again 100. Also note that the predicted value for a boy

$$a_0(1) + a_1(1) + a_2(0) = 45 + 10 = 55$$

and for a girl

$$a_1(0) + a_2(1) = 45 - 10 = 35$$

are the same as in model (5.3). No other numerical values for the weights will produce an error sum of squares less than 100. However, it is easy to see that other values for the weights exist that will produce an error sum of squares equal to 100. For example, if the following solution is chosen

$$a_0 = 0$$
$$a_1 = 55$$
$$a_2 = 35$$

the error sum of squares will clearly be equal to 100 (see model 5.3).

As a matter of fact, an unlimited number of least-squares solutions exist for model (5.4). Other possible solutions are shown in Table 5.1. It is important to recognize that although an infinite number of solutions exist that will yield an error sum of squares *equal* to 100, no solution exists that will yield a value *less* than 100. Moreover, every possible least-squares solution to model (5.4) will produce the same predicted values and the same error sum of squares.

Table 5.1 ALTERNATIVE LEAST-SQUARES SOLUTIONS FOR MODEL (5.4)

			Predicted Values		Error
a_0	a_1	a_2	Boy	Girl	Sum of squares
100	-45	-65	55	35	100
-500	555	535	55	35	100
51.8584	3.1416	-16.8584	55	35	100

5.6
HYPOTHESIS TESTING USING A MODEL
WITH AN INFINITE NUMBER OF SOLUTIONS

Suppose the validity of the claim of equal expected values for boys and girls was investigated, using model (5.4) as the full model. Observe that the predicted value for a boy, expressed symbolically, is

$$a_0(1) + a_1(1) + a_2(0)$$

and for a girl

$$a_0(1) + a_1(0) + a_2(1)$$

The hypothesis implies that these two expressions should be equal. If these expressions are set equal and then simplified, we derive the restriction

$$a_1 = a_2$$

Substituting this restriction in the full model yields

$$\mathbf{Y} = a_0\mathbf{U} + a_2\mathbf{X}^{(b)} + a_2\mathbf{X}^{(g)} + \mathbf{R}^{(2)}$$

$$\mathbf{Y} = a_0\mathbf{U} + a_2[\mathbf{X}^{(b)} + \mathbf{X}^{(g)}] + \mathbf{R}^{(2)}$$

But $\mathbf{X}^{(b)} + \mathbf{X}^{(g)} = \mathbf{U}$. Therefore,

$$\mathbf{Y} = a_0\mathbf{U} + a_2\mathbf{U} + \mathbf{R}^{(2)}$$

which can be written as

$$\mathbf{Y} = (a_0 + a_2)\mathbf{U} + \mathbf{R}^{(2)}$$

Note that the weight associated with $\mathbf{U}$ is unknown at this point. Therefore, the expression $a_0 + a_2$ can be replaced by a single symbol (say) b_0, and we can write

$$\mathbf{Y} = b_0\mathbf{U} + \mathbf{R}^{(2)} \tag{5.5}$$

This model (5.5) is identical to model (3.5). Therefore, we can see that the error sum of squares in the restricted model is the same when we ask the same question—whether or not we begin with a model that has a unique solution.

5.7
CHARACTERISTICS OF MODELS WITH UNIQUE
AND NONUNIQUE LEAST-SQUARES SOLUTIONS

We have shown that model (5.3) has a unique least-squares solution and that model (5.4) does not. The reason is that in model (5.3) neither $\mathbf{X}^{(g)}$

nor $\mathbf{X}^{(b)}$ can be expressed as a linear combination of the other. When this condition exists, the predictors are said to be a *linearly independent* set of vectors. *Any model that has a linearly independent set of predictors will have a unique least-squares solution.*

In model (5.4), however, the set of predictors is not a linearly independent set. Any one of the predictors is expressible as a linear combination of the other two.

$$\mathbf{U} = 1\mathbf{X}^{(g)} + 1\mathbf{X}^{(b)}$$

$$\mathbf{X}^{(g)} = 1\mathbf{U} - 1\mathbf{X}^{(b)}$$

$$\mathbf{X}^{(b)} = 1\mathbf{U} - 1\mathbf{X}^{(g)}$$

When this condition exists, the predictors are said to be a *linearly dependent* set of vectors. *Any model that has a linearly dependent set of predictors will have an infinite number of least-squares solutions, but every one of them will yield the same predicted values, the same residual or error vector, and the same error sum of squares.*

Definition of Linear Independence and Dependence

Given a set of vectors

$$\mathbf{X}^{(1)}, \mathbf{X}^{(2)}, \ldots, \mathbf{X}^{(r)}$$

if *any one* of the vectors can be expressed as a linear combination of one or more of the others, the *set of vectors is linearly dependent.* If *none* of the vectors can be expressed as a linear combination of one or more of the others, the *set of vectors is linearly independent.*

5.8
DESIRABILITY
OF A UNIQUE SOLUTION

Least-squares solutions to a model have been shown to produce the same predicted values and error sums of squares, *whether or not a unique solution exists.* So long as we are content with the formulation of our model, there is little reason to seek a unique solution—except for three points.

1. Generally speaking, there are computational advantages when a model has a unique solution. The computer program described in Chapter 14 will find a least-squares solution to a model (whether or not it has a unique solution), so we will not belabor the point.

2. In some situations, we may want to formulate a model in such a way that the weights themselves are of interest. For example, in model (5.4), the first solution given yielded a_0 as the average of the boy and girl averages and a_1 and a_2 as the deviations from this average. However, since model (5.4) has an infinite number of solutions, it is difficult to guarantee that the solution obtained will produce weights having the desired properties. This difficulty can generally be circumvented by "parameterizing" the model (see Appendix D) so that the predictors are a linearly independent set.

3. If we intend to use an F test as a decision rule, it is imperative that the number of linearly independent predictors in both the full and restricted models be identified.

5.9
PARTITIONING PREDICTOR VECTORS INTO INDEPENDENT AND REDUNDANT SUBSETS

We accomplish the identification of the number of linearly independent predictor vectors by partitioning the predictor vectors into an **independent subset** and a **redundant subset**.

Consider a set of k predictor vectors, $\mathbf{X}^{(1)}, \mathbf{X}^{(2)}, \ldots, \mathbf{X}^{(k)}$, each of dimension n. As noted in Section 5.7, some predictors may be expressed as linear combinations of others. (Of course, it is possible that none can be expressed as a linear combination of other vectors.) This set of predictor vectors will be partitioned into two subsets, I and R. Subset I, to be called the *independent subset*, contains vectors, no one of which can be expressed as a linear combination of any other vectors in I. We will assume that there are p vectors in I. Subset R, to be called the *redundant subset*, contains vectors each one of which *can* be expressed as a linear combination of the vectors in I. Since there are p vectors in subset I, subset R must have $k - p$ vectors. As a practice example, consider the following set of $k = 5$ vectors.

$$
\begin{array}{ccccc}
\mathbf{U} & \mathbf{X}^{(1)} & \mathbf{X}^{(2)} & \mathbf{X}^{(3)} & \mathbf{X}^{(4)} \\
\begin{bmatrix} 1 \\ 1 \\ 1 \\ 1 \end{bmatrix} &
\begin{bmatrix} 1 \\ 1 \\ 0 \\ 0 \end{bmatrix} &
\begin{bmatrix} 0 \\ 0 \\ 1 \\ 1 \end{bmatrix} &
\begin{bmatrix} 0 \\ 1 \\ 2 \\ 3 \end{bmatrix} &
\begin{bmatrix} 9 \\ 10 \\ 11 \\ 12 \end{bmatrix}
\end{array}
$$

We can start by arbitrarily placing any one of the vectors in subset I. Let us begin with $\mathbf{U}$. Subset I now contains one vector, $\mathbf{U}$. This can be symbolized as

I   R

U		

We now ask the question: "Can $\mathbf{X}^{(1)}$ be expressed as a linear combination of vectors in subset I?" Expressed another way: "Is there a value for a_1 that will make the following expression true?"

$$\mathbf{X}^{(1)} = a_1\mathbf{U}$$

Obviously, there is not. No matter what value is chosen for a_1, the vector $a_1\mathbf{U}$ will contain a_1 as every element, whereas the elements of $\mathbf{X}^{(1)}$ are not constant. Therefore, $\mathbf{X}^{(1)}$ can be placed in subset **I**, yielding

I   R

U, $\mathbf{X}^{(1)}$		

We now consider the possibility of expressing $\mathbf{X}^{(2)}$ as a linear combination of vectors in subset I. In other words: "Are there values for a_1 and a_2 such that the following expression is true?"

$$\mathbf{X}^{(2)} = a_1\mathbf{U} + a_2\mathbf{X}^{(1)}$$

If the values $a_1 = 1$ and $a_2 = -1$ are chosen, the following expression is true.

$$\mathbf{X}^{(2)} = 1\mathbf{U} - 1\mathbf{X}^{(1)}$$

Therefore, $\mathbf{X}^{(2)}$ can be placed in the redundant subset, **R**, yielding

I   R

U, $\mathbf{X}^{(1)}$		$\mathbf{X}^{(2)}$	

Continuing the process, we see that $\mathbf{X}^{(3)}$ cannot be expressed as a linear combination of $\mathbf{U}$ and $\mathbf{X}^{(1)}$. Note that $\mathbf{U}$ and $\mathbf{X}^{(1)}$ both have 1's as the first two elements. Any linear combination of $\mathbf{U}$ and $\mathbf{X}^{(1)}$ must contain the same value as the first two elements, but $\mathbf{X}^{(3)}$ does not satisfy this condition. Therefore, $\mathbf{X}^{(3)}$ can be placed in subset **I**.

I   R

U, $\mathbf{X}^{(1)}$, $\mathbf{X}^{(3)}$		$\mathbf{X}^{(2)}$	

Furthermore, we see that

$$\mathbf{X}^{(4)} = 9\mathbf{U} + 1\mathbf{X}^{(3)}$$

or

$$\mathbf{X}^{(4)} = 9\mathbf{U} + 1\mathbf{X}^{(3)} + 0\mathbf{X}^{(1)}$$

Therefore, $\mathbf{X}^{(4)}$ can be placed in subset R.

I	R
$\mathbf{U}, \mathbf{X}^{(1)}, \mathbf{X}^{(3)}$	$\mathbf{X}^{(2)}, \mathbf{X}^{(4)}$

Since all of the vectors are now exhausted, the partitioning process has been completed. Note that none of the vectors in subset I can be expressed as a linear combination of other vectors in I and that every vector in subset R can be expressed as a linear combination of vectors in I. Also note that $p = 3$ is the number of vectors in subset I, and that $k - p = 5 - 3 = 2$ is the number of vectors in subset R.

5.10
ALTERNATE PARTITIONING

In general, partitioning predictor vectors into redundant and independent subsets is not unique; that is, it can be accomplished in many different ways. For example, if we had started with the vector $\mathbf{X}^{(4)}$ and worked to the left, the procedure could be summarized as follows.

I	R
$\mathbf{X}^{(4)}$	

Question: Is $\mathbf{X}^{(3)} = a_1 \mathbf{X}^{(4)}$?
Answer: No.
Action: Place $\mathbf{X}^{(3)}$ in subset **I**.

I	R
$\mathbf{X}^{(4)}, \mathbf{X}^{(3)}$	

Question: Is $\mathbf{X}^{(2)} = a_1 \mathbf{X}^{(4)} + a_2 \mathbf{X}^{(3)}$?
Answer: No.
Action: Place $\mathbf{X}^{(2)}$ in subset I.

I	R
$\mathbf{X}^{(4)}, \mathbf{X}^{(3)}, \mathbf{X}^{(2)}$	

Question: Is $\mathbf{X}^{(1)} = a_1 \mathbf{X}^{(4)} + a_2 \mathbf{X}^{(3)} + a_3 \mathbf{X}^{(2)}$?
Answer: Yes.
How: $\mathbf{X}^{(1)} = 1/9 \mathbf{X}^{(4)} - 1/9 \mathbf{X}^{(3)} - 1 \mathbf{X}^{(2)}$
Action: Place $\mathbf{X}^{(1)}$ in subset R.

I	R
$\mathbf{X}^{(4)}, \mathbf{X}^{(3)}, \mathbf{X}^{(2)}$	$\mathbf{X}^{(1)}$

Question: Is $\mathbf{U} = a_1 \mathbf{X}^{(4)} + a_2 \mathbf{X}^{(3)} + a_3 \mathbf{X}^{(2)}$?
Answer: Yes.
How: $\mathbf{U} = 1/9 \mathbf{X}^{(4)} - 1/9 \mathbf{X}^{(3)} + 0 \mathbf{X}^{(2)}$
Action: Place $\mathbf{U}$ in subset R.

I	R
$\mathbf{X}^{(4)}, \mathbf{X}^{(3)}, \mathbf{X}^{(2)}$	$\mathbf{X}^{(1)}, \mathbf{U}$

Note that the vectors in the subsets are different than in Section 5.9, but the *number* of vectors in each subset is the same. There are other ways of parti-tioning the vectors. We might have started, for example, with $\mathbf{X}^{(2)}$ and worked alternately to the left and right. Regardless of how we proceeded, however, we would find that $p = 3$ and $k - p = 2$.

In summary, there may be many ways to partition predictor vectors into an independent subset and a redundant subset. However, p (the number of independent vectors) and $k - p$ (the number of redundant vectors) are unique for any particular set of k predictor vectors. In many cases, $p = k$; that is, there are no redundant vectors. If $p = k$, the model will have a unique least-squares solution. If $p < k$, the model will have an infinite number of least-squares solutions. Obviously, $p > k$ cannot occur.

5.11
DETERMINATION OF VALUES FOR $(df)_1$ AND $(df)_2$

In our discussion of the computation of an F statistic in Section 4.8, we deferred a formal description of the way in which $(df)_1$ and $(df)_2$ are determined to this section. Let us now assume that full and restricted models have been formulated with k_1 and k_2 predictor vectors, respectively, each vector of dimension n. The k_1 predictor vectors in the full model should be partitioned into an independent subset which has n_f vectors and a redundant subset with $k_1 - n_f$ vectors. Also, the k_2 predictor vectors in the restricted model should be partitioned into an independent subset consisting of n_r vectors and a redundant subset containing $k_2 - n_r$ vectors. The numerical values for $(df)_1$ and $(df)_2$ are obtained directly from

$$(df)_1 = n_f - n_r$$
$$(df)_2 = n - n_f$$

In most problems, the values for n_f and n_r can be obtained by simply inspecting the vectors or their definitions.

5.12
EQUIVALENT MODELS

We can now be specific about exactly what the term *equivalent models* means. Given any two models, we will say they are equivalent when all of the following conditions exist.

1. Both models have the same **Y** vector.
2. Both models have the same number of linearly independent predictors.
3. Every predictor vector in the first model is a linear combination of predictors in the second model.
4. Every predictor vector in the second model is a linear combination of predictors in the first model.

Note that models (5.1) and (5.2) are equivalent, as are models (5.3) and (5.4). When models (5.4) and (5.5) are compared, we see that the first and fourth conditions are met, but the second and third are not. Therefore, models (5.4) and (5.5) are not equivalent.

Generally, one can determine if two models are equivalent by examining the vectors and/or their definitions. If two models are equivalent, a least-squares solution will yield the following results.

1. The predicted values in the two models will be identical.
2. The residual or error vector in the two models will be identical.
3. The error sum of squares in the two models will be identical.
4. The least-squares weights generally will not be the same.

EXERCISES

For Exercises 1–9, consider the following set of vectors.

U	$\mathbf{R}^{(1)}$	$\mathbf{R}^{(2)}$	$\mathbf{C}^{(1)}$	$\mathbf{C}^{(2)}$	$\mathbf{C}^{(3)}$
1	1	0	1	0	0
1	1	0	0	1	0
1	1	0	0	0	1
1	0	1	1	0	0
1	0	1	0	1	0
1	0	1	0	0	1

1. Moving from *left to right*, partition the vectors into an independent subset, I, and a redundant subset, R.

2. Express each vector in the redundant subset R (in Exercise 1) as a linear combination of vectors in the independent subset I.

3. How many vectors are in the independent subset I (in Exercise 1)?

4. How many vectors are in the redundant subset R (in Exercise 1)?

5. Moving from *right to left*, partition the vectors into an independent subset, I and a redundant subset, R.

6. Express each vector in the redundant subset R (in Exercise 5) as a linear combination of vectors in the independent subset I.

7. How many vectors are in the independent subset I (in Exercise 5)?

8. How many vectors are in the redundant subset R (in Exercise 5)?

9. Compare the answers to Exercises 3 and 7. Are they the same or different?

For Exercises 10–18, consider the following set of vectors.

U	$\mathbf{A}^{(1)}$	$\mathbf{A}^{(2)}$	$\mathbf{B}^{(1)}$	$\mathbf{B}^{(2)}$	$\mathbf{C}^{(1)}$	$\mathbf{C}^{(2)}$
1	1	0	1	0	1	0
1	1	0	1	0	0	1
1	1	0	0	1	1	0
1	1	0	0	1	0	1
1	0	1	1	0	1	0
1	0	1	1	0	0	1
1	0	1	0	1	1	0
1	0	1	0	1	0	1

10. Moving from *left to right*, partition the vectors into an independent subset, I, and a redundant subset, R.

11. Express each vector in the redundant subset R (in Exercise 10) as a linear combination of vectors in the independent subset I.

12. How many vectors are in the independent subset I (in Exercise 10)?

13. How many vectors are in the redundant subset R (in Exercise 10)?

14. Moving from *right to left*, partition the vectors into an independent subset, I, and a redundant subset, R.

15. Express each vector in the redundant subset R (in Exercise 14) as a linear combination of vectors in the independent subset I.

16. How many vectors are in the independent subset I (in Exercise 14)?

17. How many vectors are in the redundant subset R (in Exercise 14)?

18. Compare the answers to Exercises 12 and 16. Are they the same or different?

19. Using the vectors from Exercises 1–9, assume the full model

$$\mathbf{Y} = a_1\mathbf{U} + a_2\mathbf{R}^{(1)} + a_3\mathbf{R}^{(2)} + a_4\mathbf{C}^{(1)} + a_5\mathbf{C}^{(2)} + a_6\mathbf{C}^{(3)} + \mathbf{E}^{(1)}$$

where $\mathbf{E}^{(1)}$ is the error vector resulting from using least-squares values for a_1, $a_2, \ldots, a_6$.

Assume the restricted model

$$\mathbf{Y} = b_1\mathbf{U} + b_2\mathbf{R}^{(1)} + b_3\mathbf{R}^{(2)} + \mathbf{E}^{(2)}$$

where $\mathbf{E}^{(2)}$ is the error vector resulting from using least-squares values for b_1, b_2 and b_3.

Assuming that the dimension of all vectors is n, compute $(df)_1$ and $(df)_2$.

20. Using the vectors from Exercises 10–18, assume the full model

$$\mathbf{Y} = k_1\mathbf{U} + k_2\mathbf{A}^{(1)} + k_3\mathbf{A}^{(2)} + k_4\mathbf{B}^{(1)} + k_5\mathbf{B}^{(2)} + k_6\mathbf{C}^{(1)} + k_7\mathbf{C}^{(2)} + \mathbf{E}^{(1)}$$

and the restricted model

$$\mathbf{Y} = r_1\mathbf{U} + r_2\mathbf{A}^{(1)} + r_3\mathbf{A}^{(2)} + r_4\mathbf{B}^{(1)} + r_5\mathbf{B}^{(2)} + \mathbf{E}^{(2)}$$

Assuming that the dimension of all the vectors is n, compute $(df)_1$ and $(df)_2$.

21. Using the vectors from Exercises 1–9, indicate which of the following models are equivalent and where equivalent show why.

$$\mathbf{Y} = a_1\mathbf{U} + a_2\mathbf{R}^{(1)} + a_3\mathbf{R}^{(2)} + a_4\mathbf{C}^{(1)} + a_5\mathbf{C}^{(2)} + a_6\mathbf{C}^{(3)} + \mathbf{E}^{(1)}$$

$$\mathbf{Y} = b_1\mathbf{U} + b_2\mathbf{R}^{(1)} + b_3\mathbf{C}^{(1)} + b_4\mathbf{C}^{(2)} + \mathbf{E}^{(2)}$$

$$\mathbf{Y} = k_1\mathbf{R}^{(2)} + k_2\mathbf{C}^{(1)} + k_3\mathbf{C}^{(2)} + k_4\mathbf{C}^{(3)} + \mathbf{E}^{(3)}$$

$$\mathbf{Y} = s_1\mathbf{U} + s_2\mathbf{R}^{(1)} + s_3\mathbf{R}^{(2)} + s_4\mathbf{C}^{(1)} + \mathbf{E}^{(4)}$$

22. Using the vectors from Exercises 10–18, indicate which of the following models are equivalent and where equivalent show why.

$$\mathbf{Y} = k_1\mathbf{U} + k_2\mathbf{A}^{(1)} + k_3\mathbf{A}^{(2)} + k_4\mathbf{B}^{(1)} + k_5\mathbf{B}^{(2)} + k_6\mathbf{C}^{(1)} + k_7\mathbf{C}^{(2)} + \mathbf{E}$$

$$\mathbf{Y} = m_1\mathbf{U} + m_2\mathbf{A}^{(1)} + m_3\mathbf{B}^{(1)} + m_4\mathbf{C}^{(1)} + \mathbf{E}^{(2)}$$

$$\mathbf{Y} = p_1\mathbf{A}^{(2)} + p_2\mathbf{B}^{(2)} + p_3\mathbf{C}^{(1)} + p_4\mathbf{C}^{(2)} + \mathbf{E}^{(3)}$$

$$\mathbf{Y} = r_1\mathbf{U} + r_2\mathbf{A}^{(1)} + r_3\mathbf{A}^{(2)} + r_4\mathbf{B}^{(1)} + r_5\mathbf{B}^{(2)} + \mathbf{E}^{(4)}$$

$$\mathbf{Y} = t_1\mathbf{A}^{(1)} + t_2\mathbf{B}^{(1)} + t_3\mathbf{C}^{(1)} + \mathbf{E}^{(5)}$$

$$\mathbf{Y} = s_1\mathbf{A}^{(2)} + s_2\mathbf{B}^{(2)} + s_3\mathbf{C}^{(2)} + \mathbf{E}^{(6)}$$

6

A One-Attribute Model
with Ordered Categories

6.1
INTRODUCTION

In Chapter 4 we studied a one-attribute problem with four mutually exclusive categories. The problem considered typing performance of students who were in grades 9, 10, 11, and 12. Now we will consider these four categories to be **ordered categories**. We will also demonstrate the use of linearly dependent vectors for recoding information.

6.2
ANALYSIS OF A PROBLEM INVOLVING
FOUR ORDERED CATEGORIES

Consider again the typing-performance problem presented in Chapter 4 (Section 4.3). The vectors were defined as

$\mathbf{Y}$ = a vector of dimension 20 in which each element is a typing-test score from a student.

$\mathbf{X}^{(9)}$ = 1 if a 9th grader; 0 otherwise.

$\mathbf{X}^{(10)}$ = 1 if a 10th grader; 0 otherwise.

$\mathbf{X}^{(11)}$ = 1 if an 11th grader; 0 otherwise.

$\mathbf{X}^{(12)}$ = 1 if a 12th grader; 0 otherwise.

The full model was

$$\mathbf{Y} = a_9\mathbf{X}^{(9)} + a_{10}\mathbf{X}^{(10)} + a_{11}\mathbf{X}^{(11)} + a_{12}\mathbf{X}^{(12)} + \mathbf{E}^{(1)} \qquad (6.1)$$

The hypothesis was

$$a_9 = a_{10} = a_{11} = a_{12} = a_c \text{ (a common value)}$$

6.3
PERFORMANCE NOT EQUAL FOR ORDERED CATEGORIES

In Chapter 5 we concluded that the expected values (for the variable—typing performance) of the four classes were not equal. Such a conclusion may not be entirely satisfactory because it provides no information about how they differ. Although it may be true that the expected values differ, they might differ in a systematic way that can be summarized by a simple expression.

Suppose we begin by designating a_9 by another symbol, w_0. If the expected value for freshmen is not equal to the expected value for sophomores, then

$$a_{10} \neq a_9$$
$$a_{10} \neq w_0$$

Although our argument concerns relations among the expected values, we can summarize by substituting for the expected values the symbolic expressions that are estimates of the expected values. This is done to simplify the notation. A technically more accurate argument would require that we use one set of symbols to represent the expected values and another set to represent their estimates. If we wish to make an equality statement, we might say that a_{10} differs from a_9 by an amount (say w_1) and write

$$a_{10} = a_9 + w_1 = w_0 + w_1$$

Next, consider the possibility that

$$a_{11} \neq a_{10}$$

A simple way for a_{11} and a_{10} to differ is by the same amount that a_{10} differs from a_9. Such a condition can be written as

$$a_{11} = a_{10} + w_1$$

But, since

$$a_{10} = w_0 + w_1$$
$$a_{11} = (w_0 + w_1) + w_1$$
$$a_{11} = w_0 + 2w_1$$

Finally, consider the possibility that

$$a_{12} \neq a_{11}$$

It would be nice if a_{12} differs from a_{11} by the same amount (i.e., by the amount w_1) as the other adjacent categories. Then we could write

$$a_{12} = a_{11} + w_1$$
$$a_{12} = (w_0 + 2w_1) + w_1$$
$$a_{12} = w_0 + 3w_1$$

To summarize these statements, we write

$$a_9 = w_0$$
$$a_{10} = w_0 + w_1$$
$$a_{11} = w_0 + 2w_1 \tag{6.2}$$
$$a_{12} = w_0 + 3w_1$$

Note that this discussion represents a concise way of stating the argument that *the expected values differ in a simple and systematic fashion*. Because the argument has been reduced to a set of statements (6.2), which imply certain relationships among the expected values, these statements are subject to test in the usual fashion by imposing the restrictions on the full model.

6.4
THE RESTRICTED MODEL

The restrictions in (6.2) are imposed on the full model (6.1) by direct substitution.

$$\mathbf{Y} = w_0 \mathbf{X}^{(9)} + (w_0 + w_1)\mathbf{X}^{(10)} + (w_0 + 2w_1)\mathbf{X}^{(11)}$$
$$\qquad + (w_0 + 3w_1)\mathbf{X}^{(12)} + \mathbf{E}^{(3)}$$
$$\mathbf{Y} = w_0(\mathbf{X}^{(9)} + \mathbf{X}^{(10)} + \mathbf{X}^{(11)} + \mathbf{X}^{(12)})$$
$$\qquad + w_1(\mathbf{X}^{(10)} + 2\mathbf{X}^{(11)} + 3\mathbf{X}^{(12)}) + \mathbf{E}^{(3)}$$

Note that

$$\mathbf{X}^{(9)} + \mathbf{X}^{(10)} + \mathbf{X}^{(11)} + \mathbf{X}^{(12)} = \mathbf{U}$$

and let

$$\mathbf{X}^{(10)} + 2\mathbf{X}^{(11)} + 3\mathbf{X}^{(12)} = \mathbf{C}$$

Then the restricted model is

$$\mathbf{Y} = w_0\mathbf{U} + w_1\mathbf{C} + \mathbf{E}^{(3)} \tag{6.3}$$

6.5
THE LEAST-SQUARES VALUES FOR w_0 AND w_1

Using the data of Chapter 4 and the computer program described in Chapter 14, we determine that the least-squares estimates are $w_0 = 34.72$ and $w_1 = 12.32$. Using these least-squares values, we can write the restricted model

$$\mathbf{Y} = 34.72\mathbf{U} + 12.32\mathbf{C} + \mathbf{E}^{(3)}$$

The extended form of this restricted model is

$$
\begin{bmatrix} 16 \\ 48 \\ 40 \\ 40 \\ 32 \\ 40 \\ 24 \\ 64 \\ 56 \\ 48 \\ 64 \\ 56 \\ 48 \\ 72 \\ 56 \\ 80 \\ 72 \\ 72 \\ 64 \\ 72 \end{bmatrix}
= 34.72
\begin{bmatrix} 1 \\ 1 \\ 1 \\ 1 \\ 1 \\ 1 \\ 1 \\ 1 \\ 1 \\ 1 \\ 1 \\ 1 \\ 1 \\ 1 \\ 1 \\ 1 \\ 1 \\ 1 \\ 1 \\ 1 \end{bmatrix}
+ 12.32
\begin{bmatrix} 0 \\ 0 \\ 0 \\ 0 \\ 0 \\ 1 \\ 1 \\ 1 \\ 1 \\ 1 \\ 2 \\ 2 \\ 2 \\ 2 \\ 2 \\ 3 \\ 3 \\ 3 \\ 3 \\ 3 \end{bmatrix}
+
\begin{bmatrix} -18.72 \\ 13.28 \\ 5.28 \\ 5.28 \\ -2.72 \\ -7.04 \\ -23.04 \\ 16.96 \\ 8.96 \\ .96 \\ 4.64 \\ -3.36 \\ -11.36 \\ 12.64 \\ -3.36 \\ 8.32 \\ .32 \\ .32 \\ -7.68 \\ .32 \end{bmatrix}
$$

Column headers: $\mathbf{Y}$ $\mathbf{U}$ $\mathbf{C}$ $\mathbf{E}^{(3)}$

Four elements of $\mathbf{E}^{(3)}$ can be calculated as shown.

$$e_{1,3} = 16 - (34.72 + 12.32(0)) = 16 - 34.72 = -18.72$$
$$e_{6,3} = 40 - (34.72 + 12.32(1)) = 40 - 47.04 = -7.04$$
$$e_{11,3} = 64 - (34.72 + 12.32(2)) = 64 - 59.36 = 4.64$$
$$e_{16,3} = 80 - (34.72 + 12.32(3)) = 80 - 71.68 = 8.32$$

Observe that the predicted values for the four groups are

Freshman: $(34.72)(1) + (12.32)(0) = 34.72$

Sophomore: $(34.72)(1) + (12.32)(1) = 47.04$

Junior: $(34.72)(1) + (12.32)(2) = 59.36$

Senior: $(34.72)(1) + (12.32)(3) = 71.68$

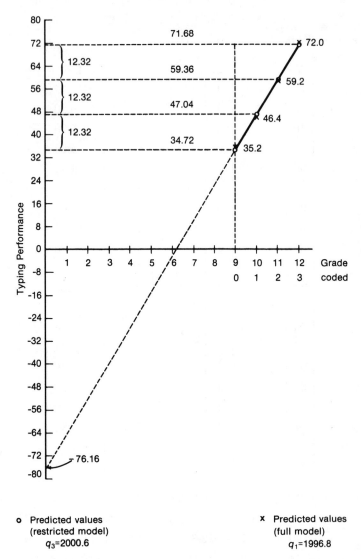

o Predicted values
(restricted model)
q_3=2000.6

x Predicted values
(full model)
q_1=1996.8

FIG. 6.1 Estimates of the Expected Values from Models (6.1), (6.3), and (6.4).

Figure 6.1 is a pictorial representation of the data.
Note that the predicted values lie on a straight line. This test is sometimes
referred to as a *test for nonlinearity* (see Glass & Stanley, 1970, pp. 150–52),
since the rejection of the hypotheses indicates that the expected values do
not lie on a straight line.

6.6
VERIFYING THE RESTRICTED MODEL

As the models we discuss become increasingly complex, the possibility of making algebraic or logical errors also increases. One way of avoiding such errors is to investigate the properties of a model and then verify that it has the desired properties.

We can investigate the properties of a model by writing the symbolic expressions that estimate the expected values and by noting whether the expressions are related in the way required for the model to have the desired properties. Consider model (6.3). The expected values are estimated by the symbolic expressions

$$\text{Freshman:} \quad w_0(1) + w_1(0) = w_0$$
$$\text{Sophomore:} \quad w_0(1) + w_1(1) = w_0 + w_1$$
$$\text{Junior:} \quad w_0(1) + w_1(2) = w_0 + 2w_1$$
$$\text{Senior:} \quad w_0(1) + w_1(3) = w_0 + 3w_1$$

Note that if w_1 is zero, the predicted values will all be equal. If w_1 is positive, then the predicted values differ by a constant amount, and the slope of the line in Figure 6.1 is positive. If w_1 is negative, the predicted values differ by a constant amount, and the slope of the line will be negative. In any event, the difference between any pair of adjacent categories is the constant w_1. Therefore, we conclude that model (6.3) has the properties required by the hypotheses (6.2).

Normally, the verification should take place before a numerical solution is attempted. However, the same verification can be made on the numerical values after the solution has been obtained. The predicted values for both the full and restricted models are shown in Table 6.1. Note the constant difference that exists in the restricted model.

Table 6.1 PREDICTED VALUES FROM MODELS (4.1) AND (6.3)

Grade	Full model	Restricted model	Difference
9	35.20	34.72	
10	46.40	47.04 →	12.32
11	59.20	59.36 →	12.32
12	72.00	71.68 →	12.32

Observe that the predicted values shown in Table 6.1 are estimates of the same parameter means based on two different models. Although the estimates are numerically quite similar, the way in which they were derived have some essential differences that are worthy of comment. In the first place, the estimates obtained in Section 4.4 are the arithmetic averages of the sampled **Y** values within each class. For example, the value 35.2 is the arithmetic average of the five students in the 9th grade. But, the value 34.72, which estimates the same parameter mean, is not the arithmetic average of any of the values in **Y**. This is a very important attribute of a model to understand because many of the models we discuss in this book produce mean estimates, which are not averages of sampled values.

The essential difference between model (4.1) and model (6.3) is that the former has four unknown parameters $(a_9, a_{10}, a_{11}, a_{12})$ and the latter has only two (w_0, w_1). In this sense, model (6.3) is a simpler model. One way of looking at every question we pose in this book is to consider whether a set of interesting means can be estimated equally well by a simple model (i.e., one with few parameters), and one less simple (i.e., one with more parameters). Generally speaking, *if the simpler model is true, the estimates will be better* (i.e., on the average, closer to the parameter means) than those produced by the less simple one. In this example, "true" refers to the relationship among the parameter means. If the parameter means do differ by a constant amount in the way described in (6.2), model (6.3) is true; otherwise it is not true.[1]

One of the reasons that the simpler model (if true) produces "better" estimates is that the estimates of the unknown parameters of the model are based on more observed values. For example, the value of a_9 in model (4.1) is based on only the first five elements in **Y**. If we were to change the last element in **Y** from 72 to (say) 60, it would not affect the predicted value (a_9) for a 9th grader at all. On the other hand, in model (6.3) the predicted value for a 9th grader is a function of both w_0 and w_1, and the values of w_0 and w_1 depend on *all* 20 observations in **Y**. If we were to change the last value in **Y**, it would affect the values of w_0 and w_1 and thus the predicted value for a 9th grader.

6.7
COMPARING THE ERROR SUMS OF SQUARES

The error sum of squares from the full model (obtained in Section 4.4) is

$$q_f = q_1 = 1996.8$$

[1]See Section 6.15 for a further discussion of this point.

The error sum of squares from the restricted model, as determined by the computer program, is

$$q_r = q_3 = 2000.6$$

There are four linearly independent vectors associated with the four coefficients of the full model: $\mathbf{X}^{(9)}$, $\mathbf{X}^{(10)}$, $\mathbf{X}^{(11)}$, $\mathbf{X}^{(12)}$. Therefore

$$n_f = 4$$

There are two linearly independent vectors, $\mathbf{U}$ and $\mathbf{C}$, associated with the two coefficients, w_0 and w_1, in the restricted model. Therefore

$$n_r = 2$$

The number of elements in each vector is 20; therefore

$$n = 20$$

Then

$$F = \frac{(q_r - q_f)/(n_f - n_r)}{q_f/(n - n_f)} = \frac{(2000.6 - 1996.8)/(4 - 2)}{1996.8/(20 - 4)}$$

$$F = 0.015$$

The probability associated with this F value is approximately 0.98. The hypotheses would be accepted on a statistical basis. In other words, the data do not contradict the notion that a constant difference in typing speed exists for adjacent classes. It is highly probable that the values in $\mathbf{Y}$ could have come from distributions whose expected values differ by a constant amount.

6.8
RECODING THE INFORMATION

In Section 6.2 the coded vector $\mathbf{C}$ contained the numerical values 0, 1, 2, and 3. The categories of grades would normally be coded 9, 10, 11, and 12, and we might want to use these values, since they are already available.

In this section we will demonstrate how these codes (9, 10, 11, and 12) provide the desired results. This is made possible by using the concept of equivalent models described in Chapter 5.

Expressing the Coded Vector in Terms of Grade

Let the vector $\mathbf{G}$ contain the grade level (9, 10, 11, 12) of each student. Then we can express $\mathbf{C}$ as a linear combination of $\mathbf{G}$ and $\mathbf{U}$.

$$\mathbf{C} = \mathbf{G} - 9\mathbf{U}$$

C	G	U
0	9	1
0	9	1
0	9	1
0	9	1
0	9	1
1	10	1
1	10	1
1	10	1
1	10	1
1	10	1
2	11	1
2	11	1
2	11	1
2	11	1
2	11	1
3	12	1
3	12	1
3	12	1
3	12	1
3	12	1

$$\mathbf{C} = \mathbf{G} - 9\mathbf{U}$$

Then substituting in the restricted model (6.2),

$$\mathbf{Y} = w_0\mathbf{U} + w_1(\mathbf{G} - 9\mathbf{U}) + \mathbf{E}^{(3)}$$

By collecting coefficients of the two vectors $\mathbf{U}$ and $\mathbf{G}$,

$$\mathbf{Y} = (w_0 - 9w_1)\mathbf{U} + w_1\mathbf{G} + \mathbf{E}^{(3)}$$

Now, rename

$$w_0 - 9w_1 = d_0$$

Then

$$\mathbf{Y} = d_0\mathbf{U} + w_1\mathbf{G} + \mathbf{E}^{(3)} \tag{6.4}$$

We can observe that the least-squares numerical value for the coefficient of $\mathbf{C}$ and $\mathbf{G}$ are the same. However, we see that the coefficient d_0 of $\mathbf{U}$ when $\mathbf{G}$ is used, is related to the coefficient w_0 of $\mathbf{U}$, when $\mathbf{C}$ is used, by

$$d_0 = w_0 - 9w_1$$

The use of either vector **C** or vector **G** produces identical predicted scores and errors. Thus models (6.3) and (6.4) are equivalent. The extended form of the restricted model is

$$
\begin{array}{cccc}
\mathbf{Y} & \mathbf{U} & \mathbf{G} & \mathbf{E}^{(3)} \\
\begin{bmatrix} 16 \\ 48 \\ 40 \\ 40 \\ 32 \\ 40 \\ 24 \\ 64 \\ 56 \\ 48 \\ 64 \\ 56 \\ 48 \\ 72 \\ 56 \\ 80 \\ 72 \\ 72 \\ 64 \\ 72 \end{bmatrix}
= -76.16
\begin{bmatrix} 1 \\ 1 \\ 1 \\ 1 \\ 1 \\ 1 \\ 1 \\ 1 \\ 1 \\ 1 \\ 1 \\ 1 \\ 1 \\ 1 \\ 1 \\ 1 \\ 1 \\ 1 \\ 1 \\ 1 \end{bmatrix}
+ 12.32
\begin{bmatrix} 9 \\ 9 \\ 9 \\ 9 \\ 9 \\ 10 \\ 10 \\ 10 \\ 10 \\ 10 \\ 11 \\ 11 \\ 11 \\ 11 \\ 11 \\ 12 \\ 12 \\ 12 \\ 12 \\ 12 \end{bmatrix}
+
\begin{bmatrix} -18.72 \\ 13.28 \\ 5.28 \\ 5.28 \\ -2.72 \\ -7.04 \\ -23.04 \\ 16.96 \\ 8.96 \\ .96 \\ 4.64 \\ -3.36 \\ -11.36 \\ 12.64 \\ -3.36 \\ 8.32 \\ .32 \\ .32 \\ -7.68 \\ .32 \end{bmatrix}
\end{array}
$$

6.9
ANOTHER EXAMINATION OF PERFORMANCE DIFFERENCES BETWEEN GRADES

In Section 6.2 we used as our starting or full model (6.1)

$$\mathbf{Y} = a_9\mathbf{X}^{(9)} + a_{10}\mathbf{X}^{(10)} + a_{11}\mathbf{X}^{(11)} + a_{12}\mathbf{X}^{(12)} + \mathbf{E}^{(1)}$$

and to test the hypothesis of a *constant difference*, we used model (6.4).

$$\mathbf{Y} = d_0\mathbf{U} + w_1\mathbf{G} + \mathbf{E}^{(3)}$$

In Chapter 4 we used (6.1) as a starting model to investigate the *equality* of the four expected values. Note that (6.4) produces four different symbolic expressions for the predicted values.

Student in Grade	Predicted Value
9	$d_0(1) + w_1(9)$
10	$d_0(1) + w_1(10)$
11	$d_0(1) + w_1(11)$
12	$d_0(1) + w_1(12)$

Thus it is possible to test the hypothesis of equality of the expected values using (6.4) as the full model if we are willing to assume that the expected differences are constant.

6.10
THE RESTRICTED MODEL

The hypothesis of interest is that the expected values for all four grades are equal. Using the predicted scores from the model, the hypothesis is

$$d_0(1) + w_1(9) = d_0(1) + w_1(10) = d_0(1) + w_1(11) = d_0(1) + w_1(12)$$

or

$$w_1(i) = w_1(j) \qquad i, j = 9, 10, 11, 12, \quad \text{and} \quad i \neq j$$

Then

$$w_1(i) - w_1(j) = 0$$

$$w_1(i - j) = 0$$

But, since $i \neq j$, it follows that the restriction implied by the hypothesis is

$$w_1 = 0$$

Imposing this restriction yields the restricted model

$$\mathbf{Y} = d_0 \mathbf{U} + \mathbf{E}^{(2)} \tag{6.5}$$

The least-squares solution to this model was obtained in Section 4.6. The value is $d_0 = 53.2$ (called a_c in Section 4.6), and the error sum of squares was 5795.2 (called q_2 in Section 4.6).

6.11
COMPARING THE ERROR SUMS OF SQUARES

The error sum of squares for the full model (obtained previously as q_3 in Section 6.7) is

$$q_f = q_3 = 2000.6$$

The error sum of squares for the restricted model is

$$q_r = q_2 = 5795.2$$

There are two linearly independent vectors associated with the unknown parameters, d_0 and w_1; therefore

$$n_f = 2$$

There is one vector, $\mathbf{U}$, in the restricted model; therefore

$$n_r = 1$$

The number of elements in each vector is 20; therefore

$$n = 20$$

Now

$$F = \frac{(q_r - q_f)/(n_f - n_r)}{q_f/(n - n_f)}$$

$$F = \frac{(5795.2 - 2000.6)/(2 - 1)}{2000.6/(20 - 2)} = 34.1$$

And the probability associated with this F value is less than 0.01.

We therefore reject the hypothesis of equality of typing performance. It is very unlikely that the values in $\mathbf{Y}$ could have arisen by random sampling from distributions whose expected values are equal. This is the same conclusion as the one reached in Chapter 4, which used a different full model.

6.12
A SYNTHESIS OF ONE-ATTRIBUTE ANALYSES

In Chapter 4 we discussed a one-attribute problem with four mutually exclusive categories. In this chapter, we have considered ordered categories and the possibility of a linear relation (or constant difference) between the vector of interest, $\mathbf{Y}$, and the students' grade level, $\mathbf{G}$. Now we will summarize and synthesize these ideas.

The General Model for Mutually Exclusive Categories

Instead of the four mutually exclusive categories considered in Chapter 4, we will generalize to k categories. Then we can write the general model

$$\mathbf{Y} = a_1 \mathbf{X}^{(1)} + a_2 \mathbf{X}^{(2)} + \cdots + a_k \mathbf{X}^{(k)} + \mathbf{E}^{(1)} \qquad (6.6)$$

where

    $\mathbf{Y}$ = the vector of interest (dimension = n).

    $\mathbf{X}^{(i)}$ = 1 if the corresponding element in $\mathbf{Y}$ is associated with category i; 0 otherwise ($i = 1, 2, \ldots, k$).

    $\mathbf{E}^{(1)}$ = the error vector.

and let

    q_1 = the error sum of squares.

The Model Containing Only the Unit Vector

In Chapter 4 and in this chapter, we used a model containing only the unit vector $\mathbf{U}$ as the predictor vector. Thus

$$\mathbf{Y} = b_0\mathbf{U} + \mathbf{E}^{(2)} \qquad (6.7)$$

where

$\mathbf{Y}$ = the vector of interest (dimension = n).

$\mathbf{U}$ = the unit vector, containing all 1's.

$\mathbf{E}^{(2)}$ = the error vector.

and let

q_2 = the error sum of squares.

The Model Assuming Constant Differences

In this chapter we used a model in which the amount of change in $\mathbf{Y}$ remained the same as we moved from one category to the next. In other words, the expected amount of change in $\mathbf{Y}$ per unit change in value of $\mathbf{G}$ (which represented student grade level in this chapter) is constant.

The model is

$$\mathbf{Y} = d_0\mathbf{U} + d_1\mathbf{G} + \mathbf{E}^{(3)} \qquad (6.8)$$

where

$\mathbf{Y}$ = the vector of interest (dimension = n).

$\mathbf{U}$ = the unit vector.

$\mathbf{G}$ = a vector containing numbers associated with each mutually exclusive category (in Section 6.8 the numbers were 9, 10, 11, and 12, which corresponded to the grade level of students).

$\mathbf{E}^{(3)}$ = the error vector.

and let

q_3 = the error sum of squares.

6.13
FLOWCHART OF ONE-ATTRIBUTE ANALYSES

Figure 6.2 summarizes the analyses that have been discussed on one-attribute problems. The sequence of these questions might vary, depending upon a particular problem. For example, it may be appropriate in some situations to test for differences first (left side of flowchart), then test for linearity.

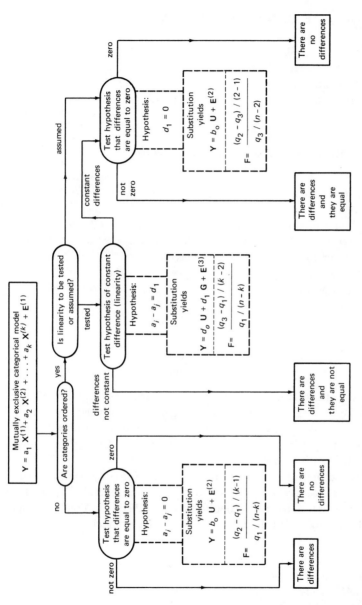

FIG. 6.2 Summary of One-Attribute Analyses.

105

6.14
THE CONCEPT OF AN ASSUMED MODEL

The problems we have discussed thus far have involved the specification of **full** and **restricted models,** but the distinction between them is somewhat arbitrary. For future discussions, it will therefore be useful to acquire an understanding of the concept of an **assumed** or **starting model**.

Desirable Attributes of a Full Model

There are two attributes that every full model should possess. First, *the model should allow you to detect the differences you are interested in examining.* For example, if you are interested in determining whether class differences exist in typing performance, you should not choose model (6.5) as the full model because it will not allow you to do this. Note that the predicted value for all four classes is d_0. But both models (6.1) and (6.4) will allow you to detect class differences. Note that the predicted values in (6.1) are a_9, a_{10}, a_{11}, and a_{12}, and in (6.4) they are

$$d_0 + w_1(9)$$
$$d_0 + w_1(10)$$
$$d_0 + w_1(11)$$
$$d_0 + w_1(12)$$

Therefore, both (6.1) and (6.4) have the first desirable property. Generally, you will be able to determine if a model has this property by writing the symbolic expressions for the predicted values. If the symbolic expressions for two different predicted values are the same, then the model will not allow you to detect a difference.

The second desirable property is that *the model should produce good estimates of the unknown parameter means* (see Sec. 5.2). In general, the model will produce good estimates if two conditions are fulfilled: the **Y** values should be sampled randomly, and the model must be a true model.

6.15
TRUE MODELS

The term **true model** refers to *the relationship that exists among the unknown parameter means.* We will examine three cases. Suppose that in a large school district where many students take typing, the typing speed averages for each grade at the end of a given year are those shown in Table 6.2.

Table 6.2 TRUE MEANS

Grade	Case I	Case II	Case III
9	28	20	32
10	36	25	32
11	42	30	32
12	43	35	32

Suppose that five students have been randomly selected from each grade level over the entire school district, and we want to use these data to estimate the true means for each grade level.

In Table 6.3 the symbolic expressions are shown from models (4.2), (6.1), and (6.4), which estimate the means shown in Table 6.2.

Table 6.3 SYMBOLIC EXPRESSIONS THAT ESTIMATE THE EXPECTED VALUES OF FOUR CLASSES USING THREE MODELS

		Model	
Grade	(6.1)	(6.4)	(4.2)
9	$a_9(1)$	$d_0 + w_1(9)$	$a_c(1)$
10	$a_{10}(1)$	$d_0 + w_1(10)$	$a_c(1)$
11	$a_{11}(1)$	$d_0 + w_1(11)$	$a_c(1)$
12	$a_{12}(1)$	$d_0 + w_1(12)$	$a_c(1)$

If the true means are related as shown under Case I, model (6.1) is a true model, but (4.2) and (6.4) are not. We can make this statement because numerical values exist for a_9, a_{10}, a_{11}, and a_{12} that make the following statements true.

$$a_9(1) = 28$$
$$a_{10}(1) = 36$$
$$a_{11}(1) = 42$$
$$a_{12}(1) = 43$$

However, there are *no* numerical values for a_c or for d_0 and w_1 that make either set of the following statements simultaneously true.

$$a_c(1) = 28 \qquad d_0 + w_1(9) = 28$$
$$a_c(1) = 36 \qquad d_0 + w_1(10) = 36$$
$$a_c(1) = 42 \qquad d_0 + w_1(11) = 42$$
$$a_c(1) = 43 \qquad d_0 + w_1(12) = 43$$

In the expressions on the left, it is clear that a_c cannot be four different values. In the expressions on the right, it is not so obvious, but an attempt to find values for d_0 and w_1 that satisfy all four conditions will lead to inconsistencies. For example, if we let $d_0 = -44$ and $w_1 = 8$, then

$$-44 + (8)(9) = 28$$
$$-44 + (8)(10) = 36$$
$$-44 + (8)(11) = 44$$
$$-44 + (8)(12) = 52$$

The first two expressions satisfy the conditions, but the last two do not. If we let $d_0 = 31$ and $w_1 = 1$, then

$$31 + (1)(9) = 40$$
$$31 + (1)(10) = 41$$
$$31 + (1)(11) = 42$$
$$31 + (1)(12) = 43$$

Now the last two expressions satisfy the conditions, but the first two do not. In short, *no values can be found that will satisfy all the conditions unless the true means differ by a constant.* Since the true means do not differ by a constant in Case I, model (6.4) is not a true model for Case I.

In Case II the true means do differ by a constant, namely five units. Therefore, if we let $d_0 = -25$ and $w_1 = 5$, then

$$-25 + (5)(9) = 20$$
$$-25 + (5)(10) = 25$$
$$-25 + (5)(11) = 30$$
$$-25 + (5)(12) = 35$$

We see that all conditions are satisfied, so model (6.4) is a true model for Case II. Note that model (6.1) is also a true model for Case II. As a matter of fact, model (6.1) is a true model no matter what relationship exists among the true means. *If an effort is being made to estimate k means, a model is necessarily true if it has k unknown parameters associated with k linearly independent predictors, and k unique patterns of values exist in the predictors.*

This assertion requires some elaboration, since it involves a very important concept. We have shown that model (6.1) is a true model no matter what relationship exists among the expected values. However, there exists an infinite set of four linearly independent vectors that are linear combinations of the predictor vectors of (6.1). Any model formulated with four linearly independent predictor vectors, each of which is a linear combination of the predictors of (6.1), would be equivalent to (6.1) and therefore a true model.

In the same sense, (6.3) is true *if* (6.4) is true because they are equivalent. Note, however, that (6.3) and (6.4) are not necessarily true because an effort is being made to estimate *four* means—but (6.3) and (6.4) contain only *two* linearly independent predictors. When we use the expression "k means," it is important to understand that *the number of unique patterns of values in the predictor vectors must be equal to or less than k.*

In (6.1) there are four unique patterns.

$$1 \ 0 \ 0 \ 0$$
$$0 \ 1 \ 0 \ 0$$
$$0 \ 0 \ 1 \ 0$$
$$0 \ 0 \ 0 \ 1$$

There are also four in (6.4).

$$1 \ 9$$
$$1 \ 10$$
$$1 \ 11$$
$$1 \ 12$$

But in (4.2) there is only one. The point is that if any one of these models had more than four unique patterns, it would produce more than four estimates.

If the true means are related, as shown in Case III, then all three models are true. This is easily demonstrated.

$$a_c = 32 \quad \text{for (4.2)}$$
$$a_9 = a_{10} = a_{11} = a_{12} = 32 \quad \text{for (6.1)}$$
$$d_0 = 32 \quad \text{and} \quad w_1 = 0 \quad \text{for (6.4)}$$

In previous chapters, we used the term *parameters* to refer to the expected values. In this chapter, we have also used the term but in a different sense. Consider Case II, as shown in Table 6.2. The values 20, 25, 30, and 35 are expected values, and they are parameters. Note, however, that these four values are expressible as

$$20 = (-25)(1) + (5)(9)$$
$$25 = (-25)(1) + (5)(10)$$
$$30 = (-25)(1) + (5)(11)$$
$$35 = (-25)(1) + (5)(12)$$

Thus we see that the four expected values are expressible as a function of the two constants (-25 and 5) and the observable values (1, 9, 10, 11, and 12). Although the constants -25 and 5 are not the expected values, they are parameters. In practice, of course, the values of these parameters will not be known, but they can be estimated by models such as (6.4). The point is that *expected values (which are unknown parameters) may be expressible as some function of other unknown parameters*, and *the unknown expected values may be estimated indirectly by obtaining estimates of the other parameters.* Many of the models in future chapters will be based on this concept.

6.16
STARTING WITH AN ASSUMED MODEL

Since we can always start with a model that is known to be true (i.e., a model with as many parameters as there are unknown means), the obvious question is why we do not always do so. For example, the full model in Section 4.4 is known to be true, but the full model in Section 6.9 is only assumed to be true. There is not enough space to discuss fully all the reasons why models are *assumed*, in part because many of the reasons are based on statistical considerations that are tangential to our primary focus. Perhaps an intuitive understanding can be gained by reflecting on the following points.

The degree to which an estimate of a parameter approximates the true value is, on the average, heavily influenced by the number of observations on which the estimate is based. In Section 6.6 we noted that the estimate of a_0 in model (6.1) was based on five criterion observations, while the estimates of d_0 and w_1 of model (6.4) are based on 20 criterion observations, although both models contain the same criterion values. The effect is that even if model (6.4) is only *approximately* true, the estimates from model (6.4) may be superior to those obtained from model (6.1)—even though it is true. For example, if the true means for Case II in Table 6.2 were 20.1, 25, 30, and 35, model (6.4) is not a true model; however, for almost any purpose imaginable, there would be little danger in treating it as though it were true.

In many situations there may be so many means to estimate that it may not be economically feasible to explore the problem at all, unless a simpler model is assumed. Also, we may want to estimate the mean for a category for which no values are available. Suppose, for example, that for some reason no values were available on members of the 11th grade in our example problem. If we restrict ourselves to model (6.1), we have no way of estimating a_{11} (note that $\mathbf{X}^{(11)}$ would contain only zeroes). However, if model (6.4) is true or approximately true, an estimate can be obtained.[2]

---

[2] See Section 13.1 for further discussion of this point.

Although we can never prove that model (6.4) is true, it can be defended on the basis of past experience or on rational arguments. The adequacy of past experience or the quality of rational argument are themselves subject to debate, but the important point to remember is that *"assumption" should not be equated with "take for granted."*

Many of the models we will discuss in subsequent sections will begin with a full model that is assumed to be true. In many cases, we will indicate ways of evaluating the appropriateness of some of the assumptions, but in other cases, we will not. A beneficial exercise in *all* cases is to ask the question: "What relationship would the true means have to possess in order for this model to be true?" In this way, if the assumptions we are making seem unreasonable, you might consider how to modify the starting model to make it more reasonable.

It is difficult to state general recommendations that adequately encompass the point we are attempting to make. On the one hand, the proof of the distribution function of F from which we derive probability values requires that the starting model be true. On the other hand, there are many questions for which "adequate" answers can be derived using the methods we recommend, even if the model is not true so long as it is not "seriously" in error. The problem is so many of these terms cannot be given precise definitions in a context-free situation. We will evade this problem frequently in future discussion by referring to an "appropriate" starting model by which we will mean a model which is true or one which is close enough to being true so that it will not lead to "inadequate" conclusions in a given situation.

There are a number of implications in this discussion that we should emphasize. *Given a particular pattern of true means, there may be a number of true models.* It is important to understand that we are not claiming the numerical values we obtain from our sample data will in fact equal the true means, but rather that on the average these estimates will be closer to the true means if the model we have formulated is true. When the term *full* model is used, it may be helpful to think of it as a *starting model* or *a model that is assumed to be true.* In effect, the procedures recommended in this book amount to assuming that *the full model is true* and that *the tests we conduct attempt to determine whether a simpler model (i.e., one with fewer parameters) is also true.*

EXERCISES

1. Use the following data to test the three hypotheses summarized in Figure 6.2. There are eight age groups, and the measure of performance, **Y,** is the *digit-symbol subtest* of the Wechsler Adult Intelligence Scale (See Glass and Stanley, 1970, p. 150).

DIGIT-SYMBOL-SUBTEST SCALED SCORES OF 28 PERSONS
IN EIGHT EQUALLY SPACED AGE GROUPS

			Age to nearest year				
10	14	18	22	26	30	34	38
7	8	9	11	9	8	7	8
8	9	10	11	10	9	9	
9	10	11	12	11	9	10	
9	11	12	12		10		
10							
Averages: 8.60	9.50	10.50	11.50	10.00	9.00	8.67	8.00

$$\text{Average of all scores} = \frac{269}{28} = 9.61$$

7

A Two-Attribute Model
with Multiple Categories

7.1
INTRODUCTION

In Chapter 3 we examined a problem in which students were described by one attribute (sex), being classified as a boy or a girl. In Chapter 4 we examined a problem in which students were described by one attribute (grade level), being in one of four grades (9, 10, 11, or 12). Now we will consider both attributes simultaneously.

We could have taken this approach quite naturally during our analysis of the boy-girl problem in Chapter 3, since those results could be questioned on the basis that girls might take typing at lower grade levels than boys. It could therefore be argued that the differences found might be due to grade level rather than sex. Consequently, it seems desirable to investigate boy-girl differences *at each and every grade level*.

The desire to investigate possible differences on one attribute at each level on other attributes is sometimes described as *holding other attributes fixed, taking out the effects of,* or *controlling for*. In summarizing the conclusions of a study, it is quite common for a researcher to make a claim similar to the statement: "Other things being equal, girls type better than boys." How can such a conclusion be justified? Our general position is that a model is simply a way of formalizing an argument. By incorporating "other things" into our model in particular kinds of ways, it becomes possible to communicate the results in a reasonably precise way—which might make such a conclusion defensible.

7.2
THE EQUALITY OF TYPING PERFORMANCE
FOR BOYS AND GIRLS WITHIN GRADE LEVEL

We will begin by defining the vectors to be used for the starting or full model. Note that the students are classified by two attributes (sex and grade simultaneously).

$\mathbf{Y}$ = a vector of dimension 20 in which each element is a typing-test score from each student.

$\mathbf{X}^{(g, 9)}$ = 1 if a girl is in the 9th grade; 0 otherwise.

$\mathbf{X}^{(b, 9)}$ = 1 if a boy is in the 9th grade; 0 otherwise.

$\mathbf{X}^{(g, 10)}$ = 1 if a girl is in the 10th grade; 0 otherwise.

$\mathbf{X}^{(b, 10)}$ = 1 if a boy is in the 10th grade; 0 otherwise.

$\mathbf{X}^{(g, 11)}$ = 1 if a girl is in the 11th grade; 0 otherwise.

$\mathbf{X}^{(b, 11)}$ = 1 if a boy is in the 11th grade; 0 otherwise.

$\mathbf{X}^{(g, 12)}$ = 1 if a girl is in the 12th grade; 0 otherwise.

$\mathbf{X}^{(b, 12)}$ = 1 if a boy is in the 12th grade; 0 otherwise.

The Full Model

The full model can be written as

$$\begin{aligned}
\mathbf{Y} = {} & a_{g, 9}\mathbf{X}^{(g, 9)} + a_{b, 9}\mathbf{X}^{(b, 9)} + a_{g, 10}\mathbf{X}^{(g, 10)} + a_{b, 10}\mathbf{X}^{(b, 10)} \\
& + a_{g, 11}\mathbf{X}^{(g, 11)} + a_{b, 11}\mathbf{X}^{(b, 11)} \\
& + a_{g, 12}\mathbf{X}^{(g, 12)} + a_{b, 12}\mathbf{X}^{(b, 12)} + \mathbf{E}^{(4)}
\end{aligned} \qquad (7.1)$$

We would like to compare the boys' typing performance with the girls' at each grade level. Does this model allow us to do that? Arriving at an answer to this question involves what we refer to in the Preface as **investigating the properties of a model**. The context of the problem requires that our model generate estimates of eight expected values. We can see that (7.1) does in fact have this property because

$\mathscr{E}(g, 9)$	is estimated by	$a_{g, 9}$
$\mathscr{E}(b, 9)$	is estimated by	$a_{b, 9}$
$\mathscr{E}(g, 10)$	is estimated by	$a_{g, 10}$
$\mathscr{E}(b, 10)$	is estimated by	$a_{b, 10}$
$\mathscr{E}(g, 11)$	is estimated by	$a_{g, 11}$
$\mathscr{E}(b, 11)$	is estimated by	$a_{b, 11}$
$\mathscr{E}(g, 12)$	is estimated by	$a_{g, 12}$
$\mathscr{E}(b, 12)$	is estimated by	$a_{b, 12}$

Moreover, because we wish to entertain the notion that the expected values may differ, the model should produce different symbolic expressions for the estimate of each expected value. We see that (7.1) also has this property.

Assuming that each of the **X** vectors has at least one nonzero value, we can easily verify that the model has eight linearly independent predictors. Therefore, the model is "true" in the sense discussed in Section 6.15, and the model should produce "good" estimates of the expected values.

7.3
THE HYPOTHESES

We would like to test the following hypotheses.

1. The expected typing performance for 9th-grade girls equals the expected typing performance for 9th-grade boys.
2. The expected typing performance for 10th-grade girls equals the expected typing performance for 10th-grade boys.
3. The expected typing performance for 11th-grade girls equals the expected typing performance for 11th-grade boys.
4. The expected typing performance for 12th-grade girls equals the expected typing performance for 12th-grade boys.

We can then translate these statements into the language of the model.

1. Expected typing score of 9th-grade girl
   = expected typing score of 9th-grade boy.

   We can symbolize this in an abbreviated form.

   $$\mathscr{E}(g, 9) = \mathscr{E}(b, 9)$$

   By substituting the corresponding estimates from (7.1), the restriction implied by the hypothesis is

   $$a_{g,9} = a_{b,9} \quad \text{or} \quad a_{g,9} - a_{b,9} = 0$$

2. $\mathscr{E}(g, 10) = \mathscr{E}(b, 10)$, which implies

   $$a_{g,10} = a_{b,10} \quad \text{or} \quad a_{g,10} - a_{b,10} = 0$$

3. $\mathscr{E}(g, 11) = \mathscr{E}(b, 11)$, which implies

   $$a_{g,11} = a_{b,11} \quad \text{or} \quad a_{g,11} - a_{b,11} = 0$$

4. $\mathscr{E}(g, 12) = \mathscr{E}(b, 12)$, which implies

   $$a_{g,12} = a_{b,12} \quad \text{or} \quad a_{g,12} - a_{b,12} = 0$$

Our basic argument is that if we can reject these hypotheses, then we can reasonably claim that boys and girls in the same grade do not type equally well. In future discussions, arguments of this type may be abbreviated to save space. For example, we might write

$$\mathscr{E}(g, i) = \mathscr{E}(b, i) \qquad i = 9, 10, 11, 12$$

which implies

$$a_{g,i} = a_{b,i} \qquad i = 9, 10, 11, 12$$

as a substitute for the more elaborate discussion.

7.4
THE RESTRICTED MODEL

We can write the restrictions implied by our hypotheses as

$a_{g,9} = a_{b,9} = a_9$ (a common value for girls and boys in the 9th grade)
$a_{g,10} = a_{b,10} = a_{10}$ (a common value for girls and boys in the 10th grade)
$a_{g,11} = a_{b,11} = a_{11}$ (a common value for girls and boys in the 11th grade)
$a_{g,12} = a_{b,12} = a_{12}$ (a common value for girls and boys in the 12th grade)

Substituting in the full model yields

$$\mathbf{Y} = a_9\mathbf{X}^{(g,9)} + a_9\mathbf{X}^{(b,9)} + a_{10}\mathbf{X}^{(g,10)} + a_{10}\mathbf{X}^{(b,10)}$$
$$+ a_{11}\mathbf{X}^{(g,11)} + a_{11}\mathbf{X}^{(b,11)} + a_{12}\mathbf{X}^{(g,12)} + a_{12}\mathbf{X}^{(b,12)} + \mathbf{E}^{(1)}$$
$$\mathbf{Y} = a_9(\mathbf{X}^{(g,9)} + \mathbf{X}^{(b,9)}) + a_{10}(\mathbf{X}^{(g,10)} + \mathbf{X}^{(b,10)})$$
$$+ a_{11}(\mathbf{X}^{(g,11)} + \mathbf{X}^{(b,11)}) + a_{12}(\mathbf{X}^{(g,12)} + \mathbf{X}^{(b,12)}) + \mathbf{E}^{(1)}$$

But we observe that

$\mathbf{X}^{(g,9)} + \mathbf{X}^{(b,9)} = \mathbf{X}^{(9)} =$ a vector with elements equal to 1 if a 9th grader; 0 otherwise.

$\mathbf{X}^{(g,10)} + \mathbf{X}^{(b,10)} = \mathbf{X}^{(10)} =$ a vector with elements equal to 1 if a 10th grader; 0 otherwise.

$\mathbf{X}^{(g,11)} + \mathbf{X}^{(b,11)} = \mathbf{X}^{(11)} =$ a vector with elements equal to 1 if an 11th grader; 0 otherwise.

$\mathbf{X}^{(g,12)} + \mathbf{X}^{(b,12)} = \mathbf{X}^{(12)} =$ a vector with elements equal to 1 if a 12th grader; 0 otherwise.

The restricted model then becomes

$$\mathbf{Y} = a_9\mathbf{X}^{(9)} + a_{10}\mathbf{X}^{(10)} + a_{11}\mathbf{X}^{(11)} + a_{12}\mathbf{X}^{(12)} + \mathbf{E}^{(1)} \tag{7.2}$$

The vectors $\mathbf{X}^{(9)}$, $\mathbf{X}^{(10)}$, $\mathbf{X}^{(11)}$ and $\mathbf{X}^{(12)}$ reflect only the grade category. We have given up the information that distinguishes sex but have maintained the possibility of grade differences.

7.5
NUMERICAL VALUES FOR THE MODELS

The data and the numerical values of all computed values for the full model are shown on the following page.

$$\mathbf{Y} = 40\,\mathbf{X}^{(g,9)} + 16\,\mathbf{X}^{(b,9)} + 56\,\mathbf{X}^{(g,10)} + 32\,\mathbf{X}^{(b,10)} + 64\,\mathbf{X}^{(g,11)} + 56\,\mathbf{X}^{(b,11)} + 72\,\mathbf{X}^{(g,12)} + 72\,\mathbf{X}^{(b,12)} + \mathbf{E}^{(4)}$$

$\mathbf{Y}$	$\mathbf{X}^{(g,9)}$	$\mathbf{X}^{(b,9)}$	$\mathbf{X}^{(g,10)}$	$\mathbf{X}^{(b,10)}$	$\mathbf{X}^{(g,11)}$	$\mathbf{X}^{(b,11)}$	$\mathbf{X}^{(g,12)}$	$\mathbf{X}^{(b,12)}$	$\mathbf{E}^{(4)}$
16	0	1	0	0	0	0	0	0	0
48	1	0	0	0	0	0	0	0	8
40	1	0	0	0	0	0	0	0	0
40	1	0	0	0	0	0	0	0	0
32	1	0	0	0	0	0	0	0	−8
40	0	0	0	1	0	0	0	0	8
24	0	0	0	1	0	0	0	0	−8
64	0	0	1	0	0	0	0	0	8
56	0	0	1	0	0	0	0	0	0
48	0	0	1	0	0	0	0	0	−8
64	0	0	0	0	0	1	0	0	8
56	0	0	0	0	0	1	0	0	0
48	0	0	0	0	0	1	0	0	−8
72	0	0	0	0	1	0	0	0	8
56	0	0	0	0	1	0	0	0	−8
80	0	0	0	0	0	0	0	1	8
72	0	0	0	0	0	0	0	1	0
72	0	0	0	0	0	0	0	1	0
64	0	0	0	0	0	0	0	1	−8
72	0	0	0	0	0	0	1	0	0

The error sum of squares is $q_4 = 768$.

The restricted model we will use to test the hypothesis is the same as the full model used in Chapter 4. The error sum of squares is $q_1 = 1996.8$.

7.6
COMPARING THE ERROR SUMS OF SQUARES

The error sum of squares for the full model is

$$q_f = q_4 = 768.0$$

The error sum of squares for the restricted model is

$$q_r = q_1 = 1996.8$$

There are eight linearly independent predictor vectors in the full model. Therefore,

$$n_f = 8$$

There are four linearly independent predictor vectors in the restricted model. Therefore,

$$n_r = 4$$

The number of elements in each vector is 20. Thus

$$n = 20$$

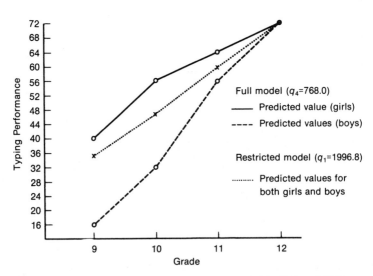

FIG. 7.1 Estimates of the Expected Values from Models (7.1) and (7.2).

Now the F value can be computed from

$$F = \frac{(q_r - q_f)/(n_f - n_r)}{q_f/(n - n_f)} = \frac{(1996.8 - 768.0)/(8 - 4)}{(768.0)/(20 - 8)}$$

$$F = 4.8$$

The probability associated with this F value is less than 0.02. The hypotheses might therefore be rejected; that is, there seems to be a difference between boys and girls within one or more of the classes.

Figure 7.1 is a pictorial representation of the data for the two models.

Note that the analysis of the differences between boys and girls in Chapter 3 indicated *no* differences between the expected performance of boys and girls. However, when we compare boys with girls *within each grade level*, we observe some possibly important differences. It would appear that girls outperform boys at the lower grade levels, but the difference vanishes at the 12th grade.

7.7
IF BOYS AND GIRLS DIFFER IN TYPING PERFORMANCE, ARE THE DIFFERENCES THE SAME FOR ALL GRADE LEVELS?

Suppose that the boys and the girls differ in typing performance at each grade level, as was the case in the numerical data used in Section 7.5. If boys and girls do differ, then it might be interesting to determine whether the difference is the same at all grade levels. This test is sometimes referred to as a **test for no interaction** between sex and grade.

The Hypothesis of No Interaction

In terms of the full model defined in Section 7.2, we can develop the hypotheses as follows. (Note the similarity between this argument and Section 6.3.)

If

$$\mathscr{E}(g, 9) - \mathscr{E}(b, 9) \neq 0$$

Then we can write

$$\mathscr{E}(g, 9) = \mathscr{E}(b, 9) + c_1$$

which implies

$$a_{g, 9} = a_{b, 9} + c_1$$

or

$$a_{g, 9} - a_{b, 9} = c_1$$

where c_1 is some unknown value. And if

$$\mathscr{E}(g, 10) - \mathscr{E}(b, 10) \neq 0$$

our hypothesis requires that the difference be the same as that at the 9th grade (i.e., c_1). Thus

$$\mathscr{E}(g, 10) - \mathscr{E}(b, 10) = c_1$$

which implies

$$a_{g, 10} - a_{b, 10} = c_1$$

or

$$a_{g, 10} = a_{b, 10} + c_1$$

Completing the argument, we have

$$\mathscr{E}(g, 11) - \mathscr{E}(b, 11) = c_1$$

which implies

$$a_{g, 11} = a_{b, 11} + c_1$$

and

$$\mathscr{E}(g, 12) - \mathscr{E}(b, 12) = c_1$$

which implies

$$a_{g, 12} = a_{b, 12} + c_1$$

Summarizing the hypotheses to be tested, we write

$$a_{g, 9} = a_{b, 9} + c_1$$
$$a_{g, 10} = a_{b, 10} + c_1$$
$$a_{g, 11} = a_{b, 11} + c_1$$
$$a_{g, 12} = a_{b, 12} + c_1$$

Substituting these restrictions in the full model yields

$$\begin{aligned}
\mathbf{Y} = & (a_{b, 9} + c_1)\mathbf{X}^{(g, 9)} + a_{b, 9}\mathbf{X}^{(b, 9)} \\
& + (a_{b, 10} + c_1)\mathbf{X}^{(g, 10)} + a_{b, 10}\mathbf{X}^{(b, 10)} \\
& + (a_{b, 11} + c_1)\mathbf{X}^{(g, 11)} + a_{b, 11}\mathbf{X}^{(b, 11)} \\
& + (a_{b, 12} + c_1)\mathbf{X}^{(g, 12)} + a_{b, 12}\mathbf{X}^{(b, 12)} + \mathbf{E}^{(5)}
\end{aligned}$$

$$\begin{aligned}
\mathbf{Y} = & a_{b, 9}(\mathbf{X}^{(g, 9)} + \mathbf{X}^{(b, 9)}) + a_{b, 10}(\mathbf{X}^{(g, 10)} + \mathbf{X}^{(b, 10)}) \\
& + a_{b, 11}(\mathbf{X}^{(g, 11)} + \mathbf{X}^{(b, 11)}) + a_{b, 12}(\mathbf{X}^{(g, 12)} + \mathbf{X}^{(b, 12)}) \\
& + c_1(\mathbf{X}^{(g, 9)} + \mathbf{X}^{(g, 10)} + \mathbf{X}^{(g, 11)} + \mathbf{X}^{(g, 12)}) + \mathbf{E}^{(5)}
\end{aligned}$$

But

$$\mathbf{X}^{(g, 9)} + \mathbf{X}^{(b, 9)} = \mathbf{X}^{(9)}$$
$$\mathbf{X}^{(g, 10)} + \mathbf{X}^{(b, 10)} = \mathbf{X}^{(10)}$$

$$\mathbf{X}^{(g,11)} + \mathbf{X}^{(b,11)} = \mathbf{X}^{(11)}$$

$$\mathbf{X}^{(g,12)} + \mathbf{X}^{(b,12)} = \mathbf{X}^{(12)}$$

$$\mathbf{X}^{(g,9)} + \mathbf{X}^{(g,10)} + \mathbf{X}^{(g,11)} + \mathbf{X}^{(g,12)} = \mathbf{X}^{(g)}$$

Then we can let

$$a_{b,9} = c_9$$

$$a_{b,10} = c_{10}$$

$$a_{b,11} = c_{11}$$

$$a_{b,12} = c_{12}$$

And by substitution, we obtain the restricted model

$$\mathbf{Y} = c_9\mathbf{X}^{(9)} + c_{10}\mathbf{X}^{(10)} + c_{11}\mathbf{X}^{(11)} + c_{12}\mathbf{X}^{(12)} + c_1\mathbf{X}^{(g)} + \mathbf{E}^{(5)} \qquad (7.3)$$

7.8
THE NUMERICAL SOLUTION FOR THE NO-INTERACTION MODEL

The data and the numerical values of the least-squares solution for the restricted model are given in this section. The results have been rounded to one decimal place.

$\mathbf{Y}$	$\mathbf{X}^{(9)}$	$\mathbf{X}^{(10)}$	$\mathbf{X}^{(11)}$	$\mathbf{X}^{(12)}$	$\mathbf{X}^{(g)}$	$\mathbf{E}^{(5)}$
16	1	0	0	0	0	−7.7
48	1	0	0	0	1	9.9
40	1	0	0	0	1	1.9
40	1	0	0	0	1	1.9
32	1	0	0	0	1	6.1
40	0	1	0	0	0	2.2
24	0	1	0	0	0	−13.8
74	0	1	0	0	1	11.8
57	0	1	0	0	1	3.8
48	0	1	0	0	1	−4.2
64	0	0	1	0	0	10.6
56	0	0	1	0	0	2.6
48	0	0	1	0	0	−5.4
72	0	0	1	0	1	4.2
56	0	0	1	0	1	−11.8
80	0	0	0	1	0	10.9
72	0	0	0	1	0	2.9
72	0	0	0	1	0	2.9
64	0	0	0	1	0	−5.1
72	0	0	0	1	1	−11.5

$$\mathbf{Y} = 23.7\,\mathbf{X}^{(9)} + 37.8\,\mathbf{X}^{(10)} + 53.4\,\mathbf{X}^{(11)} + 69.1\,\mathbf{X}^{(12)} + 14.4\,\mathbf{X}^{(g)} + \mathbf{E}^{(5)}$$

The error sum of squares is $q_5 = 1167.4$. The full-model error sum of squares, obtained from the model in Section 7.5, is $q_4 = 768.0$. Table 7.1 contains the symbolic and numerical estimates of the expected values from model (7.3). Note that the estimated difference between boys and girls at each grade is constant (i.e., 14.4).

Table 7.1 ESTIMATES OF THE EXPECTED VALUES FROM MODEL (7.3)

	Grade 9	Grade 10	Grade 11	Grade 12
Girls	$c_9 + c_1$	$c_{10} + c_1$	$c_{11} + c_1$	$c_{12} + c_1$
	$23.7 + 14.4 = 38.1$	$37.8 + 14.4 = 52.2$	$53.4 + 14.4 = 67.8$	$69.1 + 14.4 = 83.5$
Boys	c_9	c_{10}	c_{11}	c_{12}
	23.7	37.8	53.4	69.1

7.9
COMPARING THE ERROR SUMS OF SQUARES

The error sum of squares for the full model is

$$q_f = q_4 = 768.0$$

The error sum of squares for the restricted model is

$$q_r = q_5 = 1167.4$$

There are eight linearly independent predictor vectors in the full model. Therefore,

$$n_f = 8$$

There are five linearly independent predictor vectors in the restricted model. Therefore,

$$n_r = 5$$

The number of elements in each vector is 20. Then

$$n = 20$$

And the F value is

$$F = \frac{(q_r - q_f)/(n_f - n_r)}{q_f/(n - n_f)} = \frac{(1167.4 - 768.0)/(8 - 5)}{768.0/(20 - 8)}$$

$$F = 1.6$$

The probability associated with this F value is greater than 0.20. Ordinarily, such a probability value would not be acceptable as persuasive evidence of interaction.

A pictorial representation of the data is shown in Figure 7.2.

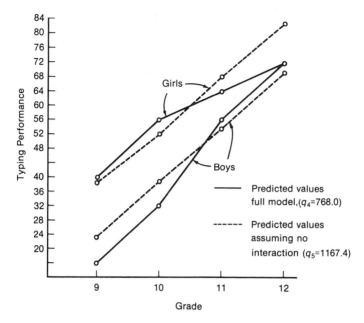

FIG. 7.2   Estimates of the Expected Values from Models (7.1) and (7.3).

7.10
ASSUMING NO INTERACTION, ARE THE EXPECTED TYPING SCORES OF BOYS AND GIRLS EQUAL AT EACH GRADE?

In some situations, it might be appropriate to use model (7.3) as a starting model to investigate the question posed in Section 7.3. Although our conclusion in Section 7.9 provides some evidence against using (7.3) as a starting model (i.e., we have some evidence that the model is not true), we will assume that (7.3) is true to indicate the nature of the argument. You will discover that the argument is identical to that presented in Section 7.3, except that the estimates of the expected values are taken from model (7.3) rather than (7.1).

7.11
THE HYPOTHESES

We wish to test the following hypotheses.

1. The expected typing performance for 9th-grade girls equals the expected typing performance for 9th-grade boys.

2. The expected typing performance for 10th-grade girls equals the expected typing performance for 10th-grade boys.

3 The expected typing performance for 11th-grade girls equals the expected typing performance for 11th-grade boys.

4. The expected typing performance for 12th-grade girls equals the expected typing performance for 12th-grade boys.

Using model (7.3), we can translate the hypotheses into mathematical language.

1. $\mathscr{E}(g, 9) - \mathscr{E}(b, 9) = 0$, which implies

$$(c_9 + c_1) - c_9 = 0$$

2. $\mathscr{E}(g, 10) - \mathscr{E}(b, 10) = 0$, which implies

$$(c_{10} + c_1) - c_{10} = 0$$

3. $\mathscr{E}(g, 11) - \mathscr{E}(b, 11) = 0$, which implies

$$(c_{11} + c_1) - c_{11} = 0$$

4. $\mathscr{E}(g, 12) - \mathscr{E}(b, 12) = 0$, which implies

$$(c_{12} + c_1) - c_{12} = 0$$

These hypotheses are true only when

$$c_1 = 0$$

Substitution in the full model gives

$$\mathbf{Y} = c_9\mathbf{X}^{(9)} + c_{10}\mathbf{X}^{(10)} + c_{11}\mathbf{X}^{(11)} + c_{12}\mathbf{X}^{(12)} + \mathbf{E}^{(1)} \qquad (7.4)$$

As in Section 7.4, the vectors $\mathbf{X}^{(9)}$, $\mathbf{X}^{(10)}$, $\mathbf{X}^{(11)}$, and $\mathbf{X}^{(12)}$ reflect only the grade category, and as before, we have given up the information distinguishing sex.

7.12
COMPARING THE ERROR SUMS OF SQUARES

We presented the numerical values for model (7.3) in Section 7.8. The value for the error sum of squares was

$$q_f = q_5 = 1167.4$$

The numerical values for the restricted model (7.4) were obtained in Section 4.4. There, the error sum of squares was

$$q_r = q_1 = 1996.8$$

The full model contains five linearly independent predictor vectors, and

$$n_f = 5$$

The restricted model contains four linearly independent predictor vectors, and

$$n_r = 4$$

Since the number of elements in each vector is

$$n = 20$$

then

$$F = \frac{(q_r - q_f)/(n_f - n_r)}{q_f/(n - n_f)}$$

$$F = \frac{(1196.8 - 1167.4)/(5 - 4)}{1167.4/(20 - 5)} = \frac{829.44}{77.82}$$

$$F = 10.7$$

The probability associated with this F value is less than 0.01. Note that in this particular case, our conclusion is the same as that reached in Section 7.6, even though we started with a questionable full model. Although such a result is not uncommon, it is important to understand that *the nature of the interaction dictates what is discoverable when a model that assumes no interaction is used as the starting model.* You will find it helpful to construct a set of data in which a comparison of models (7.1) and (7.2) yields a different conclusion than that reached in comparing models (7.3) and (7.2). Such an exercise should underscore the importance of selecting an appropriate starting model.

7.13
A SUMMARY OF THE TWO-ATTRIBUTE, MULTIPLE-CATEGORIES MODELS

In this chapter we have presented a two-attribute problem—one attribute contained *two* mutually exclusive categories and the other contained *four* mutually exclusive categories. We will now consider the general two-attribute problem, as a summary of this chapter.

General Model for Two-Attributes with Multiple Categories

We will assume that the first attribute has r mutually exclusive categories, and the second attribute has c mutually exclusive categories. Then we can write the two-attribute general model as

$$
\begin{aligned}
\mathbf{Y} = \; & a_{1,1}\mathbf{X}^{(1,1)} + a_{1,2}\mathbf{X}^{(1,2)} + \cdots + a_{1,c}\mathbf{X}^{(1,c)} \\
& + a_{2,1}\mathbf{X}^{(2,1)} + a_{2,2}\mathbf{X}^{(2,2)} + \cdots + a_{2,c}\mathbf{X}^{(2,c)} \\
& \qquad \vdots \qquad\qquad \vdots \qquad\qquad\quad \vdots \\
& + a_{r,1}\mathbf{X}^{(r,1)} + a_{r,2}\mathbf{X}^{(r,2)} + \cdots + a_{r,c}\mathbf{X}^{(r,c)} + \mathbf{E}^{(4)}
\end{aligned}
\qquad (7.5)
$$

where

$\mathbf{Y}$ = the vector of interest (dimension = n).

$\mathbf{X}^{(i,j)}$ = 1 if the corresponding element in $\mathbf{Y}$ is associated with the ith category of the first attribute and the jth category of the second attribute; 0 otherwise ($i = 1, \ldots, r; j = 1, \ldots, c$).

$\mathbf{E}^{(4)}$ = the error vector.

and

q_4 = error sum of squares.

Model Containing Only Vectors Describing One Attribute

In Section 7.4 we utilized a model containing vectors describing only one attribute (grade level), leaving four mutually exclusive categories. The general form of the one-attribute categorical model was given as model (6.6) and is written here as

$$\mathbf{Y} = a_{.1}\mathbf{X}^{(.1)} + a_{.2}\mathbf{X}^{(.2)} + \cdots + a_{.c}\mathbf{X}^{(.c)} + \mathbf{E}^{(1)} \qquad (7.6)$$

where

$\mathbf{Y}$ = the vector of interest (dimension = n).

$\mathbf{X}^{(.j)}$ = 1 if the corresponding element in $\mathbf{Y}$ is associated with the jth category of the second attribute; 0 otherwise. (Note that $\mathbf{X}^{(.j)} = \mathbf{X}^{(1,j)} + \mathbf{X}^{(2,j)} + \cdots + \mathbf{X}^{(r,j)}$.

$\mathbf{E}^{(1)}$ = the error vector.

and

q_1 = the error sum of squares.

Model Assuming No Interaction

In Section 7.7 we used a model that contained no interaction. This meant that the differences between the expected typing performance of categories on the first attribute were the same for all categories of the second attribute. The specific model for that section was designated (7.3).

The general model is

$$\mathbf{Y} = b_{1.}\mathbf{X}^{(1.)} + b_{2.}\mathbf{X}^{(2.)} + \cdots + b_{(r-1.)}\mathbf{X}^{(r-1.)}$$
$$+ b_{.1}\mathbf{X}^{(.1)} + b_{.2}\mathbf{X}^{(.2)} + \cdots + b_{.c}\mathbf{X}^{(.c)} + \mathbf{E}^{(5)} \qquad (7.7)$$

where

$\mathbf{Y}$ = the vector of interest (dimension = n).

$\mathbf{X}^{(i.)}$ = 1 if the corresponding element in $\mathbf{Y}$ is associated with the ith category of the first attribute; 0 otherwise. (Note that $\mathbf{X}^{(i.)} = \mathbf{X}^{(i,1)} + \mathbf{X}^{(i,2)} + \cdots + \mathbf{X}^{(i,c)}$).

$\mathbf{X}^{(.j)} =$ the definition given above.

$\mathbf{E}^{(5)} =$ the error vector.

and

$q_5 =$ the error sum of squares.

Note that this model does not contain the vector $\mathbf{X}^{(r.)}$. It has only $r + c$ — 1 predictor vectors. We could have included the vector $\mathbf{X}^{(r.)}$, but it would be redundant because it can be expressed as a linear combination of the others. Explicitly, we see that

$$\mathbf{X}^{(r.)} = \mathbf{X}^{(.1)} + \mathbf{X}^{(.2)} + \cdots + \mathbf{X}^{(.c)} + (-1)\mathbf{X}^{(1.)}$$
$$+ \cdots + (-1)\mathbf{X}^{(r-1.)}$$

We could have used all $r + c$ vectors as predictors. In this case, we would not change the predicted values, the error vector, or the error sum of squares. However, as we noticed in Chapter 5, there would be an infinite number of solutions for the least-squares values.

7.14
FLOWCHART OF THE TWO-ATTRIBUTE ANALYSES

Figure 7.3 summarizes, in a generalized form, the analyses performed in this chapter. But this is only one sequence of analyses. In some problems, for example, it may be appropriate to test for differences first (as on left side of the flowchart) and then test for interaction.

Numerical Examples Summarized

The mutually exclusive categorical model in Section 7.2 had one attribute (sex) with two categories (boys and girls) and one attribute (grade level) with four categories (9, 10, 11, and 12).

$$\mathbf{Y} = a_{g,9}\mathbf{X}^{(g,9)} + a_{g,10}\mathbf{X}^{(g,10)} + a_{g,11}\mathbf{X}^{(g,11)} + a_{g,12}\mathbf{X}^{(g,12)}$$
$$+ a_{b,9}\mathbf{X}^{(b,9)} + a_{b,10}\mathbf{X}^{(b,10)} + a_{b,11}\mathbf{X}^{(b,11)} + a_{b,12}\mathbf{X}^{(b,12)} + \mathbf{E}^{(4)}$$

and

$$q_4 = 768.0$$

The hypothesis of no-differences-within-categories-of-second-attribute gave us model (7.2).

$$\mathbf{Y} = a_9\mathbf{X}^{(9)} + a_{10}\mathbf{X}^{(10)} + a_{11}\mathbf{X}^{(11)} + a_{12}\mathbf{X}^{(12)} + \mathbf{E}^{(1)}$$

and

$$q_5 = 1996.8$$

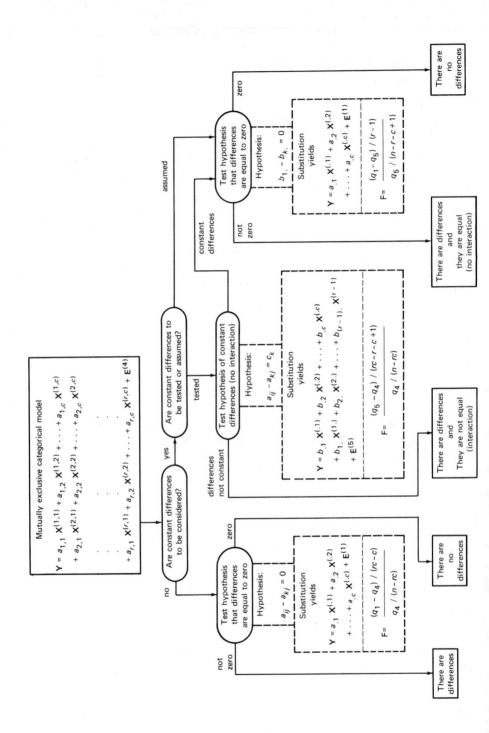

The constant difference (no-interaction) model was (7.3).

$$\mathbf{Y} = c_9\mathbf{X}^{(9)} + c_{10}\mathbf{X}^{(10)} + c_{11}\mathbf{X}^{(11)} + c_{12}\mathbf{X}^{(12)} + c_1\mathbf{X}^{(g)} + \mathbf{E}^{(5)}$$

and

$$q_5 = 1167.4$$

Now we can describe the three tests in the flowchart.

1. Using mutually exclusive model (7.1), are differences between expected **Y** values equal to zero for first-attribute categories within each second-attribute category?
   Hypothesis:

$$a_{ij} - a_{kj} = 0 \qquad \begin{aligned} i &= 1, \ldots, r-1 \\ j &= 1, \ldots, c \\ k &= 2, \ldots, r \\ i &\neq k \end{aligned}$$

In the special case (see Section 7.3),

$$a_{g,9} - a_{b,9} = 0$$

$$a_{g,10} - a_{b,10} = 0$$

$$a_{g,11} - a_{b,11} = 0$$

$$a_{g,12} - a_{b,12} = 0$$

Note that g (girls) is the first category of the first attribute (sex) and b (boys) is the second category of the first attribute. Also, note that 9, 10, 11, and 12 are the 1, 2, 3, and 4 categories of the second attribute (grade level). The F value was computed in Section 7.6.

$$F = \frac{(q_1 - q_4)/(rc - c)}{q_4/(n - rc)}$$

$$F = \frac{(1996.8 - 768.0)/(8 - 4)}{768.0/(20 - 8)}$$

$$F = 4.8$$

2. The test for interaction was described in Section 7.7.
   Hypotheses:

$$a_{g,9} - a_{b,9} = c_1$$

$$a_{g,10} - a_{b,10} = c_1$$

$$a_{g,11} - a_{b,11} = c_1$$

$$a_{g,12} - a_{b,12} = c_1$$

Note again that g (girls) is the first category of the first attribute (sex) and b (boys) is the second category of sex. Also, 9, 10, 11, and 12 are the 1, 2, 3, and 4 categories of grade level. The F value was computed in Section 7.9.

$$F = \frac{(q_5 - q_4)/(rc - r - c + 1)}{q_4/(n - rc)}$$

$$F = \frac{(1167.4 - 768.0)/(8 - 5)}{768.0/(20 - 8)}$$

$$F = 1.6$$

3. Using the model with no interaction (7.7), are differences between expected **Y** values equal to zero for first-attribute categories (boys and girls) within each second attribute category (9, 10, 11, 12)?

The general form of the hypothesis shown in Figure 7.3 is

$$b_{1.} = b_{2.} = \cdots = b_{(r-1.)} = 0$$

This hypothesis was easy to observe in Section 7.11, when only two categories (boys and girls) were present. However, when there are multiple categories on the first attribute, we should be sure that this general hypothesis is a result of statements about the expected values.

The hypothesis, in terms of the general model (7.7), is actually that for each category (j) on the second attribute, the expected values of all first-attribute categories are equal. Looking at (7.7), this is written as

$$b_{.j} + b_{1.} = b_{.j} + b_{2.} = b_{.j} + b_{3.} = \cdots = b_{.j} + b_{(r-1.)} = b_{.j}$$

Note that the predicted value for the rth category of the first attribute is $b_{.j}$. For these statements to be true, we see that it is necessary for

$$b_{1.} = b_{2.} = b_{3.} = \cdots = b_{(r-1.)} = 0$$

Then, from Section 7.12,

$$F = \frac{(q_1 - q_5)/(r + c - 1 - c)}{q_5/(n - r - c + 1)}$$

$$F = \frac{(1996.8 - 1167.4)/(5 - 4)}{1167.4/(20 - 5)} = \frac{829.40}{77.82}$$

$$F = 10.7$$

EXERCISES

In *Statistical Methods in Education and Psychology*, Glass and Stanley discuss a two-attribute problem (pp. 449–50):

All of the first-grade pupils in a school were given a reading-readiness test in September. According to the test manual, a total of 12 girls and 18 boys had scores so low that "formal reading instruction should be postponed and 'reading-readiness activities' should be substituted." A reading researcher randomly assigned the 12 girls and 18 boys in equal numbers to one of the following three conditions: (1) give 18 weeks of reading-readiness activities before beginning instruction; (2) give 9 weeks of readiness activities; (3) commence reading instruction immediately (0 weeks of readiness activities). A reading-achievement test was administered to all 30 pupils at the end of the third grade. The following grade placement scores were obtained:

READING READINESS ACTIVITIES

	18 weeks		*9 weeks*		*0 weeks*	
Boys	3.4	4.0	3.7	4.3	4.1	4.4
	4.1	3.8	4.2	3.3	3.7	3.2
	3.9	4.4	3.8	3.1	3.4	4.0
Girls	4.0	3.8	4.6	4.2	4.4	4.3
	4.3	4.7	3.9	3.6	4.0	4.6

1. Construct a six-parameter starting model.

2. For the following hypotheses:

   Write the restrictions on the parameters implied;

   Impose the restrictions and indicate the appearance of the restricted model; and

   Indicate the appearance of the F value.

   a. $\mathscr{E}(18, b) = \mathscr{E}(9, b) = \mathscr{E}(0, b)$
      $\mathscr{E}(18, g) = \mathscr{E}(9, g) = \mathscr{E}(0, g)$

   b. $\mathscr{E}(18, b) - \mathscr{E}(18, g) = c$
      $\mathscr{E}(9, b) - \mathscr{E}(9, g) = c$
      $\mathscr{E}(0, b) - \mathscr{E}(0, g) = c$

   c. Use the model developed in 2.b as the full model.
      $\mathscr{E}(18, b) = \mathscr{E}(9, b) = \mathscr{E}(0, b)$
      $\mathscr{E}(18, g) = \mathscr{E}(9, g) = \mathscr{E}(0, g)$

3. Using the computer program described in Chapter 14, find least-squares solutions to the models generated in Exercise 2 and calculate the appropriate F values.

4. Consider the number of students in each cell and the row and column totals.

	18 *weeks*	9 *weeks*	0 *weeks*	
Boys	$n_{11} = 6$	$n_{12} = 6$	$n_{13} = 6$	$n_{1.} = 18$
Girls	$n_{21} = 4$	$n_{22} = 4$	$n_{23} = 4$	$n_{2.} = 12$
	$n_{.1} = 10$	$n_{.2} = 10$	$n_{.2} = 10$	$n_{..} = 30$

Consider these hypotheses.

$$\left(\frac{n_{11}}{n_{.1}}\right)\mathscr{E}(18,b) + \left(\frac{n_{21}}{n_{.1}}\right)\mathscr{E}(18,g)$$

$$= \left(\frac{n_{12}}{n_{.2}}\right)\mathscr{E}(9,b) + \left(\frac{n_{22}}{n_{.2}}\right)\mathscr{E}(9,g)$$

$$= \left(\frac{n_{13}}{n_{.3}}\right)\mathscr{E}(0,b) + \left(\frac{n_{23}}{n_{.3}}\right)\mathscr{E}(0,g)$$

a. Rewrite the hypotheses by substituting the appropriate numerical value for the n's and the symbolic expressions that estimate the expected values from the model constructed in Exercise 1.

b. Write the restrictions on the parameters implied by the hypothesis by simplifying the expressions from a.

c. Impose the restrictions identified in b on the model constructed in Exercise 1.

d. Using the computer program described in Chapter 14, find least-squares solutions for the full and restricted models and compute the F value.

e. Compare your solution to the one given by Glass and Stanley (1970, p. 566) for a test of the effect of readiness activities.

f. Write the restrictions on the parameters that would have resulted if the cell n's had all been equal.

8

A Two-Attribute Model
with One Attribute Ordered

8.1
INTRODUCTION

In Chapter 7 our problem involved typing performance and two categorical attributes (sex and grade level). In that discussion we were not concerned about the possible ordering of one of the attributes. In this chapter we will treat the grade levels as *ordered categories*, which we discussed in Chapter 6. Our purpose is to describe the reasoning that leads to a starting model that may be more appropriate and which possesses a number of other desirable properties—particularly when the number of levels on one of the attributes is large.

8.2
ARE PERFORMANCE DIFFERENCES
BETWEEN ADJACENT GRADES EQUAL
(LINEARITY)?

Consider again the two-attribute model (7.1), involving grade level and sex. We wish to investigate the question of a linear relation between typing performance and grade level, as we did in Chapter 6. Now, however, we will consider the linearity question for both groups of students (girls and boys).

Model (7.1), which we will use as our point of departure, can be rearranged in a form that groups the girl-associated vectors together and the boy-associated vectors together.

$$
\begin{aligned}
\mathbf{Y} = {} & a_{g,9}\mathbf{X}^{(g,9)} + a_{g,10}\mathbf{X}^{(g,10)} \\
& + a_{g,11}\mathbf{X}^{(g,11)} + a_{g,12}\mathbf{X}^{(g,12)} \\
& + a_{b,9}\mathbf{X}^{(b,9)} + a_{b,10}\mathbf{X}^{(b,10)} \\
& + a_{b,11}\mathbf{X}^{(b,11)} + a_{b,12}\mathbf{X}^{(b,12)} + \mathbf{E}^{(4)}
\end{aligned}
\tag{8.1}
$$

The vectors' definitions are the same as in Section 7.2.

$\mathbf{Y}$ = a vector of dimension 20 in which each element is a typing-test score from each student.

$\mathbf{X}^{(g,9)} = 1$ if a girl is in the 9th grade; 0 otherwise.

$\mathbf{X}^{(g,10)} = 1$ if a girl is in the 10th grade; 0 otherwise.

$\mathbf{X}^{(g,11)} = 1$ if a girl is in the 11th grade; 0 otherwise.

$\mathbf{X}^{(g,12)} = 1$ if a girl is in the 12th grade; 0 otherwise.

$\mathbf{X}^{(b,9)} = 1$ if a boy is in the 9th grade; 0 otherwise.

$\mathbf{X}^{(b,10)} = 1$ if a boy is in the 10th grade; 0 otherwise.

$\mathbf{X}^{(b,11)} = 1$ if a boy is in the 11th grade; 0 otherwise.

$\mathbf{X}^{(b,12)} = 1$ if a boy is in the 12th grade; 0 otherwise.

Now, we will consider restrictions similar to those summarized in Section 6.3 for both boys and girls. Then, using model (8.1), the **hypothesis of linearity** (a constant difference between performance for adjacent grades) for girls is

$$
\begin{aligned}
a_{g,9} &= w_{g,0} \\
a_{g,10} &= w_{g,0} + w_{g,1} \\
a_{g,11} &= w_{g,0} + 2w_{g,1} \\
a_{g,12} &= w_{g,0} + 3w_{g,1}
\end{aligned}
$$

The hypothesis of linearity for boys is

$$
\begin{aligned}
a_{b,9} &= w_{b,0} \\
a_{b,10} &= w_{b,0} + w_{b,1} \\
a_{b,11} &= w_{b,0} + 2w_{b,1} \\
a_{b,12} &= w_{b,0} + 3w_{b,1}
\end{aligned}
$$

Note the similarity between these hypotheses and the hypotheses in Section 6.3. We are *simultaneously hypothesizing linearity* for both boys and girls.

8.3
TESTING FOR LINEARITY

In some situations, we may actually want to test these hypotheses. However, in other cases, the assumption of linearity may be accepted as reasonable without a statistical test. In this example, we will impose the restrictions on the full model to obtain the restricted model and will then indicate the computing expression for the F value. The procedure is similar to that shown in Section 6.4.

Imposing the restrictions on model (8.1), we get

$$\begin{aligned}
\mathbf{Y} = {} & w_{g,0}\mathbf{X}^{(g,9)} + (w_{g,0} + w_{g,1})\mathbf{X}^{(g,10)} \\
& + (w_{g,0} + 2w_{g,1})\mathbf{X}^{(g,11)} + (w_{g,0} + 3w_{g,1})\mathbf{X}^{(g,12)} \\
& + w_{b,0}\mathbf{X}^{(b,9)} + (w_{b,0} + w_{b,1})\mathbf{X}^{(b,10)} \\
& + (w_{b,0} + 2w_{b,1})\mathbf{X}^{(b,11)} + (w_{b,0} + 3w_{b,1})\mathbf{X}^{(b,12)} + \mathbf{E}^{(6)}
\end{aligned}$$

Collecting terms yields

$$\begin{aligned}
\mathbf{Y} = {} & w_{g,0}[\mathbf{X}^{(g,9)} + \mathbf{X}^{(g,10)} + \mathbf{X}^{(g,11)} + \mathbf{X}^{(g,12)}] \\
& + w_{g,1}[\mathbf{X}^{(g,10)} + 2\mathbf{X}^{(g,11)} + 3\mathbf{X}^{(g,12)}] \\
& + w_{b,0}[\mathbf{X}^{(b,9)} + \mathbf{X}^{(b,10)} + \mathbf{X}^{(b,11)} + \mathbf{X}^{(b,12)}] \\
& + w_{b,1}[\mathbf{X}^{(b,10)} + 2\mathbf{X}^{(b,11)} + 3\mathbf{X}^{(b,12)}] + \mathbf{E}^{(6)}
\end{aligned}$$

Now let

$$\mathbf{X}^{(g)} = \mathbf{X}^{(g,9)} + \mathbf{X}^{(g,10)} + \mathbf{X}^{(g,11)} + \mathbf{X}^{(g,12)} = \text{a vector with elements} \\ \text{equal to 1 if a girl.}$$

$$\mathbf{C}^{(g)} = \mathbf{X}^{(g,10)} + 2\mathbf{X}^{(g,11)} + 3\mathbf{X}^{(g,12)}$$

$$\mathbf{X}^{(b)} = \mathbf{X}^{(b,9)} + \mathbf{X}^{(b,10)} + \mathbf{X}^{(b,11)} + \mathbf{X}^{(b,12)} = \text{a vector with elements} \\ \text{equal to 1 if a boy.}$$

$$\mathbf{C}^{(b)} = \mathbf{X}^{(b,10)} + 2\mathbf{X}^{(b,11)} + 3\mathbf{X}^{(b,12)}$$

Then the restricted model is

$$\mathbf{Y} = w_{g,0}\mathbf{X}^{(g)} + w_{g,1}\mathbf{C}^{(g)} + w_{b,0}\mathbf{X}^{(b)} + w_{b,1}\mathbf{C}^{(b)} + \mathbf{E}^{(6)} \tag{8.2}$$

If we obtain the least-squares solution for the two models, the F value can then be computed.

$$F = \frac{(q_r - q_f)/(n_f - n_r)}{q_f/(n - n_f)} = \frac{(q_6 - q_4)/(8 - 4)}{q_4/(n - 8)}$$

$$F = \frac{(851.2 - 768.0)/4}{768.0/12}$$

$$F = 0.33$$

where

$q_f = q_4 =$ error sum of squares for the full model.

$q_r = q_6 =$ error sum of squares for the restricted model.

$n_f = 8 =$ number of linearly independent predictor vectors in the full model.

$n_r = 4 =$ number of linearly independent predictor vectors in the restricted model.

$n =$ number of elements in each vector.

We can compute the numerical values for the least-squares coefficients, the error sum of squares, and the F value by using the procedure described in Chapter 14. The probability value associated with an F value of 0.33 is quite large, thus supporting the notion that model (8.2) is a reasonable model.

8.4
RECODING THE INFORMATION

We will now recode information, as we did in Section 6.8. Hence the actual grades (9, 10, 11, and 12) will be used as the elements of the vectors instead of the vectors $\mathbf{C}^{(g)}$ and $\mathbf{C}^{(b)}$, which used the codes 0, 1, 2, and 3 to represent these grades.

Recall from Chapter 5 that an equivalent model can be formed that gives results identical (except for least-squares coefficients) to those of the original model. In Section 6.8 we let $\mathbf{G}$ be a vector containing the grade level (9, 10, 11, or 12) of each student. Now define

$\mathbf{G}^{(g)} = \mathbf{G} * \mathbf{X}^{(g)} =$ a vector containing the grade level if the student is a girl; 0 otherwise.

$\mathbf{G}^{(b)} = \mathbf{G} * \mathbf{X}^{(b)} =$ a vector containing the grade level if the student is a boy; 0 otherwise.

The expression

$$\mathbf{G} * \mathbf{X}^{(g)}$$

is called the **direct product** of vectors $\mathbf{G}$ and $\mathbf{X}^{(g)}$ and is defined as *a vector in which the elements are the product of the corresponding elements of* $\mathbf{G}$ *and* $\mathbf{X}^{(g)}$.

$$\mathbf{G} * \mathbf{X}^{(b)}$$

is called the **direct product** of $\mathbf{G}$ and $\mathbf{X}^{(b)}$.

The computation of $\mathbf{G}^{(g)} = \mathbf{G} * \mathbf{X}^{(g)}$ is

$\mathbf{G}$		$\mathbf{X}^{(g)}$	$=$		$=$	$\mathbf{G}^{(g)}$
9	$*$	0		9(0)		0
9		1		9(1)		9
9		1		9(1)		9
9		1		9(1)		9
9		1		9(1)		9
10		0		10(0)		0
10		0		10(0)		0
10		1		10(1)		10
10		1		10(1)		10
10		1		10(1)		10
11		0		11(0)		0
11		0		11(0)		0
11		0		11(0)		0
11		1		11(1)		11
11		1		11(1)		11
12		0		12(0)		0
12		0		12(0)		0
12		0		12(0)		0
12		0		12(0)		0
12		1		12(1)		12

The computation of $\mathbf{G}^{(b)} = \mathbf{G} * \mathbf{X}^{(b)}$ is

$\mathbf{G}$		$\mathbf{X}^{(b)}$	$=$		$=$	$\mathbf{G}^{(b)}$
9	$*$	1		9(1)		9
9		0		9(0)		0
9		0		9(0)		0
9		0		9(0)		0
9		0		9(0)		0
10		1		10(1)		10
10		1		10(1)		10
10		0		10(0)		0
10		0		10(0)		0
10		0		10(0)		0
11		1		11(1)		11
11		1		11(1)		11
11		1		11(1)		11
11		0		11(0)		0
11		0		11(0)		0
12		1		12(1)		12
12		1		12(1)		12
12		1		12(1)		12
12		1		12(1)		12
12		0		12(0)		0

Then we can let

$$\mathbf{C}^{(g)} = \mathbf{G}^{(g)} - 9\mathbf{X}^{(g)}$$

$$\mathbf{C}^{(b)} = \mathbf{G}^{(b)} - 9\mathbf{X}^{(b)}$$

Replacing $\mathbf{C}^{(g)}$ and $\mathbf{C}^{(b)}$ in model (8.2) yields

$$\mathbf{Y} = w_{g,0}\mathbf{X}^{(g)} + w_{g,1}(\mathbf{G}^{(g)} - 9\mathbf{X}^{(g)})$$
$$+ w_{b,0}\mathbf{X}^{(b)} + w_{b,1}(\mathbf{G}^{(b)} - 9\mathbf{X}^{(b)}) + \mathbf{E}^{(6)}$$

$$\mathbf{Y} = (w_{g,0} - 9w_{g,1})\mathbf{X}^{(g)} + (w_{b,0} - 9w_{b,1})\mathbf{X}^{(b)} + w_{g,1}\mathbf{G}^{(g)}$$
$$+ w_{b,1}\mathbf{G}^{(b)} + \mathbf{E}^{(6)}$$

Letting

$$(w_{g,0} - 9w_{g,1}) = d_{g,0}$$

and

$$(w_{b,0} - 9w_{b,1}) = d_{b,0}$$

Then

$$\mathbf{Y} = d_{g,0}\mathbf{X}^{(g)} + w_{g,1}\mathbf{G}^{(g)} + d_{b,0}\mathbf{X}^{(b)} + w_{b,1}\mathbf{G}^{(b)} + \mathbf{E}^{(6)} \qquad (8.3)$$

Model (8.3), equivalent to model (8.2), contains the grade values and will therefore be used as our starting model in the following discussion.

8.5
THE EQUALITY OF TYPING PERFORMANCE
FOR BOYS AND GIRLS WITHIN GRADE LEVEL

The starting model (8.3) may have been assumed true, or it may have been accepted from a statistical test. This particular starting model is sometimes used in a **covariance analysis** (see Edwards, 1962). Since certain research workers use the term covariance analysis for other procedures, it is important to know exactly what someone means if he says: "I did a covariance analysis." The argument presented here will follow the pattern beginning in Section 7.2. (You should note the similarity between the hypotheses in this chapter and those in Chapter 7. The differences are simply due to different starting models.) The starting-model vectors can be summarized as

$\mathbf{Y} =$ a vector of dimension 20 in which each element is a typing-test score from each student.

$\mathbf{X}^{(g)} = 1$ if a girl; 0 otherwise.

$\mathbf{G}^{(g)} = \mathbf{G} * \mathbf{X}^{(g)} =$ grade of student if a girl; 0 otherwise.

$\mathbf{X}^{(b)} = 1$ if a boy; 0 otherwise.

$\mathbf{G}^{(b)} = \mathbf{G} * \mathbf{X}^{(b)} =$ grade of student if a boy; 0 otherwise.

The Full Model

The full model from Section 8.4 is

$$\mathbf{Y} = d_{g,0}\mathbf{X}^{(g)} + w_{g,1}\mathbf{G}^{(g)} + d_{b,0}\mathbf{X}^{(b)} + w_{b,1}\mathbf{G}^{(b)} + \mathbf{E}^{(6)}$$

As in Section 7.2, we would like to compare the boys' typing performance with the girls' at each grade level. Does this model allow us to do so? By writing the symbolic expressions that estimate the eight expected values, you can convince yourself that it does.

8.6
THE HYPOTHESES

The statements of the hypotheses in nonmathematical form are *identical* to the statements in Section 7.3.

1. The expected typing performance for 9th-grade girls equals the expected typing performance for 9th-grade boys.
2. The expected typing performance for 10th-grade girls equals the expected typing performance for 10th-grade boys.
3. The expected typing performance for 11th-grade girls equals the expected typing performance for 11th-grade boys.
4. The expected typing performance for 12th-grade girls equals the expected typing performance for 12th-grade boys.

We can then translate these statements into the language of the model, and it is here that you will note the differences from Section 7.2.

1. $\mathscr{E}(g, 9) = \mathscr{E}(b, 9)$, which implies

$$d_{g,0} + w_{g,1}(9) = d_{b,0} + w_{b,1}(9)$$

2. $\mathscr{E}(g, 10) = \mathscr{E}(b, 10)$, which implies

$$d_{g,0} + w_{g,1}(10) = d_{b,0} + w_{b,1}(10)$$

3. $\mathscr{E}(g, 11) = \mathscr{E}(b, 11)$, which implies

$$d_{g,0} + w_{g,1}(11) = d_{b,0} + w_{b,1}(11)$$

4. $\mathscr{E}(g, 12) = \mathscr{E}(b, 12)$, which implies

$$d_{g,0} + w_{g,1}(12) = d_{b,0} + w_{b,1}(12)$$

These restrictions appear different from those obtained in Section 7.3 because we are using a different starting model, but the logic is the same. Note that the expected values being compared are the same. The difference becomes obvious when we substitute the estimates.

8.7
THE RESTRICTED MODEL

We can write these restrictions in an abbreviated form.

$$d_{g,0} + w_{g,1}(i) = d_{b,0} + w_{b,1}(i) \qquad i = 9, 10, 11, 12$$

or

$$(d_{g,0} - d_{b,0}) + (w_{g,1} - w_{b,1})i = 0$$

The only condition, then, for which the above restriction is true is if both

$$d_{g,0} = d_{b,0} = d_0 \qquad \text{(a common value for boys and girls)}$$

and

$$w_{g,1} = w_{b,1} = w_1 \qquad \text{(a common value for boys and girls)}$$

Substituting in the full model yields

$$\mathbf{Y} = d_0 \mathbf{X}^{(g)} + w_1 \mathbf{G}^{(g)} + d_0 \mathbf{X}^{(b)} + w_1 \mathbf{G}^{(b)} + \mathbf{E}^{(3)}$$

or

$$\mathbf{Y} = d_0(\mathbf{X}^{(g)} + \mathbf{X}^{(b)}) + w_1(\mathbf{G}^{(g)} + \mathbf{G}^{(b)}) + \mathbf{E}^{(3)}$$

However, since

$$\mathbf{X}^{(g)} + \mathbf{X}^{(b)} = \mathbf{U}$$

and

$$\mathbf{G}^{(g)} + \mathbf{G}^{(b)} = \mathbf{G}$$

then

$$\mathbf{Y} = d_0 \mathbf{U} + w_1 \mathbf{G} + \mathbf{E}^{(3)} \qquad (8.4)$$

The vectors now reflect only knowledge of a grade category. As in Section 7.4, we have given up the information that distinguishes sex, but we have maintained the possibility of grade differences.

8.8
NUMERICAL VALUES FOR THE MODELS

The data and the solution for the full model are shown in the following array. The weights and the residual values have been rounded to one decimal place.

Y	$X^{(g)}$	$G^{(g)}$	$X^{(b)}$	$G^{(b)}$	$E^{(6)}$
16	0	0	1	9	0.8
48	1	9	0	0	6.4
40	1	9	0	0	−1.6
40	1	9	0	0	−1.6
32	1	9	0	0	−9.6
40	0	0	1	10	5.6
24	0	0	1	10	−10.4
64	1	10	0	0	11.2
56	1	10	0	0	3.2
48	1	10	0	0	−4.8
64	0	0	1	11	10.4
56	0	0	1	11	2.4
48	0	0	1	11	−5.6
72	1	11	0	0	8.0
56	1	11	0	0	−8.0
80	0	0	1	12	7.2
72	0	0	1	12	−0.8
72	0	0	1	12	−0.8
64	0	0	1	12	−8.8
72	1	12	0	0	−3.2

$$Y = 59.3\,X^{(g)} + 11.2\,G^{(g)} + (-157.5)\,X^{(b)} + 19.2\,G^{(b)} + E^{(6)}$$

The error sum of squares for the full model is

$$q_6 = 851.2$$

The restricted model is the same as model (6.3). This error sum of squares is

$$q_3 = 2000.6$$

8.9
COMPARING THE ERROR SUMS OF SQUARES

The error sum of squares for the full model is

$$q_f = q_6 = 851.2$$

and for the restricted model the error sum of squares is

$$q_r = q_3 = 2000.6$$

The number of linearly independent predictor vectors in the full model is

$$n_f = 4$$

The number of linearly independent predictor vectors in the restricted model is

$$n_r = 2$$

The number of elements in each vector is

$$n = 20$$

Hence the F value is

$$F = \frac{(q_r - q_f)/(n_f - n_r)}{q_f/(n - n_f)} = \frac{(2000.6 - 851.2)/(4 - 2)}{(851.2)/(20 - 4)}$$
$$F = 10.8$$

The probability associated with this F value is less than 0.01, thus indicating that differences in typing performance probably exist between boys and girls within one or more of the classes.

Figure 8.1 is a pictorial representation of the data and the models.

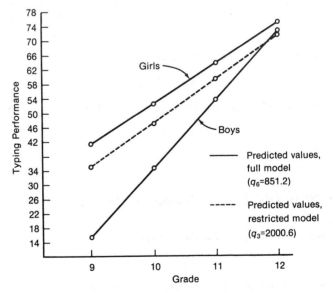

FIG. 8.1   Estimates of the Expected Values from Models (7.1) and (7.3).

8.10
IF BOYS AND GIRLS DIFFER IN TYPING PERFORMANCE, ARE DIFFERENCES THE SAME FOR ALL GRADE LEVELS?

If you believe that boys and girls differ in typing performance at each grade level, then it might be interesting to determine if the differences are the same at all grade levels. This is the *test for no interaction* between sex and grade. While the questions are the same as in Section 7.7, the form will be different because a different starting model is being used.

The Hypothesis of No Interaction

In terms of the full model (8.3), the hypothesis can be developed in the following manner. Consider the expected values for the 9th-grade girls and 9th-grade boys, the 10th-grade girls and 10th-grade boys, etc. If

$$d_{g,0} + w_{g,1}(9) \neq d_{b,0} + w_{b,1}(9)$$
$$d_{g,0} + w_{g,1}(10) \neq d_{b,0} + w_{b,1}(10)$$
$$d_{g,0} + w_{g,1}(11) \neq d_{b,0} + w_{b,1}(11)$$

or

$$d_{g,0} + w_{g,1}(12) \neq d_{b,0} + w_{b,1}(12)$$

we will then want to check the hypothesis that the differences are the same at all grade levels or that the difference at grade j is equal to the difference at grade m. That is,

$$[d_{g,0} + w_{g,1}(j)] - [d_{b,0} + w_{b,1}(j)]$$
$$= [d_{g,0} + w_{g,1}(m)] - [d_{b,0} + w_{b,1}(m)]$$

for

$$j, m = 9, 10, 11, 12 \quad \text{and} \quad j \neq m$$

The implications of this statement can be observed by rearranging the equation. Thus

$$(d_{g,0} - d_{g,0}) + (d_{b,0} - d_{b,0})$$
$$+ [w_{g,1}(j) - w_{g,1}(m)] - [w_{b,1}(j) - w_{b,1}(m)] = 0$$
$$w_{g,1}(j - m) - w_{b,1}(j - m) = 0$$
$$(w_{g,1} - w_{b,1})(j - m) = 0$$

But since $j \neq m$, then $(j - m)$ cannot be zero; therefore

$$(w_{g,1} - w_{b,1}) = 0$$

or

$$w_{g,1} = w_{b,1} = w_1 \quad \text{(a common value)}$$

Substituting the restriction

$$w_{g,1} = w_{b,1} = w_1$$

gives the restricted model

$$\mathbf{Y} = d_{g,0}\mathbf{X}^{(g)} + w_1\mathbf{G}^{(g)} + d_{b,0}\mathbf{X}^{(b)} + w_1\mathbf{G}^{(b)} + \mathbf{E}^{(7)}$$

or

$$\mathbf{Y} = d_{g,0}\mathbf{X}^{(g)} + d_{b,0}\mathbf{X}^{(b)} + w_1(\mathbf{G}^{(g)} + \mathbf{G}^{(b)}) + \mathbf{E}^{(7)}$$

But $\mathbf{G}^{(g)} + \mathbf{G}^{(b)} = \mathbf{G}$, a vector containing grades; therefore

$$\mathbf{Y} = d_{g,0}\mathbf{X}^{(g)} + d_{b,0}\mathbf{X}^{(b)} + w_1\mathbf{G} + \mathbf{E}^{(7)} \qquad (8.5)$$

Numerical Solution for the No-Interaction Model

The data and solution (rounded to one decimal place) for the no-interaction model are shown here.

Y	$\mathbf{X}^{(g)}$	$\mathbf{X}^{(b)}$	G	$\mathbf{E}^{(7)}$
16	0	1	9	−7.2
48	1	0	9	10.4
40	1	0	9	2.4
40	1	0	9	2.4
32	1	0	9	−5.6
40	0	1	10	1.6
24	0	1	10	−14.4
64	1	0	10	11.2
56	1	0	10	3.2
48	1	0	10	−4.8
64	0	1	11	10.4
56	0	1	11	2.4
48	0	1	11	−5.6
72	1	0	11	4.0
56	1	0	11	−12.0
80	0	1	12	11.2
72	0	1	12	3.2
72	0	1	12	3.2
64	0	1	12	−4.8
72	1	0	12	−11.2

$$= (-99.2)\ \mathbf{X}^{(g)} + (-113.6)\ \mathbf{X}^{(b)} + (15.2)\ \mathbf{G} + \mathbf{E}^{(7)}$$

The error sum of squares for the model is

$$q_7 = 1171.2$$

The error sum of squares (from Sec. 8.8) for the full model is

$$q_6 = 851.2$$

8.11
COMPARING THE ERROR SUMS OF SQUARES

The error sum of squares for the full model is

$$q_f = q_6 = 851.2$$

and for the restricted model is

$$q_r = q_7 = 1171.2$$

The number of linearly independent predictor vectors in the full model is

$$n_f = 4$$

The number of linearly independent predictor vectors in the restricted model

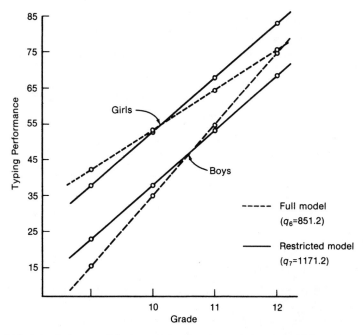

FIG. 8.2   Estimates of the Expected Values from Models (8.2), (8.3), and (8.4).

is

$$n_r = 3$$

And the number of elements in each vector is

$$n = 20$$

Hence

$$F = \frac{(q_r - q_f)/(n_f - n_r)}{q_f/(n - n_f)} = \frac{(1171.2 - 851.2)/(4 - 3)}{851.2/(20 - 4)}$$

$$F = 6.0$$

The probability associated with this F value is less than 0.03, which indicates the possibility of an interaction between sex category and grade.

On the basis of this test, the hypothesis of no interaction can be rejected. That is, we can conclude that the difference between boys and girls is not the same at every grade level. Note that this conclusion is somewhat inconsistent with the conclusion drawn in Section 7.9, where the same question was posed. The evidence there, however, was not as persuasive. A pictorial representation of the predicted values for the full and restricted models is shown in Figure 8.2.

8.12
ASSUMING NO INTERACTION, ARE THE EXPECTED TYPING SCORES OF BOYS AND GIRLS EQUAL AT EACH GRADE LEVEL?

Although the sample data of our example indicate interaction, we will illustrate the analysis that could be used assuming a no-interaction model. This procedure is similar to Section 7.10.

The Full Model

The full model is the same no-interaction model just presented.

$$\mathbf{Y} = d_{g,0}\mathbf{X}^{(g)} + d_{b,0}\mathbf{X}^{(b)} + w_1\mathbf{G} + \mathbf{E}^{(7)} \tag{8.5}$$

Hence we will want to test the same hypotheses described in Section 7.3, 7.11, and 8.6.

1. The expected typing performance for 9th-grade girls equals the expected typing performance for 9th-grade boys.
2. The expected typing performance for 10th-grade girls equals the expected typing performance for 10th-grade boys.
3. The expected typing performance for 11th-grade girls equals the expected typing performance for 11th-grade boys.

4. The expected typing performance for 12th-grade girls equals the expected typing performance for 12th-grade boys.

These hypotheses can then be translated into mathematical form. At any grade level i, the expected typing performance is the same for boys and girls. Substituting the estimates from model (8.5) yields

$$d_{g,0} + w_1(i) = d_{b,0} + w_1(i) \qquad i = 9, 10, 11, 12$$

which implies that

$$d_{g,0} = d_{b,0} = d_0 \qquad \text{(a common value)}$$

This restriction can be imposed on the full model.

The Restricted Model

Substitution gives

$$\mathbf{Y} = d_0\mathbf{X}^{(g)} + d_0\mathbf{X}^{(b)} + w_1\mathbf{G} + \mathbf{E}^{(3)}$$

or

$$\mathbf{Y} = d_0(\mathbf{X}^{(g)} + \mathbf{X}^{(b)}) + w_1\mathbf{G} + \mathbf{E}^{(3)}$$

But

$$\mathbf{X}^{(g)} + \mathbf{X}^{(b)} = \mathbf{U}$$

Then

$$\mathbf{Y} = d_0\mathbf{U} + w_1\mathbf{G} + \mathbf{E}^{(3)}$$

Note that this model is identical to model (8.4)—*it contains only grade information.*

Comparing the Error Sums of Squares

The values for the error sum of squares for the models are obtained from Section 8.11

$$q_7 = 1171.2$$

and Section 6.7

$$q_3 = 2000.6$$

The error sum of squares for the full model is

$$q_f = q_7 = 1171.2$$

and for the restricted model

$$q_r = q_3 = 2000.6$$

The full model contains three linearly independent predictor vectors and

$$n_f = 3$$

The restricted model contains two linearly independent predictor vectors and

$$n_r = 2$$

And the number of elements in each vector is

$$n = 20$$

Therefore

$$F = \frac{(q_r - q_f)/(n_f - n_r)}{q_f/(n - n_f)} = \frac{(2000.6 - 1171.2)/(3 - 2)}{1171.2/(20 - 3)}$$

$$F = 12.0$$

The probability associated with this F value is less than 0.01, which would suggest a rejection of the hypothesis. On the sample data, there are clearly differences between the performances of girls and boys at the same grade level. Furthermore, the tests for interaction and inspection of Figure 8.2 indicate that the differences are not the same at all grades.

8.13
A SUMMARY OF THE TWO-ATTRIBUTE CATEGORICAL MODEL WITH ONE ATTRIBUTE ORDERED

In this section, we will present a summary and a generalization of the analyses performed in this chapter.

General Model for Two Attributes with Multiple Categories

As in Section 7.13, we start with a general two-attribute, mutually exclusive model, with the first attribute having r categories and the second attribute having c categories.

$$\begin{aligned}
\mathbf{Y} = {}& a_{1,1}\mathbf{X}^{(1,1)} + a_{1,2}\mathbf{X}^{(1,2)} + \cdots + a_{1,c}\mathbf{X}^{(1,c)} \\
&+ a_{2,1}\mathbf{X}^{(2,1)} + a_{2,2}\mathbf{X}^{(2,2)} + \cdots + a_{2,c}\mathbf{X}^{(2,c)} \\
&\quad \vdots \qquad\qquad \vdots \qquad\qquad\qquad \vdots \\
&+ a_{r,1}\mathbf{X}^{(r,1)} + a_{r,2}\mathbf{X}^{(r,2)} + \cdots + a_{r,c}\mathbf{X}^{(r,c)} + \mathbf{E}^{(4)}
\end{aligned} \tag{8.6}$$

where

$\mathbf{Y} =$ the vector of interest (dimension $= n$).

$\mathbf{X}^{(i,j)} = 1$ if the corresponding element in $\mathbf{Y}$ is associated with the ith category of the first attribute and the jth category of the second attribute; 0 otherwise $(i = 1, \ldots, r$ and $j = 1, \ldots, c)$.

$\mathbf{E}^{(4)}$ = the error vector.

and

q_4 = the error sum of squares.

Model Assuming Constant Differences (Linearity) for the Second Attribute at Each Category of the First Attribute

The simultaneous test of linearity for all categories of the first attribute gives a model of the general form

$$\mathbf{Y} = b_1\mathbf{X}^{(1)} + c_1\mathbf{G}^{(1)} + b_2\mathbf{X}^{(2)} + c_2\mathbf{G}^{(2)}$$
$$+ \cdots + b_r\mathbf{X}^{(r)} + c_r\mathbf{G}^{(r)} + \mathbf{E}^{(6)} \tag{8.7}$$

where

$\mathbf{X}^{(i)}$ = 1 if the corresponding element of $\mathbf{Y}$ is associated with the ith category of the first attribute; 0 otherwise.

$\mathbf{G}$ = a number associated with the jth category if the corresponding element of $\mathbf{Y}$ is in the jth category.

$\mathbf{G}^{(i)} = \mathbf{X}^{(i)} * \mathbf{G}$ = the direct product of $\mathbf{X}^{(i)}$ and $\mathbf{G}$. A number associated with the jth category if the corresponding element of $\mathbf{Y}$ is from jth category of the second attribute and the ith category of the first attribute; 0 otherwise. (For example, in Sec. 8.4 the values in $\mathbf{G}^{(i)}$ were 9, 10, 11, 12.)

$\mathbf{E}^{(6)}$ = the error vector.

and

q_6 = the error sum of squares.

Model Containing Only Information about the Second Attribute

In Section 7.4 we developed model (7.2), which contained no information about the first attribute (sex). Its general form appears very much like (8.4). Note also that it is the same as model (6.7).

$$\mathbf{Y} = d_0\mathbf{U} + d_1\mathbf{G} + \mathbf{E}^{(3)} \tag{8.8}$$

where

$\mathbf{U}$ = the unit vector.

$\mathbf{G}$ = a number associated with the jth category if the corresponding element of $\mathbf{Y}$ is in the jth category.

The Model Assuming No Interaction

In Section 8.10 we obtained a model having no interaction between typing performance and grade level. The general form of the no-interaction model is

$$\mathbf{Y} = b_1\mathbf{X}^{(1)} + b_2\mathbf{X}^{(2)} + \cdots + b_r\mathbf{X}^{(r)} + w_1\mathbf{G} + \mathbf{E}^{(7)} \qquad (8.9)$$

where

$\mathbf{X}^{(i)}$ is defined by (8.7).

$\mathbf{G}$ is defined by (8.8).

8.14
FLOWCHART FOR THE TWO-ATTRIBUTE ANALYSES WITH ONE ATTRIBUTE ORDERED

Figure 8.3 summarizes the two-attribute analyses in a general form.

Model (8.6) is the general model for two attributes having multiple categories with no assumptions being made about the relationships among the expected values (i.e., a true model). Model (8.1) is a specific example of the general model with $r = 2$ and $c = 4$.

Model (8.7) is the general model for two attributes in which linearity is assumed for one of the attributes. Model (8.3) is a specific example of the general model in which the following identities can be observed.

$d_{g,0}$ corresponds to b_1

$w_{g,1}$ corresponds to c_1

$d_{b,0}$ corresponds to b_2

$w_{b,1}$ corresponds to c_2

Model (8.7) is frequently used as a starting model by assumption. When the justification is based on a statistical test, the general form of the restriction is

$$a_{ij} = b_i + (j)c_i \qquad \begin{cases} i = 1, 2, \ldots, r \\ j = 1, 2, \ldots, c \end{cases}$$

In the special case discussed in Section 8.2, the restrictions that led to model (8.3) were

$$a_{gj} = d_{g,0} + (j)w_{g,1} \qquad j = 9, 10, 11, 12$$
$$a_{bj} = d_{b,0} + (j)w_{b,1}$$

Note that the first category of sex is "girls" (g), and the second is "boys" (b).

The hypothesis of equal expected values for first-attribute categories within each second-attribute category, using (8.7) as the full model, leads to the general model (8.8) of which (8.4) is a specific example. The general form of the restrictions is

$$[b_i + c_i(j)] - [b_k + c_k(j)] = 0$$

for

$$i = 1, 2, \ldots, r - 1$$
$$k = 2, 3, \ldots, r$$
$$j = 1, 2, \ldots, c \quad \text{and} \quad i \neq k$$

The corresponding restrictions in the special case discussed in Section 8.6 were

$$[d_{g,0} + w_{g,1}(j)] - [d_{b,0} + w_{b,1}(j)] = 0 \quad j = 9, 10, 11, 12$$

The general two-attribute model in which linearity is assumed for one of the attributes with no interaction between the two attributes is (8.9). The corresponding specific example is (8.5). The restrictions on (8.7), which lead to (8.9), take the general form

$$[b_i + c_i(j)] - [b_k + c_k(j)] = [b_i + c_i(m)] - [b_k + c_k(m)]$$

for

$$i = 1, 2, \ldots, r - 1$$
$$k = 2, 3, \ldots, r$$
$$j = 1, 2, \ldots, c - 1$$
$$m = 2, 3, \ldots, c \quad \text{and} \quad i \neq k \quad j \neq m$$

In the special case discussed in Section 8.10, the restrictions were

$$[d_{g,0} + w_{g,1}(j)] - [d_{b,0} + w_{b,1}(j)] = [d_{g,0} + w_{g,1}(m)]$$
$$- [d_{b,0} + w_{b,1}(m)]$$

for

$$j = 9, 10, 11$$
$$m = 10, 11, 12 \quad \text{and} \quad j \neq m$$

The hypothesis of equal expected values for first-attribute categories within each second-attribute category using (8.9) as the full model leads to the general model (8.8) of which (8.4) is a specific example. The general form of the restrictions is

$$[b_i + w_1(j)] - [b_k + w_1(j)] = 0$$

or

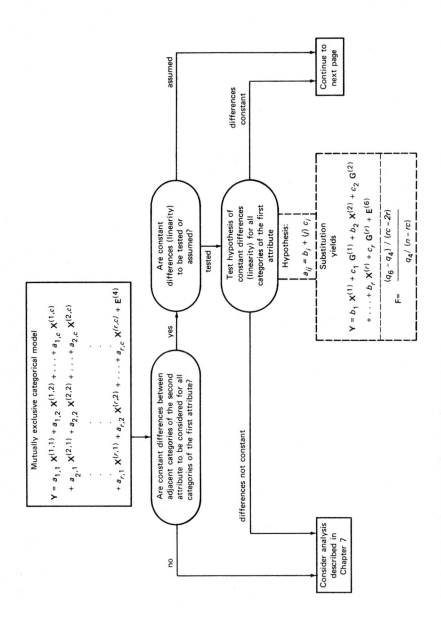

Mutually exclusive categorical model

$$Y = a_{1,1} X^{(1,1)} + a_{1,2} X^{(1,2)} + \ldots + a_{1,c} X^{(1,c)}$$
$$+ a_{2,1} X^{(2,1)} + a_{2,2} X^{(2,2)} + \ldots + a_{2,c} X^{(2,c)}$$
$$\ldots$$
$$+ a_{r,1} X^{(r,1)} + a_{r,2} X^{(r,2)} + \ldots + a_{r,c} X^{(r,c)} + E^{(4)}$$

Are constant differences between adjacent categories of the second attribute to be considered for all categories of the first attribute?

no → Consider analysis described in Chapter 7

yes

Are constant differences (linearity) to be tested or assumed?

assumed → Continue to next page

tested

Test hypothesis of constant differences (linearity) for all categories of the first attribute

Hypothesis:

$$a_{ij} = b_i + (j) \, c_i$$

Substitution yields

$$Y = b_1 X^{(11)} + c_1 G^{(1)} + b_2 X^{(2)} + c_2 G^{(2)}$$
$$+ \ldots + b_r X^{(r)} + c_r G^{(r)} + E^{(6)}$$

$$F = \frac{(q_6 - q_4) \, / \, (rc - 2r)}{q_4 \, / \, (n - rc)}$$

differences not constant → Consider analysis described in Chapter 7

differences constant → Continue to next page

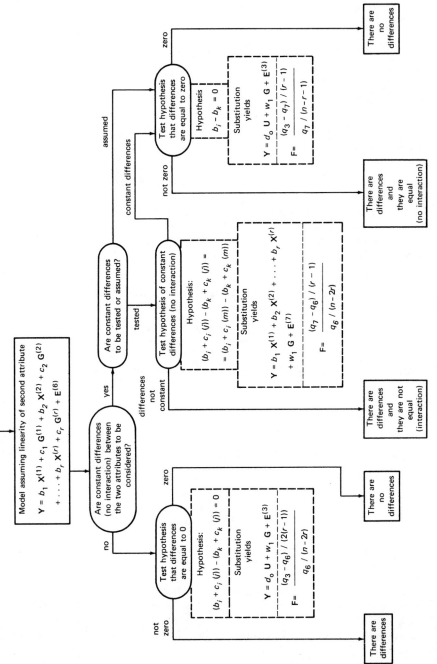

FIG. 8.3 Summary of Two-Attribute Analyses with One Attribute Ordered.

$$b_i - b_k = 0 \quad \begin{cases} i = 1, 2, \ldots, r - 1 \\ k = 2, 3, \ldots, r \\ j = 1, 2, \ldots, c \quad \text{and} \quad i \neq k \end{cases}$$

The corresponding restriction in the special case discussed in Section 8.12 was

$$d_{g,0} - d_{b,0} = 0$$

EXERCISES

Glass and Stanley (1970, p. 451) discuss a two-attribute problem in which it is reasonable to consider one of the attributes as ordered.

A sample of 40 tenth-grade pupils drawn randomly from either public or parochial schools (second attribute) can be classified as of either high, middle, or low socioeconomic status (first attribute). The pupils earned the following grade placement scores on a mathematics achievement test.

Socioeconomic Status	Type of School			
	Public		Parochial	
High	9.5	10.1	10.4	8.5
	8.7	10.4	11.6	10.3
			9.3	10.2
Middle	8.4	11.4	10.4	11.1
	10.5	10.6	9.4	10.3
	9.8	10.4	10.6	10.6
	10.6		11.0	10.7
Low	8.6	8.9	10.0	9.9
	7.3	9.7	9.5	10.6
	10.2	10.0	8.9	10.4
	9.5	7.1		
	9.8			

In natural language, our question is: If the effects of socioeconomic status are removed, do students attending public and parochial schools perform equally well in mathematics?

Letting the symbols p and q represent public and parochial schools and h, m, and l represent high, middle, low socioeconomic status, we argue that a rejection of the following hypotheses makes a "no" answer defensible.

$$\mathcal{E}(p, h) = \mathcal{E}(q, h)$$
$$\mathcal{E}(p, m) = \mathcal{E}(q, m)$$
$$\mathcal{E}(p, l) = \mathcal{E}(q, l)$$

Following the logic of Figure 8.3, investigate these hypotheses and state your conclusion. The computer program described in Chapter 14 can be used to find numerical solutions for the model.

9

A Two-Attribute Model
with Both Attributes Ordered

9.1
INTRODUCTION

In Chapter 8 the problem of interest involved one categorical attribute (sex) and one ordered attribute (grade level). In this chapter we will consider a two-attribute problem in which it is reasonable to consider both attributes as ordered. In this problem typing performance is the variable of interest, and the predictor information consists of two ordered variables—amount of practice and finger dexterity.

The observations of typing performance were made at various combinations of five hours of practice and four levels of finger dexterity. The five levels of practice were 5, 10, 15, 20, and 25 hours. The finger-dexterity measures were obtained prior to the beginning of practice. Our primary problem will be to determine whether *different* amounts of practice (h_1 and h_2) have had different effects on the typing performance of individuals who had the *same* level of finger-dexterity (f) at the beginning of the typing instruction.

Symbolically, this question can be expressed as:

$$\text{Does} \quad \mathscr{E}(h_1, f) = \mathscr{E}(h_2, f)$$

Note that we have posed the question before proposing a starting model.

As in Chapter 8, it is possible to consider our question within the context of a number of possible starting models. But, for the reasons we discussed in Section 6.16, the most desirable starting model is the simplest one possible that seems appropriate. Our choice may be based on assumption or on preliminary investigation. We will begin here by conducting some preliminary investigation with a starting model that is known to be true.

Sample data for 25 students are shown in Table 9.1

Table 9.1 TYPING SCORES OBSERVED AT EACH COMBINATION
OF PRACTICE AND FINGER DEXTERITY

Hours of Typing Practice	*Finger Dexterity*			
	1	2	3	4
5	12	18	21	25, 30
10	13	20, 24	31	40
15	21	24	34, 38	42
20	23	37	41	50, 56
25	23, 28	37	48	59

9.2
IS THE EXPECTED CHANGE IN TYPING PERFORMANCE PER UNIT CHANGE IN FINGER DEXTERITY CONSTANT?

Our problem involves mutually exclusive categories. Thus the criterion and predictor vectors are defined as

$\mathbf{Y}$ = a vector containing measures of typing performance (dimension = 25).

$\mathbf{X}^{(i,j)}$ = a vector with elements equal to 1 if the corresponding element of $\mathbf{Y}$ was observed on a student with a finger dexterity score j after i hours of practice (i = 5, 10, 15, 20, 25, and j = 1, 2, 3, 4).

There are 20 mutually exclusive categories. We can therefore consider the model

$$\mathbf{Y} = a_{5,1}\mathbf{X}^{(5,1)} + a_{5,2}\mathbf{X}^{(5,2)} + \cdots + a_{25,3}\mathbf{X}^{(25,3)} \\ + a_{25,4}\mathbf{X}^{(25,4)} + \mathbf{E}^{(8)} \tag{9.1}$$

As with other mutually exclusive categorical models, the least squares value for a_{ij} is the average of the values in $\mathbf{Y}$ that are associated with category ij. For example, the least squares value for $a_{5,1}$ is 12, and for $a_{20,4}$ it is 53. Note that we are interested in finding an estimate of 20 different expected values. Model (9.1) has 20 linearly independent predictors, so it is a true model. No assumptions are being made about the relationships among the expected values. On the other hand, 13 of the expected values are being

estimated on the basis of a single observation, and none are based on more
than two observations. Better estimates are likely to be obtained if the model
can be simplified. In practice, of course, a larger number of observations
at each level of the two attributes would be preferable. Problems do arise,
however, in which it may be excessively expensive or impossible to obtain
more than a few observations at each level.

First, we will look at this problem, using an approach similar to that in
Chapter 8. For each amount of practice separately, we will consider the
possibility that there is a constant difference in performance between adjacent dexterity levels. As indicated before, this constant difference between
adjacent categories is referred to as *linearity*. Hence we are considering
linearity for each amount of practice.

The hypotheses of a linear relation between performance and dexterity
for five hours of practice can be expressed in terms of (9.1) as

$$a_{5,1} = b_5 + (1)c_5$$
$$a_{5,2} = b_5 + (2)c_5$$
$$a_{5,3} = b_5 + (3)c_5$$
$$a_{5,4} = b_5 + (4)c_5$$

or

$$a_{5,j} = b_5 + (j)c_5 \qquad j = 1, 2, 3, 4$$

Considering each of the other amounts of practice, we can write

$$a_{10,j} = b_{10} + (j)c_{10} \qquad j = 1, 2, 3, 4$$
$$a_{15,j} = b_{15} + (j)c_{15} \qquad j = 1, 2, 3, 4$$
$$a_{20,j} = b_{20} + (j)c_{20} \qquad j = 1, 2, 3, 4$$
$$a_{25,j} = b_{25} + (j)c_{25} \qquad j = 1, 2, 3, 4$$

We are considering a separate linear relation for each practice category.
Note that the logic is identical to that used in Sections 6.3 and 8.2. The
apparent increase in complexity is the result of having five levels of practice,
which requires a more elaborate notation.

9.3
IMPOSING THE RESTRICTIONS

In some situations, these hypotheses are assumed to be true. In other
cases, it might be desired to test the hypotheses by using the F value. If a
statistical test is desired, we can proceed in a straightforward manner by
imposing the restrictions on (9.1).

$$\mathbf{Y} = [b_5 + (1)c_5]\mathbf{X}^{(5,1)} + [b_5 + (2)c_5]\mathbf{X}^{(5,2)} + [b_5 + (3)c_5]\mathbf{X}^{(5,3)}$$
$$+ [b_5 + (4)c_5]\mathbf{X}^{(5,4)} + [b_{10} + (1)c_{10}]\mathbf{X}^{(10,1)}$$
$$+ \cdots + [b_{10} + (4)c_{10}]\mathbf{X}^{(10,4)} + [b_{15} + (1)c_{15}]\mathbf{X}^{(15,1)}$$
$$+ \cdots + [b_{15} + (4)c_{15}]\mathbf{X}^{(15,4)} + [b_{20} + (1)c_{20}]\mathbf{X}^{(20,1)}$$
$$+ \cdots + [b_{20} + (4)c_{20}]\mathbf{X}^{(20,4)} + [b_{25} + (1)c_{25}]\mathbf{X}^{(25,1)}$$
$$+ \cdots + [b_{25} + (4)c_{25}]\mathbf{X}^{(25,4)} + \mathbf{E}^{(9)}$$

Collecting the vectors that have the same coefficients, we have

$$\mathbf{Y} = b_5\mathbf{X}^{(5)} + c_5\mathbf{D}^{(5)} + b_{10}\mathbf{X}^{(10)} + c_{10}\mathbf{D}^{(10)} + b_{15}\mathbf{X}^{(15)} + c_{15}\mathbf{D}^{(15)}$$
$$+ b_{20}\mathbf{X}^{(20)} + c_{20}\mathbf{D}^{(20)} + b_{25}\mathbf{X}^{(25)} + c_{25}\mathbf{D}^{(25)} + \mathbf{E}^{(9)} \qquad (9.2)$$

where

$\mathbf{X}^{(i)} = 1$ if an observation in $\mathbf{Y}$ is at practice hours i; 0 otherwise ($i = 5, 10, 15, 20, 25$).

$\mathbf{D}^{(i)} =$ the finger dexterity level if the observation in $\mathbf{Y}$ is at practice hours i; 0 otherwise ($i = 5, 10, 15, 20, 25$).

Then if we obtain the least-squares solution for the full model (9.1) and the restricted model (9.2), the F value can be computed as

$$F = \frac{(q_r - q_f)/(n_f - n_r)}{q_f/(n - n_f)} = \frac{(q_9 - q_8)/(20 - 10)}{q_8/(25 - 20)}$$

where

$q_f = q_8 =$ error sum of squares for the full model.

$q_r = q_9 =$ error sum of squares for the restricted model.

$n_f = 20 =$ number of linearly independent predictor vector in the full model.

$n_r = 10 =$ number of linearly independent predictor vectors in the restricted model.

$n = 25 =$ number of elements in each vector.

If desired, we can compute the numerical values for the least-squares coefficients, the error sum of squares, and the F value by using the procedure described in Chapter 14.

9.4
IS THE EXPECTED CHANGE IN TYPING PERFORMANCE PER UNIT CHANGE IN PRACTICE A CONSTANT?

We could study model (9.2) in a manner similar to that in Chapter 8. That is, we could continue to treat the practice levels as mutually exclusive categories. However, it is sometimes appropriate to assume (or to test) that there is a linear relationship between typing performance and hours of practice. We wish to consider the possibility that, for each finger-dexterity level, there is a constant change in typing performance for each practice-hour change. We can express this hypothesis by considering any finger dexterity level, f, and by making statements about the expected values in terms of model (9.2).

First, observe model (9.2), and then write the predicted typing value for a student with finger dexterity $(f = 1, 2, 3, 4)$ who practiced five hours.

$$b_5(1) + c_5(f)$$

or

$$b_5 + c_5(f)$$

Now, create an expression of the same general form as the predicted scores [e.g., $b_5 + c_5(f)$]. This expression will be in terms of unknown coefficients and will represent the predicted score of a student with finger dexterity f who has received 0 hours of practice. We will designate this by

$$b_0 + c_0(f)$$

where b_0 and c_0 are unknown coefficients. Note that this value depends upon the particular value of f.

Next, we will create another expression of the same form. This expression will represent the amount of *change* in performance to be expected for each additional hour of practice. This change is written as

$$d_0 + k_0(f)$$

where d_0 and k_0 are unknown coefficients. Note again that this change value depends upon the particular value of f. Now, by using the above expressions, we can express

$$b_5 + c_5(f) = [b_0 + c_0(f)] + (5)[d_0 + k_0(f)]$$

This expression says that the expected performance of a student with finger dexterity f and five hours of practice [$b_5 + c_5(f)$] is expressible as the expected performance of a student with finger dexterity f and 0 hours of practice [$b_0 + c_0(f)$] *plus* five times the amount of change in typing performance expected for *each* hour of practice [$d_0 + k_0(f)$].

If the difference in performance is constant as each additional hour of practice is added, then we can say

$$b_{10} + c_{10}(f) = [b_0 + c_0(f)] + (10)[d_0 + k_0(f)]$$

This expression says that the expected performance of a student with finger dexterity f and ten hours of practice [$b_{10} + c_{10}(f)$] is expressible as the expected performance of a student with finger dexterity f and 0 hours of practice [$b_0 + c_0(f)$] *plus* ten times the amount of change in typing performance expected for *each* hour of practice $[d_0 + k_0(f)]$. Similarly, for the other levels of practice, we can write

$$b_{15} + c_{15}(f) = [b_0 + c_0(f)] + (15)[d_0 + k_0(f)]$$
$$b_{20} + c_{20}(f) = [b_0 + c_0(f)] + (20)[d_0 + k_0(f)]$$
$$b_{25} + c_{25}(f) = [b_0 + c_0(f)] + (25)[d_0 + k_0(f)]$$

In summary, the hypotheses can be expressed as

$$b_i + c_i(f) = [b_0 + c_0(f)] + (i)[d_0 + k_0(f)] \qquad (9.3)$$

for $i = 5, 10, 15, 20, 25$ and $f = 1, 2, 3, 4$.

Having written the hypotheses in terms of predicted scores from the model, we can now examine the resulting implications about the coefficients. Rewrite (9.3) as

$$[b_i - b_0 - (i)d_0] + (f)[c_i - c_0 - (i)k_0] = 0$$

But, since this must be true for all values of f, then

$$b_i - b_0 - (i)d_0 = 0$$

and

$$c_i - c_0 - (i)k_0 = 0$$

Hence implications of the hypotheses can be stated as

$$b_i = b_0 + (i)d_0$$
$$c_i = c_0 + (i)k_0$$

for $i = 5, 10, 15, 20, 25$. Imposing these restrictions on (9.2) gives

$$\begin{aligned}
\mathbf{Y} = {}& [b_0 + (5)d_0]\mathbf{X}^{(5)} + [c_0 + (5)k_0]\mathbf{D}^{(5)} \\
&+ [b_0 + (10)d_0]\mathbf{X}^{(10)} + [c_0 + (10)k_0]\mathbf{D}^{(10)} \\
&+ [b_0 + (15)d_0]\mathbf{X}^{(15)} + [c_0 + (15)k_0]\mathbf{D}^{(15)} \\
&+ [b_0 + (20)d_0]\mathbf{X}^{(20)} + [c_0 + (20)k_0]\mathbf{D}^{(20)} \\
&+ [b_0 + (25)d_0]\mathbf{X}^{(25)} + [c_0 + (25)k_0]\mathbf{D}^{(25)} + \mathbf{E}^{(10)}
\end{aligned}$$

Collecting the vectors associated with the coefficients b_0, d_0, c_0, and k_0 gives

$$\begin{aligned}
\mathbf{Y} = {}& b_0[\mathbf{X}^{(5)} + \mathbf{X}^{(10)} + \mathbf{X}^{(15)} + \mathbf{X}^{(20)} + \mathbf{X}^{(25)}] \\
&+ d_0[(5)\mathbf{X}^{(5)} + (10)\mathbf{X}^{(10)} + (15)\mathbf{X}^{(15)} + (20)\mathbf{X}^{(20)} + (25)\mathbf{X}^{(25)}] \\
&+ c_0[\mathbf{D}^{(5)} + \mathbf{D}^{(10)} + \mathbf{D}^{(15)} + \mathbf{D}^{(20)} + \mathbf{D}^{(25)}] \\
&+ k_0[(5)\mathbf{D}^{(5)} + (10)\mathbf{D}^{(10)} + (15)\mathbf{D}^{(15)} + (20)\mathbf{D}^{(20)} + (25)\mathbf{D}^{(25)}] + \mathbf{E}^{(10)}
\end{aligned}$$

Now let

$$\mathbf{U} = \mathbf{X}^{(5)} + \mathbf{X}^{(10)} + \mathbf{X}^{(15)} + \mathbf{X}^{(20)} + \mathbf{X}^{(25)} = \text{the unit vector.}$$
$$\mathbf{H} = (5)\mathbf{X}^{(5)} + (10)\mathbf{X}^{(10)} + (15)\mathbf{X}^{(15)} + (20)\mathbf{X}^{(20)} + (25)\mathbf{X}^{(25)} =$$
$$\text{the vector with elements equal to hours of practice.}$$

$\mathbf{D} = \mathbf{D}^{(5)} + \mathbf{D}^{(10)} + \mathbf{D}^{(15)} + \mathbf{D}^{(20)} + \mathbf{D}^{(25)} =$ vector with elements equal to finger-dexterity level.

$\mathbf{H} * \mathbf{D} = (5)\mathbf{D}^{(5)} + (10)\mathbf{D}^{(10)} + (15)\mathbf{D}^{(15)} + (20)\mathbf{D}^{(20)} + (25)\mathbf{D}^{(25)} =$ the vector with elements equal to *products* of the corresponding elements of $\mathbf{H}$ and $\mathbf{D}$. (This was defined in Section 8.4 as the direct product of $\mathbf{H}$ and $\mathbf{D}$.)

The model can then be written as

$$\mathbf{Y} = b_0 \mathbf{U} + d_0 \mathbf{H} + c_0 \mathbf{D} + k_0 (\mathbf{H} * \mathbf{D}) + \mathbf{E}^{(10)} \tag{9.4}$$

It should be pointed out that the way we have imposed the restrictions is not the only way it could have been accomplished. In going from (9.1) to (9.4), the number of parameters has been reduced from 20 to 4. Another way of saying this is that we have imposed 16 restrictions on the parameters of (9.1), which reflect assumptions about relations among the 20 expected values. If you found the algebra hard to follow, you might find it useful to identify the 16 restrictions in terms of expected values, then substitute their symbolic estimates, and impose the restrictions one at a time. Although your final model may look quite different from (9.4), it should contain four linearly independent predictors, and it should be equivalent to (9.4). In any event, it is always desirable to verify that the model has the desired properties as described in Section 9.5.

If we want to test these hypotheses, the F value can be computed.

$$F = \frac{(q_r - q_f)/(n_f - n_r)}{q_f/(n - n_f)} = \frac{(q_{10} - q_9)/(10 - 4)}{q_9/(25 - 10)}$$

where

$q_f = q_9 =$ error sum of squares for the full model.

$q_r = q_{10} =$ error sum of squares for the restricted model.

$n_f = 10 =$ number of linearly independent predictor vectors in the full model.

$n_r = 4 =$ number of linearly independent predictor vectors in the restricted model.

$n = 25 =$ number of elements in each vector.

The numerical values can be computed by using the procedure in Chapter 14. In many situations, it is appropriate to use model (9.4) as a starting model. We will use (9.4) as a full model and proceed to answer questions similar to those in Sections 8.5, 8.10, and 8.12.

The appearance of the **direct product vector** $(\mathbf{H} * \mathbf{D})$ might lead someone to ask whether our model really has the desired properties. Before continuing to the analyses, therefore, we will examine model (9.4) to verify that it actually does possess the properties that were imposed in the previous sections.

9.5
VERIFYING THE PROPERTIES OF THE MODEL

We have claimed two properties for model (9.4).

1. For each practice hour level, there is a constant change in typing performance for each unit-change in finger dexterity.
2. For each finger-dexterity level, there is a constant change in typing performance for each hour-change in hours of practice.

First, consider any practice level, h, and any two different finger-dexterity levels, f_1 and f_2 ($f_1 = 1, 2, 3, 4$; $f_2 = 1, 2, 3, 4$; $f_1 \neq f_2$). Second, consider the same practice level, h, and any two different finger dexterity levels, f_3 and f_4 ($f_3 = 1, 2, 3, 4$; $f_4 = 1, 2, 3, 4$; $f_3 \neq f_4$). Note the restrictions that $f_1 \neq f_2$ and $f_3 \neq f_4$. This makes it possible that $f_1 = f_3$. Now write the predicted typing scores in terms of (9.4).

1. At practice level h and dexterity level f_1, the predicted typing performance is

$$b_0(1) + d_0(h) + c_0(f_1) + k_0(h)(f_1).$$

2. At practice level h and dexterity level f_2, the predicted typing performance is

$$b_0(1) + d_0(h) + c_0(f_2) + k_0(h)(f_2).$$

3. At practice level h and dexterity level f_3, the predicted typing performance is

$$b_0(1) + d_0(h) + c_0(f_3) + k_0(h)(f_3).$$

4. At practice level h and dexterity level f_4, the predicted typing performance is

$$b_0(1) + d_0(h) + c_0(f_4) + k_0(h)(f_4).$$

The expected change in typing performance per unit-change in finger dexterity (going from f_1 to f_2) is

$$\frac{[b_0(1) + d_0(h) + c_0(f_1) + k_0(h)(f_1)] - [b_0(1) + d_0(h) + c_0(f_2) + k_0(h)(f_2)]}{(f_1 - f_2)}$$

Simplified it is

$$\frac{f_1[c_0 + k_0(h)] - f_2[c_0 + k_0(h)]}{(f_1 - f_2)}$$

or

$$\frac{(f_1 - f_2)[c_0 + k_0(h)]}{(f_1 - f_2)}$$

or

$$c_0 + k_0(h) \tag{9.5}$$

Next, consider the expected change in typing performance per unit-change in finger dexterity (going from f_3 to f_4) at the same practice level, h.

$$\frac{[b_0(1) + d_0(h) + c_0(f_3) + k_0(h)(f_3)] - [b_0(1) + d_0(h) + c_0(f_4) + k_0(h)(f_4)]}{(f_3 - f_4)}$$

Simplified it is

$$\frac{f_3[c_0 + k_0(h)] - f_4[c_0 + k_0(h)]}{(f_3 - f_4)}$$

or

$$\frac{(f_3 - f_4)[c_0 + k_0(h)]}{(f_3 - f_4)}$$

or

$$c_0 + k_0(h) \tag{9.6}$$

Since (9.5) = (9.6), we can conclude that for any given hour of practice, h, the expected change in performance per unit-change in dexterity level is constant for all values of finger dexterity. Note that the amount of change may depend upon the value of h.

Now consider any dexterity level, f, and any two different practice hours, h_1 and h_2 ($h_1 = 5, 10, 15, 20, 25$; $h_2 = 5, 10, 15, 20, 25$; $h_1 \neq h_2$), and the same dexterity level, f, and two different practice hours, h_3 and h_4 ($h_3 = 5, 10, 15, 20, 25$; $h_4 = 5, 10, 15, 20, 25$; $h_3 \neq h_4$). Then, at dexterity level f, write the expected change in typing performance per unit-change in hours of practice (going from h_1 to h_2).

$$\frac{[b_0(1) + d_0(h_1) + c_0(f) + k_0(h_1)(f)] - [b_0(1) + d_0(h_2) + c_0(f) + k_0(h_2)(f)]}{(h_1 - h_2)}$$

Simplified it is

$$\frac{h_1[d_0 + k_0(f)] - h_2[d_0 + k_0(f)]}{(h_1 - h_2)}$$

or

$$\frac{(h_1 - h_2)[d_0 + k_0(f)]}{(h_1 - h_2)}$$

or

$$d_0 + k_0(f) \tag{9.7}$$

Now, for the same fixed-finger dexterity level, f, consider the expected change in typing performance per unit-change in hours of practice (going from h_3 to h_4).

$$\frac{[b_0(1) + d_0(h_3) + c_0(f) + k_0(h_3)(f)] - [b_0(1) + d_0(h_4) + c_0(f) + k_0(h_4)(f)]}{(h_3 - h_4)}$$

Simplified it is

$$\frac{h_3[d_0 + k_0(f)] - h_4[d_0 + k_0(f)]}{(h_3 - h_4)}$$

or

$$\frac{(h_3 - h_4)[d_0 + k_0(f)]}{(h_3 - h_4)}$$

or

$$d_0 + k_0(f) \tag{9.8}$$

Since $(9.7) = (9.8)$, we can conclude that for any given dexterity level, f, the amount of change in typing performance per hour-change in practice is constant for all values of hours of practice. Note that the amount of change may be different for different values of f. We conclude that model (9.4) actually does have the properties implied by the restrictions that were imposed.

9.6
IS EXPECTED TYPING PERFORMANCE THE SAME FOR STUDENTS WHO PRACTICE DIFFERENT AMOUNTS BUT WHO HAVE THE SAME FINGER DEXTERITY?

The question posed in this section is similar to that in Sections 7.2 and 8.5. But the mathematical form is different because we are using a different full model.

The Full Model

The full model used here is (9.4). This model assumes a linear relation between typing performance level and both *ordered* attributes.

$$\mathbf{Y} = b_0\mathbf{U} + d_0\mathbf{H} + c_0\mathbf{D} + k_0(\mathbf{H} * \mathbf{D}) + \mathbf{E}^{(10)}$$

We wish to compare the expected typing performance of students who have different amounts of practice but who have the same finger dexterity.

The Hypotheses

The nonmathematical statement of the hypotheses is: The expected typing performance of students who have practiced h_1 hours and who have finger dexterity f is equal to the expected typing performance for students who have practiced h_2 hours and who also have finger dexterity f. Note that finger dexterity is held constant (f) but hours of practice vary $(h_1$ and $h_2)$. Now, we can translate this into the language of model (9.4). The expected performance for practice hours h_1 and finger dexterity f is estimated by

$$b_0 + d_0(h_1) + c_0(f) + k_0(h_1)(f).$$

The expected performance for practice hours h_2 and finger dexterity f is estimated by

$$b_0 + d_0(h_2) + c_0(f) + k_0(h_2)(f)$$

Then the hypothesis can be written as

$$b_0 + d_0(h_1) + c_0(f) + k_0(h_1)(f) = b_0 + d_0(h_2) + c_0(f) + k_0(h_2)(f)$$

for $h_1 = 5, 10, 15, 20, 25$; $h_2 = 5, 10, 15, 20, 25$; $h_1 \neq h_2$; $f = 1, 2, 3, 4$.

The Restricted Model

The restrictions imply that

$$h_1[d_0 + k_0(f)] = h_2[d_0 + k_0(f)]$$
$$(h_1 - h_2)[d_0 + k_0(f)] = 0$$

But, if $h_1 \neq h_2$, then

$$d_0 + k_0(f) = 0$$

However, for this statement to be true for all values of finger dexterity, f, then $d_0 = 0$ and $k_0 = 0$. Imposing these restrictions on model (9.4) gives

$$\mathbf{Y} = b_0\mathbf{U} + c_0\mathbf{D} + \mathbf{E}^{(11)} \qquad (9.9)$$

None of the vectors in this model reflect knowledge of hours of practice. The model contains only information about finger dexterity.

9.7
NUMERICAL VALUES FOR THE MODELS

The data and solution for the full model (9.4) are shown here, rounded to two decimals. The solution was obtained using the computer program described in Chapter 14.

$$
\mathbf{Y} = 3.55\,\mathbf{U} + 0.46\,\mathbf{H} + 4.24\,\mathbf{D} + 0.28\,\mathbf{H*D} + \mathbf{E}^{(10)}
$$

Y	U	H	D	H*D	E^(10)
12	1	5	1	5	.53
13	1	10	1	10	−2.16
21	1	15	1	15	2.16
23	1	20	1	20	.48
23	1	25	1	25	−3.20
28	1	25	1	25	1.80
18	1	5	2	10	.88
20	1	10	2	20	−2.21
24	1	10	2	20	1.79
24	1	15	2	30	−3.29
37	1	20	2	40	4.62
37	1	25	2	50	−.46
21	1	5	3	15	−1.77
31	1	10	3	30	1.75
34	1	15	3	45	−1.74
38	1	15	3	45	2.26
41	1	20	3	60	−1.23
48	1	25	3	75	−.72
25	1	5	4	20	−3.41
30	1	5	4	20	1.59
40	1	10	4	40	3.70
42	1	15	4	60	−2.20
50	1	20	4	80	−2.09
56	1	20	4	80	3.91
59	1	25	4	100	−.98

The error sum of squares for the full model (9.4) is

$$q_{10} = 134.2$$

The solution for the restricted model (9.9) yields

$$b_0 = 11.76$$

$$c_0 = 7.83$$

$$q_{11} = 1950.5$$

Comparing the Error Sums of Squares

The error sum of squares for the full model is

$$q_f = q_{10} = 134.2$$

The error sum of squares for the restricted model is

$$q_r = q_{11} = 1950.5$$

The number of linearly independent predictor vectors in the full model is

$$n_f = 4$$

The number of linearly independent predictor vectors in the restricted model is

$$n_r = 2$$

The number of elements in each vector is

$$n = 25$$

Then, the F value is

$$F = \frac{(q_r - q_f)/(n_f - n_r)}{q_f/(n - n_f)} = \frac{(1950.5 - 134.2)/(4 - 2)}{134.2/(25 - 4)}$$

$$F = 142.1$$

The probability associated with this F value is less than 0.01, which would lead to the rejection of the hypotheses. We can therefore conclude that there are differences in typing performance for students having the same finger dexterity but who have had different amounts of practice.

Figure 9.1 is a pictorial representation of models (9.4) and (9.9).

In natural language, we can claim that practice has an *effect* on typing performance even if we take out the effect of finger dexterity. It is important to understand that the previous sentence is an inference drawn from the analysis. We have in no way "proved" that practice will cause individuals to type faster. On the contrary, all we have is an opinion based on a rather subtle argument. We assume that if practice *does not* cause improved performance, individuals who had practiced for different amounts of time would not be expected to differ in performance. The data, however, strongly suggest that individuals who practice for different amounts *do* differ in performance. Therefore, we can conclude that practice cannot be excluded as a cause of improved performance. On the other hand, it seems reasonable

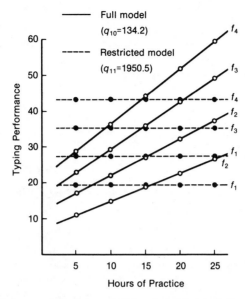

FIG. 9.1   Estimates of the Expected Values from Models (9.4) and (9.9).

to believe that individuals with greater finger dexterity will type faster than individuals with less finger dexterity. We have shown in the analysis that there is reason to believe that individuals with different amounts of practice will differ in their performance even if they have the same finger dexterity. Furthermore, it should be clear that the inference about the effect of practice is limited to the range of practice (5 to 25 hr).

9.8
IF THERE ARE DIFFERENCES IN TYPING PERFORMANCE, ARE THE DIFFERENCES THE SAME AT ALL FINGER DEXTERITIES?

If we believe that different amounts of practice result in different levels of typing performance, it might be interesting to determine whether the differences are the same at every level of finger dexterity. This *test for no interaction* is similar to the tests in Sections 7.7 and 8.10. The question of interest is identical, but the mathematical form is different because of the different full model.

The Hypothesis of No Interaction

Referring to the full model (9.4), the hypotheses can then be developed. First, consider the expected typing performance for the following students:

1. If practice hours $= h_1$ and finger dexterity $= f_1$, then $\mathscr{E}(h_1, f_1)$ can be estimated by the expression

$$b_0 + d_0(h_1) + c_0(f_1) + k_0(h_1)(f_1).$$

2. If practice hours $= h_1$ and finger dexterity $= f_2$, then $\mathscr{E}(h_1, f_2)$ can be estimated by

$$b_0 + d_0(h_1) + c_0(f_2) + k_0(h_1)(f_2).$$

3. If practice hours $= h_2$ and finger dexterity $= f_1$, then $\mathscr{E}(h_2, f_1)$ can be estimated by

$$b_0 + d_0(h_2) + c_0(f_1) + k_0(h_2)(f_1).$$

4. If practice hours $= h_2$ and finger dexterity $= f_2$, then $\mathscr{E}(h_2, f_2)$ can be estimated by

$$b_0 + d_0(h_2) + c_0(f_2) + k_0(h_2)(f_2)$$

Now, we will investigate the hypothesis that the expected change in typing performance per unit-change in practice is the same at all finger dexterities. We hypothesize that the difference between performance for h_1 and h_2 hours of practice at any finger dexterity f_1 is equal to the difference between performance for h_1 and h_2 at any other finger-dexterity level f_2. This hypothesis, stated in terms of the foregoing mathematical expressions, implies

$$[b_0 + d_0(h_1) + c_0(f_1) + k_0(h_1)(f_1)] - [b_0 + d_0(h_2) + c_0(f_1) + k_0(h_2)(f_1)]$$
$$= [b_0 + d_0(h_1) + c_0(f_2) + k_0(h_1)(f_2)] - [b_0 + d_0(h_2) + c_0(f_2) + k_0(h_2)(f_2)]$$

Simplification of this statement implies that

$$k_0(h_1 - h_2)(f_1) - k_0(h_1 - h_2)(f_2) = 0$$
$$k_0(h_1 - h_2)(f_1 - f_2) = 0$$

But, since $h_1 \neq h_2$ and $f_1 \neq f_2$, the restriction implied by the hypothesis is

$$k_0 = 0$$

Substituting this restriction gives

$$\mathbf{Y} = b_0\mathbf{U} + d_0\mathbf{H} + c_0\mathbf{D} + \mathbf{E}^{(12)} \tag{9.10}$$

The Numerical Solution for the No-Interaction Model

A solution for model (9.10), using the computer program in Chapter 14, yields

$$b_0 = -7.57$$
$$d_0 = 1.16$$
$$c_0 = 8.55$$
$$q_{12} = 271.3$$

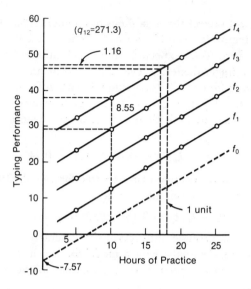

FIG. 9.2   Estimates of the Expected Values from Model (9.10).

A graphical presentation of the solution is shown in Figure 9.2.

Comparing the Error Sums of Squares

The error sum of squares for the full model (from Section 9.7) is

$$q_f = q_{10} = 134.2$$

and for the restricted model

$$q_r = q_{12} = 271.3$$

The number of linearly independent predictor vectors in the full model is

$$n_f = 4$$

and in the restricted model it is

$$n_r = 3$$

The number of elements in each vector is

$$n = 25$$

And the F value is

$$F = \frac{(q_r - q_f)/(n_f - n_r)}{q_f/(n - n_f)} = \frac{(271.3 - 134.2)/(4 - 3)}{134.2/(25 - 4)}$$

$$F = 21.5$$

The probability associated with this F value is less than 0.01, which would probably lead us to reject the hypothesis of no interaction. This information and a look at Figure 9.1 would lead us to believe that the improvement in typing performance to be expected from an additional hour of practice is different at one finger-dexterity level than it is at another. We might say that practice has different effects for students with different finger dexterities. To be specific, the expected gain in typing performance for one additional hour of practice for an individual with a finger dexterity score of one is estimated to be

$$d_0 + k_0(1) = 0.46 + 0.28 = 0.74$$

[See (9.7).] The corresponding gain expected for an individual with a finger dexterity score of four is estimated to be

$$d_0 + k_0(4) = 0.46 + (0.28)(4) = 1.58$$

Even though the example data reveal that interaction is present, we will proceed to indicate the analysis for a model for which the hypotheses of no interaction has been accepted, since the analysis might be appropriate in another situation.

9.9
ASSUMING NO INTERACTION, IS EXPECTED TYPING PERFORMANCE THE SAME FOR STUDENTS WHO PRACTICE DIFFERENT AMOUNTS BUT WHO HAVE THE SAME FINGER DEXTERITY?

The question in this section is the same as in Section 9.6. However, we will use model (9.10) as the full model.

$$\mathbf{Y} = b_0\mathbf{U} + d_0\mathbf{K} + c_0\mathbf{D} + \mathbf{E}^{(12)}$$

In Section 9.6 we used a model that allowed for interaction by including the direct product vector $(\mathbf{H} * \mathbf{D})$.

The Hypothesis

The natural language form of the hypothesis is the same as in Section 9.6, but the mathematical form is expressed in a different full model. The hypothesis is that the expected typing performance for students who have practiced h_1 hours and who have finger dexterity f is equal to the expected typing performance for students who have practiced h_2 hours and who also have finger dexterity f. In terms of the expected values, the hypothesis can be written

$$\mathscr{E}(h_1, f) = \mathscr{E}(h_2, f)$$

Substituting the estimates from (9.10) yields

$$b_0 + d_0(h_1) + c_0 f = b_0 + d_0(h_2) + c_0 f$$

which simplifies to

$$d_0(h_1 - h_2) = 0$$

But, since $h_1 \neq h_2$, then

$$d_0 = 0$$

This restriction can be imposed on the full model (9.10).

The Restricted Model

Substitution of the restriction $d_0 = 0$ gives

$$Y = b_0 U + c_0 D + E^{(11)}$$

This is identical to (9.9). Again notice that this model has *only finger dexterity information*.

Comparing the Error Sums of Squares

The error sum of squares for the full model (Section 9.8) is

$$q_f = q_{12} = 271.3$$

and for the restricted model (Section 9.7), it is

$$q_r = q_{11} = 1950.5$$

The number of linearly independent predictor vectors in the full model is

$$n_f = 3$$

and the number in the restricted model is

$$n_r = 2$$

The number of elements in each vector is

$$n = 25$$

Therefore,

$$F = \frac{(q_r - q_f)/(n_f - n_r)}{q_f/(n - n_f)} = \frac{(1950.5 - 271.3)/(3 - 2)}{271.3/(25 - 3)}$$

$$F = 136.2$$

The probability associated with this F value is less than 0.01, which indicates that there are differences in expected typing performance for students with different amounts of practice but with the same finger dexterity. Using the no-interaction model as the full model yielded a conclusion similar to that in Section 9.6, where a model containing the direct product vector $(H * D)$ was used to allow for possible interaction.

In the context of this two-attribute problem, practice would be regarded as a controllable variable (discussed in Chapter 1). Finger dexterity can be observed (measured) but not controlled. Although we may be able to select individuals with specified finger-dexterity scores, we might not be able to modify the scores. In the context of many problems, the controllable variable is a *treatment variable,* and the uncontrollable variable is a *contaminator.* Ordinarily, we are primarily interested in the *effect of the treatment,* but we must also be concerned about the possibility that our conclusions may be contaminated if the contaminator is not in the model. In the problem we have just been discussing, for example, someone might claim that the higher typing-speed scores, which are associated with a greater amount of practice, are really due to the fact that those individuals who practiced the most also had the highest finger-dexterity scores. This argument can be countered if it can be shown that individuals with the *same* finger-dexterity scores differ in performance as a function of practice. Another typical way of anticipating this argument is to assign students at random to groups that will be allowed to practice only a specified amount of time. Then, one can argue that there is no reason to expect any one group to have greater finger dexterity than any other. To the extent that it is possible to do so, the practice of *random assignment of subjects* to treatment groups should always be followed. On the other hand, failure to do so does not necessarily mean that erroneous conclusions will be drawn, particularly if *relevant contaminators* are included in the model. Moreover, there are other reasons for including contaminator variables in the model. In the context of this problem, for example, failure to include finger dexterity would not enable a practice/finger-dexterity interaction to be detected. Yet it seems intuitively reasonable to expect that individuals with greater "ability" will profit more from additional practice than individuals with less ability. In addition, the inclusion of a relevant contaminator can have a decided impact on the denominator of the F value. The reason for this is that the variability in typing performance for individuals with (say) 15 hours of practice who have a finger-dexterity score of four is likely to be less than the variability of individuals with 15 hours of practice who may have any finger-dexterity score.[1]

The decision to include a contaminator along with the treatment variable in the model enables the investigator to anticipate that he will be able to test the following hypothesis:

$$\mathscr{E}(h_1, f) = \mathscr{E}(h_2, f)$$

However, it does not help him decide what model to use to estimate the expected values. An examination of the literature leads to the inference that many investigators choose their starting model primarily on the basis of

---

[1]See Appendix, Section B.6, for additional discussion of this point.

the number of levels that the two attributes take on. For example, if the number of levels of both attributes is small, a model such as (9.1) is used, and the investigator usually reports that he performed an *analysis of variance*. If the number of levels of both attributes is large, a model such as (9.4) or, more typically, (9.10) is used, and the investigator will then report that he performed a *regression analysis*. If the number of levels of the treatment variable is small and the number of levels of the contaminator is large, a model such as (8.3) or (8.5) is frequently used. In this case, the investigator would report that an *analysis of covariance* was conducted. The essential differences among these models involve assumptions about linearity and interaction. Surprisingly, we have been unable to locate a single study in the literature that used a starting model that assumed a linear relation for the treatment variable but not the contaminator.[2]

9.10
A SUMMARY OF THE TWO-ATTRIBUTE CATEGORICAL MODEL WITH BOTH ATTRIBUTES ORDERED

This section contains a summary and a generalization of the analyses performed in this chapter. The development is similar to that in Chapter 8; however, in this chapter we considered linearity not only for the second attribute but also for the first attribute.

General Model for Two Attributes with Multiple Categories

We started, as in Sections 7.13 and 8.13, with a general two-attribute mutually exclusive categorical model.

$$
\begin{aligned}
\mathbf{Y} = a_{1,1}\mathbf{X}^{(1,1)} + a_{1,2}\mathbf{X}^{(1,2)} + \cdots + a_{1,c}\mathbf{X}^{(1,c)} \\
+ a_{2,1}\mathbf{X}^{(2,1)} + a_{2,2}\mathbf{X}^{(2,2)} + \cdots + a_{2,c}\mathbf{X}^{(2,c)} \\
\vdots \qquad\qquad \vdots \qquad\qquad \vdots \\
+ a_{r,1}\mathbf{X}^{(r,1)} + a_{r,2}\mathbf{X}^{(r,2)} + \cdots + a_{r,c}\mathbf{X}^{(r,c)} + \mathbf{E}^{(8)}
\end{aligned}
\tag{9.11}
$$

remembering that

$\mathbf{X}^{(i,j)} = 1$ if ith category of the first attribute and jth category of the second attribute.

$\mathbf{E}^{(8)} =$ the error vector. (Note that the designation "8" corresponds

[2]See Ward, 1969, and the Exercise at the end of this chapter.

to the specific model (9.1) used in this chapter. In Chapters 7 and 8, the error vector was called $\mathbf{E}^{(6)}$, since it was associated with different data.)

and

$q_8 =$ the error sum of squares

Model Assuming Constant Differences (Linearity) for the Second Attribute at Each Category of the First Attribute

As in Chapter 8, the test of linearity for all categories of the first attribute gives a model of the general form

$$\mathbf{Y} = b_1 \mathbf{X}^{(1)} + c_1 \mathbf{D}^{(1)} + b_2 \mathbf{X}^{(2)} + c_2 \mathbf{D}^{(2)}$$
$$+ \cdots + b_r \mathbf{X}^{(r)} + c_r \mathbf{D}^{(r)} + \mathbf{E}^{(9)} \tag{9.12}$$

remembering that

$\mathbf{X}^{(i)} = 1$ if the ith category of the first attribute; 0 otherwise.

$\mathbf{D} =$ a number associated with the jth category if the corresponding element of $\mathbf{Y}$ is in the jth category.

$\mathbf{D}^{(i)} = \mathbf{X}^{(i)} * \mathbf{D} =$ the direct product of $\mathbf{X}^{(i)}$ and $\mathbf{D}$.

Model Assuming Linearity for Both Attributes

The model assuming linearity in both attributes (developed in Section 9.4) has the general form

$$\mathbf{Y} = b_0 \mathbf{U} + d_0 \mathbf{H} + c_0 \mathbf{D} + k_0 (\mathbf{H} * \mathbf{D}) + \mathbf{E}^{(10)} \tag{9.13}$$

where

$\mathbf{U} =$ the unit vector.

$\mathbf{H} =$ a vector with elements that are numbers associated with each category on the first attribute.

$\mathbf{D} =$ a vector with elements that are numbers associated with each category of the second attribute.

$\mathbf{H} * \mathbf{D} =$ the direct product of $\mathbf{H}$ and $\mathbf{D}$.

Model Containing Only Information about the Second Attribute

When we use model (9.12) and hypothesize that there are no differences between expected $\mathbf{Y}$ values of first-attribute categories at all levels of second-attribute categories, we have the general model

$$\mathbf{Y} = b_0 \mathbf{U} + c_0 \mathbf{D} + \mathbf{E}^{(11)} \tag{9.14}$$

Model with No Interaction

The model with no interaction between the two attributes has the general form

$$\mathbf{Y} = b_0\mathbf{U} + d_0\mathbf{H} + c_0\mathbf{D} + \mathbf{E}^{(12)} \qquad (9.15)$$

9.11
FLOWCHART FOR THE TWO-ATTRIBUTE
ANALYSES WITH BOTH ATTRIBUTES ORDERED

Figure 9.3 summarizes the two-attribute analyses, when both are considered to have a linear relation with the $\mathbf{Y}$ vector.

Table 9.2 contains a summary of the interesting quantities from the five models discussed in this chapter. Referring to Figure 9.3 and Section 9.10, we can see that (9.1) is a special case of the general model (9.11), and model (9.2) is a special case of the general model (9.12). Model (9.12) is developed from (9.11) by imposing restrictions of the general form

$$a_{ij} = b_i + (j)c_i \qquad \begin{cases} i = 1, 2, \ldots, r \\ j = 1, 2, \ldots, c \end{cases}$$

In the special case discussed in Sections 9.2 and 9.3, model (9.2) was developed from (9.1) by using the above restrictions, but where

$$i = 5, 10, 15, 20, 25$$
$$j = 1, 2, 3, 4$$

Model (9.4) is a special case of the general model (9.13). Model (9.13) was developed from (9.12) by imposing restrictions of the general form

$$\left. \begin{array}{l} b_i = b_0 + (i)d_0 \\ c_i = c_0 + (i)k_1 \end{array} \right\} \qquad i = 1, 2, \ldots, r$$

In the special case discussed in Section 9.4, model (9.4) was developed from (9.2) by imposing these restrictions, but where

$$i = 5, 10, 15, 20, 25$$

Model (9.9) is a special case of the general model (9.14). Model (9.14) was developed from (9.13) by imposing restrictions of the general form

$$d_0 = 0$$
$$k_0 = 0$$

The logic for choosing these restrictions was developed in Section 9.6 for the special case of models (9.4) and (9.9).

Model (9.10) is a special case of (9.15). Model (9.15) was developed from (9.13) by imposing the restriction

$$k_0 = 0$$

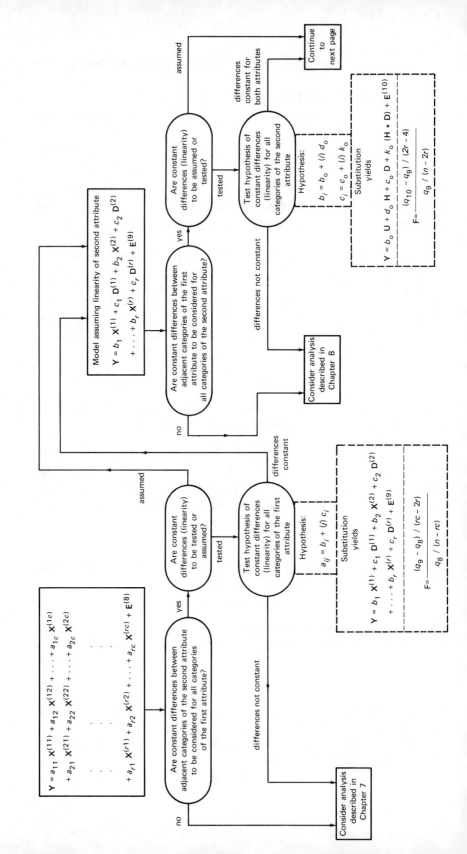

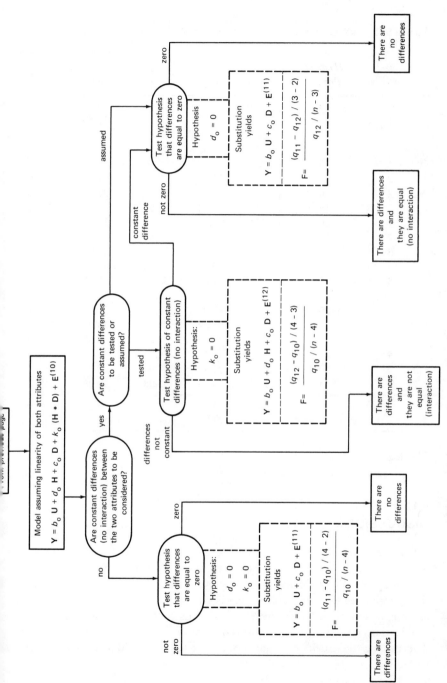

FIG. 9.3   Summary of Two-Attribute Analyses with One Attribute Ordered.

179

Table 9.2 PREDICTED VALUES ASSUMING FIVE DIFFERENT MODELS

Finger Dexterity	Hours of Practice	Model Number				
		9.1	9.2	9.4	9.9	9.10
1	5	12.0	12.18	11.47	19.59	6.81
1	10	13.0	13.04	15.16	19.59	12.63
1	15	21.0	19.61	18.84	19.59	18.46
1	20	23.0	24.33	22.52	19.59	24.28
1	25	25.5	25.56	26.20	19.59	30.10
2	5	18.0	17.20	17.12	27.42	15.36
2	10	22.0	22.01	22.21	27.42	21.19
2	15	24.0	27.23	27.29	27.42	27.01
2	20	37.0	33.81	32.38	27.42	32.83
2	25	37.0	36.76	37.46	27.42	38.66
3	5	21.0	22.21	22.77	35.25	23.92
3	10	31.0	30.99	29.26	35.25	29.74
3	15	36.0	34.85	35.74	35.25	35.56
3	20	41.0	43.30	42.23	35.25	41.39
3	25	48.0	47.95	48.72	35.25	47.21
4	5	27.5	27.22	28.41	43.08	32.47
4	10	40.0	39.96	36.31	43.08	38.29
4	15	42.0	42.47	44.20	43.08	44.12
4	20	53.0	52.78	52.09	43.08	49.94
4	25	59.0	59.14	59.98	43.08	55.77
No. of Parameters:		20	10	4	2	3
Error Sum of Squares:		59.0	93.9	134.2	1950.5	271.3

The logic for choosing this restriction was developed in Section 9.8 for the special case of models (9.4) and (9.10).

9.12
DISCUSSION

Perhaps the arguments that preceded the specification of the various models in this chapter seemed overly elaborate and unnecessarily notationally complex. We could have saved a great deal of space by simply stating the question and then defining the vectors of the models we would use to answer the question. However, it is our feeling that the process of stating the implications of a hypothesis in terms of relations among expected values and determining the restrictions that result is the best way of developing both the confidence to attempt and the skill to generate models that are useful in a specific problem area. In short, we are convinced that serious attention to model development is a prerequisite to accurate inferences and useful decisions.

Occasionally, a restricted model will result that is quite different from the one that might have been *guessed*. The practice of arbitrarily setting coefficients equal to zero or equal to other coefficients to see *what will happen* is particularly unappealing, and in many cases, it can lead to unjustifiable inferences.

If an individual is willing to limit his conclusion to the statement, "something happened!" it is difficult to argue with him—if you are satisfied with his starting (full) model. Generally, however, we want to draw a conclusion or make a claim that is more specific, in which case an elaborate argument will inevitably be required in defense of our model and methods.

Although it is impossible to give a recipe that will prove useful in all cases, it is possible (by example) to show what might happen when an argument is overly abbreviated. Consider model (9.4) again. A person might reason: "The coefficient associated with the measure of finger dexterity is c_0, and I will use that as my measure of the *effect* of finger dexterity. Therefore, if $c_0 = 0$, I can claim that finger dexterity has no effect on typing performance." Suppose it turned out that in his data c_0 was equal to zero. Would he have a valid claim?

The answer to this question is not simple because, in a technical sense, the answer is yes; but from a common-sense point of view, the answer is no. Technically, it can be argued that the claim is valid by definition (i.e., the effect of finger dexterity $= c_0$ and $c_0 = 0$). It then becomes necessary to back up to see if we agree with the definition. The problem is related to the one faced by a psychologist who is attempting to determine if hungry rats learn to run a maze more quickly than sated rats. The psychologist cannot very well ask a rat if he is hungry. If the psychologist is not allowed to define operationally what he means by a hungry rat (e.g., a rat that has not eaten for 24 hrs), then he simply cannot proceed. In most problem situations, an investigator will be required to make assumptions and to *make up* definitions. But, although we can easily verify that such devices have led to useful conclusions, specific assumptions and definitions should not be exempt from criticism.

Figure 9.4 shows a possible result using model (9.4) with $c_0 = 0$. Our hypothetical investigator could conclude that finger dexterity has no effect on typing performance. Do you agree with him? Note that at every level of practice (in the range of 5 to 25 hrs), individuals with higher finger-dexterity scores have higher expected (predicted) typing speeds than individuals with lower finger-dexterity scores.

The kind of argument used by our hypothetical investigator is deceptively appealing for a number of reasons. First, he saves considerable space, time, and mental effort because he is able to condense his argument to two short sentences. The restriction is quite simple, and little algebraic effort is required to generate a restricted model. The argument we would recommend, however, would require the investigator to state (in terms of the expected values)

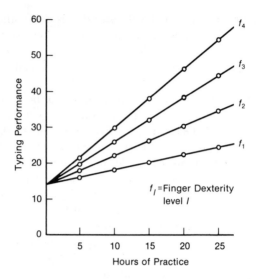

FIG. 9.4   Possible Pattern of Predicted Values from Model (9.4) When $c_0 = 0$.

what relationship would have to exist before he could claim *no effect*. Such an argument would undoubtedly be more elaborate.

Another reason the simple argument is appealing is that very frequently a complex set of statements will reduce to a very simple set of restrictions. Section 9.8 contains a good example. The algebraic expressions initially appear to be quite complex, but the restriction turns out to be quite simple. Because this phenomenon is so common, it is quite tempting to take the short cut and *guess*. Although one's ability to make this leap intuitively increases with practice, the dangers should be obvious. In any event, intuition is no substitute for a logical argument.

EXERCISES

1. In Section 9.9, we mentioned that we had been unable to locate a study that used a starting model that assumed linearity on the treatment variable but not the contaminator. Suppose you were interested in investigating the hypothesis

$$\mathscr{E}(h_1, f) = \mathscr{E}(h_2, f)$$

Furthermore, suppose you were willing to assume that the expected change in typing performance per unit change in practice was a constant at each level of finger dexterity (but not necessarily the same constant at each level), but you were not willing to assume that the expected change in performance per unit change in finger dexterity was a constant at each level of practice.

(a) Write a starting model that incorporates the assumptions you are willing to accept about relations among the expected values. *Hint*: Of the approaches that might be used to arrive at a model with the specified properties, one is to write a model similar to (9.2) but with the predictor vector definitions reversed. If you choose this method, be sure to verify that the model has the desired properties (see Sec. 9.5). Another possibility is to entertain tentatively (9.1) as a starting model and impose on the parameters of that model the restrictions that result from accepting

$$\mathscr{E}(i,j) = b_i + c_j(i) \qquad \begin{cases} i = 5, 10, 15, 20, 25 \\ j = 1, 2, 3, 4 \end{cases}$$

By substituting the estimates from (9.1)

$$a_{5,1} = b_1 + c_1(5)$$
$$a_{10,1} = b_1 + c_1(10)$$
$$\vdots$$
$$a_{25,1} = b_1 + c_1(25)$$
$$a_{5,2} = b_2 + c_2(5)$$
$$\vdots$$
$$a_{25,4} = b_4 + c_4(25)$$

There are a number of other ways in which a model with the desired properties could be generated, but the model should have eight linearly independent predictors (i.e., eight parameters).

(b) Using the model generated in (a) as the full model, write the restrictions on the parameters required to test the hypothesis

$$\mathscr{E}(h_1, f) = \mathscr{E}(h_2, f)$$

Hint: There should be four restrictions.

(c) Impose the restrictions and indicate the appearance of the restricted model and the *F*-value. *Hint*: There should be four predictor vectors in the restricted model.

(d) Using the model generated in (a) as the full model, write the restrictions on the parameters required to test for a practice/finger-dexterity interaction. *Hint*: There should be three restrictions.

(e) Impose the restrictions, write the restricted model, and indicate the appearance of the *F*-value. *Hint*: The restricted model should have five predictor vectors.

(f) Using the model generated in (e), write the restrictions required to test the hypothesis

$$\mathscr{E}(h_1, f) = \mathscr{E}(h_2, f)$$

Hint: There should be one restriction.

(g) Impose the restrictions, write the restricted model, and indicate the appearance of the *F*-value. *Hint*: The restricted model should be equivalent to the one generated in (c).

10

Applications of the Principles of Model Development to One-Attribute Problems

10.1 INTRODUCTION

This chapter contains examples of how the principles of model development, discussed in previous chapters, can be generalized to specific problems. Our purpose is to illustrate the wide variety of problems that can be investigated with the general approach. An appropriate model must be developed for each new problem that is encountered. After a model has been developed to fit a *particular* problem of interest, you may find that a similar model has already been developed for a previous problem. In this case, the old model can be reused. Care should be taken not to make a new problem fit an old model—unless the old model is appropriate. The appropriateness of a model in any specific situation is always debatable. Thus, in the examples that follow, you may be able to detect ways of improving the models.

In order to cover as many examples as possible, we have not provided sample data. You might therefore find it helpful to generate sample data for some of the problems and to find solutions to the models using the computer program described in Chapter 14. Each problem will follow an eight-step outline.

1. problem description
2. statement of the hypothesis
3. definition of vectors

4. full-model definition
5. implications of the hypothesis
6. restricted model definition
7. comparison of the models
8. comments

10.2
PROBLEM DESCRIPTION: GROUPING BASEBALL PLAYERS BY AGE

Baseball programs for young people are frequently organized into leagues based on age. A problem arises in deciding which age groups are to be assigned to the various leagues. A possible grouping might be

League	Age of Boys
1	9, 10
2	11, 12
3	13, 14
4	15, 16, 17

The justification for this grouping is based on the notion that members of each league have similar physical development. To investigate how reasonable this particular grouping is, a test of physical development is selected as the variable of interest, and a sample of boys at each age is given the test.

Hypothesis

It is argued that a rejection of the hypothesis

$$\mathscr{E}(9) = \mathscr{E}(10)$$
$$\mathscr{E}(11) = \mathscr{E}(12)$$
$$\mathscr{E}(13) = \mathscr{E}(14) \qquad (10.1)$$
$$\mathscr{E}(15) = \mathscr{E}(16) = \mathscr{E}(17)$$

would indicate that a more appropriate grouping might be found. On the other hand, a failure to reject it would indicate the proposed grouping is not unreasonable.

Definition of Vectors

$\mathbf{Y}$ = a vector of dimension n containing physical development scores.

$\mathbf{X}^{(i)}$ = 1 if the corresponding element in $\mathbf{Y}$ was observed on a boy who is i years old; 0 otherwise ($i = 9, 10, \ldots, 17$).

$\mathbf{L}^{(j)} = 1$ if the corresponding element in $\mathbf{Y}$ was observed on a boy in league j; 0 otherwise $(j = 1, 2, 3, 4)$.

The Full Model

$$\mathbf{Y} = a_9\mathbf{X}^{(9)} + a_{10}\mathbf{X}^{(10)} + \cdots + a_{17}\mathbf{X}^{(17)} + \mathbf{E}^{(1)} \qquad (10.2)$$

Implications of the Hypothesis

Substituting for the expected values in (10.1), the estimates from (10.2) yield the restrictions

$$a_9 = a_{10} = b_1 \qquad \text{(a common value for league 1)}$$
$$a_{11} = a_{12} = b_2 \qquad \text{(a common value for league 2)}$$
$$a_{13} = a_{14} = b_3 \qquad \text{(a common value for league 3)}$$
$$a_{15} = a_{16} = a_{17} = b_4 \qquad \text{(a common value for league 4)}$$

The Restricted Model

Substitution of these restrictions gives

$$\mathbf{Y} = b_1(\mathbf{X}^{(9)} + \mathbf{X}^{(10)}) + b_2(\mathbf{X}^{(11)} + \mathbf{X}^{(12)}) + b_3(\mathbf{X}^{(13)} + \mathbf{X}^{(14)})$$
$$+ b_4(\mathbf{X}^{(15)} + \mathbf{X}^{(16)} + \mathbf{X}^{(17)}) + \mathbf{E}^{(2)}$$

or

$$\mathbf{Y} = b_1\mathbf{L}^{(1)} + b_2\mathbf{L}^{(2)} + b_3\mathbf{L}^{(3)} + b_4\mathbf{L}^{(4)} + \mathbf{E}^{(2)} \qquad (10.3)$$

Comparison of the Models

Letting q_1 and q_2 be the error sum of squares associated with models (10.2) and (10.3), the models can be compared using the F value.

$$F = \frac{(q_r - q_f)/(n_f - n_r)}{q_f/(n - n_f)} = \frac{(q_2 - q_1)/(9 - 4)}{q_1/(n - 9)}$$

Comments

Accepting this hypothesis does not necessarily imply that another grouping might make the groups more homogeneous in terms of physical development. On the other hand, a rejection of this hypothesis does not necessarily imply that any other hypothesis would be accepted.[1]

---

[1] Appendix B (Section B.6) contains a description of a decision rule that might be more appropriate for this problem.

10.3
PROBLEM DESCRIPTION: LINEARITY OVER A RANGE

In previous chapters we have indicated the simplicity that can be achieved in a model if the hypothesis of linearity is found to be tenable. In some situations where this hypothesis is rejected, it may be possible to find a range in which it is tenable.

Suppose that a typing-aptitude test has been developed to predict performance in typing. The aptitude score is reported in deciles $(1, 2, \ldots, 9, 10)$ in which the lowest 10% of the aptitude scores are designated decile 1, the next highest 10% are decile 2, and the highest 10% are decile 10.

Previous analyses have indicated that the relation between typing performance and aptitude is not linear; that is, the difference in expected typing performance between adjacent deciles is not the same for all deciles. Someone observes that the plot of the average typing-performance values at each decile is the one shown in Figure 10.1.

Hypothesis

The hypothesis to be explored is whether the relation is linear in the range decile 2 to decile 9. Specifically,

$$\mathscr{E}(d) = b_0 + (d)b_1 \qquad (d = 2, 3, \ldots, 9) \qquad (10.4)$$

Definition of Vectors

$\mathbf{Y} =$ typing performance.

$\mathbf{X}^{(i)} = 1$ if the corresponding element of $\mathbf{Y}$ is from decile i; 0 otherwise $(i = 1, 2, \ldots, 10)$.

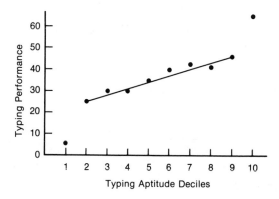

FIG. 10.1   Average Typing Scores at Various Levels of Aptitude.

$\mathbf{D} = $ typing aptitude deciles (values $1, 2, \ldots, 10$).

$\mathbf{X}^{(2-9)} = 1$ if the corresponding element of $\mathbf{Y}$ is from deciles 2 through 9; 0 otherwise.

$\mathbf{D}^{(2-9)} = \mathbf{D} * \mathbf{X}^{(2-9)} = $ the direct product of $\mathbf{D}$ and $\mathbf{X}^{(2-9)}$. The elements in $\mathbf{D}^{(2-9)}$ are aptitude decile values if the decile value is 2 or 3 or 4 ... or 9; 0 otherwise.

The Full Model

$$\mathbf{Y} = a_1 \mathbf{X}^{(1)} + a_2 \mathbf{X}^{(2)} + \cdots + a_{10} \mathbf{X}^{(10)} + \mathbf{E}^{(1)} \qquad (10.5)$$

Implications of the Hypothesis

Substituting for the expected values in (10.4), the estimates from (10.5) yield

$$a_2 = b_0 + (2)b_1$$
$$a_3 = b_0 + (3)b_1$$
$$\begin{array}{cc} \cdot & \cdot \\ \cdot & \cdot \\ \cdot & \cdot \end{array}$$
$$a_9 = b_0 + (9)b_1$$

The Restricted Model

Imposing these restrictions gives the restricted model

$$\mathbf{Y} = a_1 \mathbf{X}^{(1)} + [b_0 + (2)b_1]\mathbf{X}^{(2)} + [b_0 + (3)b_1]\mathbf{X}^{(3)}$$
$$+ \cdots + [b_0 + (9)b_1]\mathbf{X}^{(9)} + a_{10}\mathbf{X}^{(10)} + \mathbf{E}^{(2)}$$
$$\mathbf{Y} = a_1 \mathbf{X}^{(1)} + b_0[\mathbf{X}^{(2)} + \mathbf{X}^{(3)} + \cdots + \mathbf{X}^{(9)}]$$
$$+ b_1[2\mathbf{X}^{(2)} + 3\mathbf{X}^{(3)} + \cdots + 9\mathbf{X}^{(9)}] + a_{10}\mathbf{X}^{(10)} + \mathbf{E}^{(2)}$$

Then, substitution of vectors $\mathbf{X}^{(2-9)}$ and $\mathbf{D}^{(2-9)}$ gives

$$\mathbf{Y} = a_1 \mathbf{X}^{(1)} + b_0 \mathbf{X}^{(2-9)} + b_1 \mathbf{D}^{(2-9)} + a_{10}\mathbf{X}^{(10)} + \mathbf{E}^{(2)}$$

Comparison of the Models

If an F value is desired,

$$F = \frac{(q_r - q_f)/(n_f - n_r)}{q_f/(n - n_f)} = \frac{(q_2 - q_1)/(10 - 4)}{q_1/(n - 10)}$$

Comments

The least-squares values for a_1 and a_{10} are the typing performance averages for members of decile group 1 and 10, respectively. The least-squares values for a_1 and a_{10} are the same in both the *full* and the *restricted* models. The value of b_1 is an estimate of the expected change in performance per unit-change in aptitude in the aptitude range 2 through 9.

10.4
PROBLEM DESCRIPTION: LINEARITY OVER TWO RANGES

We will now consider a one-attribute problem in which it is reasonable to explore the possibility that there is *one* constant difference between adjacent categories over part of the range and a *second* constant difference over the rest of the range. Specifically, consider a study in which salaries earned at age 40 are to be predicted from the number of years of formal education completed at age 25. It is conjectured that there is a constant change in salary for each added year of education prior to high school graduation. Also, there is a constant change in salary for each added year of education beyond high school graduation. Moreover, we will assume that these two constant rates of change might be different and that the years of education to be considered are from 1 through 20.

The Hypothesis

$$\mathscr{E}(e) = c_0 + (e)c_1 \qquad e = 1, 2, \ldots, 11$$
$$\mathscr{E}(e) = d_0 + (e)d_1 \qquad e = 12, 13, \ldots, 20$$

$$(10.6)$$

Definition of Vectors

$\mathbf{Y}$ = salaries earned at age 40.

$\mathbf{X}^{(i)}$ = 1 if the corresponding element in $\mathbf{Y}$ is from a person who has completed i years of education; 0 otherwise $(i = 1, 2, \ldots, 20)$.

$\mathbf{X}^{(1-11)}$ = 1 if the corresponding element of $\mathbf{Y}$ is associated with years of education 1 through 11; 0 otherwise $[\mathbf{X}^{(1-11)} = \mathbf{X}^{(1)} + \mathbf{X}^{(2)} + \cdots + \mathbf{X}^{(11)}]$.

$\mathbf{X}^{(12-20)}$ = 1 if the corresponding element of $\mathbf{Y}$ is associated with years of education 12 through 20; 0 otherwise $[\mathbf{X}^{(12-20)} = \mathbf{X}^{(12)} + \mathbf{X}^{(13)} + \cdots + \mathbf{X}^{(20)}]$.

$\mathbf{R}$ = the number of years of education associated with the corresponding element in $\mathbf{Y}$.

$\mathbf{R}^{(1-11)} = \mathbf{R} * \mathbf{X}^{(1-11)}$ = the direct product of $\mathbf{R}$ and $\mathbf{X}^{(1-11)}$.
$\mathbf{R}^{(12-20)} = \mathbf{R} * \mathbf{X}^{(12-20)}$ = the direct product of $\mathbf{R}$ and $\mathbf{X}^{(12-20)}$.

The Full Model

$$\mathbf{Y} = a_1\mathbf{X}^{(1)} + a_2\mathbf{X}^{(2)} + \cdots + a_{20}\mathbf{X}^{(20)} + \mathbf{E}^{(1)} \qquad (10.7)$$

Implications of the Hypothesis

Substituting for the expected values in (10.6), the estimates from (10.7) yield

$$a_1 = c_0 + (1)c_1$$
$$a_2 = c_0 + (2)c_1$$
$$\cdot \qquad \cdot$$
$$\cdot \qquad \cdot$$
$$\cdot \qquad \cdot$$
$$a_{11} = c_0 + (11)c_1$$
$$a_{12} = d_0 + (12)d_1$$
$$a_{13} = d_0 + (13)d_1$$
$$\cdot \qquad \cdot$$
$$\cdot \qquad \cdot$$
$$\cdot \qquad \cdot$$
$$a_{20} = d_0 + (20)d_1$$

The Restricted Model

Substitution of these restrictions gives

$$\mathbf{Y} = [c_0 + (1)c_1]\mathbf{X}^{(1)} + [c_0 + (2)c_1]\mathbf{X}^{(2)} + \cdots + [c_0 + (11)c_1]\mathbf{X}^{(11)}$$
$$+ [d_0 + (12)d_1]\mathbf{X}^{(12)} + [d_0 + (13)d_1]\mathbf{X}^{(13)}$$
$$+ \cdots + [d_0 + (20)d_1]\mathbf{X}^{(20)} + \mathbf{E}^{(2)}$$

or

$$\mathbf{Y} = c_0[\mathbf{X}^{(1)} + \mathbf{X}^{(2)} + \cdots + \mathbf{X}^{(11)}] + c_1[(1)\mathbf{X}^{(1)} + (2)\mathbf{X}^{(2)}$$
$$+ \cdots + (11)\mathbf{X}^{(11)}] + d_0[\mathbf{X}^{(12)} + \mathbf{X}^{(13)} + \cdots + \mathbf{X}^{(20)}]$$
$$+ d_1[(12)\mathbf{X}^{(12)} + (13)\mathbf{X}^{(13)} + \cdots + (20)\mathbf{X}^{(20)}] + \mathbf{E}^{(2)}$$

Substituting the defined vectors gives

$$\mathbf{Y} = c_0\mathbf{X}^{(1-11)} + c_1\mathbf{R}^{(1-11)} + d_0\mathbf{X}^{(12-20)} + d_1\mathbf{R}^{(12-20)} + \mathbf{E}^{(2)} \qquad (10.8)$$

Comparison of the Models

The F value can be computed as

$$F = \frac{(q_r - q_f)/(n_f - n_r)}{q_f/(n - n_f)} = \frac{(q_2 - q_1)/(20 - 4)}{q_1/(n - 20)}$$

Comments

In this problem, we were concerned about whether two possibly different linear relations could exist between $\mathbf{Y}$ (salary earned) and years of education.

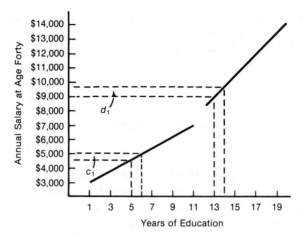

FIG. 10.2   Annual Salary as a Function of Education.

The plot of estimated expected values from the restricted model might look like the one shown in Figure 10.2.

The vectors of the restricted model might take the form of

$\mathbf{X}^{(1-11)}$	$\mathbf{R}^{(1-11)}$	$\mathbf{X}^{(12-20)}$	$\mathbf{R}^{(12-20)}$
1	9	0	0
1	4	0	0
1	6	0	0
1	4	0	0
1	7	0	0
1	11	0	0
0	0	1	12
0	0	1	14
0	0	1	17
0	0	1	20
0	0	1	13
0	0	1	15
0	0	1	18

Note that a significant F value would lead to the inference that the relationship between income and education is not linear in either one or both of the ranges. On the other hand, a high probability value associated with F does not lead to the inference that separate parameters for the two ranges are required. It may be quite possible to simplify the model even more. A high-probability value would tend to indicate that model (10.8) is adequate—relative to model (10.7).

10.5
PROBLEM DESCRIPTION: DETECTING
A DISCONTINUITY

Consider the problem described in Section 10.4. Frequently, there is a discussion concerning the value of completing the twelfth year of education (high school graduate). We might conjecture that the salary increment in going from the eleventh to twelfth year of education is different from the salary increment associated with any one of the earlier years of education. To pursue this question, let's describe a possible analysis.

The Hypothesis

$$\mathscr{E}(12) - \mathscr{E}(11) = \mathscr{E}(t) - \mathscr{E}(t-1) \qquad t = 11, 10, \ldots, 2 \qquad (10.9)$$

Note that the expression on the left is the increment in annual expected salary for completing the twelfth year over completing only the eleventh year, and the expression on the right is the expected increment for any previous pair of adjacent years, t and $(t-1)$.

Definition of Vectors

$$\mathbf{Y} = \text{salaries earned at age 40.}$$
$$\mathbf{X}^{(1-11)} = \text{defined in Section 10.4.}$$
$$\mathbf{X}^{(12-20)} = \text{defined in Section 10.4.}$$
$$\mathbf{R} = \text{defined in Section 10.4.}$$
$$\mathbf{R}^{(1-11)} = \mathbf{R} * \mathbf{X}^{(1-11)} = \text{defined in Section 10.4.}$$
$$\mathbf{R}^{(12-20)} = \mathbf{R} * \mathbf{X}^{(12-20)} = \text{defined in Section 10.4.}$$

The Full Model

We will use model (10.8) as the full model.

$$\mathbf{Y} = c_0 \mathbf{X}^{(1-11)} + c_1 \mathbf{R}^{(1-11)} + d_0 \mathbf{X}^{(12-20)} + d_1 \mathbf{R}^{(12-20)} + \mathbf{E}^{(1)} \qquad (10.10)$$

Note that we are designating the error vector for this full model as $\mathbf{E}^{(1)}$ instead of $\mathbf{E}^{(2)}$, which was its designation when it was a restricted model.

Implications of the Hypothesis

Substituting for the expected values in (10.9) the estimates in (10.10), the restricted model can then be developed. The expected salary for a person with 12 years of education is estimated by

$$d_0 + d_1(12)$$

The expected salary for a person with 11 years of education is estimated by

$$c_0 + c_1(11)$$

The salary increment associated with the final year of high school education is then estimated by

$$\text{Inc } [12 - 11] = [d_0 + d_1(12)] - [c_0 + c_1(11)]$$

Next, consider the expected salary for a person with t years of education $(t \leq 11)$, which is estimated by

$$c_0 + c_1(t)$$

Then consider the expected salary for a person with $(t - 1)$ years of education, which is estimated by

$$c_0 + c_1(t - 1)$$

The salary increment associated with going from $(t - 1)$ years of education to t years of education is

$$\text{Inc } [t - (t - 1)] = [c_0 + c_1(t)] - [c_0 + c_1(t - 1)]$$
$$\text{Inc } [t - (t - 1)] = c_1$$

Then the question of interest can be expressed by stating the hypothesis

$$\text{Inc } [12 - 11] = \text{Inc } [t - (t - 1)]$$

Substitution gives

$$[d_0 + d_1(12)] - [c_0 + c_1(11)] = c_1 \qquad (10.11)$$

or

$$d_0 = c_0 + c_1(12) - d_1(12)$$

The Restricted Model

Substitution in model (10.10) gives

$$\mathbf{Y} = c_0 \mathbf{X}^{(1-11)} + c_1 \mathbf{R}^{(1-11)} + [c_0 + c_1(12) - d_1(12)]\mathbf{X}^{(12-20)} + d_1 \mathbf{R}^{(12-20)} + \mathbf{E}^{(2)}$$

Since $\mathbf{X}^{(1-11)} + \mathbf{X}^{(12-20)} = \mathbf{U}$, then

$$\mathbf{Y} = c_0 \mathbf{U} + c_1[\mathbf{R}^{(1-11)} + (12)\mathbf{X}^{(12-20)}] + d_1[\mathbf{R}^{(12-20)} - (12)\mathbf{X}^{(12-20)}] + \mathbf{E}^{(2)} \qquad (10.12)$$

The vectors $[\mathbf{R}^{(1-11)} + (12)\mathbf{X}^{(12-20)}]$ and $[\mathbf{R}^{(12-20)} - (12)\mathbf{X}^{(12-20)}]$ are easily developed within the computer SUBROUTINE DATRAN, described in Chapter 15.

Comparison of the Models

The F value can be computed as

$$F = \frac{(q_r - q_f)/(n_f - n_r)}{q_f/(n - n_f)} = \frac{(q_2 - q_1)/(4 - 3)}{q_1/(n - 4)}$$

Comments

The restricted model contains three vectors: the familiar unit vector $\mathbf{U}$ and two others. For example,

$$[\mathbf{R}^{(1-11)} + (12)\mathbf{X}^{(12-20)}] \qquad [\mathbf{R}^{(12-20)} - (12)\mathbf{X}^{(12-20)}]$$

$[\mathbf{R}^{(1-11)} + (12)\mathbf{X}^{(12-20)}]$	$[\mathbf{R}^{(12-20)} - (12)\mathbf{X}^{(12-20)}]$
9	0
4	0
6	0
4	0
7	0
11	0
12	0
12	2
12	5
12	8
12	1
12	3
12	6

Since these vectors are so unusual, how can we be sure that the restricted model is correct? We can examine model (10.12) and verify that this model has the desired properties.

[Predicted value for 12 years] $-$ [Predicted value for 11 years]
$= [c_0 + 12c_1 + d_1(12 - 12)] - [c_0 + 11c_1] = c_1$

[Predicted value for t years] $-$ [Predicted value for $(t - 1)$ years]
$= [c_0 + c_1(t)] - [c_0 + c_1(t - 1)] = c_1 \qquad t \leq 11$

A pictorial representation of the restricted model is shown in Figure 10.3.

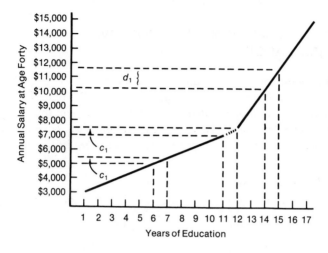

FIG. 10.3   Estimated Expected Values from Model (10.12).

An entire chapter could be devoted to comments about the arguments and models associated with this problem, since it exemplifies so many of the critical decisions that an investigator is required to make in arriving at decisions. Consider model (10.10), used as the starting model. Clearly, this model allows us to detect the difference of interest (Section 6.14) because the expression on the left in (10.11) is not equal to the expression on the right. However, it is not so clear that model (10.10) will produce good estimates of the expected values (Section 6.15). The decision to accept (10.10) as a starting model could have been based on the results of the test conducted in Section 10.4. On the other hand, we could have used (10.7) as a starting model. Note what happens if we examine the implications of (10.9) in terms of (10.7) by substitution.

$$(a_{12} - a_{11}) = (a_{11} - a_{10}) = (a_{10} - a_9) = \cdots = (a_2 - a_1)$$

In order to test these hypotheses, we would have to impose 10 restrictions. A rejection could be caused by the falsity of any one or more of the 10 hypotheses. As a result, we can conclude that a decision about (10.9) based on a comparison of models (10.10) and (10.12) is much less ambiguous than the alternative approach. (Note that there is only one restriction.) In order to justify this simplicity, however, we need to be reasonably confident that (10.10) is an adequate substitute for (10.7), which is known to be true. The major point is that the question of crucial interest should be tested against the simplest possible model that is an adequate substitute for a model known to be true.

10.6
PROBLEM DESCRIPTION: LINEARITY OVER AN ENTIRE RANGE

Consider again the situation discussed in Section 10.5. We will use the same full model, but the question of interest will be different. To determine if "something special happens at the twelfth year," we will hypothesize that the salary change from 11 to 12 years of education is the same as the salary change expected between *any other two years of education* in the entire range.

The Hypothesis

$$\mathscr{E}(12) - \mathscr{E}(11) = \mathscr{E}(t) - \mathscr{E}(t-1) = \mathscr{E}(s) - \mathscr{E}(s-1) \qquad (10.13)$$

with $t = 11, 10, \ldots, 2$ and $s = 20, 19, \ldots, 13$.

Definition of Vectors

$\mathbf{Y}$ = salaries earned at age 40.

$\mathbf{X}^{(1-11)}$ = 1 if years of education is 1 through 11; 0 otherwise.

$\mathbf{X}^{(12-20)}$ = 1 if years of education is 12 through 20; 0 otherwise.

$\mathbf{R}$ = years of education.

$\mathbf{R}^{(1-11)} = \mathbf{R} * \mathbf{X}^{(1-11)}$

$\mathbf{R}^{(12-20)} = \mathbf{R} * \mathbf{X}^{(12-20)}$

The Full Model

$$\mathbf{Y} = c_0 \mathbf{X}^{(1-11)} + c_1 \mathbf{R}^{(1-11)} + d_0 \mathbf{X}^{(12-20)} + d_1 \mathbf{R}^{(12-20)} + \mathbf{E}^{(1)} \qquad (10.14)$$

Implications of the Hypothesis

By substituting for the expected values in (10.13) the estimates in (10.14), the restrictions can then be developed.

$$\text{Inc } [12 - 11] = [d_0 + d_1(12)] - [c_0 + c_1(11)]$$

$$\text{Inc } [t - (t-1)] = [c_0 + c_1(t)] - [c_0 + c_1(t-1)] = c_1$$
$$t = 11, 10, \ldots, 2$$

$$\text{Inc } [s - (s-1)] = [d_0 + d_1(s)] - [d_0 + d_1(s-1)] = d_1$$
$$s = 20, 19, \ldots, 13$$

The hypothesis is

$$\text{Inc } [12 - 11] = \text{Inc } [t - (t-1)] = \text{Inc } [s - (s-1)]$$

$$[d_0 + d_1(12)] - [c_0 + c_1(11)] = c_1 = d_1$$

$$(d_0 - c_0) + d_1(12) - c_1(11) - c_1 = 0$$

$$(d_0 - c_0) + d_1(12) - c_1(11) - d_1 = 0$$
$$(d_0 - c_0) + 12(d_1 - c_1) = 0$$
$$(d_0 - c_0) + 11(d_1 - c_1) = 0$$

This implies that the restrictions are

$$d_0 = c_0 = k_0 \quad \text{(a common value)}$$
$$d_1 = c_1 = k_1 \quad \text{(a common value)}$$

The Restricted Model

Substitution of the restriction in (10.14) gives

$$\mathbf{Y} = k_0 \mathbf{X}^{(1-11)} + k_1 \mathbf{R}^{(1-11)} + k_0 \mathbf{X}^{(12-20)} + k_1 \mathbf{R}^{(12-20)} + \mathbf{E}^{(2)}$$
$$\mathbf{Y} = k_0 \mathbf{U} + k_1 \mathbf{R} + \mathbf{E}^{(2)} \tag{10.15}$$

Comparison of the Models

The F value is

$$F = \frac{(q_2 - q_1)/(4 - 2)}{q_1/(n - 4)}$$

Comments

In this problem, we hypothesized that the relationship between salary and education for 12 or more years of education is a continuation of the relationship between salary and education for 11 or less years of education. (A pictorial representation of (10.15) would contain a single straight line.) Note that in the analysis of the problem in Section 10.5, *we did not hypothesize* that the change in salary after 12 years of education was the same as before 12. We only hypothesized that the change from 11 to 12 was the same as the early years.

10.7
PROBLEM DESCRIPTION: A PARAMETER IS EQUAL TO A SPECIFIED NONZERO VALUE

A business school claims that within the range of 0 to 50 hours, each additional hour of supervised training results in an 0.8 words/minute improvement in typing proficiency.

The Hypothesis

$$\frac{\mathscr{E}(p) - \mathscr{E}(q)}{p - q} = 0.8 \tag{10.16}$$

For any pair of hours, p and q, $p \neq q$.

Definition of Vectors

$\mathbf{Y}$ = typing proficiency in words/min.

$\mathbf{U}$ = the unit vector.

$\mathbf{H}$ = hours of practice.

The Full Model

The full model assumes that the relation between typing proficiency and hours of practice is linear.

$$\mathbf{Y} = a_0\mathbf{U} + a_1\mathbf{H} + \mathbf{E}^{(1)} \tag{10.17}$$

Implications of the Hypothesis

By substituting for the expected values in (10.16) the estimates in (10.17), the restrictions implied by the hypothesis can then be developed. Consider two amounts of practice, p and q, and the corresponding expected typing performance estimated by

$$a_0 + a_1(p) \quad \text{and} \quad a_0 + a_1(q)$$

Then the hypothesis is

$$\frac{[a_0 + a_1(p)] - [a_0 + a_1(q)]}{p - q} = 0.8$$

or

$$\frac{a_1(p - q)}{(p - q)} = 0.8$$

or

$$a_1 = 0.8$$

The Restricted Model

Substitution in the full model gives

$$\mathbf{Y} = a_0\mathbf{U} + (0.8)\mathbf{H} + \mathbf{E}^{(2)}$$

But, since the only coefficient to be solved for by the least-squares procedure is a_0, we can write

$$\mathbf{Y} - (0.8)\mathbf{H} = a_0\mathbf{U} + \mathbf{E}^{(2)} \tag{10.18}$$

We can then solve for a_0, $\mathbf{E}^{(2)}$, and q_2 by predicting the vector $[\mathbf{Y} - 0.8\mathbf{H}]$ from the unit vector.

Comparisons of the Models

The F value is

$$F = \frac{(q_r - q_f)/(n_f - n_r)}{q_f/(n - n_f)} = \frac{(q_2 - q_1)/(2 - 1)}{q_1/(n - 2)}$$

Comments

This is the first problem in which some predictor vectors (one, in this case) are associated with unknown coefficients, and other predictor vectors (also one, in this case) are associated with known coefficients. Whenever the restricted model contains vectors that are not associated with an unknown coefficient, they can be moved to combine with the $\mathbf{Y}$ vector and form a new composite vector. This new vector [$(\mathbf{Y} - 0.8\mathbf{H})$, in this problem] can then be used as the criterion vector to solve for the least-squares coefficients.

11

Applications to One-Attribute Problems Using Polynomial Forms

11.1
INTRODUCTION TO POLYNOMIAL FORMS

In Chapter 6 we considered a one-attribute, ordered problem in which there might have been a constant difference in the expected $\mathbf{Y}$ value (typing performance) when one unit was changed on the ordered attribute (grade level). We started with the mutually exclusive categorical model

$$\mathbf{Y} = a_1\mathbf{X}^{(1)} + a_2\mathbf{X}^{(2)} + \cdots + a_k\mathbf{X}^{(k)} + \mathbf{E}^{(1)} \qquad (11.1)$$

where $\mathbf{X}^{(i)} = 1$ if from category i; 0 otherwise. We then considered the possibility that

$$a_i = d_0 + (i)d_1 \qquad i = 1, \ldots, k$$

which led to a restricted model

$$\mathbf{Y} = d_0\mathbf{U} + d_1\mathbf{G} + \mathbf{E}^{(2)}$$

where

$\mathbf{U}$ = the unit vector.

$\mathbf{G}$ = a vector containing numbers (9–12) associated with the categories (grades 9–12).

The Polynomial Hypothesis

Now suppose we conclude that the restriction

$$a_i = d_0 + (i)d_1$$

is not acceptable on either theoretical, practical, or statistical grounds. What is the next simplest possibility?

If the change d_1 is not the same at all categories of the ordered attribute, then we may let the change vary (depending on the particular category). A simple adjustment of d_1 would be to replace d_1 by $d_1 + (i)d_2$ and then write the restriction

$$a_i = d_0 + (i)[d_1 + (i)d_2]$$

or

$$a_i = d_0 + (i)d_1 + (i^2)d_2$$

But, if this restriction is not acceptable, we may replace d_2 by $d_2 + (i)d_3$ and write

$$a_i = d_0 + (i)d_1 + (i^2)[d_2 + (i)d_3]$$

or

$$a_i = d_0 + (i)d_1 + (i^2)d_2 + (i^3)d_3$$

This restriction can be extended to form

$$a_i = d_0 + (i)d_1 + (i^2)d_2 + (i^3)d_3 + \cdots + (i^p)d_p \qquad (11.2)$$

The hypothesis implied by these restrictions is referred to as **the hypothesis of a polynomial of degree p**. When we impose the restrictions in (11.2) on the full model (11.1), we get the restricted model

$$\mathbf{Y} = d_0\mathbf{U} + d_1\mathbf{G} + d_2(\mathbf{G}^2) + d_3(\mathbf{G}^3) + \cdots + d_p(\mathbf{G}^p) + \mathbf{E}^{(3)}$$

where

$\mathbf{G}$ = a vector containing numbers associated with each mutually exclusive category.

$\mathbf{G}^2 = \mathbf{G} * \mathbf{G}$ = a vector containing the squares of the element of $\mathbf{G}$.

$\mathbf{G}^3 = \mathbf{G} * \mathbf{G}^2$ = a vector containing the cubes of the elements of $\mathbf{G}$.

.   .
.   .
.   .

$\mathbf{G}^p = \mathbf{G} * \mathbf{G}^{p-1}$ = a vector containing the pth power of the elements of $\mathbf{G}$.

We will now examine some pictorial representations of the predicted $\mathbf{Y}$ values resulting from the use of polynomial models.

11.2
POLYNOMIAL FORMS

To indicate some of the characteristics of polynomial forms, several different models are shown. But only that portion of the function that illustrates important characteristics of the polynomial form is shown. In general, a polynomial form of degree p *may display* as many as $(p - 1)$

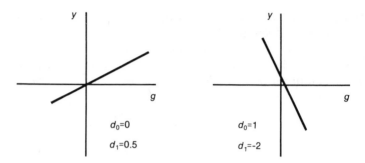

FIG. 11.1   Polynomial Forms with $p = 1$.

changes in direction of the curve. The expression *change in direction* refers to either a change from an upward to a downward movement or from a downward to an upward movement. As we will see, the sign and magnitude of the coefficients determine the precise orientation of the curve. The expected (or predicted) values are expressed as a function of g.

In Chapter 6 we examined the case of $p = 1$. There we indicated that when $p = 1$, y is said to be a linear function of g. As shown in Figure 11.1, the point at which the line crosses the y axis is given by d_0, and the slope of the line is given by d_1.

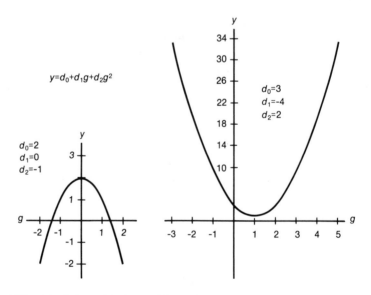

FIG. 11.2   Polynomial Forms with $p = 2$.

In Figure 11.2 we observe that there is one change of direction of the functions. The value d_0 indicates the point at which the curve crosses the y axis. When $d_1 = 0$, the curve is symmetric about the y axis. When $d_1 \neq 0$, the curve is displaced to the right or left of this axis. The values of both d_1 and d_2 determine the direction and amount of displacement. The general shape of the curve is strongly influenced by the absolute value of d_2—the larger the value, the sharper the curve. If d_2 is a positive number, the curve opens upward; if d_2 is negative, the curve opens downward.

In one of the curves shown in Figure 11.3, we observe that a polynomial form *may have* two changes in direction. A necessary but not sufficient condition for two changes in the direction of the curve is that $d_1 \neq 0$ or $d_2 \neq 0$. The form of the curve when both d_1 and d_2 are zero is illustrated by one of the curves in Figure 11.3. As was the case when $p = 2$, the sign and magnitude of the values of both d_1 and d_2 influence the general shape of curves having two changes in direction. However, a curve may appear quite different from the illustrations. The curve might be inverted, moving from upper left to lower right; it might be compressed or elongated in the regions where the changes in direction take place; or the entire curve might be displaced horizontally and vertically.

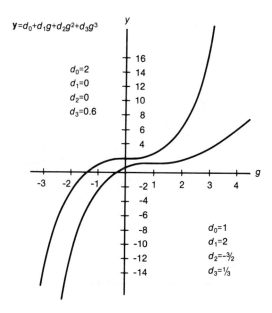

FIG. 11.3 Polynomial Forms with $p = 3$.

11.3
PROBLEM DESCRIPTION: THE EFFECT
OF ANXIETY ON PROBLEM-SOLVING
PERFORMANCE

A study was designed to investigate the relationship of anxiety to problem-solving performance. At the outset of the experiment, each subject was given a paper-and-pencil test designed to assess his general level of anxiety. All subjects were then asked to solve a problem that required complex reasoning. The problem-solving performance of each subject was measured in terms of the time required to solve the problem.

According to one theoretical position, subjects whose anxiety level is neither extremely high nor extremely low will tend to have the best problem-solving performances. This theory suggests that as the anxiety level increases from a very low to an intermediate value, the time required to solve the problem will decrease; but as anxiety level increases from the intermediate value to a higher value, the time required to solve the problem will increase. An illustration of this is the solid curved line in Figure 11.4. This theory suggests that the change in performance as anxiety increases is *not constant*. Furthermore, the theory suggests one change in direction. It is therefore hypothesized that a polynomial of degree two will adequately describe the situation.

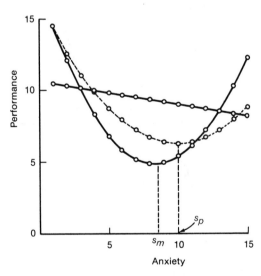

FIG. 11.4 Problem Solving Performance as a Function of Anxiety with Three Different Models.

The Hypothesis

$$\mathscr{E}(i) = d_0 + (i)d_1 + (i^2)d_2 \tag{11.3}$$

where $\mathscr{E}(i)$ is the expected time required to solve the problem for individuals with an anxiety score of i, with i taking on all values of anxiety.

Definition of Vectors

$\mathbf{Y}$ = a vector having as elements the time required to solve the reasoning problem.

$\mathbf{X}^{(i)}$ = 1 if the element in $\mathbf{Y}$ is from a person who received an anxiety score of i; 0 otherwise. (We assume that in the data there will be more than one student attaining some anxiety scores; that is, the dimension of $\mathbf{Y}$ is greater than the number of $\mathbf{X}$ vectors.)

$\mathbf{S}$ = a vector having as elements the anxiety test score of the person with corresponding element in vector $\mathbf{Y}$.

$\mathbf{S}^2 = \mathbf{S} * \mathbf{S}$ = a vector with elements that are the squared values of the corresponding elements in $\mathbf{S}$.

The Full Model

The full model is the mutually exclusive categorical model

$$\mathbf{Y} = a_1\mathbf{X}^{(1)} + a_2\mathbf{X}^{(2)} + \cdots + a_k\mathbf{X}^{(k)} + \mathbf{E}^{(1)} \tag{11.4}$$

Implications of the Hypothesis

The restrictions can be derived by substituting for the expected values in (11.3) the estimates from (11.4).

$$a_i = d_0 + (i)d_1 + (i^2)d_2$$

where

i = an anxiety test score.

d_0, d_1, d_2 = the unknown values to be estimated by the least-squares procedure.

The Restricted Model

Imposing the above restrictions and simplifying gives

$$\mathbf{Y} = d_0\mathbf{U} + d_1\mathbf{S} + d_2\mathbf{S}^2 + \mathbf{E}^{(2)}$$

Comparing the Models

The F value is

$$F = \frac{(q_r - q_f)/(n_f - n_r)}{q_f/(n - n_f)} = \frac{(q_2 - q_1)/(k - 3)}{q_1/(n - k)}$$

Comments

It is important to recognize that the number of elements (n) in each vector must be greater than the number of unique anxiety scores (k); that is, n must be greater than k. After the least-squares values for d_0, d_1, and d_2 are obtained, we can examine the sign of d_2. If $d_2 > 0$, the shape of the curve is similar to the solid curve in Figure 11.4, which represents a solution with the values

$$d_0 = 17.39$$
$$d_1 = -2.96$$
$$d_2 = 0.17$$

If we want to estimate the anxiety score(call it s_m) at which the expected solution time is minimum, it can be calculated by

$$
\begin{aligned}
s_m &= -d_1/2d_2 \\
&= -(-2.96)/(2)(0.17) \\
&= 8.70
\end{aligned}
$$

This result can be derived by using elementary calculus.

11.4
PROBLEM DESCRIPTION: IS EQUAL INCREMENT IN ANXIETY LEVEL ASSOCIATED WITH CONSTANT DECREMENT IN PROBLEM-SOLVING PERFORMANCE?

Suppose that the theory described in Section 11.3 is challenged. The alternate theory offered is that the problem-solving time decrement will be the same for each unit-change in anxiety level over the entire range of anxiety-level scores. This is the linearity condition discussed in Chapter 6. We can investigate this theory by comparing the rate of performance change per unit of anxiety-test-score difference for any two arbitrarily chosen ranges of anxiety-score values.

The Hypothesis

$$\frac{\mathscr{E}(s_2) - \mathscr{E}(s_1)}{s_2 - s_1} = \frac{\mathscr{E}(s_4) - \mathscr{E}(s_3)}{s_4 - s_3} \qquad (11.5)$$

where s_i represents any four anxiety scores, and

$$s_1 < s_2 \quad \text{and} \quad s_3 < s_4$$

Definition of Vectors

The vectors are the same as those defined in Section 11.3.

The Full Model

We could use a mutually exclusive categorical model for our full model. This would give an analysis exactly like that in Chapter 6. However, in this example, we will use the second-degree model to illustrate the use of a different full model to test for *linearity*. The full model is

$$\mathbf{Y} = d_0\mathbf{U} + d_1\mathbf{S} + d_2\mathbf{S}^2 + \mathbf{E}^{(1)} \tag{11.6}$$

Note that $\mathbf{E}^{(1)}$ is used to designate the error vector, since this is the full model.

Implications of the Hypothesis

The restricted model is developed by substituting for the expected values in (11.5) the estimates from (11.6). We consider two ranges of anxiety, defined by four different anxiety-test scores (s_1, s_2, s_3, and s_4). The first range is defined by s_1 and s_2; the second by s_3 and s_4. We further assume that s_2 is greater than s_1, and s_4 is greater than s_3. Then the hypothesis can be expressed as

$$\frac{[d_0 + d_1(s_2) + d_2(s_2)^2] - [d_0 + d_1(s_1) + d_2(s_1)^2]}{(s_2 - s_1)}$$
$$= \frac{[d_0 + d_1(s_4) + d_2(s_4)^2] - [d_0 + d_1(s_3) + d_2(s_3)^2]}{(s_4 - s_3)}$$

or

$$\frac{d_1[s_2 - s_1] + d_2[(s_2)^2 - (s_1)^2]}{(s_2 - s_1)} = \frac{d_1[s_4 - s_3] + d_2[(s_4)^2 - (s_3)^2]}{(s_4 - s_3)}$$

Then

$$\frac{(s_2 - s_1)[d_1 + d_2(s_2 + s_1)]}{(s_2 - s_1)} = \frac{(s_4 - s_3)[d_1 + d_2(s_4 + s_3)]}{(s_4 - s_3)}$$

or

$$d_2[(s_2 + s_1) - (s_4 + s_3)] = 0$$

But, in general, $[(s_2 + s_1) - (s_4 + s_3)] \neq 0$. Thus, the hypothesis implies that $d_2 = 0$.

The Restricted Model

Imposing the restriction on model (11.6) gives

$$\mathbf{Y} = d_0\mathbf{U} + d_1\mathbf{S} + \mathbf{E}^{(2)}$$

Comparing the Models

The F value is

$$F = \frac{(q_r - q_f)/(n_f - n_r)}{q_f/(n - n_f)} = \frac{(q_2 - q_1)/(3 - 2)}{q_1/(n - 3)}$$

Comments

The solid straight line in Figure 11.4 is an illustration of a possible solution where

$$d_0 = 10.40$$

$$d_1 = -0.15$$

Note the difference between the two solid lines in Figure 11.4. Such a marked difference should lead to a large difference between q_1 and q_2 and a large F value.

11.5
PROBLEM DESCRIPTION: TEST FOR MAXIMUM OR MINIMUM AT A SPECIFIC POINT

Assume that in the study of problem-solving performance and anxiety (Sections 11.3 and 11.4) we hypothesize that the best problem-solving performance (minimum amount of time) is attained at a specific anxiety-score value (s_p).

Definition of Vectors

The vectors are the same as those defined in Section 11.4.

The Full Model

The full model is

$$\mathbf{Y} = d_0\mathbf{U} + d_1\mathbf{S} + d_2\mathbf{S}^2 + \mathbf{E}^{(1)} \tag{11.7}$$

Implications of the Hypothesis

Elementary calculus will show us that the maximum or minimum of a second-degree function is located at the point where the slope is equal to zero. The slope at any value such as s_p is given by

$$\text{Slope} = d_1 + 2d_2(s_p)$$

(s_p could be any specified value of anxiety score s, such as 12, 18, 15.6, etc.) Since our hypothesis is that at s_p the slope is equal to zero, the hypothesis can be written as

$$d_1 + 2d_2(s_p) = 0$$

or

$$d_1 = -2d_2(s_p)$$

The Restricted Model

Substitution of the above restriction into (11.7) yields

$$\mathbf{Y} = d_0\mathbf{U} + [-2d_2(s_p)]\mathbf{S} + d_2\mathbf{S}^2 + \mathbf{E}^{(2)}$$
$$\mathbf{Y} = d_0\mathbf{U} + d_2[\mathbf{S}^2 - (2s_p)\mathbf{S}] + \mathbf{E}^{(2)}$$

Comparing the Models

The F value is

$$F = \frac{(q_r - q_f)/(n_f - n_r)}{q_f/(n - n_f)} = \frac{(q_2 - q_1)/(3 - 2)}{q_1/(n - 3)}$$

Comments

The acceptance of this hypothesis indicates that we can reasonably conclude that a maximum or minimum expected problem-solving time occurs at an anxiety score of s_p. By examining the sign of d_2, we can determine if the value is a maximum or a minimum (in the full model). The value is

Maximum if $d_2 < 0$.

Minimum if $d_2 > 0$.

A rejection of the hypothesis leads to the inference that problem-solving time is neither maximum nor minimum at anxiety level s_p. The curved dashed line in Figure 11.4 is an example of a solution where s_p was specified to be 10, and

$$d_0 = 16.39$$
$$d_2 = 0.10$$

Note that the predicted time at anxiety score 10 is

$$d_0 + d_2(-10^2)$$
$$16.39 + 0.1(-100) = 6.39$$

11.6
PROBLEM DESCRIPTION: USE OF A
THIRD-DEGREE POLYNOMIAL FORM OVER
A RESTRICTED RANGE

The graphic representations of the curves shown in Section 11.2 suggest that the curves could be extended indefinitely. At first, this may seem to present a logical difficulty in applying polynomial forms to problems, when the range of scores is known to be restricted. Yet such restrictions exist in most situations. It is seldom possible for meaningful predictor values or meaningful values of the variable of interest (**Y**) to be outside certain ranges. Values outside a given range may be impossible to interpret. Negative values are sometimes meaningless. Moreover, the nature of the measures may be such as to place some limit on the values that can be observed. But these considerations do not automatically eliminate the possibility of using a polynomial form. As long as the investigator is aware that *a polynomial form stated to be characteristic of the relationship between the predictor and the variable of interest is applicable only to a specified range of values,* he need not reject its use.

An example is presented to illustrate the use of a third-degree polynomial over a specified range. Some theory might lead to the following hypothesized relationships.

1. As values of the predictor increase at the low end of the predictor range, the values of the variable of interest (**Y**) increase almost imperceptibly.
2. With further increases in the predictor values, the **Y** values increase rapidly.

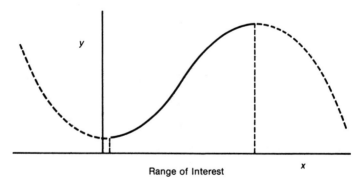

Range of Interest

FIG. 11.5 Example of a Third-Degree Polynomial with a Restricted Range of Interest.

3. As the predictor values approach the upper range limit, the increases in **Y** values taper off and finally become negligible.

A graphic representation of these characteristics is shown in a portion of the curve in Figure 11.5. Examination of Figure 11.5 shows a cubic (third degree) polynomial that has two changes of direction. The solid portion of the curve has the three hypothesized characteristics. The dotted part of the curve is outside the range of interest and is not essential.

We will now test this hypothesis on a set of data coming from a group of ordered categories. Assume that we wish to study typing performance as a function of hours of practice, and we wish to test the hypothesis that a cubic form adequately describes the relationship. We would proceed in a manner similar to that of Section 11.3.

The Hypothesis

$$\mathscr{E}(h_i) = d_0 + (h_i)d_1 + (h_i^2)d_2 + (h_i^3)d_3 \qquad (11.8)$$

where $\mathscr{E}(h_i)$ is the expected typing performance of an individual with h_i hours of practice.

Definition of Vectors

$\mathbf{Y}$ = vector of typing-performance scores.

$\mathbf{X}^{(i)}$ = 1 if the element in $\mathbf{Y}$ is from a person who practiced i hours; 0 otherwise $(i = 1, \ldots, k)$.

$\mathbf{H}$ = a vector of practice hours.

$\mathbf{H}^2 = \mathbf{H} * \mathbf{H}$ = a vector of squares of practice hours.

$\mathbf{H}^3 = \mathbf{H} * \mathbf{H} * \mathbf{H}$ = a vector of cubes of practice hours.

The Full Model

The full model is the mutually exclusive categorical model

$$\mathbf{Y} = a_1\mathbf{X}^{(1)} + a_2\mathbf{X}^{(2)} + \cdots + a_k\mathbf{X}^{(k)} + \mathbf{E}^{(1)} \qquad (11.9)$$

Implication of the Hypothesis

The restricted model can be derived by substituting for the expected values in (11.8) the estimates from (11.9).

$$a_i = d_0 + (h_i)d_1 + (h_i^2)d_2 + (h_i^3)d_3$$

where

h_i = the hours of practice associated with the ith-category hours of practice.

d_0, d_1, d_2, d_3 = unknown values to be estimated by the least-squares procedure.

The Restricted Model

Imposing these restrictions and simplifying gives

$$\mathbf{Y} = d_0 \mathbf{U} + d_1 \mathbf{H} + d_2 \mathbf{H}^2 + d_3 \mathbf{H}^3 + \mathbf{E}^{(2)}$$

Comparing the Models

The F value is

$$F = \frac{(q_2 - q_1)/(k - 4)}{q_1/(n - k)}$$

Comments

A rejection of the hypothesis would infer that this theory is erroneous. On the other hand, a failure to reject does not necessarily lead to the inference that the theory is correct. A simpler theory might adequately account for the data.

A possible solution that would lend support to the theory is shown by the solid curve in Figure 11.6, where

$$d_0 = 11.18$$
$$d_1 = -4.39$$
$$d_2 = 0.69$$
$$d_3 = -0.02$$

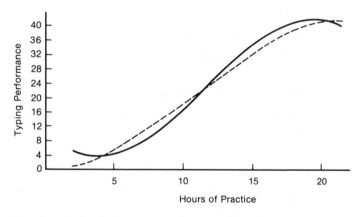

FIG. 11.6   Typing Performance as a Function of Practice.

11.7
PROBLEM DESCRIPTION: SIMPLIFYING
A MODEL INVOLVING A THIRD-DEGREE
POLYNOMIAL

In previous discussions, we have tried to indicate (by example) the delicate nature of the conflict that arises in searching for a model that can satisfactorily account for the data in a specified problem area. On the one hand, we are tempted to increase the complexity of the model to arrive at a more satisfactory account. On the other hand, we recognize that complex models entail a loss in parsimony, an increase in the difficulty of interpretation, and qualified conclusions. Moreover, conducting studies in problem areas requiring relatively complex models is usually more expensive. We must therefore search for ways of simplifying models that do not substantially impair their explanatory power.

In this book we have emphasized the simplification that results when certain regularity conditions involving linearity and lack of interaction exist. But there are many other conditions that can lead to model simplification. Consider, for example, the model involving a third-degree polynomial in Section 11.6. An examination of Figure 11.6 reveals that the slope of the line is relatively flat at low levels of practice. If we can show that a model that requires the slope to be equal to zero at a specified low level of practice (say h_p) is reasonable, then a simpler model is tenable in the sense that it has one less parameter. Intuitively, it seems reasonable to choose $h_p = 0$ as the specified low level of practice. The analysis is similar to that of Section 11.5.

Definition of Vectors

The vectors are the same as in Section 11.6.

The Full Model

The full model is the restricted model of Section 11.6.

$$\mathbf{Y} = d_0\mathbf{U} + d_1\mathbf{H} + d_2\mathbf{H}^2 + d_3\mathbf{H}^3 + \mathbf{E}^{(1)}$$

Note that the error vector for the model is called $\mathbf{E}^{(1)}$, since the model in this problem is used as a full model.

Implications of the Hypothesis

The hypothesis is that the slope of the curve is equal to zero at $h_p = 0$. The slope of the polynomial for any specific value (h_p) is

$$\text{Slope at } h_p = d_1 + 2d_2(h_p) + 3d_3(h_p)^2$$

and at $h_p = 0$

$$\text{Slope at } 0 = d_1 + 2d_2(0) + 3d_3(0)$$
$$= d_1$$

The hypothesis is that this slope is zero, or

$$d_1 = 0$$

The Restricted Model

The restricted model becomes

$$\mathbf{Y} = d_0 \mathbf{U} + d_2 \mathbf{H}^2 + d_3 \mathbf{H}^3 + \mathbf{E}^{(2)} \tag{11.10}$$

Comparing the Models

The F value is

$$F = \frac{(q_2 - q_1)/(4 - 3)}{q_1/(n - 4)}$$

Comments

We can observe from this example (and by reexamining the problem in Section 11.5) that the hypothesis that the slope of the curve is zero at a predictor value equal to zero can be tested by setting $d_1 = 0$.

The curve for the predicted values in the restricted model might look like the broken curve in Figure 11.6, where

$$d_0 = -0.25$$
$$d_2 = 0.27$$
$$d_3 = -0.01$$

It is quite likely that in some learning studies model (11.10) might reasonably be *assumed* to be a full model.

11.8
PROBLEM DESCRIPTION: DIFFERENT
SECOND-DEGREE POLYNOMIALS
FOR DIFFERENT RANGES

We will again examine the problem discussed in Section 10.4—this time testing to see if a second-degree polynomial is possible for each of the two educational ranges.

Definition of Vectors

$\mathbf{Y}$ = salaries earned at age 40.

$\mathbf{X}^{(i)}$ = 1 if the corresponding element in $\mathbf{Y}$ is from a person who has completed i years of education; 0 otherwise $(i = 1, 2, \ldots, 20)$.

$\mathbf{X}^{(1-11)}$ = 1 if the corresponding element of $\mathbf{Y}$ is associated with years of education 1 through 11; 0 otherwise $[\mathbf{X}^{(1-11)} = \mathbf{X}^{(1)} + \mathbf{X}^{(2)} + \cdots + \mathbf{X}^{(11)}]$.

$\mathbf{X}^{(12-20)}$ = 1 if the corresponding element of $\mathbf{Y}$ is associated with years of education 12 through 20; 0 otherwise $[\mathbf{X}^{(12-20)} = \mathbf{X}^{(12)} + \mathbf{X}^{(13)} + \cdots + \mathbf{X}^{(20)}]$.

$\mathbf{R}$ = the number of years of education associated with the corresponding element in $\mathbf{Y}$.

$\mathbf{R}^{(1-11)} = \mathbf{R} * \mathbf{X}^{(1-11)}$ = the direct product of $\mathbf{R}$ and $\mathbf{X}^{(1-11)}$.

$\mathbf{R}^{(12-20)} = \mathbf{R} * \mathbf{X}^{(12-20)}$ = the direct product of $\mathbf{R}$ and $\mathbf{X}^{(12-20)}$.

$[\mathbf{R}^{(1-11)}]^2 = \mathbf{R}^{(1-11)} * \mathbf{R}^{(1-11)}$ = a vector with elements equal to the squares of the elements of $\mathbf{R}^{(1-11)}$.

$[\mathbf{R}^{(12-20)}]^2 = \mathbf{R}^{(12-20)} * \mathbf{R}^{(12-20)}$ = a vector with elements equal to the squares of the elements of $\mathbf{R}^{(12-20)}$.

The Full Model

$$\mathbf{Y} = a_1\mathbf{X}^{(1)} + a_2\mathbf{X}^{(2)} + \cdots + a_{20}\mathbf{X}^{(20)} + \mathbf{E}^{(1)}$$

Implications of the Hypothesis

The hypothesis (similar to that in Section 10.4) for the range 1 through 11 is

$$a_1 = c_0 + (1)c_1 + (1)^2 c_2$$
$$a_2 = c_0 + (2)c_1 + (2)^2 c_2$$
$$\cdot \quad \cdot \quad \cdot$$
$$\cdot \quad \cdot \quad \cdot$$
$$\cdot \quad \cdot \quad \cdot$$
$$a_{11} = c_0 + (11)c_1 + (11)^2 c_2$$

and for education range 12 through 20, it is

$$a_{12} = d_0 + (12)d_1 + (12)^2 d_2$$
$$a_{13} = d_0 + (13)d_1 + (13)^2 d_2$$
$$\begin{matrix} \cdot & \cdot & \cdot \\ \cdot & \cdot & \cdot \\ \cdot & \cdot & \cdot \end{matrix}$$
$$a_{20} = d_0 + (20)d_1 + (20)^2 d_2$$

The Restricted Model

Substitution of these restrictions gives

$$\mathbf{Y} = c_0 \mathbf{X}^{(1-11)} + c_1 \mathbf{R}^{(1-11)} + c_2 [\mathbf{R}^{(1-11)}]^2$$
$$+ d_0 \mathbf{X}^{(12-20)} + d_1 \mathbf{R}^{(12-20)} + d_2 [\mathbf{R}^{(12-20)}]^2 + \mathbf{E}^{(2)}$$

Comparison of the Models

The F value is

$$F = \frac{(q_2 - q_1)/(k - 6)}{q_1/(n - k)}$$

Comments

A possible graph of the predicted $\mathbf{Y}$ values from the restricted model is shown in Figure 11.7. The graph represents the following solution:

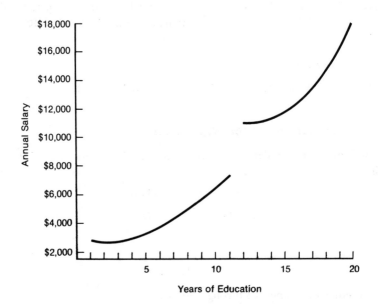

FIG. 11.7   Annual Salary as a Function of Education over Two Ranges.

$$c_0 = 28.62$$
$$c_1 = -1.73$$
$$c_2 = 0.53$$
$$d_0 = 324.92$$
$$d_1 = -33.83$$
$$d_2 = 1.33$$

11.9
PROBLEM DESCRIPTION: DISCONTINUITY
BETWEEN TWO SECOND-DEGREE POLYNOMIALS

We will now consider a problem similar to the one in Section 10.5, except here we will assume a second-degree model (as we did in Section 11.8). The hypothesis in Section 10.5 was that the salary increment in going from the eleventh to twelfth years of education is the same as the salary change expected between any other adjacent year of education in the entire range. In this problem we will observe that there is not a constant change in salary for each year of education from 1 through 11 years nor a constant change in salary from 12 through 20 years. As a result of using a model that has a changing increment in salary (shown in Figure 11.7), we must express our problem in a slightly different form. In natural language, the question is: "Did something special happen in going from the eleventh to twelfth year of education?" A possible argument for developing a restricted model can be devised.

We might say that "nothing unusual occurs"—if the expected salary for 12 years of education, using the prediction system for the 1 through 11 range of education, is equal to the expected salary for 12 years of education, using the prediction system for the 12 through 20 range of education, and if the expected salary for 11 years of education, using the prediction system for the 1 through 11 range of education, is equal to the expected salary for 11 years of education, using the prediction system for the 12 through 20 range of education.

Definition of Vectors
The vectors are the same as in Section 11.8.

The Full Model
The full model will be the restricted model of Section 11.8.

$$\mathbf{Y} = c_0 \mathbf{X}^{(1-11)} + c_1 \mathbf{R}^{(1-11)} + c_2 [\mathbf{R}^{(1-11)}]^2$$
$$+ d_0 \mathbf{X}^{(12-20)} + d_1 \mathbf{R}^{(12-20)} + d_2 [\mathbf{R}^{(12-20)}]^2 + \mathbf{E}^{(1)} \qquad (11.11)$$

Note that the error vector for this model is designated $\mathbf{E}^{(1)}$, instead of $\mathbf{E}^{(2)}$ as it was in Section 11.8, because it is used in a full model.

Implications of the Hypothesis

Consider the following expected values and their estimates from (11.11).

1. Expected salary for 12 years of education, using the prediction system for the range 1 through 11, is

$$\mathscr{E}[12, (1{-}11)] = c_0 + c_1(12) + c_2(12)^2$$

2. Expected salary for 12 years of education, using the prediction system for the range 12 through 20, is

$$\mathscr{E}[12, (12{-}20)] = d_0 + d_1(12) + d_2(12)^2$$

3. Expected salary for 11 years of education, using the prediction system for the range 1 through 11, is

$$\mathscr{E}[11, (1{-}11)] = c_0 + c_1(11) + c_2(11)^2$$

4. Expected salary for 11 years of education, using the prediction system for the range 12 through 20, is

$$\mathscr{E}[11, (12{-}20)] = d_0 + d_1(11) + d_2(11)^2$$

The hypothesis can then be expressed as

$$\mathscr{E}[12, (1{-}11)] = \mathscr{E}[12, (12{-}20)]$$

and

$$\mathscr{E}[11, (1{-}11)] = \mathscr{E}[11, (12{-}20)]$$

$$c_0 + c_1(12) + c_2(12)^2 = d_0 + d_1(12) + d_2(12)^2 \tag{11.12}$$

$$c_0 + c_1(11) + c_2(11)^2 = d_0 + d_1(11) + d_2(11)^2 \tag{11.13}$$

But, in order to simplify the substitution, we first take the difference between the two equalities.

$$c_1(12{-}11) + c_2[(12)^2 - (11)^2] = d_1(12{-}11) + d_2[(12)^2 - (11)^2]$$

$$c_1 + (23)c_2 = d_1 + (23)d_2 \tag{11.14}$$

Next, multiply (11.12) by 11 and (11.13) by 12, obtaining

$$11c_0 + c_1(11)(12) + c_2(11)(12)^2 = 11d_0 + d_1(11)(12) + d_2(11)(12)^2 \tag{11.15}$$

$$12c_0 + c_1(12)(11) + c_2(12)(11)^2 = 12d_0 + d_1(12)(11) + d_2(12)(11)^2 \tag{11.16}$$

Then, subtraction of (11.15) from (11.16) gives

$$c_0 + (11)(12)c_2(11{-}12) = d_0 + (11)(12)d_2(11{-}12)$$

$$c_0 - (132)c_2 = d_0 - (132)d_2 \tag{11.17}$$

Summarizing the restrictions from (11.14) and (11.17) gives

$$c_1 = d_1 + (23)d_2 - (23)c_2$$
$$c_0 = d_0 - (132)d_2 + (132)c_2$$

The Restricted Model

Substitution of these restrictions gives

$$\begin{aligned}
\mathbf{Y} = &\; [d_0 - (132)d_2 + (132)c_2]\mathbf{X}^{(1-11)} \\
&+ [d_1 + (23)d_2 - (23)c_2]\mathbf{R}^{(1-11)} \\
&+ c_2[\mathbf{R}^{(1-11)}]^2 + d_0\mathbf{X}^{(12-20)} \\
&+ d_1\mathbf{R}^{(12-20)} + d_2[\mathbf{R}^{(12-20)}]^2 + \mathbf{E}^{(2)} \\
\mathbf{Y} = &\; c_2[132\mathbf{X}^{(1-11)} - 23\mathbf{R}^{(1-11)} + (\mathbf{R}^{(1-11)})^2] \\
&+ d_0[\mathbf{X}^{(1-11)} + \mathbf{X}^{(12-20)}] + d_1[\mathbf{R}^{(1-11)} + \mathbf{R}^{(12-20)}] \\
&+ d_2[-132\mathbf{X}^{(1-11)} + 23\mathbf{R}^{(1-11)} + (\mathbf{R}^{(12-20)})^2] + \mathbf{E}^{(2)}
\end{aligned}$$

Simplifying provides the restricted model

$$\begin{aligned}
\mathbf{Y} = &\; c_2[132\mathbf{X}^{(1-11)} - 23\mathbf{R}^{(1-11)} + (\mathbf{R}^{(1-11)})^2] + d_0\mathbf{U} + d_1\mathbf{R} \\
&+ d_2[-132\mathbf{X}^{(1-11)} + 23\mathbf{R}^{(1-11)} + (\mathbf{R}^{(12-20)})^2] + \mathbf{E}^{(2)}
\end{aligned} \quad (11.18)$$

The required vectors can easily be generated by using the DATRAN subroutine described in Chapter 15.

Comparison of the Models

The F value is

$$F = \frac{(q_2 - q_1)/(6 - 4)}{q_1/(n - 6)}$$

Comments

Assuming that the full model produced the results shown in Figure 11.7, a possible result for the restricted model might look like Figure 11.8, where

$$d_0 = -53.62$$
$$d_1 = 12.76$$
$$c_2 = 0.54$$
$$d_2 = -0.07$$

The solid curve represents the two intersecting curves, and the broken curves represent extrapolations of these two curves.

Note that the implication (11.14)

$$c_1 + 23c_2 = d_1 + 23d_2$$

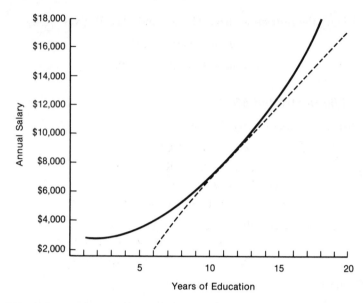

FIG. 11.8   Estimated Expected Values from Model (11.18).

is the hypothesis that states: the slope of the prediction system 1 through 11 at education 11.5 is equal to the slope of the prediction system 12 through 20 at education 11.5.[1] This can be observed because the slope at 11.5, using prediction system 1 through 11, is

$$c_1 + 2c_2(11.5) = c_1 + 23c_2$$

and the slope at 11.5, using prediction system for years 12 through 20, is

$$d_1 + 2d_2(11.5) = d_1 + 23d_2$$

Verification of the Restricted Model

It is not necessarily obvious that model (11.18) has the properties implied by the hypothesis. If any doubt exists, you should always verify the model, using the procedure described in Sections 6.6 and 9.5. We find that by using model (11.18),

$$\left.\begin{array}{l}\text{Predicted score at educational} \\ \text{level 12, using prediction sys-} \\ \text{tem for years 1 through 11.}\end{array}\right\} = \left\{\begin{array}{l}\text{Predicted score at educational} \\ \text{level 12, using prediction sys-} \\ \text{tem for years 12 through 20.}\end{array}\right.$$

---

[1]The concepts that produced these slopes are based on calculus; however it is not necessary in this discussion to understand how these slopes were obtained.

$$c_2[(132)(1) - (23)(12) + (12)^2]$$
$$+ d_0(1) + d_1(12) + d_2[(-132) + (23)(12)]$$
$$= d_0(1) + d_1(12) + d_2(12)^2$$
$$c_2(132 - 276 + 144) + d_0 + d_1(12) + d_2(144)$$
$$= d_0 + d_1(12) + d_2(144)$$
$$d_0 + d_1(12) + d_2(144)$$
$$= d_0 + d_1(12) + d_2(144)$$

Again, using (11.18), we find that

Predicted score at educational level 11, using prediction system for years 1 through 11. $\bigg\} = \bigg\{$ Predicted score at educational level 11, using prediction system for years 12 through 20.

$$c_2[(132)(1) - (23)(11) + (11)^2]$$
$$+ d_0(1) + d_1(11) + d_2[(-132) + (23)(11)]$$
$$= d_0(1) + d_1(11) + d_2(11)^2$$
$$c_2(132 - 253 + 121) + d_0 + d_1(11) + d_2(121)$$
$$= d_0 + d_1(11) + d_2(121)$$
$$d_0 + d_1(11) + d_2(121)$$
$$= d_0 + d_1(11) + d_2(121)$$

Observe that we have fitted two second-degree polynomials over two different ranges and that these two polynomials intersect at two points—years of education equal to 12 and to 11.

11.10
PROBLEM DESCRIPTION: ANOTHER DEFINITION OF CHANGE BETWEEN TWO SECOND-DEGREE POLYNOMIALS

We will now consider another approach to the "nothing-unusual-occurs" hypothesis, mentioned in Section 11.9. We might choose to say that "nothing unusual occurs" if two conditions are satisfied. First, the expected salary for 11.5 years of education, using the prediction system for the 1 through 11 range of education, is equal to the expected salary for 11.5 years of education, using the prediction system for the 12 through 20 range of education. Secondly, the amount of change in salary earned per year of education (the slope) at 11.5 years of education, using the 1 through 11 polynomial form, is equal to the amount of change in salary earned per years of education (the slope) at 11.5 years of education, using the 12 through 20 range polynomial form.

Definition of Vectors

The vectors are the same as in Sections 11.8 and 11.9.

The Full Model

The full model is the same as in Section 11.9.

$$\mathbf{Y} = c_0 \mathbf{X}^{(1-11)} + c_1 \mathbf{R}^{(1-11)} + c_2 [\mathbf{R}^{(1-11)}]^2$$
$$+ d_0 \mathbf{X}^{(12-20)} + d_1 \mathbf{R}^{(12-20)} + d_2 [\mathbf{R}^{(12-20)}]^2 + \mathbf{E}^{(1)} \qquad (11.19)$$

Implications of the Hypothesis

The hypothesis can be expressed as it was in Section 11.9.

$$\mathscr{E}[11.5, (1\text{–}11)] = \mathscr{E}[11.5, (12\text{–}20)]$$

Substituting the estimates from (11.19) yields

$$c_0 + c_1(11.5) + c_2(11.5)^2 = d_0 + d_1(11.5) + d_2(11.5)^2 \qquad (11.20)$$

And the requirement that the slopes be equal at 11.5 is given by

$$c_1 + 2c_2(11.5) = d_1 + 2d_2(11.5)$$

or

$$c_1 + 23c_2 = d_1 + 23d_2 \qquad (11.21)$$

We observed in Section 11.9 that the hypothesis implied this same restriction—the slopes of the two different prediction systems are equal at 11.5 years of education. Now multiply (11.21) by 11.5, and subtract the result from (11.20).

$$c_0 + c_1(11.5) + c_2(11.5)^2 = d_0 + d_1(11.5) + d_2(11.5)^2$$
$$(11.5)c_1 + (11.5)(23)c_2 = (11.5)d_1 + (11.5)(23)d_2$$

Subtraction gives

$$c_0 + c_2(11.5)(11.5 - 23) = d_0 + d_2(11.5)(11.5 - 23)$$

or

$$c_0 - (132.25)c_2 = d_0 - (132.25)d_2 \qquad (11.22)$$

Summarizing the restrictions from (11.21) and (11.22) gives

$$c_1 = d_1 + 23d_2 - 23c_2$$
$$c_0 = d_0 - (132.25)d_2 + (132.25)c_2$$

The Restricted Model

Substitution of these restrictions produces a model very similar to the one in Section 11.9.

$$\mathbf{Y} = c_2[132.25\mathbf{X}^{(1-11)} - 23\mathbf{R}^{(1-11)} + (\mathbf{R}^{(1-11)})^2] + d_0\mathbf{U} + d_1\mathbf{R}$$
$$+ d_2[-132.25\mathbf{X}^{(1-11)} + 23\mathbf{R}^{(1-11)} + (\mathbf{R}^{(12-20)})^2] + \mathbf{E}^{(2)} \qquad (11.23)$$

Note that this model has 132.25, where model (11.18) has 132.

Comparison of the Models

The F value is

$$F = \frac{(q_2 - q_1)/(6 - 4)}{q_1/(n - 6)}$$

Comments

Assuming that the full model yielded a graph similar to Figure 11.7, the restricted model would produce a configuration very similar to Figure 11.8. Furthermore, the restriction is closely related to the mathematical concept of continuity, and the hypothesis can be expressed in a general form.

Let

$\mathbf{X}^{(1)} = 1$ if an element in $\mathbf{Y}$ is in the *first* range of points; 0 otherwise.

$\mathbf{X}^{(2)} = 1$ if an element in $\mathbf{Y}$ is in the *second* range of points; 0 otherwise.

$\mathbf{R} =$ the coded vector (e.g., years of education).

$\mathbf{R}^{(1)} = \mathbf{R} * \mathbf{X}^{(1)}$.

$\mathbf{R}^{(2)} = \mathbf{R} * \mathbf{X}^{(2)}$.

And let r_p be the value of the coded vector for which we hypothesize:

1. The predicted values of $\mathbf{Y}$ from the two different equations are equal.
2. The slopes of the two predictor equations are equal.

The full model is

$$\mathbf{Y} = c_0\mathbf{X}^{(1)} + c_1\mathbf{R}^{(1)} + c_2[\mathbf{R}^{(1)}]^2 + d_0\mathbf{X}^{(2)} + d_1\mathbf{R}^{(2)} + d_2[\mathbf{R}^{(2)}]^2 + \mathbf{E}^{(1)}$$

and the restricted model is

$$\mathbf{Y} = b_0\mathbf{U} + b_1\mathbf{R} + b_2[(\mathbf{R}^{(1)})^2 - 2(r_p)\mathbf{R}^{(1)} + (r_p)^2\mathbf{X}^{(1)}]$$
$$+ b_3[(\mathbf{R}^{(2)})^2 - 2(r_p)\mathbf{R}^{(2)} + (r_p)^2\mathbf{X}^{(2)}] + \mathbf{E}^{(2)}$$

The vectors needed in these two models can be generated by using the DATRAN subroutine, described in Chapter 15.

The distinction between Sections 11.9 and 11.10 is primarily a different operational definition or translation of the natural language term *unusual*. Although in this particular problem it would probably make very little difference whether (11.17) or (11.22) was used as the restricted model, the point is that different conclusions might be reached, depending on how *unusual* is defined.

11.11
PROBLEM DESCRIPTION: DOES CHANGE OCCUR IMMEDIATELY FOLLOWING AN INNOVATION?

In this problem we will assume that an extensive advertising campaign has been introduced to discourage cigarette smoking. We want to determine if the cigarette sales in the year immediately following the beginning of the advertising campaign deviates from the trend of cigarette sales. (The data is illustrated in Figure 11.9.)

We will assume that the campaign starts at year 10, and we will therefore want to test the hypothesis that the sales of year 11 are on the extrapolated sales curve.

Definition of Vectors

Assuming that a second-degree polynomial fits the data of years 1 through 10, we define

$$X^{(1-10)} = 1 \text{ if the sales value in } Y \text{ is associated with any year 1 through 10; 0 otherwise.}$$

$$R = \text{year of sales (elements of } R \text{ have values } 1, 2, \ldots, 11).$$

$$R^2 = \text{square of year of sales (elements of } R^2 \text{ have values } 1, 4, \ldots, 121).$$

$$R^{(1-10)} = R * X^{(1-10)} = \text{year of sales if year is } 1, 2, \ldots, 10; 0 \text{ otherwise.}$$

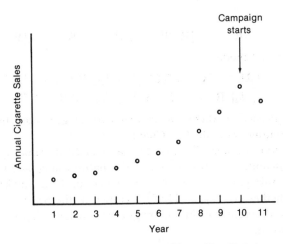

FIG. 11.9 Annual Cigarette Sales over an Eleven Year Period.

$[\mathbf{R}^{(1-10)}]^2 = \mathbf{R}^2 * \mathbf{X}^{(1-10)} =$ square of year of sales if year is 1, 2, ..., 10; 0 otherwise.

$\mathbf{X}^{(11)} = 1$ if the sales value in $\mathbf{Y}$ comes from year 11; 0 otherwise.

The Full Model

The full model is

$$\mathbf{Y} = a_1\mathbf{X}^{(1-10)} + a_2\mathbf{R}^{(1-10)} + a_3[\mathbf{R}^{(1-10)}]^2 + a_4\mathbf{X}^{(11)} + \mathbf{E}^{(1)}$$

The least-squares value for a_4 is equal to the observed $\mathbf{Y}$ value at year 11.

Implications of the Hypothesis

The hypothesis is that the expected value at the eleventh year is equal to the expected value using the extrapolated trend line. Thus the expected value at the eleventh year is estimated by

$$a_4$$

and the expected value at the eleventh year using the trend line is estimated by

$$a_1 + a_2(11) + a_3(11)^2$$

Then the hypothesis can be expressed as

$$a_4 = a_1 + a_2(11) + a_3(11)^2$$

The Restricted Model

This restriction gives

$$\mathbf{Y} = a_1\mathbf{X}^{(1-10)} + a_2\mathbf{R}^{(1-10)} + a_3[\mathbf{R}^{(1-10)}]^2$$
$$+ [a_1 + a_2(11) + a_3(11)^2]\mathbf{X}^{(11)} + \mathbf{E}^{(2)}$$
$$\mathbf{Y} = a_1[\mathbf{X}^{(1-10)} + \mathbf{X}^{(11)}] + a_2[\mathbf{R}^{(1-10)} + 11\mathbf{X}^{(11)}]$$
$$+ a_3[(\mathbf{R}^{(1-10)})^2 + (11)^2\mathbf{X}^{(11)}] + \mathbf{E}^{(2)}$$

But

$$\mathbf{X}^{(1-10)} + \mathbf{X}^{(11)} = \mathbf{U}$$
$$\mathbf{R}^{(1-10)} + 11\mathbf{X}^{(11)} = \mathbf{R}$$
$$[\mathbf{R}^{(1-10)}]^2 + [(11)^2\mathbf{X}^{(11)}] = \mathbf{R}^2$$

Therefore, the restricted model is

$$\mathbf{Y} = a_1\mathbf{U} + a_2\mathbf{R} + a_3\mathbf{R}^2 + \mathbf{E}^{(2)}$$

This restricted model has given up information that distinguishes the eleventh year from all others.

Comparison of the Models

The F value is

$$F = \frac{(q_2 - q_1)/(4 - 3)}{q_1/(n - 4)}$$

Comments

This type of analysis might be useful in a wide variety of situations in which some new method has been introduced to a particular group. In such situations, there would be no "control group" for comparison. This approach could be used when new laws are introduced into the total community or new procedures are used in an entire school.

From a technical viewpoint, the use of the F value as a decision rule for this problem could be criticized. The use of F requires the assumption (see Appendix B) that the $\mathbf{Y}$ observations are randomly selected values from specified populations. In this problem the values in $\mathbf{Y}$ are actually parameter values, except perhaps for measurement error. In other words, the value in $\mathbf{Y}$ associated with the ith year is actually the number of cigarettes sold in the ith year—not a random observation from a distribution of values. On the other hand, it is not at all clear what value of a_4 would be required to defend the conclusion that the advertising had some impact on cigarette smoking. The advertising campaign either did or did not have an *impact* on cigarette sales, but even if the value of a_4 were *substantially* lower than the value predicted from the trend line, the result might have been *caused* by something other than the campaign. As a result, any conclusion may be in error no matter what decision rule is used. Despite the shaky statistical base, one possibility would be to conclude that the campaign was effective if the probability value associated with the F value is *small*.

These reservations about the use of F are also relevant to the next problem.

11.12
PROBLEM DESCRIPTION: DETECTION
OF OSCILLATION

An extension of the model in Section 11.11 can be used to determine if several expected values lay on an extrapolated trend. For example, assume that a person is resting quietly and that a series of five blood-pressure readings are taken at times 1, 2, 3, 4, and 5. Then a loud noise is produced, and the blood pressure is recorded at times 6, 7, and 8. We want to determine if the expected values at 6, 7, and 8 are equal to the expected values from

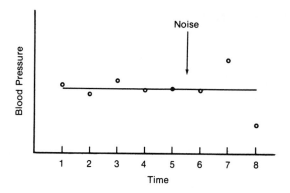

FIG. 11.10   Recorded Blood Pressure over an Eight Interval Time Period.

extrapolation of the blood-pressure level prior to the noise. (We will assume that the pre-noise data lay on a horizontal line; see Fig. 11.10).

Definition of Vectors

$\mathbf{X}^{(1-5)} = 1$ if the blood pressures were recorded during time 1 through 5; 0 otherwise.

$\mathbf{X}^{(6)} = 1$ if the blood pressure was observed at time 6; 0 otherwise.

$\mathbf{X}^{(7)} = 1$ if the blood pressure was observed at time 7; 0 otherwise.

$\mathbf{X}^{(8)} = 1$ if the blood pressure was observed at time 8; 0 otherwise.

The Full Model

The full model is

$$\mathbf{Y} = a_0\mathbf{X}^{(1-5)} + a_6\mathbf{X}^{(6)} + a_7\mathbf{X}^{(7)} + a_8\mathbf{X}^{(8)} + \mathbf{E}^{(1)}$$

The least-squares value for a_0 is the average of the five elements of $\mathbf{Y}$ associated with times 1 through 5. The least-squares values for a_6, a_7, and a_8 are the $\mathbf{Y}$ elements associated with times 6, 7, and 8, respectively.

Implications of the Hypothesis

Time	Expected Pressure	Extrapolated Value
6	a_6	a_0
7	a_7	a_0
8	a_8	a_0

The hypothesis is

$$a_6 = a_7 = a_8 = a_0$$

The Restricted Model

Substitution of the restrictions gives

$$\mathbf{Y} = a_0 \mathbf{X}^{(1-5)} + a_0 \mathbf{X}^{(6)} + a_0 \mathbf{X}^{(7)} + a_0 \mathbf{X}^{(8)} + \mathbf{E}^{(2)}$$

$$\mathbf{Y} = a_0 [\mathbf{X}^{(1-5)} + \mathbf{X}^{(6)} + \mathbf{X}^{(7)} + \mathbf{X}^{(8)}] + \mathbf{E}^{(2)}$$

or

$$\mathbf{Y} = a_0 \mathbf{U} + \mathbf{E}^{(2)}$$

Comparison of the Models

The F value is

$$F = \frac{(q_2 - q_1)/(4 - 1)}{q_1/(n - 4)}$$

Comments

A test made at only one time—time 6—(see the problem in Section 11.11) would not have detected a change. Furthermore, if we had tested to see whether the horizontal line before time 6 was the same as *another* horizontal line fitting the three data values (times 6, 7, and 8), we would have detected no change. That is, if we had used the full model

$$\mathbf{Y} = a_0 \mathbf{X}^{(1-5)} + b_0 \mathbf{X}^{(6-8)} + \mathbf{E}$$

where $\mathbf{X}^{(6-8)} = \mathbf{X}^{(6)} + \mathbf{X}^{(7)} + \mathbf{X}^{(8)}$, and tested the hypothesis $a_0 = b_0$, we would not reject it.

11.13
OTHER FUNCTIONAL FORMS

The models in this chapter should not necessarily be regarded as the most appropriate ones for the specific problems discussed. Rather, they should be regarded as examples of a way of thinking about particular problems. Moreover, it should be obvious that an unlimited number of example applications could be discussed and that any particular selection is arbitrary.

An important class of problems that we have not discussed involves the definition of vectors whose elements are not powers but *some other function* of elements in other vectors. For example, suppose x_i is an element of a predictor vector $\mathbf{X}$ and w_i is the corresponding element of another vector $\mathbf{W}$, generated by some rule of correspondence. The following list contains a few examples[2]

---

[2]Additional examples can be found in a U.S. Forest Service research paper by Freese (1964).

of the many ways in which a rule of correspondence might be defined between an element of **W** and the corresponding element of **X**.

$$w_i = \sqrt{x_i}$$

$$w_i = 1/x_i$$

$$w_i = \cos x_i$$

$$w_i = k^{x_i} \qquad \text{(where } k \text{ is some constant)}$$

$$w_i = \log x_i$$

12

Applications to Two-Attribute Problems

12.1
PROBLEM DESCRIPTION: ESTIMATION
OF UNAVAILABLE CENSUS DATA FROM
ADJACENT CENSUS TRACTS

12.1
PROBLEM DESCRIPTION: ESTIMATION
OF UNAVAILABLE CENSUS DATA FROM
ADJACENT CENSUS TRACTS

Assume that the years of formal education attained by all males over 30 years of age have been collected for a random sample of males in *eight* census tracts (represented by the check marks in this array).

Column

		1	2	3	4
R	1	✓	✓		✓
o	2		✓	✓	
w	3	✓		✓	✓

Assume also that no information is available from the unchecked census tracts, due to lack of money and/or time. We now want to estimate the expected years of formal eduction attained by males over 30 for the missing tracts.

In order to discuss the expected values, we will use $\mathscr{E}(11)$ to represent the expected value of education for row 1, column 1, and similar notation for all other known tracts. Note that information is available to estimate directly $\mathscr{E}(11)$, $\mathscr{E}(12)$, $\mathscr{E}(14)$, $\mathscr{E}(22)$, $\mathscr{E}(23)$, $\mathscr{E}(31)$, $\mathscr{E}(33)$, and $\mathscr{E}(34)$. We will use $\mathscr{M}(13)$ to represent the expected value for the missing tract in row 1, column 3, and similar notation for the other missing tracts. Note, however, that we do not have direct estimates for $\mathscr{M}(13)$, $\mathscr{M}(21)$, $\mathscr{M}(24)$, and $\mathscr{M}(32)$.

Now recall Chapter 7 in which the hypothesis of no interaction between two attributes was discussed. If no interaction exists, it might be possible to obtain a reasonable estimate for the missing information. The hypothesis of no interaction could be expressed as

$$\mathscr{E}(11) - \mathscr{E}(31) = \mathscr{E}(12) - \mathscr{M}(32)$$
$$= \mathscr{M}(13) - \mathscr{E}(33) = \mathscr{E}(14) - \mathscr{E}(34) \tag{12.1}$$

$$\mathscr{E}(11) - \mathscr{M}(21) = \mathscr{E}(12) - \mathscr{E}(22)$$
$$= \mathscr{M}(13) - \mathscr{E}(23) = \mathscr{E}(14) - \mathscr{M}(24) \tag{12.2}$$

Column

		1	2	3	4
R	1	$\mathscr{E}(11)$	$\mathscr{E}(12)$	$\mathscr{M}(13)$	$\mathscr{E}(14)$
o	2	$\mathscr{M}(21)$	$\mathscr{E}(22)$	$\mathscr{E}(23)$	$\mathscr{M}(24)$
w	3	$\mathscr{E}(31)$	$\mathscr{M}(32)$	$\mathscr{E}(33)$	$\mathscr{E}(34)$

If this hypothesis is true, then the unknown expected values could be estimated as

$$\mathscr{M}(13) = \mathscr{E}(12) - \mathscr{E}(22) + \mathscr{E}(23)$$
$$\mathscr{M}(21) = \mathscr{E}(11) - \mathscr{E}(12) + \mathscr{E}(22)$$
$$\mathscr{M}(24) = \mathscr{E}(14) - \mathscr{E}(12) + \mathscr{E}(22) \tag{12.3}$$
$$\mathscr{M}(32) = \mathscr{E}(12) - \mathscr{E}(11) + \mathscr{E}(31)$$

Now examine the implications that the hypothesis of no interaction (12.1) and (12.2) has on the expected values for which estimates can be obtained. From (12.1) we observe that

$$\mathscr{E}(11) - \mathscr{E}(31) = \mathscr{E}(14) - \mathscr{E}(34) \tag{12.4}$$

and by subtracting (12.2) from (12.1), we observe that

$$[\mathscr{E}(11) - \mathscr{E}(31)] - [\mathscr{E}(12) - \mathscr{E}(22)] = [\mathscr{M}(13) - \mathscr{E}(33)]$$
$$- [\mathscr{M}(13) - \mathscr{E}(23)]$$

or

$$\mathscr{E}(11) - \mathscr{E}(31) = \mathscr{E}(12) - \mathscr{E}(22) + \mathscr{E}(23) - \mathscr{E}(33) \tag{12.5}$$

These implications can be arrayed as

Column

		1	2	3	4
R	1	$\mathscr{E}(11)$	$\mathscr{E}(12)$		$\mathscr{E}(14)$
o	2		$\mathscr{E}(22)$	$\mathscr{E}(23)$	
w	3	$\mathscr{E}(31)$		$\mathscr{E}(33)$	$\mathscr{E}(34)$

If (12.1) and (12.2) are true, then (12.4) and (12.5) are necessarily true. But, although (12.4) and (12.5) are true, we cannot say for sure that all of the other statements in (12.1) and (12.2) are true. However, if we can accept (12.4) and (12.5), we will feel more confident in our estimation of the missing census data.

Definition of Vectors

Let

Y = years of formal education attained by the sampled males.

$X^{(i,j)}$ = 1 if the element in Y is from the tract indicated as row i and column j; 0 otherwise.

$R^{(i)}$ = 1 if the element in Y is from a tract in row i; 0 otherwise.

$C^{(j)}$ = 1 if the element in Y is from a tract in column j; 0 otherwise.

The Full Model

The full model is

$$Y = a_{11}X^{(11)} + a_{12}X^{(12)} + a_{14}X^{(14)} + a_{22}X^{(22)} + a_{23}X^{(23)}$$
$$+ a_{31}X^{(31)} + a_{33}X^{(33)} + a_{34}X^{(34)} + E^{(1)} \tag{12.6}$$

Implications of the Hypothesis

Observing the hypothesis expressed as (12.4) and (12.5) and substituting for the expected values their estimates from (12.6), we can write

$$\mathscr{E}(11) - \mathscr{E}(31) = \mathscr{E}(14) - \mathscr{E}(34)$$
$$a_{11} - a_{31} = a_{14} - a_{34} \tag{12.7}$$

and

$$\mathscr{E}(11) - \mathscr{E}(31) = \mathscr{E}(12) - \mathscr{E}(22) + \mathscr{E}(23) - \mathscr{E}(33)$$
$$a_{11} - a_{31} = a_{12} - a_{22} + a_{23} - a_{33} \tag{12.8}$$

The Restricted Model

As we have pointed out in previous discussions, the restrictions implied by a hypothesis can usually be imposed in more than one way. The appearance of the restricted model will depend on the way the restrictions are imposed, but if no algebraic errors are made, the resulting model should have the appropriate properties, which are verifiable. Although it will not affect the conclusions that are drawn, there may be advantages in imposing the restrictions in a particular way. To demonstrate this point, we will create two equivalent restricted models by imposing the restrictions in different ways.

The restrictions in (12.7) and (12.8) can be written as

$$a_{14} = a_{11} - a_{31} + a_{34}$$

$$a_{12} = a_{11} - a_{31} + a_{22} - a_{23} + a_{33}$$

and imposed by direct substitution.

$$\mathbf{Y} = a_{11}\mathbf{X}^{(11)} + (a_{11} - a_{31} + a_{22} - a_{23} + a_{33})\mathbf{X}^{(12)}$$
$$+ (a_{11} - a_{31} + a_{34})\mathbf{X}^{(14)} + a_{22}\mathbf{X}^{(22)} + a_{23}\mathbf{X}^{(23)}$$
$$+ a_{31}\mathbf{X}^{(31)} + a_{33}\mathbf{X}^{(33)} + a_{34}\mathbf{X}^{(34)} + \mathbf{E}^{(2)}$$

Collecting terms yields

$$\mathbf{Y} = a_{11}[\mathbf{X}^{(11)} + \mathbf{X}^{(12)} + \mathbf{X}^{(14)}] + a_{22}[\mathbf{X}^{(22)} + \mathbf{X}^{(12)}]$$
$$+ a_{23}[\mathbf{X}^{(23)} - \mathbf{X}^{(12)}] + a_{31}[\mathbf{X}^{(31)} - \mathbf{X}^{(12)} - \mathbf{X}^{(14)}] \quad (12.9)$$
$$+ a_{33}[\mathbf{X}^{(33)} + \mathbf{X}^{(12)}] + a_{34}[\mathbf{X}^{(34)} + \mathbf{X}^{(14)}] + \mathbf{E}^{(2)}$$

Verification of (12.9) will show that it has the desired properties, but it is not so easy to see what expression should be used to estimate the expected values $\mathscr{M}(13)$, $\mathscr{M}(21)$, $\mathscr{M}(24)$, and $\mathscr{M}(32)$. Recall that if the hypothesis is true, we can claim the following relationship to be tenable.

$$\mathscr{M}(13) = \mathscr{E}(12) - \mathscr{E}(22) + \mathscr{E}(23)$$

Using (12.9), $\mathscr{E}(12)$ is estimated by

$$a_{11} + a_{22} - a_{23} - a_{31} + a_{33}$$

$\mathscr{E}(22)$ is estimated by

$$a_{22}$$

and $\mathscr{E}(23)$ is estimated by

$$a_{23}$$

Therefore, $\mathscr{M}(13)$ can be estimated by

$$a_{11} + a_{22} - a_{23} - a_{31} + a_{33} - a_{22} + a_{23}$$

which simplifies to

$$a_{11} - a_{31} + a_{33}$$

The other missing values in (12.3) can be estimated by following the same logic.

This kind of argument can be considerably shortened if the restrictions are rewritten in a different form before they are imposed on the full model. Consider the expressions

$$a_{11} = b_1 + d_1$$
$$a_{12} = b_1 + d_2$$
$$a_{14} = b_1$$
$$a_{22} = b_2 + d_2$$
$$a_{23} = b_2 + d_3 \qquad (12.10)$$
$$a_{31} = b_3 + d_1$$
$$a_{33} = b_3 + d_3$$
$$a_{34} = b_3$$

If the expressions on the right are used as estimates of the expected values, we can show that they are related as required by the hypothesis. For example,

$$\mathscr{E}(11) - \mathscr{E}(31) = \mathscr{E}(14) - \mathscr{E}(34)$$

is estimated by

$$(b_1 + d_1) - (b_3 + d_1) = b_1 - b_3$$

and

$$\mathscr{E}(11) - \mathscr{E}(31) = \mathscr{E}(12) - \mathscr{E}(22) + \mathscr{E}(23) - \mathscr{E}(33)$$

is estimated by

$$(b_1 + d_1) - (b_3 + d_1) = (b_1 + d_2) - (b_2 + d_2) + (b_2 + d_3) - (b_3 + d_3)$$
$$b_1 - b_3 = b_1 - b_3$$

Therefore, the restrictions in (12.10) can be imposed on (12.6), which yields, after simplification,

$$\mathbf{Y} = b_1 \mathbf{R}^{(1)} + b_2 \mathbf{R}^{(2)} + b_3 \mathbf{R}^{(3)} + d_1 \mathbf{C}^{(1)} + d_2 \mathbf{C}^{(2)} + d_3 \mathbf{C}^{(3)} + \mathbf{E}^{(2)} \qquad (12.11)$$

If it is not clear why models (12.9) and (12.11) are equivalent, you can verify this fact by using the procedure described in Section 5.13.

Comparing the Models

The F value is

$$F = \frac{(q_2 - q_1)/(8 - 6)}{q_1/(n - 8)}$$

Comments

If the hypothesis is accepted as true, then we can estimate the missing census-tract expected values as

$$\text{Estimate of } \mathscr{M}(13) = b_1 + d_3$$
$$\text{Estimate of } \mathscr{M}(21) = b_2 + d_1$$

$$\text{Estimate of } \mathscr{M}(24) = b_2$$
$$\text{Estimate of } \mathscr{M}(32) = b_3 + d_2$$

The type of model just described might be useful in many situations where we want to estimate the expected response *if* data were available. Situations may arise in which it is too costly, inconvenient, or risky to actually obtain information. A reasonable estimate of the expected values based on this model might be valuable.

We should recognize that a lack of interaction is only one of many possible regularity conditions that might serve as a basis for estimating the expected values of the missing cells. For example, although interaction may exist (i.e., we reject model (12.11) as tenable), it is quite possible that within each row there is a constant difference between columns (linearity). A model incorporating these implications could then be compared with (12.6) to determine its tenability. Generally speaking, *the fewer the number of missing cells relative to the number of available cells, the more confident one can be in his estimates.* Also, the *pattern of missing cells* is a crucial consideration. For example, we would feel much better about investigating the linearity question if there were one more cell available in the second row.

12.2
PROBLEM DESCRIPTION: USE OF SECOND-DEGREE POLYNOMIAL FOR A STUDY OF ANXIETY AMONG BOYS AND GIRLS

The problem in Section 11.3 involved the use of a second-degree polynomial in a study of the effect of anxiety on problem solving. Now we will add a second attribute (sex) and assume that one second-degree polynomial is appropriate for boys and another is appropriate for girls. Using the two second-degree polynomials as the full model, we will test to see if there are differences between boys and girls who have the same level of anxiety.

Definition of Vectors

$\mathbf{Y}$ = a vector of times required to solve the reasoning problem.

$\mathbf{X}^{(g)}$ = 1 if the element in $\mathbf{Y}$ is from a girl; 0 otherwise.

$\mathbf{X}^{(b)}$ = 1 if the element in $\mathbf{Y}$ is from a boy.; 0 otherwise.

$\mathbf{S}$ = anxiety-test score vector.

$\mathbf{S}^2 = \mathbf{S} * \mathbf{S}$ = squares of test scores.

$\mathbf{S}^{(g)} = \mathbf{X}^{(g)} * \mathbf{S}.$

$\mathbf{S}^{(b)} = \mathbf{X}^{(b)} * \mathbf{S}.$

$$[\mathbf{S}^{(g)}]^2 = \mathbf{X}^{(g)} * \mathbf{S}^2.$$
$$[\mathbf{S}^{(b)}]^2 = \mathbf{X}^{(b)} * \mathbf{S}^2.$$

The Full Model

The full model assumes two second-degree polynomials: one for boys and one for girls.

$$\mathbf{Y} = a_1\mathbf{X}^{(g)} + a_2\mathbf{S}^{(g)} + a_3[\mathbf{S}^{(g)}]^2$$
$$+ b_1\mathbf{X}^{(b)} + b_2\mathbf{S}^{(b)} + b_3[\mathbf{S}^{(b)}]^2 + \mathbf{E}^{(1)} \tag{12.12}$$

Implications of the Hypothesis

Consider the expected performance for a girl at any anxiety score, i, and for a boy at the same anxiety score—where i can assume all possible values. Then the hypothesis can be written symbolically.

$$\mathscr{E}[\text{girl}, i] = \mathscr{E}[\text{boy}, i]$$

Substituting the estimates from (12.12) yields

$$a_1 + a_2(i) + a_3(i^2) = b_1 + b_2(i) + b_3(i^2)$$

or

$$(a_1 - b_1) + i[a_2 - b_2] + i^2[a_3 - b_3] = 0$$

If this is true for all values of i, then

$$a_1 - b_1 = 0$$
$$a_2 - b_2 = 0$$
$$a_3 - b_3 = 0$$

or

$$a_1 = b_1 = c_1 \quad \text{(a common value)}$$
$$a_2 = b_2 = c_2 \quad \text{(a common value)}$$
$$a_3 = b_3 = c_3 \quad \text{(a common value)}$$

The Restricted Model

Imposing these restrictions gives

$$\mathbf{Y} = c_1\mathbf{X}^{(g)} + c_2\mathbf{S}^{(g)} + c_3[\mathbf{S}^{(g)}]^2$$
$$+ c_1\mathbf{X}^{(b)} + c_2\mathbf{S}^{(b)} + c_3[\mathbf{S}^{(b)}]^2 + \mathbf{E}^{(2)}$$
$$\mathbf{Y} = c_1[\mathbf{X}^{(g)} + \mathbf{X}^{(b)}] + c_2[\mathbf{S}^{(g)} + \mathbf{S}^{(b)}]$$
$$+ c_3([\mathbf{S}^{(g)}]^2 + [\mathbf{S}^{(b)}]^2) + \mathbf{E}^{(2)}$$
$$\mathbf{Y} = c_1\mathbf{U} + c_2\mathbf{S} + c_3\mathbf{S}^2 + \mathbf{E}^{(2)} \tag{12.13}$$

Comparing the Models

The F value is

$$F = \frac{(q_2 - q_1)/(6 - 3)}{q_1/(n - 6)}$$

Comments

A graph of the predicted values for the full model is illustrated by the solid curves in Figure 12.1.

The restricted model can be graphed as a single curve similar to the broken curve in Figure 12.1. Note that the hypothesis

$$\mathscr{E}(\text{girl}, i) = \mathscr{E}(\text{boy}, i)$$

is identical to the one explored by a number of different models in Chapters 7 and 8. We emphasize again that a particular question can be investigated using a number of different starting models, and except for the points discussed in Section 6.14, nothing about the question itself is of much help in choosing the appropriate starting model.

An investigation of the properties of (12.12) reveals that the difference between boys and girls may not be constant; that is, interaction may exist. Thus, using the logic of Section 8.10, little difficulty should be encountered in an investigation of interaction if (12.12) is chosen as the full model.

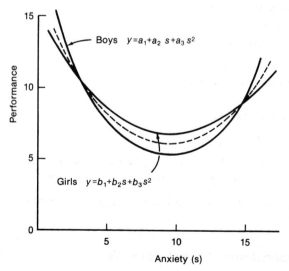

FIG. 12.1   Problem Solving Performance as a Function of Anxiety for Boys and Girls.

12.3
PROBLEM DESCRIPTION: INTERACTION AND SECOND-DEGREE POLYNOMIALS IN A STUDY OF TYPING PERFORMANCE AS A FUNCTION OF FINGER DEXTERITY AND PRACTICE

In Section 9.4 a study of typing performance as a function of finger dexterity and hours of practice used the model

$$\mathbf{Y} = b_0\mathbf{U} + d_0\mathbf{H} + c_0\mathbf{D} + k_0(\mathbf{H} * \mathbf{D}) + \mathbf{E}^{(10)} \tag{12.14}$$

This model was based on the assumption that at any value of finger dexterity the amount of change in typing performance per unit-change in practice was constant. The amount of change in performance per unit-change in practice can be different at different finger-dexterity levels; that is, interaction is possible.

Instead of assuming constant differences (linearity), we will assume that differences change by a constant amount and therefore use a second-degree polynomial as the full model. In this problem, we will test the hypothesis of no interaction: the difference in performance among students with different amounts of practice is the same at all finger-dexterity levels.

Definition of Vectors

$\mathbf{Y}$ = typing performance.

$\mathbf{H}$ = hours of practice.

$\mathbf{D}$ = finger dexterity.

$\mathbf{H}^2$ = squares of hours of practice.

$\mathbf{D}^2$ = squares of finger-dexterity scores.

The Full Model

The full model to be used is

$$\mathbf{Y} = a_0\mathbf{U} + a_1\mathbf{H} + a_2\mathbf{D} + a_3(\mathbf{H} * \mathbf{D}) + a_4\mathbf{H}^2 + a_5\mathbf{D}^2$$
$$+ a_6(\mathbf{H} * \mathbf{D}^2) + a_7(\mathbf{H}^2 * \mathbf{D}) + a_8(\mathbf{H}^2 * \mathbf{D}^2) + \mathbf{E}^{(1)} \tag{12.15}$$

The expected values at three levels of finger dexterity are illustrated in Figure 12.2.

Implications of the Hypothesis

The hypothesis of no interaction states that the difference between the expected performance of two students with finger dexterity f_1 who practice

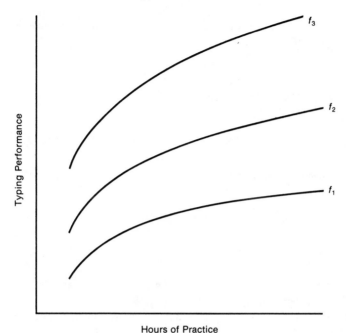

FIG. 12.2   Typing Performance as a Function of Practice at Various Levels of Finger Dexterity.

h_1 and h_2 hours, respectively, is equal to the difference between the expected performance of two students with a finger dexterity f_2 who practice h_1 and h_2 hours. The hypothesis can be written as

$$\mathscr{E}[h_1 f_1] - \mathscr{E}[h_2 f_1] = \mathscr{E}[h_1 f_2] - \mathscr{E}[h_2 f_2]$$

Substituting for the expected values the estimates from (12.15) yields

$$
\begin{aligned}
&[a_0 + a_1(h_1) + a_2(f_1) + a_3(h_1)(f_1) + a_4(h_1)^2 + a_5(f_1)^2 \\
&\quad + a_6(h_1)(f_1)^2 + a_7(h_1)^2(f_1) + a_8(h_1)^2(f_1)^2] \\
&\quad - [a_0 + a_1(h_2) + a_2(f_1) + a_3(h_2)(f_1) + a_4(h_2)^2 + a_5(f_1)^2 \\
&\quad + a_6(h_2)(f_1)^2 + a_7(h_2)^2(f_1) + a_8(h_2)^2(f_1)^2] \\
&= [a_0 + a_1(h_1) + a_2(f_2) + a_3(h_1)(f_2) + a_4(h_1)^2 + a_5(f_2) \\
&\quad + a_6(h_1)(f_2)^2 + a_7(h_1)^2(f_2) + a_8(h_1)^2(f_2)^2] \\
&\quad - [a_0 + a_1(h_2) + a_2(f_2) + a_3(h_2)(f_2) + a_4(h_2)^2 + a_5(f_2) \\
&\quad + a_6(h_2)(f_2)^2 + a_7(h_2)^2(f_2) + a_8(h_2)^2(f_2)^2]
\end{aligned}
$$

This expression can then be written as

$$
\begin{aligned}
&a_3(f_1 - f_2)(h_1 - h_2) + a_6[(f_1)^2 - (f_2)^2](h_1 - h_2) \\
&\quad + a_7(f_1 - f_2)[(h_1)^2 - (h_2)^2] + a_8[(f_1)^2 - (f_2)^2][(h_1) - (h_2)^2] = 0
\end{aligned}
$$

If this expression is true for all values of finger dexterity and hours of practice, then the hypothesis implies that

$$a_3 = a_6 = a_7 = a_8 = 0$$

The Restricted Model

This restriction results in

$$\mathbf{Y} = a_0\mathbf{U} + a_1\mathbf{H} + a_2\mathbf{D} + a_4\mathbf{H}^2 + a_5\mathbf{D}^2 + \mathbf{E}^{(2)} \qquad (12.16)$$

Comparing the Models

The F value is

$$F = \frac{(q_2 - q_1)/(9 - 5)}{q_1/(n - 9)}$$

Comments

We have eliminated all vectors having elements that are the direct products of finger dexterity and hours of practice.

The predicted values of the restricted model are illustrated in Figure 12.3. Note that the difference between f_1 and f_2 is constant across the range of practice and that the difference between f_2 and f_3 is constant—but by a different constant.

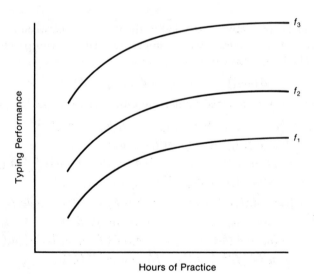

FIG. 12.3 Typing Performance as a Function of Practice and Finger Dexterity with No Interaction.

12.4
PROBLEM DESCRIPTION: ANOTHER STUDY OF TYPING PERFORMANCE AS A FUNCTION OF FINGER DEXTERITY AND PRACTICE

In this problem we will assume that model (12.16) is an appropriate model; that is, no interaction exists. We will test the hypothesis that at all levels of finger dexterity, there is no difference between the expected typing performance of students who practice different amounts.

Definition of Vectors
The vectors are the same as in Section 12.3.

The Full Model

$$\mathbf{Y} = a_0\mathbf{U} + a_1\mathbf{H} + a_2\mathbf{D} + a_4\mathbf{H}^2 + a_5\mathbf{D}^2 + \mathbf{E}^{(1)} \qquad (12.17)$$

Note that the residual vector is designated $\mathbf{E}^{(1)}$, since it is used in this problem as the full model.

Implications of the Hypothesis
The hypothesis is that two students with the same finger dexterity, f, but different amounts of practice, h_1 and h_2, will have the same expected typing performance. This can be abbreviated.

$$\mathscr{E}(h_1 f) = \mathscr{E}(h_2 f)$$

Substituting the estimates from (12.17) gives

$$a_0 + a_1(h_1) + a_2(f) + a_4(h_1)^2 + a_5(f)^2$$
$$= a_0 + a_1(h_2) + a_2(f) + a_4(h_2)^2 + a_5(f)^2$$

which can be written as

$$a_1(h_1 - h_2) + a_4[(h_1)^2 - (h_2)^2] = 0$$

If this hypothesis is true for all values of h_1 and h_2, then it is necessary that

$$a_1 = a_4 = 0$$

The Restricted Model
These restrictions, imposed on (12.17), give

$$\mathbf{Y} = a_0\mathbf{U} + a_2\mathbf{D} + a_5\mathbf{D}^2 + \mathbf{E}^{(2)} \qquad (12.18)$$

Comparing the Models

The F value is

$$F = \frac{(q_2 - q_1)/(5 - 3)}{q_1/(n - 5)}$$

Comments

In this problem the restricted model contains only information about finger dexterity. The relation between performance and finger dexterity is still expressed as a second-degree polynomial.

13

Application to Problems
Involving Several Attributes

13.1
INTRODUCTION

The application of the problem-solving principles discussed in this book to areas where the question leads to a classification scheme involving more than two attributes is conceptually straightforward, but implementation can often be difficult. For example, in the next section we will consider a problem in which the nature of the question causes us to classify students on three attributes.

> Sex of student: boy or girl
> Method Student Taught By: 1 or 2
> Initial Reading Level of Student: 20 through 80

Thus, there are potentially $2 \times 2 \times 61 = 244$ mutually exclusive categories (populations) of concern, and we are interested in comparing the expected values of these 244 populations in various ways. Conceptually, it is fairly simple to identify a true starting model that has 244 unknown parameters, and we could always consider less complex models (following the logic of Chapters 7 through 12).

In practice, however, the implementation of such a process may well be impossible (e.g., no boy students with initial reading scores of 28 can be found) or prohibitively expensive and time consuming. If we are willing to assume that the expected values on reading performance can be expressed as a linear function of initial reading performance within each of the four categories defined by the first two attributes, we can start with a model that has only eight parameters (see Section 13.2)—a reduction of 236 parameters.

The major point is that as the number of attributes and the number of levels within each attribute increase, you will be forced to make some simplifying assumptions in order to make the problem manageable. If the simplifying assumptions are seriously in error, the conclusions drawn will likely be erroneous—even if the logical argument is faultless and the numbers are calculated accurately.

13.2
PROBLEM DESCRIPTION: READING PERFORMANCE AS A FUNCTION OF METHOD OF INSTRUCTION, SEX, AND PRE-EXPERIMENT PERFORMANCE—ARE DIFFERENCES BETWEEN METHODS CONSTANT?

We wish to compare the effectiveness of two methods of reading instruction on a measure of reading performance. In this study we will determine whether the differences in reading performance between the two methods are the same for boys and girls. Furthermore, we will determine whether the performance differences between the two methods are the same for all pre-experiment reading-performance levels.

After testing to determine if the performance differences are constant, we will check to see (in the next section) if the differences between methods are zero for both sexes at all pre-experiment performance levels.

Definition of Vectors

We will assume that the relation between final reading performance and pre-experiment reading performance is linear. Let

$\mathbf{Y}$ = final reading performance measured after reading instruction has been completed.

$\mathbf{P}$ = reading performance measured before beginning the two methods of reading instruction.

$\mathbf{X}^{(g)}$ = 1 if an element in $\mathbf{Y}$ is from a girl; 0 otherwise.

$\mathbf{X}^{(b)}$ = 1 if an element in $\mathbf{Y}$ is from a boy; 0 otherwise.

$\mathbf{R}^{(1)}$ = 1 if an element in $\mathbf{Y}$ is from reading method 1; 0 otherwise.

$\mathbf{R}^{(2)}$ = 1 if an element in $\mathbf{Y}$ is from reading method 2; 0 otherwise.

$\mathbf{X}^{(g1)} = \mathbf{X}^{(g)} * \mathbf{R}^{(1)}$.

$\mathbf{X}^{(g2)} = \mathbf{X}^{(g)} * \mathbf{R}^{(2)}$.

$\mathbf{X}^{(b1)} = \mathbf{X}^{(b)} * \mathbf{R}^{(1)}$.

$\mathbf{X}^{(b2)} = \mathbf{X}^{(b)} * \mathbf{R}^{(2)}.$

$\mathbf{P}^{(g1)} = \mathbf{X}^{(g1)} * \mathbf{P}.$

$\mathbf{P}^{(g2)} = \mathbf{X}^{(g2)} * \mathbf{P}.$

$\mathbf{P}^{(b1)} = \mathbf{X}^{(b1)} * \mathbf{P}.$

$\mathbf{P}^{(b2)} = \mathbf{X}^{(b2)} * \mathbf{P}.$

The Full Model

$$\mathbf{Y} = a_{g1}\mathbf{X}^{(g1)} + a_{g2}\mathbf{X}^{(g2)} + a_{b1}\mathbf{X}^{(b1)} + a_{b2}\mathbf{X}^{(b2)}$$
$$+ c_{g1}\mathbf{P}^{(g1)} + c_{g2}\mathbf{P}^{(g2)} + c_{b1}\mathbf{P}^{(b1)} + c_{b2}\mathbf{P}^{(b2)} + \mathbf{E}^{(1)} \qquad (13.1)$$

Implications of the Hypothesis

We wish to compare differences in expected performance between the two methods at all combinations of sex and pre-experiment performance. Specifically, we want to determine if

$$\mathscr{E}(\text{boys, method 1, } k) - \mathscr{E}(\text{boys, method 2, } k)$$
$$= \mathscr{E}(\text{girls, method 1, } k) - \mathscr{E}(\text{girls, method 2, } k) \qquad (13.2)$$

and if

$$\mathscr{E}(s, \text{ method 1, } k) - \mathscr{E}(s, \text{ method 2, } k)$$
$$= \mathscr{E}(s, \text{ method 1, } m) - \mathscr{E}(s, \text{ method 2, } m)$$

We can translate these statements into natural language.

1. The expected final performance of a boy in method 1 (at pre-experiment level k) minus the expected final performance of a boy in method 2 (at pre-experiment level k) is equal to the expected final performance of a girl in method 1 (at pre-experiment level k) minus the expected final performance of a girl in method 2 (at pre-experiment level k).

2. The expected final performance of a student of sex category s in method 1 (at pre-experiment level k) minus the expected final performance of a student of sex category s in method 2 (at pre-experiment level k) is equal to the corresponding difference at any other pre-experiment level, m.

Then substituting the estimates of the expected values from (13.1) yields

$$[a_{b1} + c_{b1}(k)] - [a_{b2} + c_{b2}(k)] = [a_{g1} + c_{g1}(k)] - [a_{g2} + c_{g2}(k)] \qquad (13.3)$$

and

$$[a_{s1} + c_{s1}(k)] - [a_{s2} + c_{s2}(k)] = [a_{s1} + c_{s1}(m)] - [a_{s2} + c_{s2}(m)] \qquad (13.4)$$

Rewriting (13.3), we have

$$(a_{b1} - a_{b2} - a_{g1} + a_{g2}) + k(c_{b1} - c_{b2} - c_{g1} + c_{g2}) = 0$$

If this is true for all values of k, then

$$a_{b1} - a_{b2} - a_{g1} + a_{g2} = 0 \qquad (13.5)$$

and

$$c_{b1} - c_{b2} - c_{g1} + c_{g2} = 0 \qquad (13.6)$$

Observing (13.4), we see that

$$(c_{s1} - c_{s2})(k - m) = 0$$

Since $k \neq m$, then the restriction implies that

$$c_{s1} = c_{s2} \qquad \text{for } s = \text{boys and girls} \qquad (13.7)$$

or

$$c_{b1} - c_{b2} = 0$$

and

$$c_{g1} - c_{g2} = 0$$

Subtracting these two restrictions gives

$$c_{b1} - c_{b2} - c_{g1} + c_{g2} = 0$$

which is identical to restriction (13.6). Therefore, we have three restrictions implied by our hypothesis.

$$a_{b1} - a_{b2} - a_{g1} + a_{g2} = 0$$

$$c_{b1} - c_{b2} = 0$$

$$c_{g1} - c_{g2} = 0$$

Imposing these restrictions yields the restricted model.

The Restricted Model

$$\mathbf{Y} = d_1\mathbf{R}^{(1)} + a_g[\mathbf{X}^{(g1)} + \mathbf{X}^{(g2)}] + a_b[\mathbf{X}^{(b1)} + \mathbf{X}^{(b2)}]$$
$$+ c_g[\mathbf{P}^{(g1)} + \mathbf{P}^{(g2)}] + c_b[\mathbf{P}^{(b1)} + \mathbf{P}^{(b2)}] + \mathbf{E}^{(2)}$$

Letting

$$\mathbf{X}^{(g)} = \mathbf{X}^{(g1)} + \mathbf{X}^{(g2)}$$

$$\mathbf{X}^{(b)} = \mathbf{X}^{(b1)} + \mathbf{X}^{(b2)}$$

$$\mathbf{P}^{(g)} = \mathbf{P}^{(g1)} + \mathbf{P}^{(g2)}$$

$$\mathbf{P}^{(b)} = \mathbf{P}^{(b1)} + \mathbf{P}^{(b2)}$$

the restricted model is

$$\mathbf{Y} = d_1\mathbf{R}^{(1)} + a_g\mathbf{X}^{(g)} + a_b\mathbf{X}^{(b)} + c_g\mathbf{P}^{(g)} + c_b\mathbf{P}^{(b)} + \mathbf{E}^{(2)} \qquad (13.8)$$

Comparison of the Models

The F value is computed from

$$F = \frac{(q_2 - q_1)/(8 - 5)}{q_1/(n - 8)}$$

Comments

Even though the restricted model has no interaction between the instructional methods and the other attributes, we observe that interaction is still possible between sex and pre-experiment reading performance. Whether this interaction actually exists may not be important. The important question involves the interaction between methods and the other attributes; if there is no interaction, the differences between methods are the same for all sexes and pre-experiment reading levels. Consequently, it is not necessary to have knowledge of sex category or pre-experiment reading level to choose the best method of instruction.

The estimated values, using the restricted model, are illustrated in Figure 13.1.

Note that the full model has eight parameters. A possible graph of the full model would require that the predicted values lie on straight lines, but it is also possible that there would be four different intercepts

$$a_{g1}, a_{g2}, a_{b1}, a_{b2}$$

and four different slopes

$$c_{g1}, c_{g2}, c_{b1}, c_{b2}.$$

The restricted model, on the other hand, has only five parameters, thus allowing four different intercepts

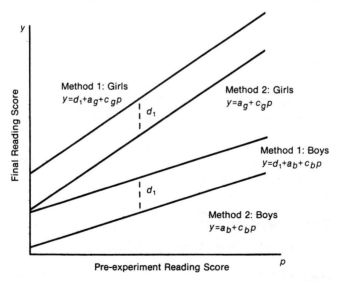

FIG. 13.1   Final Reading Performance as a Function of Method of Instruction, Sex, and Initial Performance.

$$d_1 + a_g \quad \text{for girls in method 1}$$
$$d_1 + a_b \quad \text{for boys in method 1}$$
$$a_g \quad \text{for girls in method 2}$$
$$a_b \quad \text{for boys in method 2}$$

and two different slopes

$$c_g \quad \text{for girls in either method}$$
$$c_b \quad \text{for boys in either method}$$

Note the constraint on the intercepts, which requires a common difference (d_1) between methods for both boys and girls.

You will recall that in Section 9.9 we tried to draw a distinction between *treatment variables* (ordinarily controllable) and *contaminator variables* (may not be controllable but can be observed or measured). In the context of this problem, method of instruction would be regarded as a treatment variable; it is controllable in the sense that we can assign individuals to groups that will be taught by a specific method. Sex and initial performance would be regarded as contaminators (uncontrollable but measureable). In this section we are trying to mold the model into a form that will allow us to make an unqualified recommendation of either method 1 or 2 for every student— whatever the sex or initial performance. If model (13.8) is rejected, then we would have to make a qualified recommendation or perhaps no recommendation at all. By a *qualified recommendation*, we mean that the decision about which method a student should be taught by would depend on the sex of the student, the initial performance, or both.

13.3
PROBLEM DESCRIPTION: READING PERFORMANCE AS A FUNCTION OF METHOD OF INSTRUCTION, SEX, AND PRE-EXPERIMENT PERFORMANCE —ARE THERE DIFFERENCES BETWEEN METHODS?

We will use the restricted model in Section 13.2 as the full model for this problem and test the hypothesis that the differences in final performance between methods are zero for all patterns of sex and pre-experiment performance.

Definition of Vectors

The vectors are the same as in Section 13.2.

The Full Model

$$\mathbf{Y} = d_1\mathbf{R}^{(1)} + a_g\mathbf{X}^{(g)} + a_b\mathbf{X}^{(b)} + c_g\mathbf{P}^{(g)} + c_b\mathbf{P}^{(b)} + \mathbf{E}^{(1)} \quad (13.9)$$

Implications of the Hypothesis

The hypothesis can be expressed as

$$\mathscr{E}(s, \text{method } 1, k) - \mathscr{E}(s, \text{method } 2, k) = 0$$

which can be translated to mean that the difference between the expected performance of two individuals from different methods but same sex and pre-experiment performance is equal to zero. Substituting for the expected values the estimates from (13.9) yields

$$[d_1 + a_s + c_s(k)] - [a_s + c_s(k)] = 0 \qquad s = g, b$$

or

$$d_1 = 0 \tag{13.10}$$

Substitution of this restriction gives the restricted model.

The Restricted Model

$$\mathbf{Y} = a_g \mathbf{X}^{(g)} + a_b \mathbf{X}^{(b)} + c_g \mathbf{P}^{(g)} + c_b \mathbf{P}^{(b)} + \mathbf{E}^{(2)} \tag{13.11}$$

Comparison of the Models

The F value is

$$F = \frac{(q_2 - q_1)/(5 - 4)}{q_1/(n - 5)} \tag{13.12}$$

Comments

The restricted model contains no information about the instructional method, but the model still allows for possible interaction between sex category and pre-experiment performance. Figure 13.2 illustrates a possible result using the restricted model.

The analysis proposed for this problem bears certain similarities to a procedure called **factorial analysis of covariance**. Winer (1962, pp. 595–606), for example, discusses a problem involving two different methods of teaching map reading (first attribute), three instructors (second attribute), and initial performance (third attribute), with final performance as the variable of interest ($\mathbf{Y}$). Although Winer does not describe any preliminary tests, as in Section 13.2, it is possible to investigate the properties of the model he discusses by using the procedures recommended in Appendix D. If this is done, you will discover that some important differences exist between his model and (13.9). This is not to imply that either of the models is *wrong* but that they are *different*.

We raise this point to emphasize that the uncritical acceptance of models

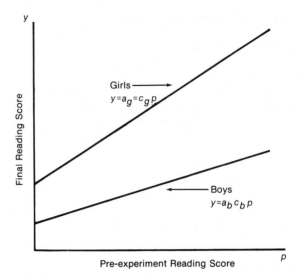

FIG. 13.2   Estimates of the Expected Values from Model (13.11).

formulated by others may not lead to the most relevant answers within the context of a given problem. For example, let us examine how the model that can be inferred from Winer's discussion will function within the context of the reading experiment. Using the vector definitions in Section 13.2 yields

$$\mathbf{Y} = a_{g1}\mathbf{X}^{(g1)} + a_{g2}\mathbf{X}^{(g2)} + a_{b1}\mathbf{X}^{(b1)} + a_{b2}\mathbf{X}^{(b2)} + b_1\mathbf{P} + \mathbf{E}^{(1)} \qquad (13.13)$$

Note the difference between (13.13) and (13.9). Although both models have five unknown parameters (five linearly independent predictor vectors), they are not equivalent. Model (13.13) requires a common slope (b_1) for all four groups, while model (13.9) allows different slopes for boys and girls. However, subject to the constraint that slopes be equal, model (13.13) puts no constraints on differences among the intercepts, but model (13.9) does.

The computing procedures recommended by Winer for testing *method effects* lead to a result that can be obtained by imposing the following restriction on (13.13).

$$a_{g1} + a_{g2} = a_{b1} + a_{b2}$$

If the error sum of squares in the restricted model is denoted q_2, then the test statistic

$$F = \frac{(q_2 - q_1)/(5 - 4)}{q_1/(n - 5)}$$

appears to be the same as (13.12). In general, however, the result will be different because of the dissimilarity of both the full and restricted models.

13.4
PROBLEM DESCRIPTION: A STUDY
OF JUDGMENT AND DECISION MAKING

Management personnel must often base judgments and decisions upon complex arrays of information. If they could state explicitly how they used this information, these decision makers—and others—could replicate their judgments in subsequent situations in which the same types of information are available. As a rule, however, managers cannot explain precisely how they use information to reach their decisions.

If we can obtain all the information available to decision makers and an adequate sample of their decisions, we can frequently formulate a mathematical model that satisfactorily accounts for the decision. Although this model may not use the items of information in the same way as the human judges, it does *simulate* their decision-making policy, since it leads to decisions similar to those in the sample. Once a model is formulated (assuming it predicts the sample of decisions accurately), we can use it to obtain innumerable decisions without the variability that results from fatigue or the other factors affecting human judgments. In addition, if a judgment process is adequately expressed in a mathematical model, it is possible to test hypotheses about the relevance of the information to the judgment process. This approach to the simulation of judgment is illustrated here in a problem that involves the determination of salaries.

Consider a situation in which a business executive is responsible for determining the annual salaries of the employees of a company. The problem is to formulate a model that will satisfactorily predict his judgments with respect to these salaries. Then a hypothesis will be tested concerning the relevance of educational information to salary estimation. Assume that we have selected a random sample of n jobs and have assembled information about the jobs and the individuals performing them. (We will consider only a small number of attributes that might be relevant to the situation.) The information may include educational level, amount of responsibility for expenditure of funds, number of persons supervised, irregularity of working hours, years of experience, marital status, etc. All this information is given to the company official, who must then decide the salary he would recommend paying each of the persons who fill the n jobs in the sample.

Definition of Vectors

$\mathbf{Y}$ = a vector of dimension n in which the elements are the salary recommendations of the company executive.

$\mathbf{X}^{(1)}$ = the number of people supervised by the employee who is in the job being judged.

$\mathbf{X}^{(2)}$ = the number of years of education that the employee has.

$$\mathbf{X}^{(3)} = \text{the number of years of experience for each employee.}$$

$\mathbf{X}^{(4)}, \ldots, \mathbf{X}^{(p)} = $ other vectors that might be appropriate.

It might be appropriate to define vectors that represent possible interaction between certain types of information. This could be accomplished by forming the appropriate direct products.

The Full Model

The full model can be written as

$$\mathbf{Y} = a_0\mathbf{U} + a_1\mathbf{X}^{(1)} + a_2\mathbf{X}^{(2)} + a_3\mathbf{X}^{(3)} + \cdots + a_p\mathbf{X}^{(p)} + \mathbf{E}^{(1)} \quad (13.14)$$

Implications of the Hypothesis

Even though our primary purpose may be to develop a good prediction system, we will test the hypothesis that there is no difference in judged salary between individuals who have *different* amounts of education (say k_1 and k_2) but who are the same on all other attributes. In terms of model (13.14), we express this as

$$a_0 + a_1(i) + a_2(k_1) + \cdots + a_p(s) = a_0 + a_1(i) + a_2(k_2) + \cdots + a_p(s)$$

or

$$a_2(k_1 - k_2) = 0$$

Since $k_1 \neq k_2$, then the restriction implied by the hypothesis is

$$a_2 = 0$$

The Restricted Model

Imposing this restriction gives

$$\mathbf{Y} = a_0\mathbf{U} + a_1\mathbf{X}^{(1)} + a_3\mathbf{X}^{(3)} + \cdots + a_p\mathbf{X}^{(p)} + \mathbf{E}^{(2)} \quad (13.15)$$

Comparison of the Models

The F value is

$$F = \frac{(q_2 - q_1)/(p + 1 - p)}{q_1/[n - (p + 1)]}$$

Comments

On the basis of this test, we could decide whether different amounts of education result in recommended differences in salary. Similar questions can be asked about other information. This technique[1] can be used in many situations in which it is appropriate to express "fuzzy" attributes (such as salary, quality, value) in terms of other attributes that are more clearly understood.

---

[1]Additional discussion of this technique can be found in articles by Christal (1968) and Ward (1962).

13.5
PROBLEM DESCRIPTION: THE EQUALITY
OF SEVERAL PREDICTION SYSTEMS

We will assume that we have developed the prediction system described in Section 13.4 for k different judges or decision makers. Each judge examines the files of the same n employees and recommends a salary. We wish to determine if it is reasonable to believe that different judges will recommend the same salary for employees with the same predictor characteristics. This hypothesis is useful in determining whether reasonable agreement among several decision makers exists.

Definition of Vectors

$\mathbf{Y}$ = the vector of judgments containing nk elements. (The first n elements are from policy-maker 1, and the second n elements from policy-maker 2, etc.)

$\mathbf{X}^{(i,0)}$ = 1 if the corresponding element in $\mathbf{Y}$ is from policy-maker i; 0 otherwise $(i = 1, \ldots, k)$.

$\mathbf{X}^{(j)}$ = vectors containing elements corresponding with predictor vector j. [These vectors may be either binary (1–0) or other coded vectors $(j = 1, \ldots, p)$.]

$\mathbf{X}^{(i,j)} = \mathbf{X}^{(i,0)} * \mathbf{X}^{(j)}$.

For $k = 3$ and $p = 2$, the vectors might be

Y	$\mathbf{X}^{(1,0)}$	$\mathbf{X}^{(2,0)}$	$\mathbf{X}^{(3,0)}$	$\mathbf{X}^{(1,1)}$	$\mathbf{X}^{(1,2)}$	$\mathbf{X}^{(2,1)}$	$\mathbf{X}^{(2,2)}$	$\mathbf{X}^{(3,1)}$	$\mathbf{X}^{(3,2)}$
y_{11}	1	0	0	x_{11}	x_{12}	0	0	0	0
y_{21}	1	0	0	x_{21}	x_{22}	0	0	0	0
.	.	.	.	.	.	.	.	.	.
.	.	.	.	.	.	.	.	.	.
.	.	.	.	.	.	.	.	.	.
y_{n1}	1	0	0	x_{n1}	x_{n2}	0	0	0	0
y_{12}	0	1	0	0	0	x_{11}	x_{12}	0	0
y_{22}	0	1	0	0	0	x_{21}	x_{22}	0	0
.	.	.	.	.	.	.	.	.	.
.	.	.	.	.	.	.	.	.	.
y_{n2}	0	1	0	0	0	x_{n1}	x_{n2}	0	0
y_{13}	0	0	1	0	0	0	0	x_{11}	x_{12}
y_{23}	0	0	1	0	0	0	0	x_{21}	x_{22}
.	.	.	.	.	.	.	.	.	.
.	.	.	.	.	.	.	.	.	.
y_{n3}	0	0	1	0	0	0	0	x_{n1}	x_{n2}

Note that y_{mi} is the salary recommended by the ith policy maker for the mth employee $(i = 1, 2, \ldots k; m = 1, 2, \ldots, n)$. The symbol x_{mj} represents the value observed on the mth employee on the jth predictor $(m = 1, 2, \ldots, n; j = 1, \ldots, p)$. Furthermore, note that the symbol x_{mj} appears k times—once for each policy maker.

The Full Model

The full model can be written as

$$
\begin{aligned}
\mathbf{Y} = a_{1,0}\mathbf{X}^{(1,0)} &+ a_{2,0}\mathbf{X}^{(2,0)} + \cdots + a_{k,0}\mathbf{X}^{(k,0)} \\
&+ a_{1,1}\mathbf{X}^{(1,1)} + a_{1,2}\mathbf{X}^{(1,2)} + \cdots + a_{1,p}\mathbf{X}^{(1,p)} \\
& \quad\quad \vdots \\
&+ a_{k,1}\mathbf{X}^{(k,1)} + a_{k,2}\mathbf{X}^{(k,2)} + \cdots + a_{k,p}\mathbf{X}^{(k,p)} + \mathbf{E}^{(1)}
\end{aligned}
\tag{13.16}
$$

Implications of the Hypothesis

The hypothesis is that for all k judges the expected salaries recommended are equal for employees with identical values on the predictors. In terms of (13.16), this is expressed as

$$
\begin{aligned}
a_{1,0}(1) &+ a_{1,1}(v_1) + a_{1,2}(v_2) + \cdots + a_{1,p}(v_p) \\
= a_{2,0}(1) &+ a_{2,1}(v_1) + a_{2,2}(v_2) + \cdots + a_{2,p}(v_p) \\
& \quad\quad \vdots \\
= a_{k,0}(1) &+ a_{k,1}(v_1) + a_{k,2}(v_2) + \cdots + a_{k,p}(v_p)
\end{aligned}
$$

For this to be true for all values of the predictors, we must have

$$
\begin{aligned}
a_{1,0} &= a_{2,0} = \cdots = a_{k,0} = b_0 \\
a_{1,1} &= a_{2,1} = \cdots = a_{k,1} = b_1 \\
& \quad\quad \vdots \\
a_{1,p} &= a_{2,p} = \cdots = a_{k,p} = b_p
\end{aligned}
$$

The Restricted Model

Substitution of these restrictions gives up all information that distinguishes between policy makers.

$$
\begin{aligned}
\mathbf{Y} = b_0\mathbf{X}^{(1,0)} &+ b_0\mathbf{X}^{(2,0)} + \cdots + b_0\mathbf{X}^{(k,0)} \\
&+ b_1\mathbf{X}^{(1,1)} + b_1\mathbf{X}^{(1,2)} + \cdots + b_1\mathbf{X}^{(1,p)} \\
& \quad\quad \vdots \\
&+ b_p\mathbf{X}^{(k,1)} + b_p\mathbf{X}^{(k,2)} + \cdots + b_p\mathbf{X}^{(k,p)} + \mathbf{E}^{(2)}
\end{aligned}
$$

or

$$\mathbf{Y} = b_0\mathbf{U} + b_1\mathbf{X}^{(1)} + \cdots + b_p\mathbf{X}^{(p)} + \mathbf{E}^{(2)} \qquad (13.17)$$

Comparing the Models

The F value is

$$F = \frac{(q_2 - q_1)/[kp - (p + 1)]}{q_1/(nk - kp)}$$

Comments

In some situations, it may be appropriate to seek groups of individuals who have similar equations. A procedure that is useful for seeking such models is described by Bottenberg and Christal (1962).

14

The Computer
Solution of Models

14.1
INTRODUCTION

The computations required to find least-squares solutions for the models we have described can be quite simple in some cases but quite formidable in others. We did not emphasize detailed computing procedures in the earlier chapters in order to concentrate on the general principles of model formulation. Our aim was to show that an individual can learn to formulate understandable models and can apprehend the utility of a numerical solution without getting involved in the detailed computational procedures that lead to a numerical solution. One of the reasons for this is that different classes of models have unique properties, thus making certain computing algorithms superior to others in terms of speed, accuracy, convenience, etc. Moreover, we believe that *an investigator's primary concern should be to formulate a model that adequately represents his thinking about a research problem.* Only when he is satisfied with the adequacy of the model should he consider computational feasibility. If the computational requirements are excessive, the model can then be modified (while still retaining the essential features of the problem).

For most of the models in this book, the computer program described in this chapter can be executed rapidly and with reasonable accuracy. We could probably write a more efficient program for each particular model, and at many computing installations, such routines are available. The major advantages of this program, however, are *its generality* and *the ease with which a model can be translated into computer output.*

14.2
SCOPE OF THE PROGRAM

Any model of the general form

$$\mathbf{Y} = a_1\mathbf{X}^{(1)} + a_2\mathbf{X}^{(2)} + \cdots + a_k\mathbf{X}^{(k)} + \mathbf{E}$$

where $\mathbf{Y}$ and the $\mathbf{X}^{(i)}$ are known and $\mathbf{E}$ and the a_i are unknown, can be solved using the program—providing that *one of the* $\mathbf{X}^{(i)}$ *is the unit vector* or that *the unit vector is a linear combination of the* $\mathbf{X}^{(i)}$. There is no requirement that the $\mathbf{X}^{(i)}$ be linearly independent. If the $\mathbf{X}^{(i)}$ are linearly independent, a unique solution will be determined for the a_i; otherwise, one of the infinite solutions will be found. The error sum of squares and the predicted values are unique (the same) in either case.

The algorithm used in this program (see Appendix C) is iterative, and the solution is approximate. The degree of accuracy is determined, in part, by the wordsize of the machine and the specific properties of the model. Our experience indicates that a machine having at least a 32-bit wordsize is sufficiently accurate for most practical models. Accuracy can be controlled to some degree by modifying one of the parameters of the program. A source-language listing of the program can be found in Appendix E.

14.3
INPUT CARD PREPARATION

Generally, the user will be required to provide *six* types of input cards. These cards are described in detail in Sections 14.4–14.9, where they are used in an example problem originally presented in Chapter 4. A listing of the required input cards for the sample problem is given in Figure 14.1.

In this description frequent references are made to SUBROUTINE DATRAN—for now, they can be ignored.[1]

14.4
TITLE CARD(S)

The first card listed in Figure 14.1 is called a **title card**. It is used only for *descriptive purposes*, and it may contain any legal FORTRAN characters. For most systems, the legal characters will be the numeric punches 0 through 9, alphabetics A through Z, and such special characters as $+$, $-$, $*$, $/$, $($, $)$, $=$, ., commas, and blank. The first 24 columns of the title card cannot be

---

[1] DATRAN is a subroutine of the main program described in this chapter. After reading Chapter 15, which explains SUBROUTINE DATRAN, we suggest that you reread this chapter.

```
SAMPLE PROBLEMS FROM CHAPTERS 4 AND 6.◄──────Title Card          9
   20      6    ◄────────────────────────── Parameter Card
(11X,  F2.0,  1X,  5F2.0) ◄────────────────── Format Card
SUBJECT   1 16   9 1 0 0 0      1   ╲
SUBJECT   2 48   9 1 0 0 0      0    ╲
SUBJECT   3 40   9 1 0 0 0      0
SUBJECT   4 40   9 1 0 0 0      0
SUBJECT   5 32   9 1 0 0 0      0
SUBJECT   6 40  10 0 1 0 0      1
SUBJECT   7 24  10 0 1 0 0      1
SUBJECT   8 64  10 0 1 0 0      0
SUBJECT   9 56  10 0 1 0 0      0
SUBJECT  10 48  10 0 1 0 0      0     ⎬  Data Cards
SUBJECT  11 64  11 0 0 1 0      1
SUBJECT  12 56  11 0 0 1 0      1
SUBJECT  13 48  11 0 0 1 0      1
SUBJECT  14 72  11 0 0 1 0      0
SUBJECT  15 56  11 0 0 1 0      0
SUBJECT  16 80  12 0 0 0 1      1
SUBJECT  17 72  12 0 0 0 1      1
SUBJECT  18 72  12 0 0 0 1      1
SUBJECT  19 64  12 0 0 0 1      1    ╱
SUBJECT  20 72  12 0 0 0 1      0   ╱
4.1         001001003006 ⎫ Model Cards
6.4         002001002002 ⎭
SEC. 6.7    999001002004002 ⎫
SEC. 4.9    999001050004001 ⎬  F— Value Cards
SEC. 6.11   999002050002001 ⎭
                         ⎬ Two Blank Cards
```

FIG. 14.1   Listing of Required Input Cards for Sample Problems from Chapters 4 and 6.

entirely blank. Output from the program will include an image listing of this card—except for column 80, which is not printed. Any number of title cards can be used (in Figure 14.1, there is only one). All title cards but the last must be blank in column 80; the last title card must *not* be blank in column 80.

14.5
PARAMETER CARD

The second card in the sample input is called a **parameter card**. It has the following format.

Columns	Contents
1–5	Dimension of the vectors in the models. In the example, the number 20 is punched in columns 4 and 5. The five columns (1 through 5) are referred to as a **five-column field**. When some value is punched in the rightmost positions of a field, the term **right-justified** is used.
6–10	Number of elements on each input data record. In the example, this number is 6, and it is punched right-justified. This value is given the symbolic name NC in DATRAN.
11–15	Number of vectors (criteria and predictors but not residuals) in the models to be solved. If all of the vectors are punched on the data cards,

the standard version of SUBROUTINE DATRAN (see Chapter 15) is used, and this field may be left blank. In the example, we use standard DATRAN, so this field has been left blank. In DATRAN this value is given the symbolic name NV. If this field is blank (or zero), NV is assumed equal to NC.

16–20   This field is used to control the *retention* of the input data. If this field is nonzero, the data are not saved, and the predicted value option on the model card (see Section 14.8) cannot be used. If the field is zero or blank, the input data are retained in memory (or on tape), and the predicted-value option can be exercised. In the example, the field is blank.

14.6
FORMAT CARD

The third card in the example is called a **format card**. It allows the user to specify the *location* of the data elements on the data cards. This feature of the program permits data cards to be punched in a variety of formats.

Space does not permit an extensive discussion of the powerful and flexible variable-format capability of FORTRAN. Fortunately, most formats can be specified with a minimum amount of information.[2] FORTRAN compilers vary slightly with respect to legal format specifications, but a FORTRAN reference manual for your particular system should resolve all difficulties.

Data values will normally be punched in *consecutive columns* across a data card. The columns can be logically subdivided into *fields*. For example, each data card in the example has a value from 9 through 12 punched in columns 15 and 16, which is a two-column field. In specifying the format, the user generally needs to "skip" certain columns and "pick up" certain fields.

Consider the format card

(11X, F2.0, 1X, 5F2.0)

A format card will *always* contain a left parenthesis as the first nonblank character and a right parenthesis as the last nonblank character. The characters between the parentheses can be read as

11X: Skip the first 11 columns.

F2.0:   Pick up the next two columns, and store the value in memory with no decimals. This value is stored in a memory location given the symbolic name C(1) in DATRAN. In other words, the 1st data value from the cards is obtained from columns 12 and 13.

---

[2] Detailed information about writing format specifications can be found in Veldman (1967).

1X: Skip one column (i.e., column 14).

5F2.0: Pick up five fields, each two columns wide, and store each value with no decimals. These values are stored in memory in locations C(2) through C(6).

Note that the format specifies six fields, and the number 6 is punched in column 10 of the parameter card. In general, k columns are skipped by the specification kX, and data fields are picked up by the specification nF$c.d$, where c is the number of columns in a field and d is the number of columns to be treated as decimal values. For example, if the values punched in columns 12 and 13 were logically 4.8, 4.0, etc., the format specification would be F2.1—not F2.0. The value of n indicates that there are n fields, each of which has the same specification. If n is not specified, it is understood to be *one*. Blank columns in numeric fields of the data cards are interpreted by the computer as zeroes. The characters punched in the format card can begin in any column and end in any column. Blanks are ignored, and commas are required. If any doubt exists about the presence of blanks in columns 17, 19, 21, and 23, these columns can be skipped by using either the format

(11X, F2.0, 1X, F2.0, 1X, F1.0, 1X, F1.0, 1X, F1.0, 1X, F1.0)

or

(11X, F2.0, 1X, F2.0, 4(1X, F1.0))

Column 30 contains additional information not needed for this problem, but this information is ignored by the computer because it is not specified on the format card.

14.7
DATA CARDS

In the example, the 20 cards that follow the format card are called **data cards**. Generally, the number of data cards will be punched right-justified, in columns 1 through 5 of the parameter card. Situations may arise in which two or more data cards are required to contain all the data for a given subject. This problem can be handled by using one or more slashes (/) on the format card.[3]

In general, if there are n subjects with k data cards for each subject, columns 1 through 5 of the parameter card will contain the number n, but there will be n times k data cards, and the format card will contain $k - 1$ slashes.

For many of the models discussed in this book, vectors are required that are not likely to be punched on data cards. In the example, the last four vectors would not normally be punched. By using SUBROUTINE DATRAN,

---

[3]A description of the use of slashes on format cards can be found in any FORTRAN manual.

however, the user can define almost any vector he can imagine with a minimum of keypunching on the data cards.

14.8
MODEL CARDS AND *F*-VALUE CARDS

The format of a model card is:

Columns	Contents
1–10	Identification. Any legal FORTRAN characters. The first model card in Figure 14.1 contains the characters 4.1, and the second contains 6.4.
11–13	Model number. Any value between 1 and 50 punched right-justified. This field may be left blank, in which case a model number is computed by adding one to the previous model number. In the example, the models are numbered 001 and 002.
14–16	Criterion vector number. In the example, vector one is the criterion or **Y**.
17–76	A series of three-column fields of the form $i, j, k, l, \ldots m, n$ that specifies which vectors are to be used as predictors in the model. Vectors i through j and k through l and . . . m through n are used as predictors. Any fields not needed to specify the predictors may be left blank. In the example, the first model requires vectors three through six as predictors and the specification is accomplished by punching 003006 into columns 17 through 22. Since columns 23 through 76 are not needed to complete the specification, they have been left blank. The second model requires that only vector two be specified as a predictor, which is accomplished by punching 002002 into columns 17 through 22.
77–79	Blank.
80	Predicted-value option. If column 80 is blank or zero, a vector of predicted values will be printed. This option can be exercised *only* if columns 16 through 20 of the parameter card are blank or zero.

The model card allows almost unlimited flexibility in the specification of vectors comprising a model. If the standard version of SUBROUTINE DATRAN is used, the order of the vectors is the same as their order on the data cards. If the user writes his own SUBROUTINE DATRAN, the vectors can be arranged in any order desired.

An Example of the Use of the Model Card. Suppose that some problem created the need for 20 vectors. For a particular model (say model 22), however, only vectors 3, 4, 5, 12, 16, 17, and 19 are to be used as predictors, and vector 9 is the criterion. Columns 11 through 40 would be punched

$$022009003005012012016017019019$$

This can be read as: For model 22, vector 9 is specified as the criterion (or **Y**) vector, and the predictor vectors are 3 through 5, 12 through 12, 16 through 17, and 19 through 19.

The format of an F-value (shown as "F-test" on printout) card is

Columns	Contents
1–10	Identification. Any legal FORTRAN characters.
11–13	Punch 999.
14–16	Model number of the full model (see columns 11 through 13 of model card).
17–19	Model number of the restricted model (see columns 11 through 13 of model card).
20–22	Number of linearly independent predictors in the full model.
23–25	Number of linearly independent predictors in the restricted model.
26–80	Blank.

The first F-value card in the example specifies model 1 as the full model, with four linearly independent predictors, and model 2 as the restricted model, with two linearly independent predictors (see Section 6.7). Model and F-value cards can be interspersed in any order, so long as the models referenced on the F-value card *precede* it. There is only one exception to this rule: Anytime a full model is to be compared with a restricted model containing a unit vector as the only predictor, it is not necessary to provide a model card for the restricted model. Instead, the comparison is accomplished by specifying *any number less than 51* (not previously used as a model number) as the restricted model number on the F-value card. In the example problem, model 1 is compared to model 050, which is a test of the equality of the expected values of the four classes (see Section 4.9). Also, model 2 is compared to model 050, which is a test of the equality of the expected values of the four classes using a different full model (see Section 6.11).

Note that model 2 (as formulated in Section 6.4) contains a unit vector, but the model card does not specify a unit vector as one of the predictors. The program assumes that every model contains a unit vector predictor, so the user is not required to include it. But he should be aware of this feature.

A *blank* card should follow the last model or F-value card. This card causes the program to cease its search for additional model cards. A title card for a new problem should then follow the blank card. If this new title card is blank, computer activity will cease. Otherwise, the card-input sequence will be repeated for the new problem.

14.9
COMPUTER OUTPUT

The output that would be generated by our sample input is shown in Figure 14.2.

The initial part of the output provides **a summary of the input,** and most of the more typical user errors can be detected by a detailed examination of this summary. The first line of output is an image listing of the title

SAMPLE PROBLEMS FROM CHAPTERS 4 AND 6.

     20 = DIMENSION OF VECTORS (N).
      6 = NO. OF DATA ELEMENTS ON EACH INPUT RECORD (NC).
      6 = NO. OF VECTORS (NV).

DATA FORMAT

(11X, F2.0, 1X, 5F2.0)

VECTORS

	Y	G	$X^{(9)}$	$X^{(10)}$	$X^{(11)}$	$X^{(12)}$
	1.	2.	3.	4.	5.	6.
1.	16.00	9.00	1.00	0.00	0.00	0.00
2.	48.00	9.00	1.00	0.00	0.00	0.00
3.	40.00	9.00	1.00	0.00	0.00	0.00
4.	40.00	9.00	1.00	0.00	0.00	0.00
5.	32.00	9.00	1.00	0.00	0.00	0.00
6.	40.00	10.00	0.00	1.00	0.00	0.00
7.	24.00	10.00	0.00	1.00	0.00	0.00
8.	64.00	10.00	0.00	1.00	0.00	0.00
9.	56.00	10.00	0.00	1.00	0.00	0.00
10.	48.00	10.00	0.00	1.00	0.00	0.00
11.	64.00	11.00	0.00	0.00	1.00	0.00
12.	56.00	11.00	0.00	0.00	1.00	0.00
13.	48.00	11.00	0.00	0.00	1.00	0.00
14.	72.00	11.00	0.00	0.00	1.00	0.00
15.	56.00	11.00	0.00	0.00	1.00	0.00
16.	80.00	12.00	0.00	0.00	0.00	1.00
17.	72.00	12.00	0.00	0.00	0.00	1.00
18.	72.00	12.00	0.00	0.00	0.00	1.00
19.	64.00	12.00	0.00	0.00	0.00	1.00
20.	72.00	12.00	0.00	0.00	0.00	1.00

VAR.NO.	MEAN	SIGMA	VARIANCE
1	53.2000	17.0223	289.7600
2	10.5000	1.1180	1.2500
3	.2500	.4330	.1875
4	.2500	.4330	.1875
5	.2500	.4330	.1875
6	.2500	.4330	.1875

CORRELATION MATRIX

	1.	2.	3.	4.	5.	6.
1.	1.000	.809	-.611	-.231	.204	.638
2.	.809	1.000	-.775	-.258	.258	.775
3.	-.611	-.775	1.000	-.333	-.333	-.333
4.	-.231	-.258	-.333	1.000	-.333	-.333
5.	.204	.258	-.333	-.333	1.000	-.333
6.	.638	.775	-.333	-.333	-.333	1.000

```
* * * * * * * * * *   MODEL NO.    1   * * * * * * * * * * *

4.1                  ITERATION TOLERANCE- .00000010

CRITERION          1
PREDICTORS       3 -  6
```

VAR.NO.	CORRECTION	RSQ.	ERROR S.S.	ERROR MSQ.	ITER.
6	.6376436	.4065894	3438.9333	191.0519	1
5	.3760462	.6013252	2310.4000	135.9059	2
3	-.2663137	.6524353	2014.2071	125.8879	3
5	-.0552597	.6553690	1997.2054	124.8253	4
3	-.0120080	.6554354	1996.8207	124.8013	5
5	-.0018653	.6554388	1996.8010	124.8001	6
3	-.0006142	.6554390	1996.8001	124.8000	7

```
        RSQ.=  .6554390    R=  .8095919                              7
        ESS.=     1996.8000    STD.ERROR OF EST.=    11.1714
        ERROR MEAN SQUARE =   124.8000  ( 4 PARAMETERS ASSUMED.)
```

VAR.NO.	RAW WT.	STD. WT.	ERROR	ENTRY	VALIDITY
3	-11.1987	-.2849	0.0000	3	-.6105
4	0.0000	0.0000	.0000	0	-.2306
5	12.8040	.3257	-.0001	2	.2035
6	25.6000	.6512	.0000	1	.6376

```
              46.3987  UNIT VECTOR WEIGHT

                                    35.2 = 46.4 - 11.2
```

ID NO	Y VECTOR	PRED. VALUE	RESIDUAL VECTOR	PREDICTOR VECTORS			
1.	16.00	35.200	-19.2000	1	1	0	0	0
2.	48.00	35.200	12.8000	1	1	0	0	0
3.	40.00	35.200	4.8000	1	1	0	0	0
4.	40.00	35.200	4.8000	1	1	0	0	0
5.	32.00	35.200	-3.2000	1	1	0	0	0
6.	40.00	46.399	-6.3987	1	0	1	0	0
7.	24.00	46.399	-22.3987	1	0	1	0	0
8.	64.00	46.399	17.6013	1	0	1	0	0
9.	56.00	46.399	9.6013	1	0	1	0	0
10.	48.00	46.399	1.6013	1	0	1	0	0
11.	64.00	59.203	4.7973	1	0	0	1	0
12.	56.00	59.203	-3.2027	1	0	0	1	0
13.	48.00	59.203	-11.2027	1	0	0	1	0
14.	72.00	59.203	12.7973	1	0	0	1	0
15.	56.00	59.203	-3.2027	1	0	0	1	0
16.	80.00	71.999	8.0013	1	0	0	0	1
17.	72.00	71.999	.0013	1	0	0	0	1
18.	72.00	71.999	.0013	1	0	0	0	1
19.	64.00	71.999	-7.9987	1	0	0	0	1
20.	72.00	71.999	.0013	1	0	0	0	1

```
___ Error Vector                  U   X⁽⁹⁾  X⁽¹⁰⁾ X⁽¹¹⁾ X⁽¹²⁾
```

Error Vector   U $X^{(9)}$ $X^{(10)}$ $X^{(11)}$ $X^{(12)}$

```
* * * * * * * * * *  MODEL NO.    2   * * * * * * * * * * *

 6.4                 ITERATION TOLERANCE- .00000010

 CRITERION          1
 PREDICTORS        2 -  2

VAR.NO. CORRECTION    RSO.           ERROR S.S.     ERROR MSO.    ITER.

    2      .8091825      .6547764       2000.6400      111.1467       1

      RSO.=  .6547764    R=  .8091825                                 1

      ESS.=        2000.6400      STD.ERROR OF EST.=    10.5426
      ERROR MEAN SQUARE =    111.1467  ( 2 PARAMETERS ASSUMED.)

 VAR.NO.   RAW WT.    STD. WT.       ERROR    ENTRY VALIDITY

    2      12.3200      .8092       0.0000       1        .8092

          -76.1600 UNIT VECTOR WEIGHT
```

34.72 = -76.16 +(12.32) (9)

| ID | Y | PRED. | RESIDUAL | PREDICTOR | |
NO	VECTOR	VALUE	VECTOR	VECTORS	
1.	16.00	34.720	-18.7200	1	9
2.	48.00	34.720	13.2800	1	9
3.	40.00	34.720	5.2800	1	9
4.	40.00	34.720	5.2800	1	9
5.	32.00	34.720	-2.7200	1	9
6.	40.00	47.040	-7.0400	1	10
7.	24.00	47.040	-23.0400	1	10
8.	64.00	47.040	16.9600	1	10
9.	56.00	47.040	8.9600	1	10
10.	48.00	47.040	.9600	1	10
11.	64.00	59.360	4.6400	1	11
12.	56.00	59.360	-3.3600	1	11
13.	48.00	59.360	-11.3600	1	11
14.	72.00	59.360	12.6400	1	11
15.	56.00	59.360	-3.3600	1	11
16.	80.00	71.680	8.3200	1	12
17.	72.00	71.680	.3200	1	12
18.	72.00	71.680	.3200	1	12
19.	64.00	71.680	-7.6800	1	12
20.	72.00	71.680	.3200	1	12

──────── U — G ────────

```
.  .  .  .  .  .  .  .  .  .  .  .  .  .  .  .  .  .  .  .  .  .  .  .  .  .  .  .  .  .  .  .
.                                                                                            .
.   FTEST-SEC. 6.7                                                                           .
.                                                                                            .
.   MODEL      RSQ.        SS(ERROR)      MEAN SQUARES         F         PROB                 .
.                                                                                            .
.   FULL    1   .6554       1996.8000      124.8000               .0154   .9847              .
.   REST    2   .6548       2000.6400                                                        .
.   DIFF.       .0007          3.8400        1.9200     DF1=  2 DF2=    16                    .
.                                                                                            .
.  .  .  .  .  .  .  .  .  .  .  .  .  .  .  .  .  .  .  .  .  .  .  .  .  .  .  .  .  .  .  .


.  .  .  .  .  .  .  .  .  .  .  .  .  .  .  .  .  .  .  .  .  .  .  .  .  .  .  .  .  .  .  .
.                                                                                            .
.   FTEST-SEC. 4.9                                                                           .
.                                                                                            .
.   MODEL      RSQ.        SS(ERROR)      MEAN SQUARES         F         PROB                 .
.                                                                                            .
.   FULL    1   .6554       1996.8000      124.8000          10.1453   .0006                 .
.   REST   50  0.0000       5795.2000                                                        .
.   DIFF.       .6554       3798.4000       1266.1333    DF1=  3 DF2=    16                   .
.                                                                                            .
.  .  .  .  .  .  .  .  .  .  .  .  .  .  .  .  .  .  .  .  .  .  .  .  .  .  .  .  .  .  .  .


.  .  .  .  .  .  .  .  .  .  .  .  .  .  .  .  .  .  .  .  .  .  .  .  .  .  .  .  .  .  .  .
.                                                                                            .
.   FTEST-SEC. 6.11                                                                          .
.                                                                                            .
.   MODEL      RSQ.        SS(ERROR)      MEAN SQUARES         F         PROB                 .
.                                                                                            .
.   FULL    2   .6548       2000.6400      111.1467          34.1401   .0000                 .
.   REST   50  0.0000       5795.2000                                                        .
.   DIFF.       .6548       3794.5600       3794.5600    DF1=  1 DF2=    18                   .
.                                                                                            .
.  .  .  .  .  .  .  .  .  .  .  .  .  .  .  .  .  .  .  .  .  .  .  .  .  .  .  .  .  .  .  .
```

111.15 = 2000.64/18

3794.56 = (5795.20 - 2000.64) /1

34.14 = (3794.56/111.15)

FIG. 14.2   Output Generated by Input for Sample Problems from Chapters 4 and 6.

card. The next three lines summarize the information that was punched on the parameter card, followed by an image listing of the format card. Every element in each vector is then listed. Note that each vector contains 20 elements. The first vector is **Y**, and the last four are $X^{(9)}$, $X^{(10)}$, $X^{(11)}$, and $X^{(12)}$—all from Section 4.3. The second vector is **G**—from Section 6.8. If tape is being used for temporary storage, the vectors will not be listed.

Following the listing of the vectors is **a table of averages, standard deviations** (sigma), and **variances**. The average for each vector is calculated by taking the sum of the elements in the vector and dividing this sum by the dimension of the vector. The variance is obtained by taking the sum of the squared deviations of each element from the average and dividing this sum by the dimension of the vectors. The standard deviation is the square root of the variance.

In many cases, the user will have a reasonably good idea about the relative magnitudes of the averages. Frequently, input errors can be detected by examining the averages. For example, the sum of the averages of vectors 3 through 6 is 1.0, which will always be the case when the vectors are mutually exclusive, categorical vectors. This is a particularly useful check when the vectors are generated in DATRAN.

14.10
THE CORRELATION MATRIX

The next part of the output is a symmetric array of values called the **correlation matrix**. The values in this array are obtained by the equation used for a Pearson product-moment correlation coefficient between two variables (see Glass and Stanley, 1970, p. 114). The user should be cautious, however, in inferring any particular meaning from these values unless he is familiar with the theory and assumptions of correlation analysis. In this particular program, these values are used primarily as a computing convenience (see Draper and Smith, 1966, p. 144). In general, useful inferences from these values depend on *the distributional form of the underlying variables* (normal) and *the way in which the values were selected* (randomly). For many of the problems discussed in this book, neither of these conditions is met. As a descriptive statistic, however, these values can sometimes be informative (see Carroll, 1961).

14.11
SOLUTION TO THE MODEL

Each model card in the input deck will cause an output listing similar to "Model No. 1" shown in Figure 14.2. The identification punched in columns

1 through 10 of the model card is printed, and the criterion vector and pre-dictor vectors are identified. The numerical determination of the least-squares weights (explained in Appendix C) is accomplished by an iterative procedure that maximizes a value referred to as RSQ. On successive itera-tions, RSQ gets closer and closer to the **squared multiple-correlation coefficient** (the squared correlation between the criterion vector and a least-squares weighted composite of the predictor vectors).

In effect, the computing procedure assumes initially that every unknown weight is *zero*. On the first iteration, a modification of one of the weights is made in such a way that no other modification would yield a smaller error sum of squares. Subsequent iterations repeat this process, each time modify-ing a weight so as to minimize the error sum of squares. The relationship between RSQ and the error sum of squares (ESS) is given by the equation

$$RSQ = 1.0 - \frac{ESS}{n\sigma^2}$$

where σ^2 is the variance of the values in **Y**.

Six summary values of the iterative process are reported on the output for the first 10 iterations, unless fewer iterations are required. The symbols as-sociated with these six values are defined as

VAR. NO.: The number of the predictor vector for which the weight is being modified on the current iteration.

CORRECTION: The amount by which the weight is modified, except for a scaling factor (see Appendix C).

RSQ.: The squared correlation between the actual and predicted values after the correction has been made.

ERROR S.S.: The current value of the error sum of squares.

ERROR MSQ.: This value (see Appendix B) is calculated by dividing the current error sum of squares by the dimension of the vectors minus the number of nonzero weights. If a redundant vector exists in the set of predictors, this value can be in error.

ITER.: Iteration number.

The process continues until an iteration fails to raise the value of *RSQ* by the iteration tolerance, which is set to .0000001. Below the iteration sequence, final values are reported for RSQ, R (the square root of RSQ), ESS, the error mean square, and the standard error of estimate (the square root of the error mean square).

14.12
THE LEAST-SQUARES WEIGHTS

Under the column heading RAW WT, the least-squares weight associated with each predictor is listed along with another value labeled **unit vector weight**. This value is also called the **regression constant**. In effect, the computing algorithm used in this program *adds a unit vector to the set of predictors specified on the model card.* The implications that can be drawn from this fact must be well understood by the user.

In the first place, if a model has been formulated that does not contain a unit vector predictor (or a set of vectors of which the unit vector is a linear combination), this program will not provide the desired solution. For example, consider model (6.4), discussed in Section 6.8,

$$\mathbf{Y} = d_0\mathbf{U} + w_1\mathbf{G} + \mathbf{E}^{(3)}$$

The problem in Section 6.8 led to the restriction

$$w_1 = 0$$

Suppose, instead, that some question had led to the restriction

$$d_0 = 0$$

Imposing this restriction yields

$$\mathbf{Y} = 0\mathbf{U} + w_1\mathbf{G} + \mathbf{E}^{(4)}$$

or

$$\mathbf{Y} = w_1\mathbf{G} + \mathbf{E}^{(4)} \tag{14.1}$$

Note that (14.1) does not contain a unit vector nor is $\mathbf{U}$ a linear combination of $\mathbf{G}$; therefore, a solution for (14.1) cannot be achieved using this program. But the inference should not be drawn that something is "wrong" with model (14.1). The deficiency is in the computer program, not the model. You are not likely, however, to find this deficiency very restrictive because interesting models without a unit vector do not arise very often. When they do, alternative computing expressions are usually available (see Section 2.9). Note also that the second model card will generate a solution to model (6.4), not model (14.1).

Secondly, the addition of the unit vector to the set of predictors specified on the model card may produce a linearly dependent set of predictors, as in this example. The model that is actually being solved can be represented as

$$\mathbf{Y} = a_0\mathbf{U} + a_9\mathbf{X}^{(9)} + a_{10}\mathbf{X}^{(10)} + a_{11}\mathbf{X}^{(11)} + a_{12}\mathbf{X}^{(12)} + \mathbf{E}^{(1)} \tag{14.2}$$

where the vectors are defined the same as in Section 4.3. From the discussion in Section 5.3, we know that this model is equivalent to (4.1), but it does not have a unique solution. When the model has an infinite number of solutions, the program will provide one of them. In this example, the weights are

$$a_0 = 46.3987$$

$$a_9 = -11.1987$$

$$a_{10} = 0$$

$$a_{11} = 12.8040$$

$$a_{12} = 25.6000$$

and the predicted values are

$$a_0 + a_9 = 46.3987 - 11.1987 = 35.2$$

$$a_0 + a_{10} = 46.3987 + 0 = 46.4$$

$$a_0 + a_{11} = 46.3987 + 12.8040 = 59.2$$

$$a_0 + a_{12} = 46.3987 + 25.6000 = 72.0$$

which correspond to the values obtained in Section 4.4.

As long as the primary concern is obtaining *predicted values* (which estimate the parameter means or expected values) and error sums of squares for hypothesis testing, it makes no difference which one of the infinite solutions is found. But, if the *weights* are of interest, a great deal of care may be required in the definition of the predictor vectors (see Appendix D). Here, for example, the *differences* among the predicted values are more easily seen by looking at the weights rather than at the predicted values.

14.13
STANDARDIZED WEIGHTS

The values on the output under the column heading STD. WT. are referred to as standard or **standardized weights**. They are the values that would be obtained if **Y** and every predictor vector were converted to Z-score form (i.e., average $= 0$; standard deviation $= 1$) and a least-squares solution obtained. Since these values are not utilized in any of the problems discussed in this book, we will not pursue the purposes[4] for which they might be used —except to note that they are occasionally used in ways that are mysterious at worst, and questionable at best!

The values under the column heading ERROR are *measures* of the computational inaccuracy of the solution. The rationale for using these values as an indicator of inaccuracy can be defended by showing that the expression

---

[4]The interested reader is referred to an article by Darlington (1968) for further discussion.

$$\mathbf{W} = \mathbf{R}^{-1}\mathbf{R}^{(0)} \tag{14.3}$$

where

$\mathbf{W}$ = a $r \times 1$ vector of standardized weights.

$\mathbf{R}^{-1}$ = the $r \times r$ inverse of the matrix of intercorrelations among the predictors.

$\mathbf{R}^{(0)}$ = a $r \times 1$ vector of correlations between the criterion and the predictors. These values are frequently called the *validities*, and they are shown in the above output labeled VALIDITY.

is a solution for the standardized weights. Premultiplying both sides of 14.3 by $\mathbf{R}$ gives

$$\mathbf{RW} = \mathbf{R}^{(0)} \tag{14.4}$$

Now consider a solution for $\mathbf{W}$ (call it $\mathbf{T}$) obtained in some manner other than (14.3). If $\mathbf{T}$ is equal to $\mathbf{W}$, then $\mathbf{RT}$ should be equal to $\mathbf{R}^{(0)}$. The values in the output under the label ERROR are the elements of the vector

$$\mathbf{RT} - \mathbf{R}^{(0)}$$

The values under the column heading ENTRY reflect the *order* in which the predictors entered the equation during the iterative process.

We have devoted a great deal of space to the problem of translating *natural language* statements or questions into mathematical forms that enable us to manipulate a model. Some questions, however, that arise in natural-language form almost defy translation. Examples are the questions:

1. Which predictor variable is the most *important* in *explaining* the criterion?

2. What are the *relative contributions* of the various predictors to the prediction of the criterion?

We do not have enough space to explore all of the ramifications of this problem, but articles by Darlington (1968) and Ward (1969) do describe various ways of calculating values to reflect answers to these questions. Although it is usually not very clear exactly how these values are useful, if they are rank-ordered, the correlations between the ranks and the values reported under ENTRY will generally be quite high.

We emphasize again the desirability of expressing questions in terms of *expected values* (or translating the question into one that states a relationship among expected values). Although a colleague may disagree with your model, your translation process, or the restrictions you impose on the model, it is at least possible to reduce the argument to a level that can be communicated.

14.14
PREDICTED VALUES

The solution to each model is followed by **a listing of the predicted values**, unless this option is suppressed by a nonzero punch in column 80 of the model card. Associated with each predicted value are the corresponding observed criterion (Y) value and the values for each predictor. The residual or error vector is also shown. An examination of the residual values[5] can sometimes be instrumental in detecting errors or in improving the model.

Generally speaking, the magnitude of the errors reflects how well the model fits the data. Occasionally, one will observe a value that is much larger in absolute magnitude than any of the other errors. Such a case is sometimes referred to as an **outlier**. Scoring, measurement, or keypunching errors sometimes account for outliers. In other situations, the case or cases may be unique in some identifiable way that will lead the investigator to exclude these cases from the analysis or to modify the model in such a way as to represent this uniqueness in the model. For example, in a study of college achievement in English, an examination of the residuals might show that all outliers were foreign students. Depending on the purpose of the analysis, it would clearly be advisable either to eliminate the cases or to modify the model.

In practice, however, the predicted-value option is usually suppressed if the number of cases is large or the number of unique predictor patterns is small. Predicted values are easily calculated from the weights, and the subroutine that produces the predicted values can be easily modified to print only outliers.

14.15
F-VALUE OUTPUT

The output generated by the presence of an *F*-value card in the input is enclosed in a box of periods. The models being compared are identified by number, and the associated error sum of squares and RSQ are shown for both the full and restricted models. The degrees of freedom (DF1 and DF2) are calculated and printed.

Consider the *F*-value identified as SEC. 6.7. This comparison is discussed in Section 6.7. The value 3.84 is the *difference* between the error sum of squares in the restricted and full models. When divided by DF1 = 2, the

---

[5]An excellent discussion of the examination of residuals can be found in Draper and Smith (1966).

value 1.92 is obtained. This value is referred to as the *numerator mean square* because it is the numerator of the F ratio. The *denominator mean square* (124.8) is obtained by dividing the error sum of squares of the full model (1996.8) by DF2 (16).

Also shown on the output are the *comparisons* discussed in Section 4.9 and 6.11. Note that in each case, model 50 is referred to as the restricted model, but no model card was included for model 50. This comparison is possible because a model that is specified on the F-value card as having only one predictor is assumed by the program to have only a unit-vector predictor. The error sum of squares for such a model can be calculated directly by the expression

$$\underset{\text{(Dimension of } \mathbf{Y})}{20} \times \underset{\text{(Variance of } \mathbf{Y})}{289.76} = 5795.2$$

which is the value shown in Section 4.6 for the error sum of squares.

15

Subroutine DATRAN

15.1
INTRODUCTION

An important feature of the computer program discussed in Chapter 14 is a subroutine called DATRAN (from DATA TRANsformation). A complete understanding of this routine will enable the user to handle easily problems that are logically simple but frequently troublesome in practice. A standard version of DATRAN is used when the data cards contain all of the values needed for the vectors required in each model.

15.2
STANDARD VERSION OF SUBROUTINE
DATRAN

The standard version of DATRAN is composed of five cards. When listed on a line printer, the cards appear in the following sequence:

```
SUBROUTINE DATRAN (C, NC, V, NV)
DIMENSION C(1), V(1)
CALL MOVE (C, NC, V)
RETURN
END
```

Punching begins in column 7 in these cards, and spaces thereafter are irrelevant. These cards contain what are referred to as FORTRAN statements.

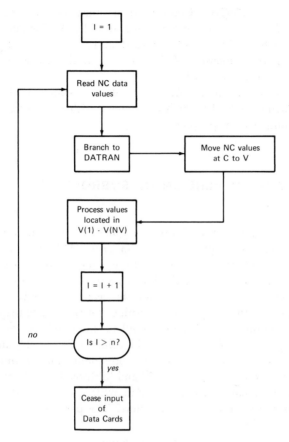

FIG. 15.1   Flowchart of Standard DATRAN.

FORTRAN is a very powerful—but easily learned—programming language.[1] Fortunately, most of the problems that occur in writing statements in DATRAN can be understood through the use of examples.

In the program NC data values are read from a data card and stored in memory locations C(1), C(2), . . . C(NC). SUBROUTINE DATRAN is called at this point. In the standard version, the statement

CALL MOVE (C, NC, V)

causes the NC values stored beginning at C(1) to be moved to memory loca-

---

[1] An excellent treatment of FORTRAN can be found in Veldman (1967).

tions $V(1), V(2), \ldots V(NC)$. Control is then returned to the program, which processes the NV values stored beginning at $V(1)$. At this point, NC data values are read from the second data card, and SUBROUTINE DATRAN is executed again. If the dimension of the vectors is n, this process is repeated n times, as shown in Figure 15.1.

If the user wishes to modify the input values in some way, he can easily do so by replacing the CALL MOVE statement with any FORTRAN statement that will accomplish this purpose.

15.3
A NONSTANDARD VERSION OF SUBROUTINE DATRAN

Many models discussed in this book require vectors containing elements that are not likely to be punched on data cards. Although the data cards can be punched so that they contain all the values needed (as described in Chapter 14), the user will usually find it more convenient to write a nonstandard version of DATRAN to generate the vectors he needs.

To demonstrate the simplicity of writing FORTRAN statements to insert in DATRAN, consider the sample problem discussed in the preceding chapter. Suppose the binary vectors in columns 18, 20, 22, and 24 had not been punched on the data cards. The only data values of interest on the data cards are in columns 12 through 13 and 15 through 16. By modifying the parameter and format cards slightly and writing a nonstandard DATRAN, we can generate the same output as before. The parameter card beginning in column 1 would be

000200000200006

and the format card would be

(10X, 2F3.0)

Or, if we were not sure that columns 11 and 14 were blank,

(11X, F2.0, 1X, F2.0)

the DATRAN subroutine could assume the following sequence:

```
      SUBROUTINE DATRAN (C, NC, V, NV)
      DIMENSION C(1), V(1)
1     CALL ZERO (V(3), 4)
2     V(1) = C(1)
3     V(2) = C(2)
4     K = C(2) - 6.0
```

```
5    V(K) = 1.0
     RETURN
     END
```

The numbers on the left are called **statement numbers**. Although not required for this problem, they are permissible, and they serve as reference points in discussing the statements. When used, statement numbers should appear in the first five columns, and the text of the statements should begin in some column greater than six.

Statement No.	*Purpose*
1	This statement is a SUBROUTINE CALL statement. It causes four locations beginning at V(3) to be set to zero. As a result, V(3), V(4), V(5), and V(6) now contain zeroes.
2	This statement is an assignment statement. It causes location V(1) to be assigned the value currently located at C(1).
3	Another assignment statement, which causes V(2) to be assigned the value currently located at C(2). Note that we could replace statements 2 and 3 by a single statement: CALL MOVE (C(1), 2, V(1)).
4	This statement causes a memory location named K to be assigned the current value of C(2) minus 6. Note that C(2) will contain the values punched in columns 15 and 16, (namely, 9 through 12). Therefore, K will take on the value $9 - 6 = 3$ for the first five data cards; $10 - 6 = 4$ for the second set of five data cards; $11 - 6 = 5$ for the third set of five data cards; and $12 - 6 = 6$ for the last five data cards.
5	This statement causes location V(K) to be assigned the value of one. Note that this statement will cause either V(3), V(4), V(5), or V(6) to be assigned the value one, depending on the value of K, which depends on the value in C(2).

The RETURN statement causes control to be returned to the main program, and the END statement is always the last statement in the subroutine.

The parameter card and the format card specify that only two values will be read into C from each card, but six vectors are needed. The subroutine will be executed 20 times—once for each data card. The following listing summarizes the contents of the various memory locations, after SUBROUTINE DATRAN has been executed for each data card.

Data Card No.	C(1)	C(2)	K	V(1)	V(2)	V(3)	V(4)	V(5)	V(6)
1	16	9	3	16	9	1	0	0	0
2	48	9	3	48	9	1	0	0	0
3	40	9	3	40	9	1	0	0	0

4	40	9	3	40	9	1	0	0	0
5	32	9	3	32	9	1	0	0	0
6	40	10	4	40	10	0	1	0	0
7	24	10	4	24	10	0	1	0	0
8	64	10	4	64	10	0	1	0	0
9	56	10	4	56	10	0	1	0	0
10	48	10	4	48	10	0	1	0	0
11	64	11	5	56	11	0	0	1	0
12	56	11	5	56	11	0	0	1	0
13	48	11	5	48	11	0	0	1	0
14	72	11	5	72	11	0	0	1	0
15	56	11	5	56	11	0	0	1	0
16	80	12	6	80	12	0	0	0	1
17	72	12	6	72	12	0	0	0	1
18	72	12	6	72	12	0	0	0	1
19	64	12	6	64	12	0	0	0	1
20	72	12	6	72	12	0	0	0	1

15.4
ANOTHER EXAMPLE OF DATRAN

In Sections 11.8 and 11.9, we defined a number of vectors, which were used in a study of income and education. Using those definitions, we will now generate the following vectors by writing nonstandard DATRAN.

Defined Vectors	DATRAN Reference
$\mathbf{Y}$	V(1)
$\mathbf{R}$	V(2)
$\mathbf{X}^{(i)}$ with $i = 1, 20$	V(3) through V(22)
$\mathbf{X}^{(1-11)}$	V(23)
$\mathbf{X}^{(12-20)}$	V(24)
$\mathbf{R}^{(1-11)}$	V(25)
$\mathbf{R}^{(12-20)}$	V(26)
$(\mathbf{R}^{(1-11)})^2$	V(27)
$(\mathbf{R}^{(19-20)})^2$	V(28)
$(132\mathbf{X}^{(1-11)} - 23\mathbf{R}^{(1-11)} + (\mathbf{R}^{(1-11)})^2)$	V(29)
$(132\mathbf{X}^{(1-11)} + 23\mathbf{R}^{(1-11)} + (\mathbf{R}^{(12-20)})^2)$	V(30)

In this particular problem, data cards would normally contain only annual salary and years of education. Suppose that columns 11 through 15 contain annual salary, that columns 68 through 69 contain years of education, and that data are available on 220 individuals. The parameter and format cards would be

00220000020003000001
(10X, F5.0, 52X, F2.0)

On each read cycle, the salary data would be stored in $C(1)$, and years of education would be stored in $C(2)$. The subroutine to generate the desired vectors could be written in a number of different ways. For example,

```
SUBROUTINE DATRAN (C, NC, V, NV)
DIMENSION C(1), V(1)
CALL ZERO (V, NV)
V(1) = C(1)
R = C(2)
V(2) = R
K = R + 2.
V(K) = 1.
K = R/12.
V(K + 23) = 1.
V(K + 25) = R
V(K + 27) = R * R
V(29) = 132. * V(23) - 23. * V(25) + V(27)
V(30) = 132. * V(23) + 23. * V(25) + V(28)
RETURN
END
```

Model and *F*-value cards would be

```
F ULL MODEL001001003022
MODEL1 1 . 1 1002001023028
F  1  VS .  2  999001002020006
MODEL1 1 . 18008001020020029030
F  2  VS .  8  999002008006004
```

Accuracy problems are sometimes encountered when dealing with models that produce highly intercorrelated predictor vectors and with polynomial forms in general. Generally, this problem can be circumvented by *reparameterizing* (see Appendix D) the model, thus reducing the correlations among the predictors. The ideal is to achieve a reparameterization that yields predictor vectors that are *mutually orthogonal* (see Appendix A). With polynomial forms, one way of accomplishing this orthogonalization is to use a table of coefficients of orthogonal polynomials (Draper & Smith, 1966) or a subroutine that will generate them and then reparameterize the model in DATRAN.

15.5
OTHER USES OF DATRAN

DATRAN need not be limited to generating vectors. Since any legal FORTRAN statement can appear in the subroutine, accomplished programmers can devise numerous ways of using the routine. For example, range and validity checks on the data can be made, and in some cases, errors can be corrected by substituting legal values. If desired, a corrected deck could be punched within the subroutine, or a frequency count of records with specified characteristics could be generated and printed. Since NC can be greater than NV, it is possible to read in a large number of values that will not be used for generating vectors but may be used for some other purpose. For example, with multiple card input per subject, an alphabetic identification field might be selected from each card (using A mode format rather than F mode), along with a card number and a match and sequence check made in DATRAN.

If it is likely that files having a large number of records will be dealt with, a slight change in the program will pay rich dividends. This modification adds statements in the subroutine that will call DATRAN and that will recognize a flag (returned from DATRAN) to signal an invalid record and then skip the processing associated with these records. Such a feature can be particularly useful when input is from tape, thus obviating the need for a separate pass to select specified records.

Although information about order can be used in DATRAN, card or tape sorts will almost never be required. An example in which order might be used involves changing the format in the middle of a job. Suppose that two files contain the same information but have different formats, and both files are required for a particular job. Furthermore, suppose that the first file contains m records. The format for the first file would appear on the format card, and a record count would be kept in DATRAN. After the mth record has been processed in DATRAN, another format card can be read or otherwise stored in the array holding the format. The records of the second file will then be read using the new format. Even with minimal programming skills, the possibilities are unlimited.

As we indicated in Section 14.8, it is possible to stack jobs so that a number of sets of data can be processed in a single run. If a nonstandard DATRAN is required for the jobs, it may be that the statements needed to generate the desired vectors for one job are not the same as for another job. The main routine automatically keeps track of the current job number, and it can be made available to DATRAN through common storage. An example is shown here.

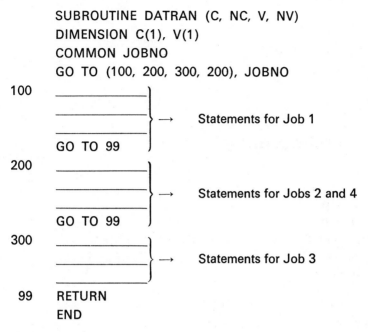

```
        SUBROUTINE DATRAN (C, NC, V, NV)
        DIMENSION C(1), V(1)
        COMMON JOBNO
        GO TO (100, 200, 300, 200), JOBNO
100     _____ ⎫
        _____ ⎬ →   Statements for Job 1
        _____ ⎪
        GO TO 99    ⎭
200     _____ ⎫
        _____ ⎬ →   Statements for Jobs 2 and 4
        _____ ⎪
        GO TO 99    ⎭
300     _____ ⎫
        _____ ⎬ →   Statements for Job 3
        _____ ⎭
99      RETURN
        END
```

Bibliography

Ackoff, Russell L. *Scientific Method*. New York: Wiley, 1962.

Anscombe, F. J. "Topics in the Investigation of Linear Relations Fitted by the Method of Least Squares." *J. Royal Stat. Soc.*, Ser. B (Methodological), 29:1 (1967), pp. 1–52.

Bashaw, W. L. *Mathematics for Statistics*. New York: Wiley, 1969.

Bottenberg, R. A., and J. H. Ward, Jr. *Applied Multiple Linear Regression*. PRL-TDR-63-6, AD-413 128, Lackland AFB, Tex.: Personnel Research Laboratory, Aerospace Medical Division, March 1963. (Available from Clearinghouse for Federal Scientific and Technical Information, U.S. Department of Commerce, Wash. D.C.)

———, and R. Christal "Grouping Criteria—A Method Which Retains Maximum Predictive Efficiency." *J. Exper. Ed.*, 36:4 (Summer, 1968), pp. 28–34.

Carroll, John B. "The Nature of the Data, or How to Choose a Correlation Coefficient." *Psychometrika*, 26:4 (December, 1961), pp. 347–72.

Christal, R. E. "Selecting a Harem—and Other Applications of the Policy Capturing Model." *J. Exper. Ed.*, 36:4 (Summer, 1968), pp. 35–41.

——— "JAN: A Technique for Analyzing Group Judgment." *J. Exper. Ed.*, 36:4 (Summer, 1968), pp. 24–27.

Darlington, Richard "Multiple Regression in Psychological Research and Practice." *Psychol. Bull.*, 69 (1968), pp. 161–82.

Draper, Norman, and Harry Smith *Applied Regression Analysis*. New York: Wiley, 1966.

Edwards, A. L. *Experimental Design in Psychological Research*. New York: Holt, 1962.

Engelhart, M. D. "A Note on the Analysis of Gains and Posttest Scores." *Ed. and Psychol. Measurement*, 27:2 (1967), pp. 257–60.

Freese, Frank *Linear Regression Methods for Forest Research*. U.S. Forest Service Research Paper, FPL 17, U.S. Department of Agriculture, Forest Products Laboratory, Madison, Wisconsin, 1964.

Glass, G. V., and J. C. Stanley *Statistical Methods in Education and Psychology*. Englewood Cliffs, N.J.: Prentice-Hall, 1970.

Greenberger, Martin H., and J. H. Ward, Jr. "An Iterative Technique for Multiple Correlation Analysis." Technical Newsletter No. 12, IBM Applied Science Division, IBM Corp., 590 Madison Ave., New York, 1956.

Jennings, Earl "Fixed Effects Analysis of Variance by Regression Analysis." *Multivariate Behav. Res.*, 2 (January, 1967), pp. 95–108.

Kelly, T. L., and F. S. Salisbury "An Iteration Method for Determining Multiple Correlation Constants." *J. Amer. Stat. Ass.*, 21 (1926), pp. 282–92.

McCornack, Robert L. "A Comparison of Three Predictor Selection Techniques in Multiple Regression." *Psychometrika*, 35:2 (June, 1970), pp. 257–71.

McNeill, Keith A. "Meeting the Goals of Research with Multiple Linear Regression." *Multivariate Behav. Res.*, 5 (July 1970), pp. 375–86.

Murdoch, D. C. *Linear Algebra for Undergraduates*. New York: Wiley, 1957.

Seal, Hilary L. "Studies in the History of Probability and Statistics. XV. The Historical Development of the Gauss Linear Model." *Biometrika*, 54 (1967), pp. 1–24.

Scheffé, Henry *The Analysis of Variance*. New York: Wiley, 1959.

Veldman, Donald J. FORTRAN *Programming for the Behavioral Sciences*. New York: Holt, 1967.

Ward, J. H., Jr. "Multiple Linear Regression Models" in *Computer Applications in the Behavioral Sciences* (H. Borko, ed.) Englewood Cliffs, N.J.: Prentice-Hall, 1962.

———— "Synthesizing Regression Models—An Aid to Learning Effective Problem Analysis." *Amer. Statistician*, 23:2 (April, 1969), pp. 14–20.

———— "Partitioning of Variance and Contribution or Importance of a Variable: A Visit to a Graduate Seminar." *Amer. Ed. Res. Journal*, 6:3 (May, 1969), pp. 467–74.

————, and Kathleen Davis "Teaching a Digital Computer to Assist in Making Decisions." PRL-TR-63-16, AD-407 322, Lackland AFB, Tex.: Personnel Research Laboratory, Aerospace Medical Division, June 1963.

Winer, B. J. *Statistical Principles in Experimental Design*. New York: McGraw-Hill, 1962.

Wishart, J. "Statistics in Agricultural Research," *J. R. Stat. Soc. Supp.*, 1 (1934), pp. 26–61.

Appendix A

Computation of Least-Squares Coefficients

In this appendix, several topics related to the computation of least-squares coefficients will be discussed.

A.1
THE MODEL IN MATRIX FORM

Our models usually take the form of

$$\mathbf{Y} = a_1\mathbf{X}^{(1)} + a_2\mathbf{X}^{(2)} + \cdots + a_k\mathbf{X}^{(k)} + \mathbf{E}$$

Letting $\mathbf{X}$ be a matrix whose columns are $\mathbf{X}^{(1)}, \mathbf{X}^{(2)}, \ldots, \mathbf{X}^{(k)}$ and $\mathbf{A}$ be a column vector with elements $a_1, a_2, \ldots, a_k$, we can write the model in the matrix form

$$\underset{(n \times 1)}{\mathbf{Y}} = \underset{(n \times k)}{\mathbf{X}} \underset{(k \times 1)}{\mathbf{A}} + \underset{(n \times 1)}{\mathbf{E}}$$

A.2
INNER PRODUCT OF TWO VECTORS

The inner product of two column vectors, $\mathbf{S}$ and $\mathbf{T}$, can be defined. Let

$\mathbf{S}' =$ a row vector (or matrix) made from the elements of $\mathbf{S}$.

$\mathbf{T}' =$ a row vector made from $\mathbf{T}$.

Then the inner product is

$$\mathbf{S'T} = s_1 t_1 + s_2 t_2 + \cdots + s_n t_n = \sum_{i=1}^{n} s_i t_i$$

Note that $\mathbf{S'T} = \mathbf{T'S}$.

A.3
ORTHOGONALITY

Two vectors, $\mathbf{S}$ and $\mathbf{T}$, are **orthogonal** if

$$\mathbf{S'T} = 0$$

A.4
ORTHOGONALITY AND LEAST SQUARES

If in

$$\mathbf{Y} = \mathbf{XA} + \mathbf{E}$$

$\mathbf{E}$ is orthogonal to the column vectors of $\mathbf{X}$, then

$$\mathbf{E'E} = e_1^2 + e_2^2 + \cdots + e_n^2$$

is a minimum, and $\mathbf{E}$ is said to be orthogonal to the space generated by $\mathbf{X}$. Consider the expression

$$\mathbf{Y} = \mathbf{XA} + \mathbf{E} \tag{A.1}$$

with $\mathbf{E}$ orthogonal to $\mathbf{X}^{(1)}, \mathbf{X}^{(2)}, \ldots, \mathbf{X}^{(k)}$ or $\mathbf{X'E} = 0$

Note that the result of $\mathbf{X'E}$ is a $k \times 1$ vector with each element equal to zero. We use the symbol 0 to refer to a vector containing all zeroes.

Consider another expression

$$\mathbf{Y} = \mathbf{XB} + \mathbf{F} \tag{A.2}$$

where $\mathbf{X'F} \neq 0$. We will show that

$$\mathbf{F'F} \geq \mathbf{E'E}$$

and that the equality is true only when $\mathbf{B} = \mathbf{A}$. Subtract (A.2) from (A.1) and obtain

$$\underset{(n \times 1)}{0} = \underset{(n \times k)}{\mathbf{X}} \underset{(k \times 1)}{(\mathbf{A} - \mathbf{B})} + \underset{(n \times 1)}{\mathbf{E}} - \underset{(n \times 1)}{\mathbf{F}}$$

Then

$$\mathbf{F} = \mathbf{E} + \mathbf{X}(\mathbf{A} - \mathbf{B})$$

and

$$\mathbf{F'F} = [\mathbf{E} + \mathbf{X}(\mathbf{A} - \mathbf{B})]'[\mathbf{E} + \mathbf{X}(\mathbf{A} - \mathbf{B})]$$

$$\mathbf{F'F} = \mathbf{E'E} + 2(\mathbf{A} - \mathbf{B})'\mathbf{X'E} + (\mathbf{A} - \mathbf{B})'\mathbf{X'X}(\mathbf{A} - \mathbf{B})$$

But it is given that $\mathbf{X'E} = 0$. Therefore

$$\mathbf{F'F} = \mathbf{E'E} + (\mathbf{A} - \mathbf{B})'\mathbf{X'X}(\mathbf{A} - \mathbf{B})$$

But since $\mathbf{F'F}$, $\mathbf{E'E}$, and $(\mathbf{A} - \mathbf{B})'\mathbf{X'X}(\mathbf{A} - \mathbf{B})$ are not negative,

$$\mathbf{F'F} \geq \mathbf{E'E}$$

and

$$(\mathbf{A} - \mathbf{B})'\mathbf{X'X}(\mathbf{A} - \mathbf{B}) = 0$$

only when $\mathbf{A} = \mathbf{B}$. The least-squares values are then given by the coefficients $\mathbf{A}$ such that $\mathbf{X'E} = 0$. Thus, if

$$\mathbf{Y} = \mathbf{XA} + \mathbf{E}$$

then

$$\mathbf{X'E} = 0$$
$$\mathbf{X'(Y} - \mathbf{XA)} = 0$$
$$\mathbf{X'Y} - \mathbf{X'XA} = 0$$
$$(\mathbf{X'X})\mathbf{A} = \mathbf{X'Y}$$

If $(\mathbf{X'X})^{-1}$ exists,

$$\mathbf{A} = (\mathbf{X'X})^{-1}\mathbf{X'Y}$$

A.5
DECOMPOSING Y INTO TWO ORTHOGONAL COMPONENTS

We want to express $\mathbf{Y}$ as a multiple of a single vector, $\mathbf{X}$, plus a residual vector, $\mathbf{E}$. That is,

$$\mathbf{Y} = k_1\mathbf{X} + \mathbf{E}$$

such that

$$\mathbf{E'E} = e_1^2 + e_2^2 + \cdots + e_n^2$$

is minimum. We must minimize $\mathbf{E'E}$ by making $\mathbf{X'E} = 0$. Thus,

$$\mathbf{X'(Y} - k_1\mathbf{X)} = 0$$
$$\mathbf{X'Y} - k_1\mathbf{X'X} = 0$$
$$k_1 = \frac{\mathbf{X'Y}}{\mathbf{X'X}} = \left(\sum_{i=1}^{n} x_i y_i\right)\bigg/\left(\sum_{i=1}^{n} x_i^2\right) \tag{A.3}$$

We can then write the decomposition as

$$\mathbf{Y} = k_1\mathbf{X} + \mathbf{E} = \frac{(\mathbf{X'Y})}{(\mathbf{X'X})}\mathbf{X} + \mathbf{E}$$

and letting $\mathbf{P} = [(\mathbf{X'Y})/(\mathbf{X'X})]\mathbf{X}$, we can write

$$\mathbf{Y} = \mathbf{P} + \mathbf{E}$$

A.6
SUM OF SQUARES

Now we can compute

$$\mathbf{Y'Y} = (\mathbf{P} + \mathbf{E})'(\mathbf{P} + \mathbf{E})$$
$$\mathbf{Y'Y} = \mathbf{P'P} + \mathbf{P'E} + \mathbf{E'P} + \mathbf{E'E}$$

But because

$$\mathbf{P'E} = \mathbf{E'P} = (\mathbf{XA})'\mathbf{E} = \mathbf{A'X'E} = 0$$

we have

$$\mathbf{Y'Y} = \mathbf{P'P} + \mathbf{E'E}$$

This indicates that the total sum of squares ($\mathbf{Y'Y}$) is equal to the predicted sum of squares ($\mathbf{P'P}$) plus the error sum of squares ($\mathbf{E'E}$).

Figure A.1 shows a geometric interpretation. The length of any vector $\mathbf{V}$ is equal to $\sqrt{\mathbf{V'V}}$. Observe that $\mathbf{E}$ is perpendicular (orthogonal) to $\mathbf{X}$ and that the length of vector $\mathbf{E} = \sqrt{\mathbf{E'E}}$ is a minimum.

A.7
DECOMPOSING Y INTO A MULTIPLE OF U
AND A RESIDUAL

We wish to express

$$\mathbf{Y} = k_1\mathbf{U} + \mathbf{E}$$

such that $\mathbf{E'E} = e_1^2 + e_2^2 + \cdots + e_n^2$ is a minimum. From (A.3)

$$k_1 = \frac{\mathbf{U'Y}}{\mathbf{U'U}} = \left(\sum_{i=1}^{n} y_i\right)\bigg/n$$

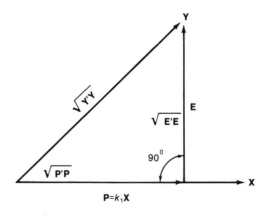

FIG. A.1   A Geometric Interpretation.

Then

$$\mathbf{Y} = \left[\left(\sum_{i=1}^{n} y_i \right) \Big/ n \right] \mathbf{U} + \mathbf{E}$$

We see that the elements of $\mathbf{E}$ are the deviations of the elements in $\mathbf{Y}$ from the average. Then

$$\mathbf{Y}'\mathbf{Y} = \mathbf{P}'\mathbf{P} + \mathbf{E}'\mathbf{E}$$

or

$$\mathbf{Y}'\mathbf{Y} = \left(\sum_{i=1}^{n} y_i \right)^2 \Big/ n + \mathbf{E}'\mathbf{E}$$

or

$$\mathbf{E}'\mathbf{E} = \left(\sum_{i=1}^{n} y_i^2 \right) - \left(\sum_{i=1}^{n} y_i \right)^2 \Big/ n$$

And the standard deviation (σ_y) is computed from

$$\sigma_y = \sqrt{\frac{\mathbf{E}'\mathbf{E}}{n}}$$

Appendix B

Assumptions Underlying the Use of the *F* Value as a Decision Rule

B.1
INTRODUCTION

Our primary purpose in this book has been to identify and exemplify certain skills that we believe are useful in model building. Very little consideration has been devoted to selecting a decision rule—this problem could easily fill another book.

Our repetitive use of the *F* value as a decision rule is based largely on convenience rather than a conviction that it has the most desirable properties for all purposes. For example, a very large sample (Section 4.10) can produce a statistically significant *F* value with very little practical consequence. On the other hand, the integration of model-building skills with statistical concepts, such as those associated with the *F* value, can add enormously to the utility of decision-making in the face of uncertainty. For this reason it seems desirable to identify in a more systematic way the conditions under which the ratio

$$\frac{(\mathrm{ESS}_r - \mathrm{ESS}_f)/(df)_1}{\mathrm{ESS}_f/(df)_2}$$

has a distribution function known as the **F distribution.**

In the discussion that follows, we will state the assumptions in a way that permits the reader to make the choice about the use of *F* as a decision rule. No effort will be made to prove the assertions that are stated.[1] Furthermore, frequent references will be made to the full (or starting) model

$$\mathbf{Y} = a_1\mathbf{X}^{(1)} + a_2\mathbf{X}^{(2)} + \cdots + a_k\mathbf{X}^{(k)} + \mathbf{E}^{(1)} \qquad (B.1)$$

and the restricted model

$$\mathbf{Y} = b_1\mathbf{Z}^{(1)} + b_2\mathbf{Z}^{(2)} + \cdots + b_m\mathbf{Z}^{(m)} + \mathbf{E}^{(2)} \qquad (B.2)$$

Each vector contains n elements. The values in the vectors $\mathbf{Y}$ and $\mathbf{X}^{(1)}$ through $\mathbf{X}^{(k)}$ are known. Each $\mathbf{Z}$ vector is a linear combination of one or more of the $\mathbf{X}$ vectors. The values in $\mathbf{E}^{(1)}$ and $\mathbf{E}^{(2)}$ are calculated by finding least-squares solutions for a_1 through a_k and b_1 through b_m.

B.2
THE STARTING MODEL

In general, the specification of the starting model and a numerical solution for the unknown values are notational and computational problems. If, in the context of a given problem, you discover that the quantities yielded by a least-squares solution to (B.1) turn out to be "useful" numbers, you should use them—whether or not the conditions that are specified later are met.

B.3
ESTIMATING EXPECTED VALUES

For all of the example problems discussed in this book, we have used a model of the general form (B.1) to estimate expected values. Model (B.1) produces "good" estimates (see Section 5.2) of the expected values if two conditions are satisfied: one concerns *sampling*, and the other concerns the *truth* of the model.

Consider an element (say the ith) of the vector $\mathbf{Y}$, which we denote y_i. If we examine the corresponding element of each $\mathbf{X}$ vector, we see that y_i is associated with the values

$$x_{i,1}, x_{i,2}, \ldots, x_{i,k}$$

These values can then be used to identify a population; y_i is a value observed on a particular member (assumed to have been selected by a random

---

[1] Proofs of most of these claims can be found in references—Graybill (1961) or Scheffé (1959).

process) of that population. To be specific, consider the extended form of model (9.4) in Section 9.7. Examine the fifteenth element of **Y**. Then,

$$y_i = y_{15} = 21$$
$$x_{i,1} = x_{15,1} = 1$$
$$x_{i,2} = x_{15,2} = 5$$
$$x_{i,3} = x_{15,3} = 3$$
$$x_{i,k} = x_{15,4} = 15$$

The number 21 is the typing-speed score of an individual who is a member of a population. Each member of this population has had 5 hrs of practice, and each member has a finger-dexterity score of 3. This particular member of the population was selected randomly from the population. Note that the fifteenth individual is the only member of this population represented in the sample. Now examine $y_{23} = 50$ and $y_{24} = 56$. Both of these individuals are members of a population characterized by having practiced 20 hrs and by having a finger-dexterity score of 4. Thus, we have two members from this population in the sample. In model (9.4) it is possible to identify 20 distinct patterns of the x values; hence, 20 different populations are represented.

The second condition—the model must be "true"—is defined in the discussion in Section 6.15. Consider model (9.4). There are 20 populations represented. Each member of each of the 20 populations has a typing score. What is the expected value of typing performance for each of the 20 populations? If we have only samples from the populations, we do not know and we cannot determine what the expected values are, but we can estimate them. In general, these estimates will be "good" if the model is true, and *a model is true if the expected values can be expressed as a linear combination of observable values and unknown parameters in the way described by the model.* For example, in order for model (9.4) to be true, the expected value of the ijth population, $\mathscr{E}(i,j)$, must be equal to

$$b_0(1) + d_0(i) + c_0(j) + k_0(i*j) \qquad \begin{cases} i = 5, 10, 15, 20, 25 \\ j = 1, 2, 3, 4 \end{cases}$$

where 1, i, and j are the observable values, and b_0, d_0, c_0, and k_0 are unknown parameters. To be specific, we assume that

$$\mathscr{E}(5, 3) = b_0 + 5d_0 + 3c_0 + 15k_0$$

and that

$$\mathscr{E}(20, 2) = b_0 + 20d_0 + 2c_0 + 40k_0$$

etc., for all of the possible values of i and j. Note that the observable values change from one expected value to another, but the parameters remain the same.

B.4
HYPOTHESIS TESTING

Although the assumptions discussed in this section are not required in many situations (particularly practical problems of prediction), they are important in instances where the primary concern is hypothesis testing and not just estimating expected values, as discussed in the preceding section.

Consider model (B.1), which contains the parameters a_1 through a_k. A restricted model is obtained by imposing one or more restrictions of a particular form on the parameters. Specifically, the restrictions must be expressible in the form

$$c_{11}a_1 + c_{12}a_2 + \cdots + c_{1k}a_k = d_1$$
$$c_{21}a_1 + c_{22}a_2 + \cdots + c_{2k}a_k = d_2$$
$$\begin{matrix} \cdot & \cdot & \cdot \\ \cdot & \cdot & \cdot \\ \cdot & \cdot & \cdot \end{matrix}$$
$$c_{r1}a_1 + c_{r2}a_2 + \cdots + c_{rk}a_k = d_r$$

where c_{ij} and d_i are specified constants.

These expressions may look more complex than they actually are. For example, suppose we wanted to test the hypothesis $a_1 - a_2 = a_3 - a_4$. This restriction can be written as

$$1a_1 - 1a_2 - 1a_3 + 1a_4 + 0a_5 + \cdots + 0a_k = 0$$

Note that

$$c_{11} = 1, \ c_{12} = -1, \ c_{13} - 1$$
$$c_{14} = 1, \ c_{15} \text{ through } c_{1k} = 0$$
$$d_1 = 0 \text{ and } r = 1$$

The major point is that *we are restricted to testing hypotheses about the parameters that can be expressed in a linear form.* For example, we could not test the following hypotheses using the methods described in this book.

$$a_1 = a_2^2$$
$$a_1 a_2 = a_3 a_4$$
$$a_1 = 4^{a_2}$$

These cannot be tested because the relations cannot be expressed in the general form just described. But any hypothesis that can be expressed in this general form is subject to test using the methods described here. You will recall from the discussion in Section 9.12, however, that logical and inferential problems can be encountered if the restrictions are not derived from relations among expected values. We therefore strongly recommend that Step 3 in the Preface not be skipped.

The restrictions can be substituted for the parameters of model (B.1), thus yielding (B.2) when the expressions are simplified. One of the effects of requiring linear restrictions is that *every predictor vector in the restricted model will be a linear combination of predictors in the full model.* Thus, every Z is a linear combination of one or more X vectors.

Suppose a least-squares solution is found for (B.1) and (B.2), and the corresponding error sum of squares, ESS_1 and ESS_2, are calculated. Furthermore, suppose that the number of linearly independent predictor vectors in the full model is $p \leq k$ and that the number of linearly independent predictor vectors in the restricted model is $q \leq m$ and $q < p$. Then the following expression is the likelihood-ratio-test statistic (see Scheffé, 1959, p. 32).

$$\frac{(ESS_2 - ESS_1)/(p - q)}{ESS_1/(n - p)}$$

It also has the F distribution with $p - q$ and $n - p$ degrees of freedom, providing the following conditions[2] are satisfied.

1. The random-sampling assumption described in Section B.3 must be satisfied.

2. The full model must be true, as described in Section B.3.

3. The restrictions must be true. This is another way of saying that the restricted model must also be true.

4. The distribution of the variable of interest within each population must be normal.

5. The variance of the variable of interest must be the same within each population.

6. The variable of interest within each population is distributed independently of any of the other populations.

If the probability value associated with a computed F is very small, there is evidence that one or more of these conditions has not been adequately satisfied. In practice, if we feel reasonably comfortable about the other conditions, we tend to reject number 3, and, as a consequence, reject the hypothesis (if $r = 1$) or the compound hypothesis (if $r > 1$) that led to the restrictions.

---

[2]This list contains some technical terms that we have not adequately discussed. In particular, the concept of *a set of normally and independently distributed variables with homogeneous (equal) variances* needs additional discussion. An excellent source for such coverage is Glass and Stanley (1970, pp. 79–84, 95–104, 141–44, 68–374, 501–08).

B.5
ROBUSTNESS OF *F*

A test statistic such as *F* is said to be *robust* if its sampling distribution is not much affected by violations of the assumptions made in its derivation. Suppose, for example, that all of the assumptions listed in Section B.4 were satisfied—except the normality assumption. Suppose that we conducted a particular investigation a very large number of times, each time with a different set of sampled values. If the frequency distribution of the obtained *F* values corresponds very closely to the *F* distribution, then we would say that *F* is robust under violation of the normality assumption; otherwise, we would say that it is not robust.[3]

B.6
USE OF THE ERROR MEAN SQUARE AS
A DECISION RULE

In certain areas of science, theoretical positions are sufficiently developed to predict the actual magnitude of parameters. In others, a theory may predict relations among parameters but not their magnitudes. In less developed areas, theory (or perhaps only intuition) may lead to the inference that the expected values of an interesting variable can be described as some function of other attributes, but the form of the function may remain completely unknown. In such cases, an investigator's activities could more properly be described as model seeking rather than hypothesis testing. The goal is to find *the simplest possible model that will account for the differences among the estimated expected values*.

A useful statistic for this purpose is a value called the **error mean square**. For any model, consider the quantity

$$\text{ESS}/(n - k)$$

where *n* is the dimension of the vectors and *k* is the number of parameters being estimated (i.e., the number of linearly independent predictor vectors). If assumptions 1, 2, and 5 in the list in Section B.4 are satisfied, this ratio can be shown to be an unbiased estimate of the common variance of the variable of interest within each population. Among a set of models, then, the one producing the smallest error mean square has appeal because the expected variance of errors of prediction is small relative to other models.

---

[3] A great deal of theoretical and empirical investigation of the robustness of *F* under various violations has been conducted. A good review of this work can be found in Glass and Stanley (1970, pp. 368–74).

Note that the expression ESS/n is the average squared error in the sample. This number has some intuitive appeal as a descriptive statistic. But as an inferential statistic it is defective, since it always takes on its minimum value when the number of parameters is equal to the number of expected values being estimated. Using the denominator $(n - k)$ has a subtle impact. Consider the values reported in Table 9.2 and summarized here.

Model	ESS	Number of Parameters	Error Mean Square
(9.1)	59.00	20	11.80
(9.2)	93.92	10	6.26
(9.4)	134.20	4	6.39
(9.9)	1950.51	2	84.80
(9.10)	271.25	3	12.33

Note that the model with only two parameters (9.9) yields an error mean square of 84.80. By adding one parameter (9.10), the value plummets to 12.33. Adding one additional parameter (9.4) lowers the value to 6.39. Adding six additional parameters (9.2) lowers the value only slightly to 6.26, and adding ten more parameters increases the value to 11.80.

On the basis of these values, we would be inclined to choose model (9.4) as the "best" model. Although the error mean square[4] is slightly smaller for model (9.2), this gain complicates the model considerably.

---

[4]A more elaborate discussion of the error mean square can be found in Draper and Smith (1966).

Appendix C

An Iterative Technique for Computing Least-Squares Coefficients

C.1
INTRODUCTION

The iterative method used in the FORTRAN program described in Chapter 14 is based on the procedure described by Greenberger and Ward (1956) and by Kelley and Salisbury (1926). The description, using matrix notation, presented here is for those who are interested in the computational details of this iterative method.

C.2
DEFINITIONS

Let

$$\mathbf{Y} = \begin{bmatrix} y_1 \\ y_2 \\ \cdot \\ \cdot \\ \cdot \\ y_n \end{bmatrix} = \text{a column vector of dimension } n.$$

$\mathbf{X} = [\mathbf{X}^{(1)} \mathbf{X}^{(2)} \cdots \mathbf{X}^{(r)}] = $ a matrix of dimensions $n \times r$, composed of column vectors $\mathbf{X}^{(1)}, \mathbf{X}^{(2)}, \ldots, \mathbf{X}^{(r)}$.

$$\mathbf{B} = \begin{bmatrix} b_1 \\ b_2 \\ \cdot \\ \cdot \\ \cdot \\ b_r \end{bmatrix} = \text{a column vector of dimension } r, \text{ representing the least-squares coefficients.}$$

$$\mathbf{E} = \begin{bmatrix} e_1 \\ e_2 \\ \cdot \\ \cdot \\ \cdot \\ e_n \end{bmatrix} = \text{a column vector of dimension } n\text{—the error vector.}$$

$$\mathbf{V} = \begin{bmatrix} v_1 \\ v_2 \\ \cdot \\ \cdot \\ \cdot \\ v_r \end{bmatrix} = \text{a column vector of dimension } r, \text{ representing an arbitrary set of coefficients.}$$

$$\mathbf{G} = \begin{bmatrix} g_1 \\ g_2 \\ \cdot \\ \cdot \\ \cdot \\ g_n \end{bmatrix} = \text{a column vector of dimension } n, \text{ representing errors using coefficients } \mathbf{V}.$$

$$\mathbf{Z}^{(0)} = \frac{1}{\sigma_y}[\mathbf{Y} - m_y\mathbf{U}] = \begin{bmatrix} \dfrac{y_i - m_y}{\sigma_y} \\ \dfrac{y_2 - m_y}{\sigma_y} \\ \cdot \\ \cdot \\ \cdot \\ \dfrac{y_n - m_y}{\sigma_y} \end{bmatrix} = \text{a column vector of dimension } n, \text{ containing standardized } \mathbf{Y} \text{ scores.}$$

where
$\sigma_y = $ standard deviation of the elements of $\mathbf{Y}$.

$m_y = $ average of the elements of $\mathbf{Y}$.

$\mathbf{U} = $ the unit vector, containing all ones.

$$\mathbf{Z}^{(j)} = \frac{1}{\sigma_j}[\mathbf{X}^{(j)} - m_j\mathbf{U}] = \begin{bmatrix} \dfrac{x_{1j} - m_j}{\sigma_j} \\ \dfrac{x_{2j} - m_j}{\sigma_j} \\ \cdot \\ \cdot \\ \cdot \\ \dfrac{x_{nj} - m_j}{\sigma_j} \end{bmatrix}$$ = a column vector of dimension n, containing standardized $\mathbf{X}^{(j)}$ scores.

$\mathbf{Z} = [\mathbf{Z}^{(1)}\mathbf{Z}^{(2)} \cdots \mathbf{Z}^{(r)}]$ = a matrix of dimensions $n \times r$ of standardized scores.

$$\mathbf{W} = \begin{bmatrix} w_1 \\ w_2 \\ \cdot \\ \cdot \\ \cdot \\ w_r \end{bmatrix}$$ = a column vector of dimension r, representing the least-squares coefficients for standardized scores.

$$\mathbf{F} = \begin{bmatrix} f_1 \\ f_2 \\ \cdot \\ \cdot \\ \cdot \\ f_n \end{bmatrix}$$ = a column vector of dimension n—the error vector for standardized scores.

$$\mathbf{T} = \begin{bmatrix} t_1 \\ t_2 \\ \cdot \\ \cdot \\ \cdot \\ t_r \end{bmatrix}$$ = a column vector of dimension r, representing an arbitrary set of coefficients for standardized scores.

$$\mathbf{H} = \begin{bmatrix} h_1 \\ h_2 \\ \cdot \\ \cdot \\ \cdot \\ h_n \end{bmatrix}$$ = a column vector of dimension n, representing errors using coefficients $\mathbf{T}$.

$\mathbf{R} = \dfrac{1}{n}[\mathbf{Z}'\mathbf{Z}]$ = intercorrelation matrix $(r \times r)$ of $\mathbf{X}^{(1)}, \mathbf{X}^{(2)}, \ldots, \mathbf{X}^{(r)}$.

$\mathbf{R}^{(0)} = \dfrac{1}{n}[\mathbf{Z}'\mathbf{Z}^{(0)}]$ = a column vector of dimension r, containing correlation coefficients of all predictors with $\mathbf{Y}$.

$\mathbf{R}^{(p)} = \dfrac{1}{n}[\mathbf{Z}'\mathbf{Z}^{(p)}]$ = a column vector of dimension r, containing correlation coefficients of all predictors with the pth predictor.

$r_{p0} = \dfrac{1}{n}[\mathbf{Z}^{(p)\prime}\mathbf{Z}^{(0)}]$ = the correlation between $\mathbf{Y}$ and $\mathbf{X}^{(p)}$.

$$a_p = \mathbf{T}'\mathbf{R}^{(p)}$$
$$\mathbf{A}' = \mathbf{T}'\mathbf{R} = [a_1 a_2 \cdots a_p \cdots a_r]$$
$$\sigma^2 = \mathbf{T}'\mathbf{R}\mathbf{T} = \mathbf{A}'\mathbf{T}$$
$$s = \mathbf{T}'\mathbf{R}^{(0)}$$

C.3
LEAST-SQUARES COEFFICIENTS

The problem is to determine the coefficients $b_1, b_2, \ldots, b_r$ that minimize

$$\sum_{i=1}^{n} e_i^2 = (\mathbf{E}'\mathbf{E})$$

where

$$\mathbf{Y} = \mathbf{X}\mathbf{B} + \mathbf{E}$$

We can minimize $\mathbf{E}'\mathbf{E}$ by making $\mathbf{E}$ orthogonal to the vector space generated by $\mathbf{X}$. Thus

$$\mathbf{X}'\mathbf{E} = 0$$

But, since

$$\mathbf{E} = \mathbf{Y} - \mathbf{X}\mathbf{B}$$

then

$$\mathbf{X}'\mathbf{X}\mathbf{B} = \mathbf{X}'\mathbf{Y}$$

And

$$\mathbf{B} = (\mathbf{X}'\mathbf{X})^{-1}\mathbf{X}'\mathbf{Y}$$

assuming that $(\mathbf{X}'\mathbf{X})^{-1}$ exists.

C.4
THE ITERATIVE METHOD USING
THE ORIGINAL VECTORS

This section describes the general iterative method. It begins with an arbitrary set of coefficients $v_1, v_2, \ldots, v_r$ and makes corrections on the coefficients that maximally decrease

$$\sum_{i=1}^{n} g_i^2 = (\mathbf{G'G})$$

This method considers making a correction on each coefficient and then selects the correction that will maximally decrease $\mathbf{G'G}$.

Let $\mathbf{X}^{(p)}$ be the vector whose coefficient is being considered for correction. Using the arbitrary coefficients $\mathbf{V}$, write

$$\mathbf{Y} = k_1(\mathbf{XV}) + k_2\mathbf{X}^{(p)} + \mathbf{G}$$

where k_1 and k_2 are coefficients to be determined by least-squares procedure. Then let

$$d = \frac{k_2}{k_1}$$

Thus

$$\mathbf{Y} = k_1[\mathbf{XV} + d\mathbf{X}^{(p)}] + \mathbf{G}$$

To minimize $\mathbf{G'G}$, make $\mathbf{G}$ orthogonal to the space generated by the vectors $\mathbf{XV}$ and $\mathbf{X}^{(p)}$

$$(\mathbf{XV})'\mathbf{G} = 0$$

$$\mathbf{X}^{(p)'}\mathbf{G} = 0$$

Then, since $\mathbf{G} = \mathbf{Y} - k_1(\mathbf{XV} + d\mathbf{X}^{(p)})$,

$$(\mathbf{XV})'[\mathbf{Y} - k_1(\mathbf{XV} + d\mathbf{X}^{(p)})] = 0$$

$$\mathbf{X}^{(p)'}[\mathbf{Y} - k_1(\mathbf{XV} + d\mathbf{X}^{(p)})] = 0$$

and

$$k_1(\mathbf{V'X'XV} + d\mathbf{V'X'X}^{(p)}) = \mathbf{V'X'Y} \tag{C.1}$$

$$k_1(\mathbf{X}^{(p)'}\mathbf{XV} + d\mathbf{X}^{(p)'}\mathbf{X}^{(p)}) = \mathbf{X}^{(p)'}\mathbf{Y} \tag{C.2}$$

Multiplying this last equation by d, we obtain

$$k_1(d\mathbf{X}^{(p)'}\mathbf{XV} + d^2\mathbf{X}^{(p)'}\mathbf{X}^{(p)}) = d\mathbf{X}^{(p)'}\mathbf{Y} \tag{C.3}$$

But, since $d(\mathbf{V'X'X}^{(p)}) = d(\mathbf{X}^{(p)'}\mathbf{XV})$, we can add (C.1) and (C.3) and write

$$k_1(\mathbf{V'X'XV} + 2d\mathbf{V'X'X}^{(p)} + d^2\mathbf{X}^{(p)'}\mathbf{X}^{(p)}) = \mathbf{V'X'Y} + d\mathbf{X}^{(p)'}\mathbf{Y}$$

Then

$$k_1 = \frac{\mathbf{V'X'Y} + d\mathbf{X}^{(p)'}\mathbf{Y}}{\mathbf{V'X'XV} + 2d\mathbf{V'X'X}^{(p)} + d^2\mathbf{X}^{(p)'}\mathbf{X}^{(p)}}$$

From (C.1) and (C.2)

$$k_1 = \frac{\mathbf{V'X'Y}}{\mathbf{V'X'XV} + d\mathbf{V'X'X}^{(p)}} = \frac{\mathbf{X}^{(p)'}\mathbf{Y}}{\mathbf{X}^{(p)'}\mathbf{XV} + d\mathbf{X}^{(p)'}\mathbf{X}^{(p)}}$$

Crossmultiplying gives

$$d\mathbf{X}^{(p)'}\mathbf{X}^{(p)}\mathbf{V}'\mathbf{X}'\mathbf{Y} + (\mathbf{V}'\mathbf{X}'\mathbf{Y})\mathbf{X}^{(p)'}\mathbf{X}\mathbf{V}$$
$$= d\mathbf{V}'\mathbf{X}'\mathbf{X}^{(p)}\mathbf{X}^{(p)}\mathbf{Y} + \mathbf{V}'\mathbf{X}'\mathbf{X}\mathbf{V}\mathbf{X}^{(p)'}\mathbf{Y}$$

$$d = \frac{(\mathbf{V}'\mathbf{X}'\mathbf{X}\mathbf{V})(\mathbf{X}^{(p)'}\mathbf{Y}) - (\mathbf{V}'\mathbf{X}'\mathbf{Y})\mathbf{X}^{(p)'}\mathbf{X}\mathbf{V}}{\mathbf{X}^{(p)'}\mathbf{X}^{(p)}\mathbf{V}'\mathbf{X}'\mathbf{Y} - \mathbf{V}'\mathbf{X}'\mathbf{X}^{(p)}\mathbf{X}^{(p)'}\mathbf{Y}}$$

The values k_1 and d can be computed for each coefficient, and the correction that maximally decreases $\mathbf{G}'\mathbf{G}$ can be made.

C.5
THE ITERATIVE METHOD USING STANDARDIZED SCORES

This section describes the actual iterative method (using standard scores) that is employed in our computer program. It begins with an arbitrary set of coefficients $t_1, t_2, \ldots, t_r$ and corrects iteratively to maximally decrease $\mathbf{H}'\mathbf{H}$ (the error sum of squares). $\mathbf{H}'\mathbf{H}$ will then approach $\mathbf{F}'\mathbf{F}$ (the minimum error sum of squares). The FORTRAN program starts with $t_1 = t_2 = \cdots = t_r = 0$.

Consider

$$\mathbf{Z}^{(0)} = c_1(\mathbf{ZT}) + c_2\mathbf{Z}^{(p)} + \mathbf{H}$$

where c_1 and c_2 are coefficients to be determined by least-squares procedure. Then let

$$\delta = \frac{c_2}{c_1}$$

Thus

$$\mathbf{Z}^{(0)} = c_1[\mathbf{ZT} + \delta\mathbf{Z}^{(p)}] + \mathbf{H}$$

To minimize $\mathbf{H}'\mathbf{H}$, make $\mathbf{H}$ orthogonal to $\mathbf{ZT}$ and $\mathbf{X}^{(p)}$.

$$(\mathbf{ZT})'\mathbf{H} = 0$$
$$\mathbf{Z}^{(p)'}\mathbf{H} = 0$$

Then, since $\mathbf{H} = \mathbf{Z}^{(0)} - c_1(\mathbf{ZT} + \delta\mathbf{Z}^{(p)})$,

$$(\mathbf{ZT})'[\mathbf{Z}^{(0)} - c_1(\mathbf{ZT} + \delta\mathbf{Z}^{(p)})] = 0$$
$$\mathbf{Z}^{(p)'}[\mathbf{Z}^{(0)} - c_1(\mathbf{ZT} + \delta\mathbf{Z}^{(p)})] = 0$$
$$c_1(\mathbf{T}'\mathbf{Z}'\mathbf{ZT} + \delta\mathbf{T}'\mathbf{Z}'\mathbf{Z}^{(p)}) = \mathbf{T}'\mathbf{Z}'\mathbf{Z}^{(0)}$$
$$c_1(\mathbf{Z}^{(p)'}\mathbf{ZT} + \delta\mathbf{Z}^{(p)'}\mathbf{Z}^{(p)}) = \mathbf{Z}^{(p)'}\mathbf{Z}^{(0)}$$

Multiplying both equations by $1/n$—using the definitions in Section C.2 and observing that $1/n(\mathbf{Z}^{(p)'}\mathbf{Z}^{(p)}) = 1$—gives

$$c_1[\sigma^2 + \delta(a_p)] = s$$

$$c_1[a_p + \delta] = r_{p0}$$

Multiplying the second equation by δ gives

$$c_1[\sigma^2 + \delta(a_p)] = s$$

$$c_1[\delta(a_p) + \delta^2] = \delta r_{p0}$$

Adding we get

$$c_1 = \frac{s + \delta(r_{p0})}{\sigma^2 + 2\delta(a_p) + \delta^2}$$

and

$$c_1 = \frac{s}{\sigma^2 + \delta(a_p)} = \frac{r_{p0}}{a_p + \delta}$$

Thus

$$\delta = \frac{\sigma^2(r_{p0}) - s(a_p)}{s - a_p(r_{p0})}$$

In order to compute the values of σ and c_1 at each iteration, we must have new values for s, σ^2, and a_j $(j = 1, 2, \ldots, r)$; these are symbolized by s^*, $(\sigma^2)^*$, and a_j^*. The values of r_{p0} (and all other correlations) are computed prior to starting the iterative sequence.

The new coefficient associated with the pth predictor is given by

$$t_p^* = t_p + \delta$$

Then s^*, $(\sigma^2)^*$, and a_j^* can be determined as follows.

Since $s = \mathbf{T'R}^{(0)}$

$$s^* = t_1 r_{10} + t_2 r_{20} + \cdots + (t_p + \delta)r_{p0} + \cdots + t_r r_{r0}$$

$$s^* = (t_1 r_{10} + \cdots + t_p r_{p0} + \cdots + t_r r_{r0}) + \delta r_{p0}$$

$$s^* = s + \delta r_{p0}$$

and since $a_j = \mathbf{T'R}^{(j)}$

$$a_j^* = t_1 r_{j1} + t_2 r_{j2} + \cdots + (t_p + \delta)r_{jp} + \cdots + t_r r_{jr}$$

$$a_j^* = (t_1 r_{j1} + t_2 r_{j2} + \cdots + t_p r_{jp} + \cdots + t_r r_{jr}) + \delta r_{jp}$$

$$a_j^* = a_j + \delta r_{jp}$$

Now, since $\sigma^2 = \mathbf{A'T}$,

$$(\sigma^2)^* = t_1 a_1^* + t_2 a_2^* + \cdots + (t_p + \delta)a_p^* + \cdots + t_r a_r^*$$

Substitution of $a_j^* = a_j + \delta r_{jp}$ gives

$$(\sigma^2)^* = t_1(a_1 + \delta r_{1p}) + t_2(a_2 + \delta r_{2p})$$
$$+ \cdots + (t_p + \delta)(a_p + \delta r_{pp}) + \cdots + t_r(a_r + \delta r_{rp})$$

$$(\sigma^2)^* = (t_1 a_1 + t_2 a_2 + \cdots + t_r a_r)$$
$$+ \delta(t_1 r_{1p} + t_2 r_{2p} + \cdots + t_r r_{rp}) + \delta(a_p + \delta)$$

and

$$(\sigma^2)^* = \sigma^2 + \delta(a_p) + \delta(a_p) + \delta^2$$

$$(\sigma^2)^* = \sigma^2 + 2\delta(a_p) + \delta^2$$

Observe that the value

$$c_1 = \frac{s + \delta(r_{p0})}{\sigma^2 + 2\delta(a_p) + \delta^2} = \frac{s^*}{(\sigma^2)^*}$$

It can also be shown that the squared correlation between $\mathbf{Z}^{(0)}$ and the vector

$$c_1 \mathbf{ZT} + c_2 \mathbf{Z}^{(p)}$$

is given by

$$\text{RSQ} = \frac{s^2}{\sigma^2} = \frac{(\mathbf{T'R}^{(0)})^2}{\mathbf{T'RT}}$$

On successive iterations, $\mathbf{RT}$ approaches $\mathbf{R}^{(0)}$, and RSQ approaches the squared correlation between $\mathbf{Z}^{(0)}$ and a composite of least squares weighted $\mathbf{Z}$. This squared correlation is frequently referred to as the **squared multiple correlation coefficient.** If $\mathbf{RT} = \mathbf{R}^{(0)}$ then

$$\text{Squared multiple correlation} = \frac{(\mathbf{T'R}^{(0)})^2}{\mathbf{TR}^{(0)}} = \mathbf{T'R}^{(0)}$$

When an iteration fails to increase RSQ by a specified tolerance, iterations cease and $c_1 \mathbf{T}$ approximates $\mathbf{W}$. The desired values of $\mathbf{B}$ are approximated by

$$b_j = w_j \left(\frac{\sigma_y}{\sigma_j} \right)$$

The general iterative procedure described in the preceding section does not require that a unit vector be one of the columns of $\mathbf{X}$. However, the procedure used in the computer program and discussed here assumes that a unit vector is one of the columns of $\mathbf{X}$. Note that the standard deviation of the unit vector is zero and that it is impossible to convert the unit vector to standard scores. The number of columns in $\mathbf{Z}$ will therefore be one less than the number of columns of $\mathbf{X}$.

C.6
STEPS IN THE ITERATIVE PROCEDURE

The steps in the iterative process are shown in the following list. On the left is the step number, and on the right is the FORTRAN statement number in SUBROUTINE REGRES (see Appendix E) in which the step is executed. The symbols used in the steps have been defined in previous sections of this appendix, while the symbols in brackets are their corresponding FORTRAN symbols.

1. Iteration Tolerance = .0000001   [STPC]   1001

2. $\mathbf{A} = 0$ [BETA]   1002

3. $\mathbf{T} = 0$ [RAWWT]   1003

4. $s = 0$ [S]   1004

5. $\sigma^2 = 0$ [SIG2]   1005

6. $\text{RSQ} = 0$ [RSQ]   1006

7. $\delta = 0$ [DEL]   1007

8. Iteration Count = 0   [IT]   1008

9. Identify predictor as a candidate for the one to   [ID]   1009
   be corrected, $(p = 1)$

10. Initialize BEST RSQ to zero   [RSQL]   25

11. $a_j^* = a_j + \delta r_{jp}$ [BETA(J)]   1010

12. Denominator of $\delta = s - a_j r_{i0}$ [DEN]   1011

13. If denominator of $\delta \neq 0$, GO TO 19   1012

14. Trial $\delta = r_{i0}$ [DELT]   30

15. Trial $s = (r_{i0})^2$ [STEST]   1013

16. Trial $\sigma^2 = (r_{i0})^2$ [SIG2T]   1014

17. Trial $\text{RSQL} = (r_{i0})^2$ [RSQT]   1015

18. GO TO 23

19. Trial $\delta = [\sigma^2(r_{i0}) - s(a_i)]/[s - a_i(r_{i0})]$ 35

20. Trial $s = s^* = s + \delta r_{i0}$ 1016

21. Trial $\sigma^2 = (\sigma^2)^* = \sigma^2 + 2\delta(a_i) + \delta^2$ 1017

22. Trial $\text{RSQL} = (s^2)^*/(\sigma^2)^*$ 1018

23. IF $\text{RSQL} \geq \text{RSQT}$ GO TO 29   40

24. Best $s = $ Trial s [SLAR]   1019

25. Best $\sigma^2 = $ Trial σ^2 [SIG2L]   1020

26. $\text{RSQL} = \text{RSQT}$ 1021

27. Best $\delta = $ Trial δ [DELTL]   1022

28. Identify current value of p as best candidate for   [IDLAR]   1023
    correction.

29. Continue   45

30. If the current value of RSQL is not greater   1024
    than RSQ by more than STPC, GO TO 39

31. $s = $ Best s 50

32. $\sigma^2 = $ Best σ^2 1025

33. $\text{RSQ} = \text{BEST RSQ}$ 1026

34. $\delta = $ Best δ 1027

35. Increase iteration count by 1   **1028**

36. Identify predictor number ID associated with **1029** best correction = IDLAR

37. Correction on $\mathbf{T}(\text{ID}) = \delta$ **55**

38. GO TO 10   **65**

39. Iteration ceases, $c_1 = s/\sigma^2$ [SDS2]   **75**

40. Calculate standard weights by multiplying   [BETA]   **1030** every value of $\mathbf{T}$ by c_1

41. Convert standard weights to original score   [RAWWT]   **85** weights

42. Compute unit vector weight   [UNIT]   **1031**

Appendix D

Model Recognition

D.1
INTRODUCTION

Many of the models discussed in this book are identical in most important respects to statistical procedures recommended in other sources, but the similarities are not always immediately apparent. In this section, we will discuss some of the ways that the essential properties of models from other sources can be recognized.

In many cases, the only difference between one of our models and one from some other source is the way the model is **parameterized**. For example, consider model (6.4), discussed in Section 6.8.

$$\mathbf{Y} = d_0\mathbf{U} + b_1\mathbf{G} + \mathbf{E}^{(3)} \tag{D.1}$$

Suppose we rewrite d_0 as $d_0 = b_0 - \bar{g}b_1$, where $\bar{g}$ is the arithmetic average of the values in the vector $\mathbf{G}$, and then substitute this expression for d_0 in (D.1).

$$\mathbf{Y} = (b_0 - \bar{g}b_1)\mathbf{U} + b_1\mathbf{G} + \mathbf{E}^{(3)}$$

$$\mathbf{Y} = b_0\mathbf{U} - b_1(\bar{g}\mathbf{U}) + b_1\mathbf{G} + \mathbf{E}^{(3)} \tag{D.2}$$

$$\mathbf{Y} = b_0\mathbf{U} + b_1(\mathbf{G} - \bar{g}\mathbf{U}) + \mathbf{E}^{(3)}$$

Note that we did not impose a restriction on d_0—we simply expressed it in a different way. Models (D.1) and (D.2) are equivalent models in the way described in Section 5.13; (D.2) can therefore be described as a **reparameterization** of (D.1), since the only important differences between them are the values of the parameters.

In some situations, there are computational advantages in using (D.2), primarily because $\mathbf{U}$ is orthogonal to the vector $(\mathbf{G} - \bar{g}\mathbf{U})$. Also, the least-squares value of b_0 is equal to the arithmetic average of the values in $\mathbf{Y}$, which can be a desirable feature.

D.2
ONE-WAY ANALYSIS OF VARIANCE

Difficulties are sometimes encountered when a model is described *only* in terms of its parameters, without identifying the vectors associated with the parameters.[1] A typical example of this is the discussion frequently associated with the **one-way analysis of variance** (Glass & Stanley, 1970, p. 340). Using the problem of Section 4.2 as an example, we could argue that the expected typing speed for a member of the ninth grade can be expressed as the sum of two components: a general mean, denoted μ, and the *effect* of being in the ninth grade, denoted by α_9. A similar statement can be made for the other three grades and summarized.

$$\mathscr{E}(\mathbf{Y}_i) = \mu + \alpha_i \qquad i = 9, 10, 11, 12$$

can be read as: "The expected value for the ith class is equal to $\mu + \alpha_i$."

Suppose we let m, a_9, a_{10}, a_{11}, and a_{12} be the estimates of μ, α_9, α_{10}, α_{11}, and α_{12}, respectively. Then we can write the model

$$\mathbf{Y} = m\mathbf{U} + a_9\mathbf{X}^{(9)} + a_{10}\mathbf{X}^{(10)} + a_{11}\mathbf{X}^{(11)} + a_{12}\mathbf{X}^{(12)} + \mathbf{E}^{(1)} \qquad (D.3)$$

where all vectors are as defined in Section 4.3.

Note that (D.3) does not have a unique least-squares solution (see Section 5.5). It can be reduced to an equivalent model that does have a unique solution by arbitrarily placing one restriction on the parameters. This particular kind of restriction, which results in a reparameterization of the model, is sometimes referred to as a **side condition**. For example, if we choose the side condition

$$m = 0$$

we get

$$\mathbf{Y} = a_9\mathbf{X}^{(9)} + a_{10}\mathbf{X}^{(10)} + a_{11}\mathbf{X}^{(11)} + a_{12}\mathbf{X}^{(12)} + \mathbf{E}^{(1)} \qquad (D.4)$$

which is identical to (4.1) and equivalent to (D.3). The most common side condition chosen is

$$a_9 + a_{10} + a_{11} + a_{12} = 0$$

which can be written as

$$a_9 = -a_{10} - a_{11} - a_{12} \qquad (D.5)$$

---

[1]For an interesting example of this difficulty, which had some important historical consequences, see Seal (1967, pp. 20–21).

Substituting (D.5) in (D.3) yields

$$\mathbf{Y} = m\mathbf{U} + (-a_{10} - a_{11} - a_{12})\mathbf{X}^{(9)} + a_{10}\mathbf{X}^{(10)}$$
$$+ a_{11}\mathbf{X}^{(11)} + a_{12}\mathbf{X}^{(12)} + \mathbf{E}^{(1)}$$

Collecting terms yields

$$\mathbf{Y} = m\mathbf{U} + a_{10}[\mathbf{X}^{(10)} - \mathbf{X}^{(9)}] + a_{11}[\mathbf{X}^{(11)} - \mathbf{X}^{(9)}]$$
$$+ a_{12}[\mathbf{X}^{(12)} - \mathbf{X}^{(9)}] + \mathbf{E}^{(1)} \tag{D.6}$$

Model (D.6) has a unique solution, and it is equivalent to both (D.3) and (D.4).

When the one-way analysis of variance is discussed in the context of a linear model, a model such as (D.6) is usually the full model. To test the hypothesis of no-grade effects, the grade effects are set to zero.

$$a_{10} = a_{11} = a_{12} = 0$$

Another way of arriving at the same restrictions is to set the predicted values equal.

$$m - a_{10} - a_{11} - a_{12} = m + a_{10} = m + a_{11} = m + a_{12}$$

The m's cancel, and we have

$$-a_{10} - a_{11} - a_{12} = a_{10}$$
$$-a_{10} - a_{11} - a_{12} = a_{11}$$
$$-a_{10} - a_{11} - a_{12} = a_{12}$$

The only condition under which all of these can be true is if

$$a_{10} = a_{11} = a_{12} = 0$$

If these restrictions are imposed on (D.6), the resulting restricted model is identical to (4.2).

Notice that a solution of (D.4) will yield values for $a_9 \ldots a_{12}$ equal to the average criterion values of the four classes. Model (D.6) has the property that m will be equal to the *average* of the four averages. If the number of observations from each class is the same, m will also be equal to the average of all the criterion values. If the n's from each class are not equal, in model (D.6), m will not be equal to the average value in $\mathbf{Y}$. In this situation, the side condition chosen may be

$$n_9 a_9 + n_{10} a_{10} + n_{11} a_{11} + n_{12} a_{12} = 0$$

which can be written

$$a_9 = -(n_{10}/n_9)a_{10} - (n_{11}/n_9)a_{11} - (n_{12}/n_9)a_{12} \tag{D.7}$$

where n_i is the number of criterion observations in the ith class.

Substituting (D.7) in (D.3) and simplifying, we achieve

$$\mathbf{Y} = m\mathbf{U} + a_{10}[\mathbf{X}^{(10)} - (n_{10}/n_9)\mathbf{X}^{(9)}] + a_{11}[\mathbf{X}^{(11)} - (n_{11}/n_9)\mathbf{X}^{(9)}]$$
$$+ a_{12}[\mathbf{X}^{(12)} - (n_{12}/n_9)\mathbf{X}^{(9)}] + \mathbf{E}^{(1)} \tag{D.8}$$

Note that (D.3), (D.4), (D.6), and (D.8) are equivalent models, having all the properties discussed in Section 5.13. In the special case of $n_9 = n_{10} = n_{11} = n_{12}$, model (D.8) reduces to (D.6). In model (D.8), m will be equal to the average of the criterion values, whether the n_i are equal or unequal.

D.3
TWO-FACTOR ANALYSIS OF VARIANCE

The computing expressions ordinarily associated with a class of models known as **two-factor analysis of variance** (Glass & Stanley, 1970, p. 403) frequently refer indirectly, if at all, to an expression that can be recognized as a model. When the topic is discussed in the context of a linear model, the parameterization chosen has desirable conceptual attributes for some purposes and computational advantages for testing certain hypotheses. We will develop the model in a way similar to that used in Section D.2. Suppose that n patients have been randomly divided into six subgroups. Each patient in each subgroup is administered one of two possible drugs at one of three possible concentration levels, and a measure of "pain reduction" is obtained on each patient. Note that there are six expected values of interest—one for each subgroup. Each expected value can be expressed as the sum of four components,

$$\mathscr{E}(\mathbf{Y}_{ij}) = \mu + \alpha_i + \beta_j + \alpha\beta_{ij}$$

where μ is a general mean, α_i is the effect due to the ith drug, β_j is the effect due to the jth concentration level, and $\alpha\beta_{ij}$ is the additional effect of receiving the ith drug at the jth concentration level ($i = 1, 2; j = 1, 2, 3.$)

We begin by defining the column vectors (all of dimension n).

$\mathbf{Y}$ = pain reduction measures.

$\mathbf{D}^{(i)} = 1$ if the corresponding value in $\mathbf{Y}$ is observed on a person receiving drug i; 0 otherwise.

$\mathbf{L}^{(j)} = 1$ if the corresponding value in $\mathbf{Y}$ is observed on a person receiving either drug at concentration level j; 0 otherwise.

$\mathbf{X}^{(ij)} = \mathbf{D}^{(i)} * \mathbf{L}^{(j)}$ ($i = 1, 2; j = 1, 2, 3$).

We now choose as estimates of μ, α_i, β_j, and $\alpha\beta_{ij}$ the symbols m, a_i, b_j, and g_{ij}, respectively, and entertain the following model.

$$\mathbf{Y} = m\mathbf{U} + a_1\mathbf{D}^{(1)} + a_2\mathbf{D}^{(2)} + b_1\mathbf{L}^{(1)} + b_2\mathbf{L}^{(2)} + b_3\mathbf{L}^{(3)} + g_{11}\mathbf{X}^{(1,1)}$$
$$+ g_{12}\mathbf{X}^{(1,2)} + g_{13}\mathbf{X}^{(1,3)} + g_{21}\mathbf{X}^{(2,1)} + g_{22}\mathbf{X}^{(2,2)} + g_{23}\mathbf{X}^{(2,3)} + \mathbf{E}^{(1)} \quad \text{(D.9)}$$

Note that there are 12 predictor vectors in the model. But, if the vectors are partitioned into independent and redundant subsets, as described in Section 5.10, there will be six vectors in the redundant subset; therefore

(D.9) does not have a unique solution. If we want a unique solution, we are free to choose six side conditions. Although the side conditions will not ordinarily affect the estimates of the expected values, they will affect the values of the coefficients. For example, if we choose the side conditions

$$m = 0$$
$$a_1 = a_2 = 0$$
$$b_1 = b_2 = b_3 = 0$$

and impose them on (D.9), we get

$$\mathbf{Y} = g_{11}\mathbf{X}^{(1,1)} + g_{12}\mathbf{X}^{(1,2)} + \cdots + g_{23}\mathbf{X}^{(2,3)} + \mathbf{E}^{(1)} \qquad (D.10)$$

Note that this model is what we have referred to as a *mutually exclusive categorical model*. It is equivalent to (D.9). The expected value for the ijth category is estimated by g_{ij}. The side conditions usually chosen, however, are

1. $a_1 + a_2 = 0$
2. $b_1 + b_2 + b_3 = 0$
3. $g_{11} + g_{12} + g_{13} = 0$
4. $g_{21} + g_{22} + g_{23} = 0$
5. $g_{11} + g_{21} = 0$
6. $g_{12} + g_{22} = 0$
7. $g_{13} + g_{23} = 0$

It appears that there are seven, not six, stated conditions. But any one of the last five is implied by the other four (i.e., if the other four are true, the fifth must be). Six of these conditions can therefore be rewritten as

1. $a_2 = -a_1$
2. $b_3 = -b_1 - b_2$
3. $g_{13} = -g_{11} - g_{12}$
5. $g_{21} = -g_{11}$
6. $g_{22} = -g_{12}$
7. $g_{23} = -g_{13} = g_{11} + g_{12}$ (from 3)

(D.11)

If we substitute (D.11) in (D.9) and simplify, we get

$$\mathbf{Y} = m\mathbf{U} + a_1[\mathbf{D}^{(1)} - \mathbf{D}^{(2)}] + b_1[\mathbf{L}^{(1)} - \mathbf{L}^{(3)}] + b_2[\mathbf{L}^{(2)} - \mathbf{L}^{(3)}]$$
$$+ g_{11}[\mathbf{X}^{(11)} - \mathbf{X}^{(13)} - \mathbf{X}^{(21)} + \mathbf{X}^{(23)}]$$
$$+ g_{12}[\mathbf{X}^{(12)} - \mathbf{X}^{(13)} - \mathbf{X}^{(22)} + \mathbf{X}^{(23)}] + \mathbf{E}^{(1)} \qquad (D.12)$$

Table D.1 contains a specification of the elements in each predictor vector for all models defined in this section. For example, the elements of the second predictor vector in (D.12) can be found on the thirteenth row of the table. Although each predictor vector contains n elements, only six unique values are possible.

Table D.1 PREDICTOR VECTOR ELEMENTS FOR DRUG-CONCENTRATION LEVEL COMBINATIONS

Vectors	Drug 1 — Drug Concentration			Drug 2 — Drug Concentration		
	1	2	3	1	2	3
U	1	1	1	1	1	1
$D^{(1)}$	1	1	1	0	0	0
$D^{(2)}$	0	0	0	1	1	1
$L^{(1)}$	1	0	0	1	0	0
$L^{(2)}$	0	1	0	0	1	0
$L^{(3)}$	0	0	1	0	0	1
$X^{(11)}$	1	0	0	0	0	0
$X^{(12)}$	0	1	0	0	0	0
$X^{(13)}$	0	0	1	0	0	0
$X^{(21)}$	0	0	0	1	0	0
$X^{(22)}$	0	0	0	0	1	0
$X^{(23)}$	0	0	0	0	0	1
$D^{(1)} - D^{(2)}$	1	1	1	-1	-1	-1
$L^{(1)} - L^{(3)}$	1	0	-1	1	0	-1
$L^{(2)} - L^{(3)}$	0	1	-1	0	1	-1
$X^{(11)} - X^{(13)} - X^{(21)} + X^{(23)}$	1	0	-1	-1	0	1
$X^{(12)} - X^{(13)} - X^{(22)} + X^{(23)}$	0	1	-1	0	-1	1
$D^{(2)} - (n_{2.}/n_{1.})D^{(1)}$	$\dfrac{-n_{2.}}{n_{1.}}$	$\dfrac{-n_{2.}}{n_{1.}}$	$\dfrac{-n_{2.}}{n_{1.}}$	1	1	1
$L^{(2)} - (n_{.2}/n_{.1})L^{(1)}$	$\dfrac{-n_{.2}}{n_{.1}}$	1	0	$\dfrac{-n_{.2}}{n_{.1}}$	1	0
$L^{(3)} - (n_{.3}/n_{.1})L^{(1)}$	$\dfrac{-n_{.3}}{n_{.1}}$	0	1	$\dfrac{-n_{.3}}{n_{.1}}$	0	1
$X^{(12)} - (n_{.2}/n_{11})X^{(11)} + (n_{12}/n_{2.})X^{(21)} - (n_{12}/n_{22})X^{(22)}$	$\dfrac{-n_{.2}}{n_{11}}$	1	0	$\dfrac{n_{12}}{n_{2.}}$	$\dfrac{-n_{12}}{n_{22}}$	0
$X^{(13)} - (n_{13}/n_{11})X^{(11)} + (n_{.3}/n_{21})X^{(21)} - (n_{13}/n_{23})X^{(23)}$	$\dfrac{-n_{13}}{n_{11}}$	0	1	0	$\dfrac{n_{.3}}{n_{21}}$	$\dfrac{-n_{13}}{n_{23}}$

Although the predictor vectors in (D.12) may look rather strange, they are easily generated by SUBROUTINE DATRAN, described in Chapter 15. In fact, a pattern exists in the predictors that enables a programmer, given only the number of levels of each factor, to write a general routine that will generate these vectors. Note, for example, that the fifth predictor (row 16, Table D.1) is the direct product of the second and third (rows 13 and 14), and the sixth is the direct product of the second and fourth. Models (D.9), (D.10), and (D.11) are all equivalent and therefore produce the same numerical values as estimates of the six expected values. The expected values using the three models are estimated by the expressions shown in Table D.2.

Table D.2 PREDICTED VALUES FROM THREE EQUIVALENT MODELS

Drug	Concentration Level	Model		
		(D.9)	(D.10)	(D.12)
1	1	$m + a_1 + b_1 + g_{11}$	g_{11}	$m + a_1 + b_1 + g_{11}$
1	2	$m + a_1 + b_2 + g_{12}$	g_{12}	$m + a_1 + b_2 + g_{12}$
1	3	$m + a_1 + b_3 + g_{13}$	g_{13}	$m + a_1 - b_1 - b_2 - g_{11} - g_{12}$
2	1	$m + a_2 + b_1 + g_{21}$	g_{21}	$m - a_1 + b_1 - g_{11}$
2	2	$m + a_2 + b_2 + g_{22}$	g_{22}	$m - a_1 + b_2 - g_{12}$
2	3	$m + a_2 + b_3 + g_{23}$	g_{23}	$m - a_1 - b_1 - b_2 + g_{11} + g_{12}$

One of the advantages of using (D.12) as a full model can be seen if we wish to test certain kinds of hypotheses. Consider the question of whether the difference between the drugs is the same at each concentration level (i.e., interaction). Translating this into the restrictions implied in terms of the predicted values from Table D.2 yields

$$(m + a_1 + b_1 + g_{11}) - (m - a_1 + b_1 - g_{11})$$
$$= (m + a_1 + b_2 + g_{12}) - (m - a_1 + b_2 - g_{12})$$
$$= (m + a_1 - b_1 - b_2 - g_{11} - g_{12}) - (m - a_1 - b_1 - b_2 + g_{11} + g_{12})$$

Cancelling wherever possible produces

$$2g_{11} = 2g_{12} = -2g_{11} - 2g_{12}$$

The only condition under which this can be true is if

$$g_{11} = g_{12} = 0$$

These restrictions are easy to impose (compared with Section 7.7), and no additional vectors need be generated. Moreover, some computational procedures take advantage of the orthogonal properties of (D.12). Note that the first two predictors are orthogonal to the last four and to each other; the third and fourth vectors are orthogonal to the other four but not to each other; and the last two are orthogonal to the other four but not to each other.

D.4
MAIN EFFECTS

Model (D.12) is ideally parameterized for testing another set of hypotheses referred to as the **main effects**. For example, the main effects for drugs are tested by imposing the restriction

$$a_1 = 0 \qquad\qquad (D.13)$$

and the main effects for concentration level are tested by imposing the restrictions

$$b_1 = b_2 = 0 \qquad\qquad (D.14)$$

Although the mechanics for testing these hypotheses are identical to those used in other models in this book, the underlying logic is somewhat different.

In Appendix B we stated that any hypothesis that could be written as a linear combination of the parameters set equal to a specified constant was subject to test. Since the expected values themselves are linear combinations of the parameters, this statement implies that *it is possible to test hypotheses involving weighted sums of the expected values.* For example, if we take (D.10) as the full model rather than (D.12), we can write the restriction for testing the presence of drug main effects as

$$(1/3)g_{11} + (1/3)g_{12} + (1/3)g_{13} = (1/3)g_{21} + (1/3)g_{22} + (1/3)g_{23}$$

where the weights used are $1/3$. This restriction can be simplified and substituted in (D.10), which will produce a restricted model equivalent to the one produced by substituting (D.13) into (D.12).

The corresponding test for concentration level main effects using (D.10) as the full model requires the restrictions

$$(1/2)g_{11} + (1/2)g_{21} = (1/2)g_{12} + (1/2)g_{22}$$
$$(1/2)g_{11} + (1/2)g_{21} = (1/2)g_{13} + (1/2)g_{23}$$

When these restrictions are simplified and substituted into (D.10), a restricted model results that is equivalent to the model produced when (D.14) is substituted in (D.12)

The results achieved depend on the weights that are chosen to multiply the parameters (Scheffé, 1959, p. 91). Unless a particular problem dictates otherwise, *equal* weights are usually used. If the number of observations in each subgroup is not the same, unequal weights are sometimes used, depending on why the n's are unequal. The unequal weighting is usually accomplished, in effect, by choosing the following side conditions for (D.9).

$$n_{1.}a_1 + n_{2.}a_2 = 0$$
$$n_{.1}b_1 + n_{.2}b_2 + n_{.3}b_3 = 0$$
$$n_{11}g_{11} + n_{12}g_{12} + n_{13}g_{13} = 0$$
$$n_{21}g_{21} + n_{22}g_{22} + n_{23}g_{23} = 0$$
$$n_{11}g_{11} + n_{21}g_{21} = 0$$
$$n_{12}g_{12} + n_{22}g_{22} = 0$$
$$n_{13}g_{13} + n_{23}g_{23} = 0$$

In these expressions, n_{ij} is the number of criterion observations available for patients receiving drug i at concentration level j $(i = 1, 2; j = 1, 2, 3)$, and

$$n_{1.} = n_{11} + n_{12} + n_{13}$$
$$n_{2.} = n_{21} + n_{22} + n_{23}$$
$$n_{.1} = n_{11} + n_{21}$$
$$n_{.2} = n_{12} + n_{22}$$
$$n_{.3} = n_{13} + n_{23}$$

These side conditions can be simplified in a number of ways and then substituted into (D.9). One possibility yields

$$\mathbf{Y} = m\mathbf{U} + a_2[\mathbf{D}^{(2)} - (n_{2.}/n_{1.})\mathbf{D}^{(1)}] + b_2[\mathbf{L}^{(2)} - (n_{.2}/n_{.1})\mathbf{L}^{(1)}]$$
$$+ b_3[\mathbf{L}^{(3)} - (n_{.3}/n_{.1})\mathbf{L}^{(1)}]$$
$$+ g_{12}[\mathbf{X}^{(12)} - (n_{.2}/n_{11})\mathbf{X}^{(11)} + (n_{12}/n_2.)\mathbf{X}^{(21)} - (n_{12}/n_{22})\mathbf{X}^{(22)}]$$
$$+ g_{13}[\mathbf{X}^{(13)} - (n_{13}/n_{11})\mathbf{X}^{(11)} + (n_{.3}/n_{21})\mathbf{X}^{(21)} - (n_{13}/n_{23})\mathbf{X}^{(23)}] + \mathbf{E}^{(1)}$$
$$\text{(D.15)}$$

Note once again that (D.15) is equivalent to (D.9), (D.10), and (D.12). However, imposing (D.13) or (D.14) on (D.15) will not produce restricted models equivalent to those produced when (D.13) or (D.14) are substituted into (D.12); so the results will be different. Suppose we let q_1 represent the error sum of squares from any of the equivalent full models, q_2 represent the error sum of squares from the model produced by imposing (D.13) on (D.15), and q_3 represent the error sum of squares from the model produced by imposing (D.14) on (D.15). Tests on the main effects can be then constructed.

$$F = \frac{(q_2 - q_1)/(6 - 5)}{q_1/(n - 4)}$$

$$F = \frac{(q_3 - q_1)/(6 - 4)}{q_1/(n - 6)}$$

Computationally, these results can be obtained with simpler models. For example, consider the following models using the vectors defined in Section D.3.

$$\mathbf{Y} = a_1\mathbf{D}^{(1)} + a_2\mathbf{D}^{(2)} + b_1\mathbf{L}^{(1)} + b_2\mathbf{L}^{(2)} + b_3\mathbf{L}^{(3)} + \mathbf{E}^{(4)}$$
$$\mathbf{Y} = a_1\mathbf{D}^{(1)} + a_2\mathbf{D}^{(2)} + \mathbf{E}^{(5)}$$
$$\mathbf{Y} = b_1\mathbf{L}^{(1)} + b_2\mathbf{L}^{(2)} + b_3\mathbf{L}^{(3)} + \mathbf{E}^{(6)}$$

Let the error sum of squares from the models be q_4, q_5, and q_6, respectively. Then it can be shown that

$$q_2 - q_1 = q_6 - q_4$$
$$q_3 - q_1 = q_5 - q_4$$

and these identities can be used in the numerators.

D.5
INFERRING MODELS FROM SOURCE TABLES

Many sources recommend computing procedures that lead to a summary table of results having the general form of Table D.3.

Table D.3 EXAMPLE OF SOURCE TABLE

Source	df	Sum of Squares	Mean Squares	F
A_1	d_1	$S_1 - B$	M_1	F_1
A_2	d_2	$S_2 - B$	M_2	F_2
.	.	.	.	.
.	.	.	.	.
.	.	.	.	.
A_k	d_k	$S_k - B$	M_k	F_k
Error:	j	B	D	
Total:	m	C		

The symbols A_i $(i = 1, k)$ represent symbols or names that correspond to certain hypotheses that have been tested. Examples of names that might appear in the table are *linear, quadratic, drug main effects*, $A \times B$ *interaction, nonadditivity*, etc. Generally, the values in the table can be found by using the following expressions.

$$F_i = M_i / D$$
$$M_i = (S_i - B)/d_i$$
$$D = B/j$$

In many cases, a more complete understanding of the results can be gained if the underlying models can be inferred. Certain values that appear in the table can be helpful in this respect. For example, if the number of criterion observations are known (say n), you can be reasonably sure that the full model has $n - j$ parameters and that the dimension of Y is n. If n is not otherwise reported, it may be possible to infer it from m, since m will usually be equal to n or $n - 1$. If m is equal to n, then $C = Y'Y$. If m is equal to $n - 1$, then C will be the error sum of squares in the model

$$Y = a_0 U + E$$

If you know anything about the scaling of the criterion values, it is frequently possible to determine whether $m = n$ or $n - 1$ by noting the magnitude of C. The value of B will generally be the error sum of squares in the full model. With a little practice, it is almost always possible to infer the full model.

The value of S_i is obtained by imposing d_i restrictions on the parameters of the full model and calculating the error sum of squares in the restricted model. The most difficult task is to determine the restrictions that produce S_i. If the hypothesis being tested is well understood, little difficulty should be encountered; otherwise, some ingenuity and effort may be required. It is precisely in those situations in which the hypothesis is not well understood that a fuller understanding of the underlying models will prove most fruitful. After you have satisfied yourself about the acceptability of the models, you may wish to adopt the recommended computational strategies rather than the more general ones, which are not necessarily ideal for any particular model.

Appendix E

Program Model

In this section, we present a FORTRAN image listing of the computer program and associated subroutines described in Chapters 14 and 15. The program has been thoroughly tested on a CDC 6600, but it should run with only minor modifications on any computer having a reasonably good FORTRAN compiler.

The arrays in the program are currently dimensioned to handle problems requiring no more than 50 vectors. The DIMENSION statements are easily modified to handle larger problems. The user will need to make a decision about the option of the program that generates a listing of the predicted and residual values. If the program is being used primarily for instructional purposes, we strongly recommend that the option be made available.

If the option is desired, the input data must be available to the program after the solution of any model. The data can be retained in memory or stored on tape. (The program is currently written to store the data in memory.) The user should be sure that the array named FILE in the main program is dimensioned at least N times NV. The subroutines WRTAPE and RDTAPE are not required if the data are retained in memory.

If the user has a scratch tape available, the amount of memory required can be significantly reduced by storing the input data on tape. This feature can be implemented by removing the C in column 1 of statements 991 and 992 in SUBROUTINE CORR and 991 in SUBROUTINE PREDIC. If tape is being used, the array FILE is used as a buffer, and it must be dimensioned at least NV in the main program. Economy in tape processing can be accomplished by making FILE as large as possible.

If the predicted-value option is not desired, FILE can be dimensioned as one in the main program, and subroutines WRTAPE, RDTAPE, and PREDIC would not be necessary.

```
       PROGRAM MODEL(INPUT, OUTPUT, TAPE2, TAPE5 = INPUT, TAPE6 = OUTPUT)     1
C--GENERAL LINEAR MODEL SOLVER                                                 2
C--      .       .       .      20 MAY 1971       .       .       .            3
       DIMENSION C(50), V(50), R(50,50), SUM(50), SIGMA(50), BETA(50), RA      4
      1WWT(51), RSQS(50), LY(50), MODE(50)                                     5
C-- IF PREDICTED VALUES ARE BEING REQUESTED FILE SHOULD BE DIMENSIONED         6
C--    AT LEAST (N*NV) IF TAPE IS NOT BEING USED.  IF TAPE IS BEING            7
C--    USED FILE  SHOULD BE DIMENSIONED (KSZ) . (SEE STATEMENT 990 IN          8
C--    SUBROUTINE CORR AND PREDIC)                                             9
       DIMENSION FILE(5000)                                                   10
       COMMON JOBNO, KOUT, IN, C, V, R, SUM, RSQS, BETA, RAWWT, SIGMA, MO     11
      1DE, FILE                                                               12
C--DEFINE THE CARD READER                                                     13
       IN = 5                                                                 14
C--DEFINE THE LINE PRINTER                                                    15
       KOUT = 6                                                               16
C--CALL THE MAIN ROUTINE                                                      17
       CALL LINEAR                                                            18
       END                                                                    19-
       SUBROUTINE LINEAR                                                 LIN   1
       DIMENSION C(50), V(50), SSCP(50,50), SUM(50), SIGMA(50), BETA(50),LIN   2
      1 RAWWT(51), RSQS(50), R(50,50), XMEAN(50), KC(50), KFMT(50), MODELLIN   3
      2(50), FILE(1), INTR(50), ID(2), LY(50)                            LIN   4
       COMMON JOBNO, KOUT, IN, C, V, R, SUM, RSQS, BETA, RAWWT, SIGMA, MOLIN   5
      1DEL, FILE                                                         LIN   6
       EQUIVALENCE (SSCP, R), (SUM, XMEAN), (C, KC), (RSQS, KFMT), (C, INLIN   7
      1TR), (C, ID), (LY, V)                                             LIN   8
       DATA   IBL/1H /                                                   LIN   9
       JOBNO = 0                                                         LIN  10
   5   JOBNO = JOBNO+1                                                   LIN  11
       WRITE (KOUT,20)                                                   LIN  12
C--READ TITLE CARDS. LAST TITLE CARD NON-BLANK IN COL. 80               LIN  13
  10   READ (IN,25) (KC(I), I = 1, 21)                                   LIN  14
       KSTOP = KC(1)-KC(2)+KC(3)-KC(4)+KC(5)-KC(6)                       LIN  15
       IF (KSTOP .EQ. 0) CALL EXIT                                       LIN  16
       WRITE (KOUT,30) (KC(I), I = 1, 20)                                LIN  17
       IF (KC(21) .EQ. IBL) GO TO 10                                     LIN  18
C      IF (KC(21) .NE. IBL) GO TO 15                                     LIN  19
C--READ PARAMETER CARD.                                                  LIN  20
       READ (IN,35) N, NC, NV, ISTORE                                    LIN  21
       IF (NV .EQ. 0) NV = NC                                            LIN  22
       WRITE (KOUT,40) N, NC, NV                                         LIN  23
       ISTAR = -20                                                       LIN  24
       ISTOP = 0                                                         LIN  25
  15   ISTOP = ISTOP+21                                                  LIN  26
       ISTAR = ISTAR+21                                                  LIN  27
C--READ VARIABLE FORMAT CARD(S)                                          LIN  28
       READ (IN,25) (KFMT(I), I = ISTAR, ISTOP)                          LIN  29
       IF (KFMT(ISTOP) .NE. IBL) GO TO 15                                LIN  30
       WRITE (KOUT,45) (KFMT(I), I = 1, ISTOP)                           LIN  31
       CALL CORR (N, NC, NV, ISTORE)                                     LIN  32
       CALL REGRES (N, NV)                                               LIN  33
       GO TO 5                                                           LIN  34
C                                                                        LIN  35
  20   FORMAT   (1H1)                                                    LIN  36
```

```
 25    FORMAT    (19A4, A3, A1)                                          LIN  37
 30    FORMAT    (5X, 19A4, A3)                                          LIN  38
 35    FORMAT    (10I5)                                                  LIN  39
 40    FORMAT    (//5X, I5,28H = DIMENSION OF VECTORS (N).,/ 5X, I5,50H = LIN  40
      1NO. OF DATA ELEMENTS ON EACH INPUT RECORD (NC).,/ 5X, I5,23H = NO.LIN  41
      2 OF VECTORS (NV). )                                               LIN  42
 45    FORMAT    (//5X, 11HDATA FORMAT,// (5X, 19A4, A3, A1))            LIN  43
       END                                                              LIN  44-
       SUBROUTINE CORR (N, NC, NV, ISTORE)                              COR   1
       DIMENSION C(50), V(50), SSCP(50,50), SUM(50), SIGMA(50), BETA(50),COR   2
      1 RAWWT(51), RSQS(50), R(50,50), XMEAN(50), KC(50), KFMT(50), MODELCOR   3
      2(50), FILE(1), INTR(50), ID(2), LY(50)                          COR   4
       COMMON JOBNO, KOUT, IN, C, V, R, SUM, RSQS, BETA, RAWWT, SIGMA, MOCOR   5
      1DEL, FILE                                                        COR   6
       EQUIVALENCE (SSCP, R), (SUM, XMEAN), (C, KC), (RSQS, KFMT), (C, INCOR   7
      1TR), (C, ID), (LY, V)                                            COR   8
       NOREC = 0                                                        COR   9
 990 KSZ = 300                                                          COR  10
       KM = NV-1                                                        COR  11
       XN = N                                                           COR  12
       DO 5 I = 1, NV                                                   COR  13
       SUM(I) = 0.                                                      COR  14
       DO 5 J = I, NV                                                   COR  15
 5     SSCP(I, J) = 0.                                                  COR  16
       DO 20 K = 1, N                                                   COR  17
C-- READ DATA CARDS.                                                    COR  18
       READ (IN,KFMT) (C(M), M = 1, NC)                                 COR  19
       CALL DATRAN (C, NC, V, NV)                                       COR  20
       IF (ISTORE .NE. 0) GO TO 15                                      COR  21
C--STORE DATA IN FILE                                                   COR  22
C--IF TAPE USED, ELIMINATE THE C IN COL. 1 OF THE NEXT TWO CARDS        COR  23
C 991 CALL WRTAPE (NOREC, V, FILE, N, NV, KSZ)                          COR  24
C 992 GO TO 15                                                          COR  25
       KAY = (K-1)*NV                                                   COR  26
       DO 10 L = 1, NV                                                  COR  27
       KL = KAY+L                                                       COR  28
 10    FILE(KL) = V(L)                                                  COR  29
 15    DO 20 I = 1, NV                                                  COR  30
       SUM(I) = SUM(I)+V(I)                                             COR  31
       DO 20 J = I, NV                                                  COR  32
 20    SSCP(I, J) = SSCP(I, J)+V(I)*V(J)                                COR  33
       DO 35 I = 1, KM                                                  COR  34
       IP = I+1                                                         COR  35
       DO 35 J = IP, NV                                                 COR  36
       DEN = SQRT((XN*SSCP(I, I)-SUM(I)*SUM(I))*(XN*SSCP(J, J)-SUM(J)*SUMCOR  37
      1(J)))                                                            COR  38
       IF (DEN) 25,25,30                                                COR  39
 25    R(I, J) = 0.                                                     COR  40
       GO TO 35                                                         COR  41
 30    R(I, J) = (XN*SSCP(I, J)-SUM(I)*SUM(J))/DEN                      COR  42
       IF (ABS(R(I, J)) .LE. 1.0) GO TO 35                             COR  43
       WRITE (KOUT,65) I, J, R(I, J)                                    COR  44
       CALL EXIT                                                        COR  45
 35    R(J, I) = R(I, J)                                                COR  46
       IF (ISTORE .NE. 0) GO TO 45                                      COR  47
```

```
          IF (NOREC .NE. 0) GO TO 45                                    COR  48
          WRITE (KOUT,70)                                               COR  49
          DO 40 K = 1, NV, 10                                           COR  50
          KSP = MINO(K+9, NV)                                           COR  51
          WRITE (KOUT,75) (J, J = K, KSP)                               COR  52
          DO 40 I = 1, N                                                COR  53
          L = (I-1)*NV+K                                                COR  54
          LSP = L+MINO(9, NV-K)                                         COR  55
   40     WRITE (KOUT,80) I, (FILE(IJ), IJ = L, LSP)                    COR  56
   45     WRITE (KOUT,85)                                               COR  57
          DO 60 I = 1, NV                                               COR  58
          XMEAN(I) = SUM(I)/XN                                          COR  59
          VAR = ((SSCP(I, I)/XN)-XMEAN(I)**2)                           COR  60
          SIGMA(I) = SQRT(VAR)                                          COR  61
          IF (SIGMA(I)) 50,50,55                                        COR  62
   50     R(I, I) = 0.                                                  COR  63
          GO TO 60                                                      COR  64
   55     R(I, I) = 1.0                                                 COR  65
   60     WRITE (KOUT,90) I, XMEAN(I), SIGMA(I), VAR                    COR  66
          WRITE (KOUT,95)                                               COR  67
          CALL PRINT (R, NV, NV, 50)                                    COR  68
          RETURN                                                        COR  69
   C                                                                    COR  70
   65     FORMAT   (/5X,28HOUT OF RANGE CORRELATION I =,I4,6H    J =,I5, COR  71
         1 6H    R =,F10.4)                                             COR  72
   70     FORMAT   (// 5X,  7HVECTORS / )                               COR  73
   75     FORMAT   (/ 8X, 10( I10,1H. ) / )                             COR  74
   80     FORMAT   (2X, I4, 1H., 1X, 10F11.4 )                          COR  75
   85     FORMAT   (//5X, 36HVAR.NO. AVERAGE     SIGMA   VARIANCE    /) COR  76
   90     FORMAT   (5X, I5, 3F10.4)                                     COR  77
   95     FORMAT   (/// 5X, 18HCORRELATION MATRIX /)                    COR  78
          END                                                          COR  79-
          SUBROUTINE REGRES (N, NV)                                     REG   1
          DIMENSION C(50), V(50), SSCP(50,50), SUM(50), SIGMA(50), BETA(50),REG  2
         1 RAWWT(51), RSQS(50), R(50,50), XMEAN(50), KC(50), KFMT(50), MODELREG  3
         2(50), FILE(1), INTR(50), IV(3), LY(50)                        REG   4
          COMMON JOBNO, KOUT, IN, C, V, R, SUM, RSQS, BETA, RAWWT, SIGMA, MOREG  5
         1DEL, FILE                                                     REG   6
          EQUIVALENCE (SSCP, R), (SUM, XMEAN), (C, KC), (RSQS, KFMT), (C, INREG  7
         1TR), (C, IV), (LY, V)                                         REG   8
          EQUIVALENCE (IDC, MODEL)                                      REG   9
   C--DEFINE NUMBER OF ITERATIONS TO PRINT                             REG  10
   5      NIT = 10                                                      REG  11
   C--DEFINE ITERATION TOLERANCE STOP CRITERION                        REG  12
   1001   STPC = .0000001                                              REG  13
          XN = N                                                        REG  14
          MN = 1                                                        REG  15
          CALL ZERO (RSQS, 50)                                          REG  16
          CALL ZERO (V, 50)                                             REG  17
   C-- READ MODEL OR F-TEST CARD. NOTE THAT COLUMN 80 CONTROLS WHETHER REG  18
   C-- OR NOT PREDICTED VALUES WILL BE CALCULATED. (SEE STATEMENT 180) REG  19
   10     READ (IN,115) IV, MODNUM, (MODEL(I), I = 1, 23)               REG  20
          IF (IDC .EQ. 0) GO TO 110                                     REG  21
          NG = 0                                                        REG  22
          DO 15 I = 2, 22                                               REG  23
```

```
       IF (MODEL(I) .EQ. 0) GO TO 20                              REG  24
       NG = NG+1                                                  REG  25
 15    CONTINUE                                                   REG  26
       WRITE (KOUT,120) IV                                        REG  27
       GO TO 10                                                   REG  28
 20    IF (NG .EQ. 3) GO TO 105                                   REG  29
       IF (MODNUM .EQ. 999) GO TO 105                             REG  30
       IF (NG .EQ. 0) GO TO 105                                   REG  31
       IF (MODNUM .NE. 0) MN = MODNUM-1                           REG  32
       MN = MN+1                                                  REG  33
       WRITE (KOUT,125) MN                                        REG  34
       KSTOP = NG+1                                               REG  35
       WRITE (KOUT,130) IV, STPC, IDC, (MODEL(K), K = 2, KSTOP)   REG  36
       CALL ZERO (C, 50)                                          REG  37
1002   CALL ZERO (BETA, NV)                                       REG  38
1003   CALL ZERO (RAWWT, NV+1)                                    REG  39
1004   S = 0.                                                     REG  40
1005   SIG2 = 0.                                                  REG  41
1006   RSQ = 0.                                                   REG  42
1007   DEL = 0.                                                   REG  43
1008   IT = 0                                                     REG  44
1009   ID = 1                                                     REG  45
       XNP = 1.0                                                  REG  46
       IF (NIT .EQ. 0) GO TO 25                                   REG  47
       WRITE (KOUT,135)                                           REG  48
 25    RSQL = 0.                                                  REG  49
       DO 45 I = 2, NG, 2                                         REG  50
       K = MODEL(I)                                               REG  51
       L = MODEL(I+1)                                             REG  52
       DO 45 J = K, L                                             REG  53
1010   BETA(J) = BETA(J)+DEL*R(J, ID)                             REG  54
1011   DEN = S-BETA(J)*R(J, IDC)                                  REG  55
1012   IF (DEN) 35,30,35                                          REG  56
 30    DELT = R(J, IDC)                                           REG  57
1013   STEST = DELT*DELT                                          REG  58
1014   SIG2T = STEST                                              REG  59
1015   RSQT = STEST                                               REG  60
       GO TO 40                                                   REG  61
 35    DELT = (SIG2*R(J, IDC)-S*BETA(J))/DEN                      REG  62
1016   STEST = S+DELT*R(J, IDC)                                   REG  63
1017   SIG2T = SIG2+2.0*BETA(J)*DELT+DELT*DELT                    REG  64
1018   RSQT = STEST*STEST/SIG2T                                   REG  65
 40    IF (RSQL .GE. RSQT) GO TO 45                               REG  66
1019   SLAR = STEST                                               REG  67
1020   SIG2L = SIG2T                                              REG  68
1021   RSQL = RSQT                                                REG  69
1022   DELTL = DELT                                               REG  70
1023   IDLAR = J                                                  REG  71
 45    CONTINUE                                                   REG  72
1024   IF (RSQL-RSQ-STPC) 70,50,50                                REG  73
 50    S = SLAR                                                   REG  74
1025   SIG2 = SIG2L                                               REG  75
1026   RSQ = RSQL                                                 REG  76
1027   DEL = DELTL                                                REG  77
1028   IT = IT+1                                                  REG  78
```

```
1029 ID = IDLAR                                                        REG  79
     IF (RAWWT(ID) .NE. 0) GO TO 55                                    REG  80
     XNP = XNP+1.                                                      REG  81
     INTR(ID) = XNP-1                                                  REG  82
  55 RAWWT(ID) = RAWWT(ID)+DEL                                         REG  83
     IF (NIT-IT) 65,60,60                                              REG  84
  60 ESS = (1.-RSQL)*(XN*SIGMA(IDC)**2)                                REG  85
     ERRMSQ = ESS/(XN-XNP)                                             REG  86
     WRITE (KOUT,140) ID, DEL, RSQL, ESS, ERRMSQ, IT                   REG  87
  65 IF (RSQL .LT. 1.001) GO TO 25                                     REG  88
     WRITE (KOUT,145)                                                  REG  89
     GO TO 10                                                          REG  90
  70 IF (SIG2 .NE. 0.) GO TO 75                                        REG  91
     SDS2 = 0.                                                         REG  92
     GO TO 80                                                          REG  93
  75 SDS2 = S/SIG2                                                     REG  94
  80 RR = SQRT(RSQL)                                                   REG  95
     ESS = (1.-RSQL)*(XN*SIGMA(IDC)**2)                                REG  96
     ERRMSQ = ESS/(XN-XNP)                                             REG  97
     SEEST = SQRT(ERRMSQ)                                              REG  98
     RSQS(MN) = RSQL                                                   REG  99
     LY(MN) = IDC                                                      REG 100
     WRITE (KOUT,150) RSQL, RR, IT                                     REG 101
     WRITE (KOUT,155) ESS, SEEST, ERRMSQ, XNP                          REG 102
     UNIT = 0.0                                                        REG 103
     DO 90 I = 2, NG, 2                                                REG 104
     K = MODEL(I)                                                      REG 105
     L = MODEL(I+1)                                                    REG 106
     DO 90 J = K, L                                                    REG 107
1030 BETA(J) = RAWWT(J)*SDS2                                           REG 108
     IF (SIGMA(J) .NE. 0) GO TO 85                                     REG 109
     RAWWT(J) = 0.                                                     REG 110
     GO TO 90                                                          REG 111
  85 RAWWT(J) = BETA(J)*SIGMA(IDC)/SIGMA(J)                            REG 112
1031 UNIT = UNIT+(BETA(J)*(XMEAN(J)/SIGMA(J)))                         REG 113
  90 CONTINUE                                                          REG 114
     WRITE (KOUT,160)                                                  REG 115
     DO 100 I = 2, NG, 2                                               REG 116
     K = MODEL(I)                                                      REG 117
     L1 = MODEL(I+1)                                                   REG 118
     DO 100 J = K, L1                                                  REG 119
     RB = 0.                                                           REG 120
     DO 95 M = 2, NG, 2                                                REG 121
     KSR = MODEL(M)                                                    REG 122
     KSP = MODEL(M+1)                                                  REG 123
     DO 95 L = KSR, KSP                                                REG 124
  95 RB = RB+R(L, J)*BETA(L)                                           REG 125
     RBLESV = R(J, IDC)-RB                                             REG 126
 100 WRITE (KOUT,165) J, RAWWT(J), BETA(J), RBLESV, INTR(J), R(IDC, J) REG 127
     UNIT = XMEAN(IDC)-SIGMA(IDC)*UNIT                                 REG 128
     WRITE (KOUT,170) UNIT                                             REG 129
     RAWWT(NV+1) = UNIT                                                REG 130
     IF (MODEL(23) .NE. 0) GO TO 10                                    REG 131
     CALL PREDIC (N, NV, NG)                                           REG 132
     GO TO 10                                                          REG 133
```

```
105   CALL FTEST (N)                                                  REG 134
      GO TO 10                                                        REG 135
110   RETURN                                                          REG 136
C                                                                     REG 137
115   FORMAT    (2A4, A2, 23I3, I1)                                   REG 138
120   FORMAT    (/5X,2A4,A2,4X, 14HBAD MODEL CARD/)                   REG 139
125   FORMAT    (1H1,5X,10(2H* ), 10H MODEL NO.I5,3X,10(2H* ), /)     REG 140
130   FORMAT    (5X,2A4, A2, 5X, 20HITERATION TOLERANCE=F10.8//5X,11H CRREG 141
     1ITERION I9, / 5X, 12H  PREDICTORSI6,2H -,I3,/(17X, I6,2H -,I3))   REG 142
135   FORMAT    ( 4X,7HVAR.NO.,1X,10HCORRECTION,3X,4HRSQ.,8X,10HERROR S.S.REG 143
     1, 5X,10HERROR MSQ.,3X, 5HITER./)                                REG 144
140   FORMAT    ( 4X,I4,2F12.7,2F15.4, I6)                            REG 145
145   FORMAT    (5X,24HRSQ IS GREATER THAN 1.0  )                     REG 146
150   FORMAT    (/ 10X, 5HRSQ.= F10.7, 3X, 2HR= F10.7, 20X, I8/)      REG 147
155   FORMAT    (10X, 5HESS.= F15.4, 5X, 18HSTD.ERROR OF EST.=F10.4/  REG 148
     1 10X, 19HERROR MEAN SQUARE =F12.4, 2H ( F3, 21H PARAMETERS ASSUMEREG 149
     2D.)  )                                                          REG 150
160   FORMAT    (/ 5X, 58HVAR.NO.    RAW WT.    STD. WT.       ERROR   ENTREG 151
     1RY VALIDITY  /)                                                 REG 152
165   FORMAT    (5X,I5, 3F12.4, I7, F10.4)                            REG 153
170   FORMAT    (/ 10X, F12.4,19H UNIT VECTOR WEIGHT )                REG 154
      END                                                             REG 155-
      SUBROUTINE PREDIC (N, NV, NG)                                   PRD   1
      DIMENSION C(50), V(50), SSCP(50,50), SUM(50), SIGMA(50), BETA(50),PRD 2
     1 RAWWT(51), RSQS(50), R(50,50), XMEAN(50), KC(50), KFMT(50), MODELPRD 3
     2(50), FILE(1), INTR(50), ID(2), LY(50)                          PRD   4
      COMMON JOBNO, KOUT, IN, C, V, R, SUM, RSQS, BETA, RAWWT, SIGMA, MOPRD 5
     1DEL, FILE                                                       PRD   6
      EQUIVALENCE (SSCP, R), (SUM, XMEAN), (C, KC), (RSQS, KFMT), (C, INPRD 7
     1TR), (C, ID), (LY, V)                                           PRD   8
      NOREC = 0                                                       PRD   9
990   KSZ = 300                                                       PRD  10
      WRITE (KOUT,15)                                                 PRD  11
      U = 1.0                                                         PRD  12
      DO 10 I = 1, N                                                  PRD  13
      II = (I-1)*NV                                                   PRD  14
C--IF TAPE USED, ELIMINATE THE C IN COL. 1 OF THE NEXT CARD           PRD  15
C 991 CALL RDTAPE (NOREC, II, FILE, N, NV, KSZ)                       PRD  16
      P = 0.                                                          PRD  17
      L = 0                                                           PRD  18
      DO 5 J = 1, NG, 2                                               PRD  19
      KSTAR = MODEL(J+1)                                              PRD  20
      KSTOP = MODEL(J+2)                                              PRD  21
      DO 5 K = KSTAR, KSTOP                                           PRD  22
      IK = II+K                                                       PRD  23
      P = P+FILE(IK)*RAWWT(K)                                         PRD  24
      L = L+1                                                         PRD  25
5     C(L) = FILE(IK)                                                 PRD  26
      P = P+RAWWT(NV+1)                                               PRD  27
      IIDC = II+MODEL(1)                                              PRD  28
      AC = FILE(IIDC)                                                 PRD  29
      ERR = AC-P                                                      PRD  30
10    WRITE (KOUT,20) I, AC, P, ERR, U, (C(M), M = 1, L)              PRD  31
      RETURN                                                          PRD  32
C                                                                     PRD  33
```

```
 15    FORMAT   (//3X,11HOBSERVATION,3X, 10HOBSERVED Y,3X, 11HPREDICTED Y,PRD   34
      1   10H  RESIDUAL 5X, 9HPREDICTOR / 6X, 6HNUMBER, 7X, 5HVALUE,`9X, PRD   35
      2  5HVALUE, 7X, 5HVALUE, 7X, 6HVALUES  /  )                      PRD   36
 20    FORMAT   (1X,I8,   F16.3, F14.3, F12.3,1X,10F7.2/(52X,10F7.2))   PRD   37
       END                                                             PRD   38-
       SUBROUTINE FTEST (N)                                            FTS    1
       DIMENSION C(50), V(50), SSCP(50,50), SUM(50), SIGMA(50), BETA(50),FTS    2
      1 RAWWT(51), RSQS(50), R(50,50), XMEAN(50), KC(50), KFMT(50), MODELFTS    3
      2(50), FILE(1), INTR(50), ID(3), LY(50)                          FTS    4
       COMMON JOBNO, KOUT, IN, C, V, R, SUM, RSQS, BETA, RAWWT, SIGMA, MOFTS    5
      1DEL, FILE                                                       FTS    6
       EQUIVALENCE (SSCP, R), (SUM, XMEAN), (C, KC), (RSQS, KFMT), (C, INFTS    7
      1TR), (C, ID), (LY, V)                                           FTS    8
       EQUIVALENCE (MODEL, NF), (MODEL(2), NR), (MODEL(3), NPF), (MODEL(4FTS    9
      1), NPR)                                                         FTS   10
       DF1 = NPF-NPR                                                   FTS   11
       DF2 = N-NPF                                                     FTS   12
       RSQF = RSQS(NF)                                                 FTS   13
       KF = LY(NF)                                                     FTS   14
       IF (NR .NE. 0) GO TO 5                                          FTS   15
       RSQR = 0.                                                       FTS   16
       KR = LY(NF)                                                     FTS   17
       GO TO 10                                                        FTS   18
 5     RSQR = RSQS(NR)                                                 FTS   19
       KR = LY(NR)                                                     FTS   20
 10    XN = N                                                          FTS   21
       B = XN*SIGMA(KF)**2                                             FTS   22
       ESSF = (1.-RSQF)*B                                              FTS   23
       IF (NPR .NE. 1) B = XN*SIGMA(KR)**2                             FTS   24
       ESSR = (1.-RSQR)*B                                              FTS   25
       DESS = ESSR-ESSF                                                FTS   26
       DRSQ = RSQF-RSQR                                                FTS   27
       SQMN = DESS/DF1                                                 FTS   28
       SQMD = ESSF/DF2                                                 FTS   29
       F = SQMN/SQMD                                                   FTS   30
       CALL PLEVEL (DF1, DF2, F, P)                                    FTS   31
       WRITE (KOUT,15)                                                 FTS   32
       WRITE (KOUT,20)                                                 FTS   33
       WRITE (KOUT,25)                                                 FTS   34
       WRITE (KOUT,30) ID                                              FTS   35
       WRITE (KOUT,25)                                                 FTS   36
       WRITE (KOUT,35)                                                 FTS   37
       WRITE (KOUT,25)                                                 FTS   38
       WRITE (KOUT,40) NF, RSQF, ESSF, SQMD, F, P                      FTS   39
       WRITE (KOUT,45) NR, RSQR, ESSR                                  FTS   40
       WRITE (KOUT,50) DRSQ, DESS, SQMN, DF1, DF2                      FTS   41
       WRITE (KOUT,25)                                                 FTS   42
       WRITE (KOUT,20)                                                 FTS   43
       RETURN                                                          FTS   44
 C                                                                     FTS   45
 15    FORMAT   (//)                                                   FTS   46
 20    FORMAT   (5X,37(2H .))                                          FTS   47
 25    FORMAT   (5X,2H .,71X, 1H.)                                     FTS   48
 30    FORMAT   (5X,10H .  FTEST-,2A4, A2, 53X, 1H.)                   FTS   49
 35    FORMAT   (5X,74H .   MODEL    RSQ.        SS(ERROR)    MEAN SQUAFTS   50
```

324

```
       1RES       F       PROB  .  )                                    FTS  51
40     FORMAT     (5X, 8H .  FULL, I4, F8.4, 5X, F11.4, F14.4,          FTS  52
      1         F14.4,        F7.4, 2X, 1H.)                            FTS  53
45     FORMAT     (5X,8H .  REST, I4, F8.4, 5X, F11.4,37X, 1H.)         FTS  54
50     FORMAT     ( 5X, 9H .  DIFF., F11.4, 5X, F11.4,      F14.4, 3X,  FTS  55
      1    5H DF1= F3.0, 5H DF2= F6.0, 2H . )                           FTS  56
       END                                                             FTS  57-
       SUBROUTINE PLEVEL (DF1, DF2, F, P)                              PLV   1
       DIMENSION Y(6), ARG(3), GAMA(3)                                 PLV   2
       DATA ARG / 1, 1, 2 /                                            PLV   3
       BASHLN(Z, X) = (X+.5)*ALOG(X)-X+.918938534+(.833333333E-1-Z*(.2777PLV   4
      177778E-2-Z*(.793650794E-3-Z*(.595238095E-3-Z*.841750842E-3))))/X PLV   5
       IF (DF1 .LT. 1 .. OR.DF2 .LT. 1 .. OR .F. LT.0.) GO TO 90       PLV   6
       IF (ARG(1) .EQ. DF1 .AND. ARG(2) .EQ. DF2) GO TO 40            PLV   7
       ARG(1) = DF1                                                    PLV   8
       ARG(2) = DF2                                                    PLV   9
       ARG(3) = DF1+DF2                                                PLV  10
       DO 35 I = 1, 3                                                  PLV  11
       IF (ARG(I) .EQ. 1.) GO TO 30                                   PLV  12
       T = ARG(I)-2.                                                   PLV  13
       J = AMOD(ARG(I), 2.)+1.                                        PLV  14
       GO TO (10,5), J                                                 PLV  15
5      U = (T-1.)*.5                                                   PLV  16
       GAMA(I) = .572364943-T*.693147181                              PLV  17
       IF (U .LT. 2.) GO TO 15                                        PLV  18
       GO TO 20                                                        PLV  19
10     T = T*.5                                                        PLV  20
       GAMA(I) = 0.                                                    PLV  21
15     IF (T .LT. 2.) GO TO 35                                        PLV  22
       GO TO 25                                                        PLV  23
20     Z = 1./(U*U)                                                    PLV  24
       GAMA(I) = GAMA(I)-BASHLN(Z, U)                                 PLV  25
25     Z = 1./(T*T)                                                    PLV  26
       GAMA(I) = GAMA(I)+BASHLN(Z, T)                                 PLV  27
       GO TO 35                                                        PLV  28
30     GAMA(I) = .572364943                                            PLV  29
35     CONTINUE                                                        PLV  30
       C = GAMA(1)+GAMA(2)-GAMA(3)-69.-.693147181                     PLV  31
       Y(1) = .4054651181                                              PLV  32
       Y(2) = -1.203972804                                            PLV  33
       Y(3) = .5877866649                                              PLV  34
       Y(4) = Y(2)                                                     PLV  35
       Y(5) = Y(1)                                                     PLV  36
40     AX = DF2/(F*DF1+DF2)                                            PLV  37
       IF (AX .GT. 0.99999900) GO TO 85                               PLV  38
       H = ATAN(SQRT(AX/(1.-AX)))/60.                                 PLV  39
       IF (H .LE. .130899694E-1) GO TO 45                            PLV  40
       H = .261799387E-1-H                                            PLV  41
       CN = DF1-1.                                                     PLV  42
       CM = (DF2-1.)*.5                                                PLV  43
       P = -1./H                                                       PLV  44
       XM = -H                                                         PLV  45
       GO TO 50                                                        PLV  46
45     CN = DF2-1.                                                     PLV  47
       CM = (DF1-1.)*.5                                                PLV  48
```

```
          P = 0.                                                       PLV   49
          XM = H                                                       PLV   50
   50     IF (CN .NE. 0.) GO TO 55                                     PLV   51
          XX = Y(2)-C                                                  PLV   52
          IF (XX .LT. 0.) GO TO 55                                     PLV   53
          P = P+EXP(XX-69.)                                            PLV   54
   55     Y(6) = -.5108256238                                          PLV   55
          X = 0.                                                       PLV   56
          DO 75 I = 1, 10                                              PLV   57
          GO TO (65,65,65,65,65,65,65,65,65,60), I                     PLV   58
   60     Y(6) = Y(2)                                                  PLV   59
   65     DO 75 J = 1, 6                                               PLV   60
          X = X+H                                                      PLV   61
          XS = SIN(X)                                                  PLV   62
          Z = Y(J)-C+CN*ALOG(XS)+CM*ALOG(1.-XS*XS)                     PLV   63
          IF (Z) 75,70,70                                              PLV   64
   70     P = P+EXP(Z-69.)                                             PLV   65
   75     CONTINUE                                                     PLV   66
          P = XM*P                                                     PLV   67
          IF (P .LT. 1.0E-05) P = 0.                                   PLV   68
   80     RETURN                                                       PLV   69
   85     P = 1.                                                       PLV   70
          GO TO 80                                                     PLV   71
   90     P = 1.                                                       PLV   72
          PRINT 95, DF1, DF2, F                                        PLV   73
          GO TO 80                                                     PLV   74
C                                                                      PLV   75
   95     FORMAT (7H1DF1 = F5.0,7H,DF2 = F5.0,5H,F = F10.5//            PLV   76
         1  48H P DOES NOT EXIST IF DF1 OR DF2 IS LESS THAN 1  /        PLV   77
         2  48H OR IF F IS LESS THAN ZERO.                    /        PLV   78
         3  48H P FOR THIS PROBLEM HAS BEEN ARBITRARILY SET   /        PLV   79
         4  48H EQUAL TO 1. AND A NORMAL RETURN HAS OCCURRED. )         PLV   80
          END                                                          PLV   81-
          SUBROUTINE WRTAPE (NOREC, V, FILE, N, NV, KSZ)               WRT    1
          DIMENSION V(1), FILE(1)                                      WRT    2
          IF (NOREC .NE. 0) GO TO 5                                    WRT    3
          REWIND 2                                                     WRT    4
          KOUNT = 0                                                    WRT    5
          NOREC = 1                                                    WRT    6
          NRECBK = KSZ/NV                                              WRT    7
          IF (NRECBK .GT. N) NRECBK = N                                WRT    8
          LSTOP = NRECBK*NV                                            WRT    9
   5      LSTAR = (NOREC-1)*NV+1                                       WRT   10
          CALL MOVE (V, NV, FILE(LSTAR))                               WRT   11
          KOUNT = KOUNT+1                                              WRT   12
          IF (KOUNT .EQ. N) GO TO 10                                   WRT   13
          IF (NOREC .LT. NRECBK) GO TO 15                              WRT   14
   10     WRITE (2) (FILE(L), L = 1, LSTOP)                            WRT   15
          NOREC = 0                                                    WRT   16
   15     NOREC = NOREC+1                                              WRT   17
          RETURN                                                       WRT   18
          END                                                          WRT   19-
          SUBROUTINE RDTAPE (NOREC, II, FILE, N, NV, KSZ)              RDT    1
          DIMENSION FILE(1)                                            RDT    2
          IF (NOREC .NE. 0) GO TO 5                                    RDT    3
```

```
      REWIND 2                                            RDT    4
      NRECBK = KSZ/NV                                     RDT    5
      IF (NRECBK .GT. N) NRECBK = N                       RDT    6
      LSTOP = NRECBK*NV                                   RDT    7
      GO TO 10                                            RDT    8
5     NOREC = NOREC+1                                     RDT    9
      IF (NOREC .LE. NRECBK) GO TO 15                     RDT   10
10    READ (2) (FILE(L), L = 1, LSTOP)                    RDT   11
      NOREC = 1                                           RDT   12
15    II = (NOREC-1)*NV                                   RDT   13
      RETURN                                              RDT   14
      END                                                 RDT   15-
      SUBROUTINE PRINT (A, NR, NC, ND)                    PRT    1
      DIMENSION A(ND,NC)                                  PRT    2
      COMMON JOBNO, KOUT                                  PRT    3
5     DO 10 L = 1, NC, 10                                 PRT    4
      M = MINO(L+9, NC)                                   PRT    5
      WRITE (KOUT,15) (J, J = L, M)                       PRT    6
      DO 10 I = 1, NR                                     PRT    7
10    WRITE (KOUT,20) I, (A(I, J), J = L, M)              PRT    8
      RETURN                                              PRT    9
C                                                         PRT   10
15    FORMAT    (/ 8X, 10(I10, 1H.) /)                    PRT   11
20    FORMAT    (2X,I4,1H., 1X, 10F11.4)                  PRT   12
      END                                                 PRT   13-
      SUBROUTINE ZERO (ARRAY, K)                          ZRO    1
      DIMENSION ARRAY(1)                                  ZRO    2
      DO 5 I = 1, K                                       ZRO    3
5     ARRAY(I) = 0.                                       ZRO    4
      RETURN                                              ZRO    5
      END                                                 ZRO    6-
      SUBROUTINE MOVE (FROM, NEL, TO)                     MOV    1
      DIMENSION FROM(1), TO(1)                            MOV    2
      DO 5 I = 1, NEL                                     MOV    3
5     TO(I) = FROM(I)                                     MOV    4
      RETURN                                              MOV    5
      END                                                 MOV    6-
      SUBROUTINE DATRAN (C, NC, V, NV)                    DAT    1
      DIMENSION C(1), V(1)                                DAT    2
      CALL MOVE (C, NC, V)                                DAT    3
      RETURN                                              DAT    4
      END                                                 DAT    5-
```

327

Index

S

Salisbury, F. S., 283
Sample, random, 57
Scheffe, Henry, 21, 283, 290
Seal, H. L., 283
Slope, 97
Smith, Harry, 279, 282
Standard deviations, 267
Stanley, J. C., 57, 67, 74, 78, 96,
    111, 130
Starting model, 111, 290
Statistical significance, 71, 73
Subscripts, 8
Superscripts, 8

T

Taking out effects, 113
Title Card(s), 257
Treatment effects in three-attribute
    problems, 248
True model, 98, 106
    definition, 108
Two-attribute models
    flow chart, 127, 151, 177
    summary, 125, 149, 175
Type I error, 67, 71
Type II error, 67

U

Unit vector
    definition, 27
    redundant, 81

V

Variable
    controlled, 3

criterion, 25
dependent, 25
expected value, 55
of interest, 5, 25, 54
    examples of, 6
Variance, 35, 267
    homogeneity, 73
Vectors
    addition, 13
    column, 7
    components, 7, 286
    decomposing into two orthogonal
        components, 286
    definition, 7
    dimension, 8
    direct product, 137, 162
    elements, 7
    equality, 10
    inner product, 284
    linear combinations, 15
    linearly independent, 68
    multiplication by a number, 12
    not associated with unknown
        coefficients, 199
    notation, 5, 8
    of interest, 27
    operations, 12
    partitioning into independent and
        redundant subsets, 84
    properties of operations, 19
    representation of information, 5
    residual, 29
    row, 7
Verifying the properties of a model,
    97, 114, 163, 220

W

Weights
    least-squares, 33
    standardized, 270
Winer, B. J., 249
Wishart, J., 5